Shipwrecks and the Bounty of the Sea

Shipwrecks and the Bounty of the Sea

DAVID CRESSY

OXFORD
UNIVERSITY PRESS

OXFORD
UNIVERSITY PRESS

Great Clarendon Street, Oxford, OX2 6DP,
United Kingdom

Oxford University Press is a department of the University of Oxford.
It furthers the University's objective of excellence in research, scholarship,
and education by publishing worldwide. Oxford is a registered trade mark of
Oxford University Press in the UK and in certain other countries

First Edition published in 2022

Published in the United States of America by Oxford University Press
198 Madison Avenue, New York, NY 10016, United States of America

British Library Cataloguing in Publication Data
Data available

Library of Congress Control Number: 2022933697

ISBN 978–0–19–286339–3

DOI: 10.1093/oso/9780192863393.001.0001

Printed and bound by
CPI Group (UK) Ltd, Croydon, CR0 4YY

Acknowledgements

This book began in healthier times and was written under the shadow of the pandemic. Many of the libraries and archives I needed had to close during 2020 and 2021. My work would have come to a halt without continuing access to online databases of the Huntington Library, the libraries of Ohio State University, the Claremont Colleges, and The National Archives. Especially valuable were State Papers Online, Early English Books Online, Eighteenth-Century Collections Online, and the Cecil Papers. Colin Greenstreet introduced me to the database of the Marine Lives Project, and shared images of depositions before the High Court of Admiralty. Archivists at the Somerset Heritage Centre, Wiltshire and Swindon History Centre, Guildhall Library, and The National Archives supplied crucial copies. Other scholars who answered queries and lent support include Amanda Bevan, Tom Cogswell, Lori Anne Ferrell, Dagmar Freist, Ian Friel, Paul Halliday, Simon Healey, Steve Hindle, Eleanor Hubbard, Krista Kesselring, Paulina Kewes, Michael Leslie, Andrea McKenzie, Geoffrey Parker, Glyn Parry, Cathryn Pearce, Nicholas Rogers, Richard Unger, and Christopher Whittick. I am grateful too to Oxford University Press for their confidence in my work, and for producing such handsome books. Valerie Cressy accompanied me to shipwreck beaches from Cornwall to Northumbria in times when travel was possible. Most memorable were the rocks of the Isles of Scilly, the steep shingles of Chesil Beach, Dorset, the chalk cliffs near Seaford, Sussex, and the low bluffs of Winterton, Norfolk. We have more journeys to make in better times.

Ships in early modern sources are generally regarded as feminine, and I retain this usage where citation requires it. Distances are given in miles, currency values in pounds, shillings, and pence. Weights and measures follow the Imperial and Avoirdupois conventions of the past. Spelling and punctuation have been modernized, except where necessary and appropriate. Dates are given 'old style', except that the year is taken to have begun on 1 January. All books were published in London, unless otherwise indicated. Standard abbreviations include BL for British Library, HCA for High Court of Admiralty, PC for Privy Council, SP for State Papers, and STAC for Star Chamber records in The National Archives, Kew.

Contents

List of Figures

'Methought I saw a thousand fearful wracks; ten thousand men that fishes gnaw'd upon'

(William Shakespeare, *Richard III*, Act 1, sc. 4)

Introduction

Shipwrecks on the shores of England were not just catastrophes for merchants and mariners, but opportunities for local inhabitants. The goods and fittings of stricken vessels, if not lost to the waves, became subject to predation by interests and agencies on land. In the eyes of seaboard communities, shipwrecks were windfalls of wealth, justified as seigneurial entitlements, fruits of office, or gifts of God. The shorelines, beaches, and intertidal zones of shipwrecks became contested spaces, as salvagers, scavengers, and survivors sought material recompense or advantage. Social history and maritime history met at the water's edge, where, as the proverb said, it was an ill wind that blew nobody any good.

This book treats shipwrecks as social events in the lives of English communities. It unites the perils of the sea with the travails of the land, and locates maritime mishaps on the coastal margins within the social, political, and economic history of England. Ranging from the 1550s to the 1750s—across the long early modern era—it introduces seafarers in distress, battered by storms, and follows their fate as their ships came wrecked ashore. It presents previously unknown testimony by coastal inhabitants about the recovery and distribution of shipwrecked goods. It challenges the myth of cruel and 'barbarous' wreckers, exposes the origins of that mischaracterization, and uses new evidence to refine the concept of the 'moral economy'. It examines the law of 'wreck of the sea' and shows how that law was interpreted and applied. It shows how goods of the world fetched up on English and Welsh shores, to be exploited by landowners, state officials, and the 'country people' as they competed for the bounty of the sea. Involving law, commerce, navigation, neighbourly relations, truth-telling, deception, and the handling of materials and commodities, *Shipwrecks and the Bounty of the Sea* illuminates a range of topics of historical and general interest. Although eighteen of England's historical counties and eight more in Wales had coastlines, and hundreds of parishes bordered the sea, their distinctive circumstances have rarely been scrutinized. This book takes coastal and maritime communities as its domain.

Lashed by the waves of the Atlantic, the Irish Sea, the North Sea, and the Channel, the sea coasts of early modern England saw countless marine tragedies. Ships by the dozen were grounded, foundered, bilged, and were wrecked, as their ladings were scattered on shore. Hundreds of seamen drowned or were ruined as their vessels were cast away, though others lived to tell their tales. As many as one in twenty voyages ended in disaster. Shipwreck, however, was a beginning as well as an end. The casting-away of commercial vessels entailed loss of life and

Shipwrecks and the Bounty of the Sea. David Cressy, Oxford University Press. © David Cressy 2022.
DOI: 10.1093/oso/9780192863393.003.0001

property, but also stimulated terrestrial interests with moral, material, legal, social, and economic consequences.

Shipwrecks dissolved ownership and reassigned property, extinguishing prior possession and establishing new entitlements, as material wealth transitioned from the sea to the shore. The volume and value of this transfer are beyond calculation, but could be reckoned in thousands of pounds. Each wreck was an emergency as well as an opportunity, testing the bonds of community, authority, morality, and discipline. Discovering who was involved, how people behaved, who benefited, in what circumstances, and to what effect, is the driving task of this book.

The expanding maritime commerce of the sixteenth, seventeenth, and eighteenth centuries brought the goods of the world to English ports, and spilled some of this lading roughly on shore. Bales of cloth, barrels of wine, fruits of the Mediterranean, and timbers of the Baltic were among the items retrieved from shipwrecks. Useful lumber, pieces of apparel, and the residue of marine furnishings and fittings were among the materials that crossed the beach. Some wrecks yielded Asian spices and Spanish treasure. Others brought gluts of tallow or fish. Popular parlance spoke of 'Godsends' or 'God's gifts', as if the harvest was a providential blessing.

Shippers insisted on their continuing rights, especially if crewmen survived, but had to negotiate in circumstances of duress. Critical observers spoke of plunder, and deemed the plunderers 'savage'. Established authority looked to the law, which attempted to adjudicate between distressed merchants and mariners, landed proprietors, holders of droits and privileges, and the prerogative rights of the crown. Law and custom also addressed the conduct of coastal commoners, who provided the labour for salvage and recovery, to determine their recompense, reward, or punishment. The law, as always, was malleable and contestable, and practical arrangements did not necessarily adhere to principles of right. Participants could appeal to statute law, customary law, moral law, and the international law of the sea for privileges, rights, and restitution.

One of the enduring concerns of social history is the degree to which communities were riven by social, cultural, and economic animosities, or were bound together by webs of mutuality, solidarity, and deference. These dimensions of experience were exposed by crises of politics, plague, dearth, and war. Shipwrecks too revealed lines of cooperation and competition. Quite apart from their significance for seafarers, these episodes were memorable events for shoreline settlements, tests of the social order, and challenges to authorities on land. Their handling disclosed rifts and ties in the politics of neighbourhoods, and the ligaments of custom, authority, and law. Shipwrecks open another window into relationships between the centre and the periphery, the powerful and the powerless, and the populace and the elite.

Reports of broken voyages, complaints by distressed mariners, and investigations into the circumstances and aftermath of shipwreck provide some of the sources that underlie this study. Court records, depositions, narratives, and contemporary commentaries expose legal dealings and social relations around the foreshore and across the coastal hinterland, where nautical and terrestrial cultures intersected. Eighteenth-century newspapers add detail and commentary. I have made extensive use of State Papers and records of the High Court of Admiralty, as well as material from Chancery, Star Chamber, and the Duchy of Lancaster, major manuscript collections, and papers in local record offices, to reveal stories, incidents, and problems.[1] The result is a populated history, rich in stories, giving voice to seamen, countryfolk, and a wide range of stakeholders. Printed primary sources—sermons, law books, voyage accounts, and newspapers—are integrated into the analysis, along with scholarship in a variety of related fields. Abundant evidence, much of it previously unexamined, illuminates the interactions of seafarers and seaboard inhabitants, state authorities, droit holders, and the so-called barbarous country people. Whether coastal commoners deserve their reputation as disorderly 'wreckers' is a question to be investigated.

Shipwrecks and Scholars

Like most historical analysis, this study is guided by previous works of scholarship as well as by primary sources. A range of writings in various disciplines bears on the subject in hand, with varying degrees of utility. Much of the literature on shipwrecks dwells on ocean adventures and castaway survival, rather than the impact of such events on coastal communities. The dominant tradition in maritime studies treats shipwrecks as accidents of the sea, as fatal conjunctures of storms and mistakes, rather than violent landfalls with complex consequences. They appear most often as moral dramas with lamentable sufferings in faraway settings, anthologized, sensationalized, and soberly entertaining. A related tradition of 'true' relations, especially popular in the eighteenth and nineteenth centuries, offers narratives of shipwreck victims, sometimes with heroic or fanciful embellishments.[2] The most comprehensive modern gazetteer is Richard and

[1] Historical scholarship on seafarers, ships, cargoes, maritime environments, wrecks, and their local management would be greatly aided by an index or calendar to the vast uncatalogued records of the High Court of Admiralty. These include twenty-eight volumes of Interrogatories, 1546–1673 (HCA 23/1–28); forty-five volumes of Answers, 1577–1770 (HCA 13/100–145); ninety volumes of Examinations and Answers, 1550–1750 (HCA 13/6–99); forty-eight volumes or boxes of Examinations on Commission, 1564–1678 (HCA 13/224–271); and sixty-seven volumes of Act Books, 1550–1749 (HCA 3/7–74). Many of these volumes have more than six hundred tightly written folios. They deal with all manner of maritime matters: charters, wages, discipline, prizes, grievances, and wrecks. Lacking adequate finding aids, even at the best of times, a lone scholar can do no more than sample. More records relating to wrecks may be found in national and local archives, which are more easily searched by date and person than by subject.

[2] Early classics in this genre include Archibald Duncan, *The Mariner's Chronicle: Being a Collection of the Most Interesting Narratives of Shipwrecks, Fires, Famines, and other Calamities Incident to a Life of Marine Enterprise*, 6 vols (1804–8); James Stanier Clarke, *Naufragia or Historical Memoirs of*

Bridget Larn, *Shipwreck Index of the British Isles* (7 volumes, 1995–2005), a guide for treasure-hunters in which early modern wrecks are under-represented.[3]

Ordeals of tempest, stranding, and abandonment provide plots and tests of character in creative works from Homer's *Odyssey* to Defoe's *Robinson Crusoe* and beyond. Classic examples of this genre attend to the tribulations of shipwreck victims, real or imagined, who coped with rough waters and distant shores. 'All lost! We split!' cried Shakespeare's mariners as their storm-tossed vessel crashed on Prospero's island. 'Be not afeard, the isle is full of noises,' the indigenous Caliban warns survivors. At least five of Shakespeare's plays involve characters who suffer and survive a shipwreck.[4] On the page and on the stage, the violent curtailment of a voyage launches adventures of discovery, betrayal, and reconciliation.

Historians of early modern England have paid limited attention to shipwrecks. The essential point of entry is John Rule's classic essay on 'Wrecking and Coastal Plunder' in *Albion's Fatal Tree: Crime and Society in Eighteenth-Century England* (1975). Though mainly concerned with 'the peak of wrecking activity' in the later Hanoverian period, taking most of its evidence from Cornwall, it sets the agenda for all subsequent studies. While observing that 'wrecking' covered a range of activities, and recognizing the role of 'substantial citizens' alongside the poor, Rule emphasizes the popular notion that salvors were entitled to whatever they could find, regardless of the law. Rightly sceptical of claims that wreckers lured ships to their doom, he nonetheless reports on their 'shameful and horrid practices'. Influenced by E. P. Thompson, Rule interprets wrecking in terms of the 'moral economy' of the crowd, as actions of resistance and redress. Focused on 'depredation' and 'plunder', he sees the stripping of ships and cargoes as disorderly activities that were legitimized by local custom.[5]

Though careful not to glamorize or excuse wreckers as protesters, Rule in later papers treats them as participants in collective 'social crime', whose spoil, though strictly illegal, enjoyed open or tacit toleration. Like poaching and smuggling, wrecking appears here as 'a means of getting or supplementing a living' that augmented 'the makeshift economy of the poor'.[6] Similarly influenced by

Shipwrecks and of the Providential Deliverance of Vessels, 2 vols (1805–6); and John Graham Dalyell, *Shipwrecks and Disasters at Sea: or, Historical Narratives of the Most Noted Calamities and Providential Deliverances which have Resulted from Maritime Enterprise*, 3 vols (Edinburgh, 1812).

[3] Richard Larn and Bridget Larn, *Shipwreck Index of the British Isles*, 7 vols (1995–2005).

[4] William Shakespeare, *Tempest* (written c.1611), Act 1, scenes 1 and 2. See also *Comedy of Errors, Twelfth Night, Pericles*, and *Winter's Tale*.

[5] John G. Rule, 'Wrecking and Coastal Plunder', in Douglas Hay, Peter Linebaugh, John G. Rule, et al. (eds), *Albion's Fatal Tree: Crime and Society in Eighteenth-Century England* (1975), 167–88; E. P. Thompson, 'The Moral Economy of the English Crowd in the Eighteenth Century', *Past & Present*, 50 (1971), 76–136.

[6] J. G. Rule, 'Social Crime in the Rural South in the Eighteenth and Early Nineteenth Centuries', *Southern History*, 1 (1979), 135–53; John Rule, 'Smuggling and Wrecking', in Philip Payton, Aston Kennerly, and Helen Doe (eds), *The Maritime History of Cornwall* (Exeter, 2014), 195–208.

Thompson, John Styles treats these 'social crimes' as tolerable 'forms of illegal appropriation' that drew on 'deep communal alliances' and 'were considered legitimate by various, broad sectors of the public'.[7] These are influential arguments, but they cover only part of the story. As this book demonstrates, the gathering of material from wrecked vessels in the Elizabethan and Stuart periods was not necessarily illegal, was not always disorderly or disreputable, and did not principally benefit poor commoners.

Engaging these issues a full generation later, Cathryn Pearce questions the 'domination/resistance model' advanced by followers of E. P. Thompson. Attending afresh to premodern Cornwall, she finds little evidence of a 'dominating relationship' between coastal lords and commoners, but rather relations 'based on mutuality as well as antagonism'. Her review of law and practice finds salvage proceeding collaboratively, though wrecking was sometimes 'hotly contested' between property owners and 'those who believed in their personal rights of harvest'. Manorial lords as well as landless tenants contributed to an economy of wrecking that was deeply engrained in far south-west England.[8]

Pearce, like Rule, discredits myths of murderous wreckers and deplores their recurrence in modern popular culture. A case in point is Bella Bathurst, *The Wreckers: A Story of Killing Seas, False Lights, and Plundered Ships* (2005), which, though widely distributed, is lightweight, derivative, and sensationalist, described in one scholarly review as an 'accretion of misinformation . . . riddled with unsubstantiated assertions and errors'.[9] Discerning readers deserve better.

A new generation of maritime historians has examined the circulation of people and goods, and 'the complex connections that existed between ship and shore', as well as the cultural consequences of voyaging. Shipwrecks have yet to figure centrally in these studies (Pearce on Cornwall excepted), but they yield fruitful examples of 'change and conflict at the water's edge'.[10] Practitioners of 'the new coastal history' similarly attend to activities along the foreshore, and in zones

[7] John Styles, '"Our traitorous money makers": The Yorkshire Coiners and the Law, 1760–83', in John Brewer and John Styles (eds), *An Ungovernable People: The English and their Law in the Seventeenth and Eighteenth Centuries* (New Brunswick, 1980), 209–10.

[8] Cathryn Pearce, *Cornish Wrecking 1700–1860: Reality and Popular Myth* (Woodbridge, 2010), 153, 165.

[9] Bella Bathurst, *The Wreckers: A Story of Killing Seas, False Lights, and Plundered Ships* (2005), also published as *The Wreckers: A Story of Killing Seas and Plundered Shipwrecks: From the 18th Century to the Present Day* (New York, 2005), reviewed by Cathryn J. Pearce, *International Journal of Maritime History*, 17 (2005), 411–12.

[10] Glen O'Hara, '"The Sea is Swinging into View": Modern British Maritime History in a Globalised World', *English Historical Review*, 124 (2009), 1109–34; Richard J. Blakemore and James Davey (eds), *The Maritime World of Early Modern Britain* (Amsterdam, 2020), 17; Lauren Benton and Nathan Perl-Rosenthal (eds), *A World at Sea: Maritime Practices and Global History* (Philadelphia, 2020), 1–14, 186–92. See also John Mack, *The Sea: A Cultural History* (2011), 165, on the ambiguity, liminality, and shifting boundaries of 'the beach'.

where the littoral and its hinterlands intermeshed.[11] These are suggestive lines of enquiry, with potential application to the local lived experience of early modern England.

Recent scholarly interest in shipwrecks has led literary scholars associated with the so-called blue humanities to focus more on 'the burden of meaning carried by the metaphorics of seafaring and shipwreck' than material incidents in the English past.[12] Such work explores 'the shifting semiotics and symbolism' of 'the shipwreck topos',[13] and the archetypal 'panorama of shipwreck narratives . . . in which drama may unfold'.[14] Kindred studies analyse 'multilayered, timeless metaphors of human existence' and the 'mimetic qualities' of 'shipwreck topoi' in 'allegorical, fictional, and polemical shipwreck texts'.[15] Most fulsome in this vein is Steve Mentz, whose *Shipwreck Modernity: Ecologies of Globalization* explores the 'melodramatic presentation, epistemological crisis, and recuperative metaphysics' of the genre.[16] Derived from deep reading in canonical texts, these works raise theoretical issues of the kind that historians seldom ponder. They are rich in ideas, but lack grounding in the documentary evidence that forms the core of this study.

Studies by medievalists on the social entanglements of *wreccum maris*—the law of wreck of the sea—provide better models for emulation.[17] Most ingeniously, Tom Johnson uses late medieval manor court rolls to show how wrecked goods were identified and appropriated. The finding and registering of materials from North Sea shipwrecks show how 'a washed-up thing without an owner' could be transformed into 'a legitimate piece of property belonging to someone' else. Goods

[11] Isaac Land, 'Tidal Waves: The New Coastal History', *Journal of Social History*, 40 (2007), 731–43; David Worthington (ed.), *The New Coastal History: Cultural and Environmental Perspectives from Scotland and Beyond* (Cham, Switzerland, 2017). See also Gérard Le Bouedec, 'La Pluriactivité dans les sociétés littorales XVIIe–XIXe siècle', *Annales de Bretagne et des Pays de l'Ouest*, 109 (2002), 61–90.

[12] Hans Blumenberg, *Shipwreck with Spectator: Paradigm of a Metaphor for Existence* (Cambridge, MA, 1997), 8.

[13] Carl Thompson (ed.), *Shipwreck in Art and Literature* (New York, 2014), 3, 15.

[14] James V. Morrison, *Shipwrecked: Disaster and Transformation in Homer, Shakespeare, Defoe, and the Modern World* (Ann Arbor, 2014), 4.

[15] Brigitte Le Juez and Olga Springer (eds), *Shipwrecks and Island Motifs in Literature and the Arts* (Leiden, 2015), 1, 7; Jennifer H. Oliver, *Shipwreck in French Renaissance Writing: The Direful Spectacle* (Oxford, 2019), 3, 21, 99, 119. See also Josiah Blackmore, *Manifest Perdition: Shipwreck Narrative and the Disruption of Empire* (Minneapolis, 2002).

[16] (Minneapolis, 2015), p. xxx. See also Steve Mentz, 'God's Storms: Shipwreck and the Meanings of Ocean in Early Modern England and America', in Thompson (ed.), *Shipwreck in Art and Literature*, 77–91; and Steve Mentz, '"We Split!": Shipwreck in Early Modern European History and Culture', in Claire Jowitt, Craig Lambert, and Steve Mentz (eds), *The Routledge Companion to Marine and Maritime Worlds, 1400–1800* (Abingdon and New York, 2020), 580–97.

[17] Frederick C. Hamil, 'Wreck of the Sea in Medieval England', in A. E. R. Boak (ed.), *University of Michigan Historical Essays* (Ann Arbor, 1937), 1–24; Rose Melikan, 'Shippers, Salvors, and Sovereigns: Competing Interests in the Medieval Law of Shipwreck', *Journal of Legal History*, 11 (1990), 163–82; Susan Raich, 'Wreck of the Sea in Law and Practice in Eleventh- and Twelfth-Century England', in Elizabeth van Houts (ed.), *Anglo-Norman Studies XXXVIII: Proceedings of the Battle Conference 2015* (2016), 141–54.

from the sea sustained a 'shipwreck economy' in parts of coastal East Anglia, which ramified around the shores of early modern England.[18]

Further insights may be gained from work on other periods and places. Most rewarding is Alain Cabantous, *Les Côtes barbares: Pilleurs d'épaves et sociétés littorals en France (1680–1830)* (Paris, 1993), which examines the social, moral, and material consequences of shipwrecks along the coasts of Atlantic France and La Manche.[19] Other valuable studies examine shipwreck environments in the seventeenth-century Mediterranean, [20] eighteenth-century Brittany,[21] the eighteenth- and nineteenth-century Baltic,[22] and much further afield.[23]

Another helpful body of scholarship locates wrecking within the 'shadowy landscapes' of the grey economy, where certain illicit activities were 'socially embedded' and enjoyed some 'social legitimacy'.[24] Beverly Lemire's *Global Trade and the Transformation of Consumer Cultures: The Material Word Remade, c.1500–1820* (Cambridge, 2018) shows how 'informal, extralegal, and customary practices' such as smuggling, scavenging, and wrecking were part of the 'material politics' of illicit acquisition.[25] Much of the history of shipwreck recovery conforms to this pattern, which is another way of imagining the 'moral economy'. Recent work on Spanish imperial sources similarly exposes the 'unspoken compromises' that coastal dwellers made to reconcile profit, morality, and law at the

[18] Tom Johnson, 'Medieval Law and Materiality: Shipwrecks, Finders, and Property on the Suffolk Coast, ca. 1380–1410', *American Historical Review*, 120 (2015), 407–32, quote at 411; Tom Johnson, 'The Economics of Shipwreck in Late Medieval Suffolk', in James P. Bowen and A. T. Brown (eds), *Custom and Commercialization in English Rural Society: Revisiting Tawney and Postan* (Hatfield, 2016), 121–38.

[19] Alain Cabantous, *Les Côtes barbares: Pilleurs d'épaves et sociétés littorals en France (1680–1830)* (Paris, 1993).

[20] Marcello Berti, 'I rischi nella circolazione marittima tra Europa nordica ed Europa mediterranea nel primo trentennio del seicento e il caso della seconda guerra anglo-olandese (1665–67)', in Simonetta Cavaciocchi (ed.), *Ricchezza del Mare: Ricchezza dal Mare: secc. XIII–XVIII* (Florence, 2006), 809–39.

[21] Sylvain Coindet, 'Les Naufrages sur L'île de Sein au XVIIIe siècle: Une lente évolution vers le sauvetage', *Annales de Bretagne et Pays de l'Ouest*, 113 (2006), 87–109; Sylvain Coindet, 'Le Temps du naufrage: Une triple vision de l'évènement dans l'amirauté de Cornouille (1720–1790)', *Annales de Bretagne et Pays de l'Ouest*, 117 (2010), 73–94.

[22] Yrjö Kaukiainen, 'Wreck-Plundering by East Finnish Coastal People—Criminal Tradition or Popular Culture?', in Lars U. Scholl and Merja-Liisa Hinkkanen (eds), *Sail and Steam: Selected Maritime Writings of Yrjö Kaukiainen* (Liverpool, 2004), 151–62; Kersti Lust, 'Wrecking Peasants and Salvaging Landlords—Or Vice Versa? Wrecking in the Russian Baltic Provinces of Estland and Livland, 1780–1870', *International Review of Social History*, 62 (2017), 67–93.

[23] Luke S. Roberts, 'Shipwrecks and Flotsam: The Foreign World in Edo-Period Topesa', *Monumenta nipponica*, 70 (2015), 83–122; Brad Duncan and Martin Gibbs, *Please God Send Me a Wreck: Responses to Shipwreck in a 19th Century Australian Community* (New York, 2015).

[24] Alexandra Hartnett and Shannon Lee Dawdy, 'The Archaeology of Illegal and Illicit Economies', *Annual Review of Anthropology*, 42 (2013), 37–51.

[25] Beverly Lemire, *Global Trade and the Transformation of Consumer Cultures: The Material Word Remade, c.1500–1820* (Cambridge, 2018), 137–89. See also David Chen Smith, 'Fair Trade and the Political Economy of Brandy Smuggling in Early Eighteenth-Century Britain', *Past & Present*, 251 (May 2021), 75–111.

margins of 'the nascent new Atlantic world'.[26] The insight that piracy, though blatantly illegal, had aiders and abettors, collaborators and investors, and that its history 'exposed tensions between local leaders on the peripheries and imperial administrators at the center of power in London', provides another framework for thinking about the plundering of wrecks.[27]

The first finders and earliest exploiters of ships that were grounded, lost, cast away, and wrecked are sometimes referred to as 'wreckers', though that word had no currency before the eighteenth century. 'Along the shore a crowd of wreckers stand I Ready to seize whatever drives to land', trilled an entertainment of 1746.[28] The word embraced hired labourers, freelance salvagers, and opportunistic plunderers, as well as some of their landlords and employers. These people, and earlier villagers like them, were coastal inhabitants, shoreline dwellers, or residents of nearby parishes whose lives were entwined with the moods and bounties of the sea. They were not criminals, rioters, or protesters, although their activity as a crowd could be boisterous, greedy, and protective of assumed 'rights'. Much of their normal business faced inland, to fields, workshops, roads, and markets; some were farmers and fishermen, others artisans, miners, quarrymen, and their wives. The arrival of bounty on their beach demanded vigorous effort, and occasioned windfall profit. Drawing all these threads together, *Shipwrecks and the Bounty of the Sea* treats shipwrecks as social and material events that touched the lives of shore folk as well as seafarers and entangled them with their neighbours and the law. The chapters are organized as follows.

Chapter 1. Ships at Risk

Early modern sailing vessels suffered 'so many manglements, that it is a very great wonder to see the providence of God in the preserving of them', marvelled the interregnum preacher Daniel Pell (*An Improvement of the Sea*, 1659). Any ship could become 'shipwreckful', a catastrophe waiting to happen. 'Even now worth this, and now worth nothing', mused a shipowner in Shakespeare's *Merchant of Venice*, as shipwreck reduced a maritime venture to rubbish.

This chapter treats ships as skilled constructions and vehicles for traffic that could be undone by misfortune. It reviews estimates of the size of the merchant fleet and the frequency and cost of shipwrecks. Evidence suggests that 4–5 per cent of voyages went amiss, costing shippers up to a quarter of a million pounds per

[26] Jesse Cromwell, *The Smugglers' World: Illicit Trade and Atlantic Communities in Eighteenth-Century Venezuela* (Chapel Hill, 2018), 1–27; Juan José Ponce Vazquez, *Islanders and Empire: Smuggling and Political Defiance in Hispaniola, 1580–1690* (Cambridge, 2020), 1–21.

[27] Mark Hanna, *Pirate Nests and the Rise of the British Empire, 1570–1740* (Chapel Hill, 2015), 3–30, 416–17.

[28] William Hyland, *The Ship-Wreck: A Dramatick Piece* (1746), prologue.

year. The price was high for the development of a global economy, but English coastal communities were among its beneficiaries, as goods from the worlds' oceans washed ashore.

Chapter 2. The Perils of the Sea

This chapter turns to the textual representation of voyaging and shipwrecks in ancient, biblical, and early modern sources, and to contemporary accounts of ships and seamen in peril. Paying particular attention to the meteorological, navigational, and cultural hazards that brought ships to grief on English and Welsh shores, it explores how shipwrecks were imagined, moralized, and experienced. Storms and shipwrecks in the Bible (Jonah, St Paul), in the classics (Homer, Vergil), and in the writings of the Renaissance (Erasmus, Rabelais, Sidney, Shakespeare) served to punish the hubris of heroes and the sins of sailors. Preachers and moralists used this maritime imagery to warn of the shipwreck of the soul or the shipwreck of the state.

While the master narrative of the age attributed disaster and deliverance to divine providence, reports by merchants and mariners described the actual mishaps of voyaging, extremities of weather, crises of foundering and abandonment, and the deaths and endurance of shipwreck victims. They told of ships being pushed beyond their handling, as mariners were overwhelmed by the fury of the waves, as navigational error, faulty seamanship, and blind misfortune played their parts.

Chapter 3. *Wreccum Maris*: The Law of 'Wreck of the Sea'

Early modern law had varied streams and currents, with useful ambiguities and flexibilities. It was axiomatic in England that the goods and materials of shipwrecks belonged by prerogative to the crown, who could assign those rights to proprietors, corporations, or individuals. A statute of Edward I, however, enshrined the complication that, 'where a man, a dog, or a cat escape quick out the ship', neither that ship, nor anything on it, should be judged a wreck. The original owners would have a year and a day to reclaim their property, subject to payment of droits, fees, and rewards. Endless enquiries, suits, and arguments followed about the circumstances of shipwreck, whether all aboard had perished or abandoned their vessel, whether 'true wreck' was proved, and how the spoils should be divided.

Different views coexisted about the legality and propriety of shoreline activities, whether salvagers worked with or against established authority, whether wrecking constituted a service, a custom, or a crime, and whether common lawyers or the civil lawyers of the Admiralty had jurisdiction. Rooted in legal commentary and the records of legal process, this chapter also engages with recent scholarship on 'law-mindedness', legal culture, and legal pluralism to show how seafarers and shore folk became entangled in disputes over wrecks. It asks questions that historians always find useful: *cui bono*? to whose benefit? and 'who is saying what to whom?'.

Chapter 4. 'The Barbarous Country People'

This chapter exposes the canard that shipwrecks occasioned gross disorder among coastal inhabitants, who were guilty of 'barbarous spoils and rapines'. It advances and modifies the discussion begun by John Rule in 1975, and joined by Cathryn Pearce in 2010, about the 'moral economy' of 'wreckers'. It reviews hostile rhetoric from a variety of historical sources, and finds it mostly exaggerated, self-serving, and misleading.

Those who denounced coastal countryfolk as 'barbarous', 'cruel', and 'inhumane' did not so much demonstrate their charge as assert it; they did not so much describe the competition for shipwrecked goods as take sides in it. The denunciation of salvagers as 'savage' belonged to a rhetoric of denigration that divided English subjects between dutiful and disorderly sorts. Close inspection of recorded episodes finds minimal evidence of violence and greed, and shows that ordinary scavengers worked as much in harness with mariners, local proprietors, and officials as against them. It is argued here and in subsequent chapters that shipwrecks may have stressed the social order, but its architecture remained intact.

Chapter 5. 'The Great Profit of the Lords of Manors'

This chapter builds on the observation by Samuel Pepys that 'the great profit of the lords of manors upon the sea coasts lay in wrecks', where they and their tenants 'do most savagely make prey of all shipwrecked persons, goods, and vessels'. Though often overlooked, the energetic assertion of seigneurial rights around the coastline supports recent observations that manorial courts and manorial claims remained active well beyond the Middle Ages.

The lords of coastal manors claimed 'benefit of wreck' on their shores and defended that right with vigour against rival proprietors, Admiralty officials, and their own tenants. Examples from Cornwall to Cumberland show aristocrats and gentlemen exploiting the materials that came ashore, filling their barns with ships' timbers and their cellars with shipwrecked wine. Many went to law to preserve their privileges, and a few involved themselves in affrays and even duels. Extensive evidence, little of it previously examined, reveals customs and procedures of wreck retrieval, the distribution of moieties and rewards, disputes about manorial boundaries and precedents, and materials brought ashore, as the elite enriched themselves from the bounty of the sea.

Chapter 6. The Lord Admiral's Droits and His Majesty's Profit

This chapter connects the economic and administrative history of shipwrecks to the high political history of Elizabethan and Stuart England and reveals that the greatest beneficiaries of *wreccum maris* were the agents and appointees of the crown.

The Lord Warden of the Cinque Ports enjoyed Admiralty rights in the richest of all wreck zones, from Essex to Sussex, including the Goodwin Sands in the narrow seas off Kent. His lieutenants, sergeants, and droit gatherers policed southern beaches and insisted on his lordship's share. Competing with him nationwide was the Lord High Admiral of England, who regarded wreck rights as a major perquisite. This rivalry was suspended when the same man held both offices, most energetically under the Duke of Buckingham in the 1620s and the Duke of York in the 1660s. Buckingham monetized the Admiralty, and after his assassination the crown took over the apparatus to maximize 'his majesty's profits' from England's coasts; its pursuit was an under-recognized element of Caroline fiscal feudalism.

Stuart monarchs were jealous of their prerogatives, and challenged encroachments by lords of manors, local vice-admirals, and other agencies. The expanding power of the state in the later seventeenth century added more layers of authority to the already crowded arena of claimants. Customs commissioners demanded duty on the ever-plentiful wine from shipwrecks, while vice-admirals and lords of manors argued against such meddling. The official, royal, and seigneurial take from shipwrecks by far exceeded the 'petty pickings' of the much-maligned country people, on whom the labour of salvage depended.

Chapter 7. Shipwreck Tales from Sea and Shore

Buried in local archives, state papers, and the barely catalogued records of the High Court of Admiralty, the correspondence of officials and the depositions of witnesses describe the removal of 'findalls and things saved' from English beaches. Vivid first-person testimonies combine the nautical perspective of mariners with the viewpoints and voices of salvors and scavengers. They show how shipwrecks happened and how shore-dwellers took advantage of them. Wreck recovery emerges here as a social process, embedded in the structures and cultures of the community, animated by relationships of neighbourliness, opportunity, authority, and law.

More than a dozen micro histories illuminate activities that were energetic but by no means 'barbarous'. Wrecking emerges as a community activity, generally supervised by bailiffs and droit collectors, and subject to the overview of councils and commissions. Local dramas unfolded over the discovery of ships in distress, the treatment of survivors, the gathering of wreckage, and the concealment and distribution of goods. Highlights include a Northumberland wreck that embroiled the governments of three countries, the looting of a pirate ship from a beach in Elizabethan Sussex, goods 'embezzled and purloined away' from wrecks on offshore sandbanks, and the plunder of the *St Jacob* at Littlehampton in 1654, authorized by the Earl of Arundel's steward.

Chapter 8. The Bounty of the *Golden Grape*

Most extraordinary of all are the depositions regarding the *Golden Grape*, which was wrecked on the coast of Dorset in 1641 with a cargo worth £10,000. Seven crewmen drowned, but at least twelve survived to lament their loss as 'the people of the country by force and violence took and carried the same away'. A subsequent examination produced 118 folios of testimony from 343 witnesses, identifying 547 individuals involved in the plunder. Identified by name, address, gender, and occupation, the deponents were a cross section of Dorset coastal society, showing a community in action. The records reveal inter-village rivalries and solidarities, teamwork and enterprise, deference and cooperation, as barrels of raisins, jars of oil, bales of silk, and sacks of silver were brought ashore.

The depositions reveal instances of intimidation and theft, but little overt violence, no 'barbarity'. Rather than a disordered frenzy, they depict a practised communal effort to take what the sea offered. Salvagers treated the survivors with courtesy, worked collaboratively with neighbours, deferred to men in authority, and told their stories for the record. Explaining themselves before the commissioners, most deponents acknowledged their roles at the wreck, but they gathered goods, they said, only for safe keeping until lawful authority arrived. None of the villagers was punished.

Chapter 9. Mariners in Distress

The sea was 'a sepulchre for thousands', as most victims of shipwrecks drowned. Reports tell of deaths by the dozen, by the hundred, and more than 1,400 lost when Sir Cloudesley Shovell's fleet was wrecked on the Isles of Scilly in 1707. Survivors were fortunate to take to their boats, or cling to floating wreckage, hoping not to fall on 'unneighbourly shores'. Their experience on the coast of England bore little relation to the shipwreck stories of literary romance.

This chapter follows the fate of 'ship-broken men' as they engaged with the people of the shoreline. It draws on evidence they presented to examiners and commissioners. Though some complained of lawless looting, and grieved at their loss of goods, most acknowledged the assistance of local inhabitants. Survivors secured shelter, clothing, and medical attention, and some owed their lives to the ministrations of wreckers. Many, like the officers of the *Golden Grape*, engaged with salvagers to preserve parts of their lading, or sold material from the ship to meet their immediate needs. A few reported being cheated by agents of the Admiralty and stewards of lords of manors who took advantage of their plight. Justices of the Peace issued passes for shipwrecked mariners, asking local officials 'not to molest or trouble' them as they travelled to convenient ports. Foreign sailors needed repatriation, and even enemies in times of war had ways to go home.

Chapter 10. Material Bounty Brought Ashore

The wreckage that came ashore from stricken vessels, and passed into the hands of villagers, gentlemen, and officials, varied enormously in content, condition, and worth. Everything consigned for passage at sea, including the ships and possessions of seaman, was at risk of loss. The transfer to shore could be chaotic, informal, and sometimes illicit, but reports, accounts, and inventories indicate the diversity of items recovered and the values sometimes attached to them. This chapter takes stock of the findalls, godsends, and gatherings that constituted the goods and gains from wrecks. Building on recent work on material culture and the 'traffic in things', it reveals interactions between maritime and terrestrial cultures, between coastal residents and officials, and between objects and their possessors.

Rich records register the commodities retrieved from wrecks and the gains they represented. Ordinary villagers did well to come clear with a few jars of oil, a few bushels of fruit, and small loads of salvaged timber, among rewards for their work. Their gentle landlords and masters more likely enriched themselves with prime pickings, abundant wine, and items of privilege. The Bacons of Norfolk and the Arundells of Cornwall, for example, stocked their storerooms with wrecked cargoes and took possession of salvageable ships. The Wardens of the Cinque Ports and agents of the Admiralty accumulated moieties and droits as fruits of office. The crown, as always, registered the most gains, especially when bullion was in view. While commoners performed the labour, and carried the opprobrium, the elite gained honour and status, as well as profit, from the bounty of the sea.

Chapter 11. Deep Recovery

Shoreline recovery extended as far into the sea as horsemen could reach with long poles. Salvagers worked with hooks and grapples in the waves. Anything deeper was lost, unless engines could be devised or divers could be found to descend. This chapter examines the organizational and technical challenges involved in the recovery of shipwrecked material from seas deeper than shoremen could reach. It tells the story of underwater recovery, from the daring free divers of the sixteenth century employed to locate anchors and cannons to the enterprising syndicates of the late Stuart period using breathing apparatus to retrieve silver bullion. Most of this book treats shipwrecks as social dramas at the juncture of land and sea; here they are also considered as sites, in the archaeological sense, from which maritime bounty could be recovered by inventors and investors.

Italian and Dutch expertise led the way in the 'weighing' or raising of ships in waters of more than ten fathoms. The Dutchman Jacob Johnson, known as Jacob the Diver, earned commissions under Charles I for retrieving treasure chests and ordnance from the Channel. Other experts assisted the navy in the 1650s and 1660s to recover cannon from the Thames and the North Sea. Well-financed operatives in the 1680s went further afield, in search of 'the treasure of the ocean', and brought home more than £200,000 worth of silver from the Caribbean, of which the crown took a tenth. A spate of late-Stuart projectors bid for diving rights in English waters, including one in 1690 promoting the 'new invention' of 'a sea crab for working in the sea to fish and take up ships' guns and goods lost or forsaken, and a pair of lungs to be fixed to a man's back for his breathing under water as he swims'.

Chapter 12. Eighteenth-Century Wrecking Revisited

Classic accounts of wrecking focus on Hanoverian Cornwall and deal primarily with episodes from the 1750s to the 1820s. This chapter concentrates on the neglected first half of the eighteenth century, and presents material from several coastlines. It builds on research in the early modern era to examine shoreline activities in a period of social, economic, and legal change. Engaging with current scholarship, it introduces fresh evidence to reveal the social breadth of participation in wrecking, as shore workers contended with their masters and betters, countrymen vied with mercantile interests, and Customs officers impounded dutiable goods. A growing volume of shipping raised the stakes and expanded opportunities. Coastal conflicts may have become more common, and more riotous, while popular culture depicted wreckers as plunderers 'blest with fortune's store'.[29]

[29] Hyland, *Ship-Wreck*, 11.

The legal environment was transformed by legislation in 1714 that threatened fines and imprisonment for anyone who boarded wrecks without permission or impeded the saving of their goods. A much harsher law in 1753 railed against the 'wicked enormities' of those who stripped shipwrecks and made unauthorized wrecking a felony punishable by death. The courts of the Admiralty played a lesser role, as Quarter Sessions, Assizes, and newspapers generated more evidence. The state's demands for revenue from Customs became more aggressive, sometimes backed by troops, while manorial proprietors continued to secure their share. It was in this period that the word 'wrecker' first appeared. Charges of 'barbarous' behaviour continued, but with no more justification than before.

The Appendix, 'Two Centuries of Shipwrecks', lists more than 850 named vessels that were wrecked or cast away on English and Welsh shores between 1550 and 1750.

1
Ships at Risk

It has long been recognized that England 'possessed the good fortune to sit athwart one of the busiest trade routes in the world', and that 'tapping into the trade that flowed around its shores was England's great opportunity' to become a global entrepot.[1] Less remarked is the windfall wealth that also accrued, or rather was reassigned, from the occasional bounty of wrecks. Wines and spirits from France and Spain, luxury fabrics from France and the Low Countries, fruits and oils from the Mediterranean, Baltic timber, Irish hides and tallow, American silver and tobacco, East India goods, and varied foodstuffs, furs, metals, coal, and manufactures all spilled onto English beaches, to be claimed or consumed by competing interests.[2] The shipper's loss was the shoreman's gain, in a world of burgeoning maritime traffic. The fittings and framings of ships themselves were also items of value to enterprising coastal dealers and scavengers.

England's commercial expansion was a marvel to admiring contemporaries. 'The gallant Englishman's rare navigating art' brought in 'fair Engleterra's wealth, her silks, her wines, her sugars, spices, stuffs, her silver and her gold, beside many other innumerable and unreckonable commodities', such as 'figs, lemons, oranges, raisins, etc.,' crowed Daniel Pell in 1659. 'The merchant ships are continually going and coming... into England and out of England, into the remote parts of the world, as bees out of an hive in summer time... above a thousand sail every year.' Yet all this wealth was at risk. Pell's primary observation was not the prosperity of maritime traffic but its vulnerability. 'The sea hath a million of

[1] Richard Price, *British Society 1680–1880* (Cambridge, 1999), 5. For English maritime commerce, see T. S. Willan, *The English Coasting Trade 1600–1750* (Manchester, 1938); Ralph Davis, 'English Foreign Trade, 1660–1700', *Economic History Review*, 7 (1954), 150–66; A. M. Millard, 'London's Imports 1587–1640', *Blackmansbury*, 4 (1967), 14–22; Kenneth R. Andrews, *Ships, Money and Politics: Seafaring and Naval Enterprise in the Reign of Charles I* (Cambridge, 1991), 16–33; W. B. Stephens, 'English Wine Imports *c.*1603–40, with Special Reference to the Devon Ports', in Todd Gray and Margery M. Rowe (eds), *Tudor and Stuart Devon: The Common Estate and Government* (1992), 141–72; Richard W. Unger, 'Ships and Sailing Routes in Maritime Trade around Europe 1300–1600', in Wim Blockmans, Mikhail Krom, and Justyna Wubs-Mrozewicz (eds), *The Routledge Handbook of Maritime Trade around Europe 1300–1699: Commercial Networks and Urban Autonomy* (2017), 17–35. See also Thomas Mun, *A Discourse of Trade, from England unto the East-Indies* (1621); John Boroughs, *The Soveraignty of the British Seas* (1651); Samuel Fortrey, *Englands Interest and Improvement: Consisting in the Increase of the Store, and Trade of this Kingdom* (Cambridge, 1663); John Houghton, *England's Great Happiness, or, A Dialogue between Content and Complaint* (1677); William Petyt, *Britannia Languens: or, A Discourse of Trade* (1680).

[2] Beverly Lemire, *Global Trade and the Transformation of Consumer Culture: The Material World Remade, c.1500–1820* (Cambridge, 2018), notes some of the cultural and economic consequences of smuggling, wrecking, and scavenging.

Shipwrecks and the Bounty of the Sea. David Cressy, Oxford University Press. © David Cressy 2022.
DOI: 10.1093/oso/9780192863393.003.0002

dangers in it', he wrote, and 'no ship is so well caulked, so well decked or planked, but may give way', and join the lost fleet of wrecks. 'Many a ship . . . swelling with a full sail in a fair day hath gone to pot before the evening.' England's sailing vessels, Pell marvelled, suffered 'so many manglements, that it is a very great wonder to see the providence of God in the preserving of them'.[3] Any ship could become 'shipwreckful', a catastrophe waiting to happen. Any voyage could succumb to the perils of the seas.[4]

Numbers and Values

Often-cited statistics show English merchant shipping expanding from 52,000 tons burden in 1572, to 115,000 tons in 1629, to 340,000 tons in 1686. The tonnage of foreign shipping grew even greater, led by the Dutch with approximately 175,000 tons of merchant shipping in 1567, and more than 600,000 tons by 1636. The combined European merchant fleet towards the later seventeenth century comprised around 1,100,000 tons.[5] Based mainly on surveys, these figures are likely to be underestimates if they leave out small vessels sailing from lesser ports. Recently revised figures from a large-scale database note 1,923 English ships in 1572 with a combined tonnage of 62,369, and even these figures underestimate

[3] Daniel Pell, *Pelagos. Nec inter Vivos, nec inter Mortuos: Neither amongst the Living, nor amongst the Dead. Or, An Improvement of the Sea* (1659), sig. B, 19, 135, 531, 543, 555–6.

[4] Josiah Blackmore, *Manifest Perdition: Shipwreck Narrative and the Disruption of Empire* (Minneapolis, 2002), 1; Jennifer H. Oliver, *Shipwreck in French Renaissance Writing: The Direful Spectacle* (Oxford, 2019), 3–21; Steve Mentz, 'God's Storms: Shipwreck and the Meanings of Ocean in Early Modern England and America', in Carl Thompson (ed.), *Shipwreck in Art and Literature* (New York, 2014), 77–91; Steve Mentz, '"We Split!": Shipwreck in Early Modern European History and Culture', in Claire Jowitt, Craig Lambert, and Steve Mentz (eds), *The Routledge Companion to Marine and Maritime Worlds, 1400–1800* (Abingdon and New York, 2020), 580–97. Early modern reflections on maritime danger include Martin Parker, *Neptunes Raging Fury, or, The Gallant Sea-Mens Suffering* (c.1655); William Johnson, *Deus Nobiscum: Or, A Sermon Preached upon a Great Deliverance at* Sea (1659); John Flavell, *A New Compass for Seamen* (1664); John Ryther, *Sea-Dangers and Deliverances Improved* (1674); *Strange and Terrible News from the Seas. Or: A True Relation of a Most Wonderful Violent Tempest* (1678); *God's Wonders in the Great Deep, or, The Seaman's Danger and Deliverance Exemplified* (1710).

[5] Figures cited in Abbot Payson Usher, 'The Growth of English Shipping 1572–1922', *Quarterly Journal of Economics*, 42 (1928), 465–78, and Ralph Davis, *The Rise of the English Shipping Industry in the Seventeenth and Eighteenth Centuries* (1962), 7, 10, 15, are modified in Richard W. Unger, 'The Tonnage of Europe's Merchant Fleets, 1300–1800', in Richard W. Unger (ed.), *Ships and Shipping in the North Sea and Atlantic, 1400–1800* (Aldershot and Brookfield, VT, 1997), 253–6, 260–1. See also Richard W. Unger (ed.), *Shipping and Economic Growth 1350–1850* (Leiden, 2011), 11, and Jan Luiten van Zanden, 'Early Modern Economic Growth: A Survey of the European Economy, 1500–1800', in Maarten Prak (ed.), *Early Modern Capitalism: Economic and Social Change in Europe, 1400–1800* (2001), 69–87, esp. table 4.4. For burden or carrying capacity, see Frederic C. Lane, 'Tonnages, Medieval and Modern', *Economic History Review*, 2nd ser., 17 (1964), 213–29, esp. 228. For tonnage and displacement, see Jan Glete, *Navies and Nations: Warships, Navies and Nations in Europe and America, 1500–1860*, 2 vols (Stockholm, 1993), i. 67–9,74–5.

the total.[6] William Petty, the father of political arithmetic, put the European figure at 2,000,000 tons in the late 1680s. The rising number and quality of naval vessels added to this sail-driven armada: 33 in the English fleet in 1626, 108 in 1666, and 233 by 1741, with much greater tonnage and heft.[7] Much of this shipping plied English coasts and sea lanes, linking the North Sea, the Channel, and the Irish Sea to the Baltic, the Atlantic, and the world beyond.[8] Estimates of its value defy all but the crudest calculation, but the wealth at risk in English waters amounted to many millions of pounds. Every ship represented a calculated investment, a skilled construction, and a vehicle for traffic, that could be undone by misfortune.

Scattered references indicate the 'worth' of particular ships, some prodigious and others old and small. The 'worth' of ten English merchantmen lost to Spanish privateers following the 'peace' of 1604 reportedly ranged from £1,300 to £15,000, with a mean of £5,500. The *Amity* of London was worth £5,600 when taken in 1605, the *Anne Gallant* worth £8,000 when lost off Florida three years later.[9] Similar valuations appear in Thomas Mun's Jacobean account of lost East Indiamen, worth an average of £5,180 per ship.[10] Five London vessels costing from £2,400 to £5,000 were sold in 1618 for £500 to £2,000 'for want of employment', registering depreciation and interruption in trade.[11] A study of shipping during Charles I's wars with Spain and France in the 1620s finds that vessels lost to the enemy or to storms had an average worth of £758 unladen, and that the average value of captured cargoes was £1,189.[12] Close to £20,000 went into the construction of an early Stuart warship like the *Prince Royal*, and a further £16,000 into its rebuilding in 1641. By the eighteenth century the cost had more than doubled.[13]

[6] Craig L. Lambert and Gary P. Baker, 'An Investigation of the Size and Geographical Distribution of the English, Welsh, and Channel Islands Merchant Fleet: A Case Study of 1571–72', in Richard J. Blakemore and James Davey (eds), *The Maritime World of Early Modern Britain* (Amsterdam, 2020), 81–103, esp. 94.

[7] SP 16/13, fos 105–6; SP 29/450, fo. 86; N. A. M. Rodger, *The Command of the Ocean: A Naval History of Britain, 1649–1815* (2004), 614. Glete, *Navies and Nations*, ii. 549–54, has the following figures for the numbers and total displacement of the English and British navy: 1590: 36 ships, 25,000 tons displacement; 1640: 43 ships, 37,900; 1660: 131 ships, 87,900 tons displacement; 1680: 133 ships, 132,100 tons displacement; 1700: 177 ships, 196,200 tons displacement; 1730: 220 ships, 189,200 tons displacement; 1750: 220 ships, 276,200 tons displacement; 1770: 235 ships, 349,800 tons displacement; 1790: 312 ships, 472,800 tons displacement; 1815: 350 ships, 609,300 tons displacement.

[8] Willan, *English Coasting Trade*; N. J. Williams, *The Maritime Trade of the East Anglian Ports 1550–1590* (Oxford, 1988).

[9] *A Declaration of His Highness, by the Advice of the Council Setting Forth, on the Behalf of this Commonwealth, the Justice of their Cause Against Spain* (1655), 10–11.

[10] Mun, *Discourse of Trade*, 39.

[11] G. V. Scammell, 'Shipowning in the Economy and Politics of Early Modern England', *Historical Journal*, 15 (1972), 389.

[12] J. S. Kepler, 'The Value of Ships Gained and Lost by the English Shipping Industry during the Wars with Spain and France, 1624–1630', *Mariner's Mirror*, 59 (1973), 218–19.

[13] *The Autobiography of Phineas Pett*, ed. W. G. Perrin, Navy Records Society (1918), pp. lxxx, lxxxi, 217; Barrington Rosier, 'The Construction Costs of Eighteenth-Century Warships', *Mariner's Mirror*, 96 (2010), 161–72.

Another representation of the value of merchant vessels appears in John Johnson's Jacobean arithmetic exercises, which posed problems involving ships costing £2,700, £3,600, and £3,616 13*s.*[14] The accounts of the seventeenth-century London shipmaster Sir Henry Johnson show that he paid £590 12*s.* 6*d.* in 1639 for 'seven sixteen parts of the good ship called the *Valentine* of London', indicating a price of £1,350, and he sold the *Hercules* for £1,800 in 1669. Johnson's investment of £500 for a 1/32 share in the 600-ton *Bengal Merchant* in 1676 suggests a valuation for that venture as high as £16,000.[15] Argosies like the great East Indiamen were not typical of the English merchant marine, though their wrecks were inclined to be spectacular. The thirty-eight merchantmen in which Henry Johnson had an interest had an average burden of 433 tons, but most commercial vessels were of less than a hundred tons. The converted colliers, wine ships, and fishery vessels that carried English emigrants to New England in the 1630s ranged in burden from 25 to 350 tons, with most around 160.[16] English ships using Restoration-era Bristol had an average burden of 45 tons, while English ships clearing London for France averaged 54.2 tons (see Figure 1).[17]

Figure 1. Wenceslas Hollar, 'Dutch Fluyt', from Navium Variae Figurae et Forma, 1647. Used courtesy of the Harris Brisbane Dick Fund, 1925, The Met.

[14] John Johnson, *Iohnsons Arithmatick* (1623), 161, 173, 287.

[15] BL, MS Add. 22,184, fos 3, 25.

[16] Charles Edward Banks, *The Planters of the Commonwealth* (Boston, 1930), 65–205; David Cressy, *Coming Over: Migration and Communication between England and New England in the Seventeenth Century* (Cambridge, 1987), 145–6.

[17] Violet Barbour, 'Dutch and English Merchant Shipping in the Seventeenth Century', *Economic History Review*, 2 (1930), 262–3; Patrick McGrath, 'Merchant Shipping in the Seventeenth Century: The Evidence of the Bristol Deposition Books', *Mariner's Mirror*, 41 (1955), 28–9. See, however, the

Estimates of value based on tonnage offer little more precision. A 250-ton merchantman could be built in England in 1676 at a cost of £7 2*s.* 6*d.* a ton, £1,781 10*s.* off the stocks. A cheaper second-hand Dutch ship of 200 tons could be bought for about £4 10*s.* a ton, close to £900.[18] Warships of that period cost £8 to £10 per ton to construct, and more than twice that amount 'set to sea'. A 600-ton frigate that cost £4,800 to build would represent an investment of £13,000 by the time it was ready for service.[19] A marine architect in the reign of Queen Anne reckoned £6 10*s.* a ton to build a ship of 216 tons, and £10 16*s.* a ton for a thousand-ton behemoth. Such ships would have values of £1,404 to £10,800, before being fitted with guns and tackle.[20] The average value of 154 ships reported to the High Court of Admiralty in the seventeenth century was £5 13*s.* 6*d.* per ton, varying with furnishing, condition, ordnance, and provisions.[21] William Petty, writing in 1677, reckoned the value 'great and small, new and old, one with another' at £8 per ton.[22]

It may therefore be reasonable, perhaps even modest, to assume for purposes of estimation that unladen merchant ships were worth an average of £6 a ton. If England's shipping in the 1620s comprised some 115,000 tons, its combined value could have been £690,000; the fleet of 340,000 tons in the 1680s would have been worth more than two million pounds. If 500,000 tons of home and foreign shipping made their way through English waters, then three million pounds worth of hulls, furnishings, and gear would be at risk. Cargo values may easily have doubled that amount. Ladings varied from ship to ship and voyage to voyage and were supplemented by undeclared items that crewmen traded on their own account.[23]

The worth of some prodigy ships became apparent only when they were wrecked or taken as prizes. Salvagers of the *George* of Flushing that broke apart in Northumberland in 1565 gathered goods worth £2,400, though unknown amounts went undeclared.[24] The Baltic trader *Marygold* was reckoned to be worth £5,000 when she was taken by privateers in 1581.[25] The *Sea Cock* of Flushing, 380 tons burden, wrecked in 1597, was rated 'a good ship,

survey of ships in the Port of London in 1628, which lists over a hundred ships of over a hundred tons, SP 16/137.

[18] Barbour, 'Dutch and English Merchant Shipping', 275. Dutch ships were built quickly and cheaply with Baltic timber. English ships were more costly, and reputably more robust, framed with seasoned oak.

[19] J. R. Tanner (ed.), *A Descriptive Catalogue of the Naval Manuscripts in the Pepysian Library at Magdalene College, Cambridge* (1903), 229.

[20] William Sutherland, *The Ship-Builders Assistant: Or, Some Essays towards Compleating the Art of Marine Architecture* (1711), 15.

[21] Colin Greenstreet, 'What was a C17th Commercial Ship Worth per Ton of Cargo Burden?', https://marinelives.academia.edu/ColinGteenstreet (accessed October 2019).

[22] Petty, *Political Arithmetick*, 5.

[23] Richard J. Blakemore, 'Pieces of Eight, Pieces of Eight: Seamen's Earnings and the Venture Economy of Early Modern Seafaring', *Economic History Review*, 70 (2017), 1153–84.

[24] SP 59/41, fos 227–8. [25] HCA 13/24, fo. 171^{v}.

worth £2,000'.[26] Owners of another ship lost in 1616 set its value at £3,000, but were lucky to get £300 from salvagers.[27]

The East Indiaman *Moon* carried spices valued at £55,000 when it foundered near Dover in 1625.[28] A Spanish Netherlander was wrecked nearby in the year following yielded £30,000 worth of treasure to the Lord Admiral, the Duke of Buckingham.[29] Goods aboard the *Society* of London, wrecked off Kent in 1636, were said to be worth more than £18,000.[30] Droit collectors from a wreck in Sussex in 1637 accounted for cargo worth £2,000, though much was retained in private hands.[31] A similar sum was retrieved from the *Golden Grape*, wrecked in Dorset in 1641, though this was only a fifth of the ship's reputed value.[32] The furniture, tackle, and lading of the 180-ton *Adventure* of London, homebound from Lisbon, were said to be worth £20,000 when taken by Dunkirkers in 1643.[33]

According to Bulstrode Whitelocke, a Dutch vessel that was wrecked near Pembroke in 1650 was 'laden with goods worth £50,000'.[34] The *Ann* of Yarmouth, bound for the king-in-exile Charles II, was said to have goods 'to the value of £80,000' when it was wrecked off Godrevy, Cornwall, in 1650.[35] Laden East Indiamen, like the *Albemarle* that was wrecked in 1708, cost the owners £40,000, according to company agents.[36] Ships of such worth were rare, and their value was sometimes exaggerated, but they indicate some of the sums at issue. Nothing compared to the £400,000 allegedly lost when the *Royal Merchant* went down in 1641, a treasure of almost mythic proportions. The Venetian ambassador in England reported her cargo as '£300,000 sterling in silver, as well as spices and goods worth quite as much', the loss leaving the mercantile community 'greatly perturbed'.[37] Most ladings, however, were more modest and mundane, though still of value to those who found them. For every cargo valued in the tens of thousands there were dozens worth only a few hundred pounds.

Lost in a wreck, beside the fortunes of merchants and mariners, was the cumulative work of skilled 'carpenters, caulkers, carvers, joiners, smiths, and other labourers' and all the measured materials that went into the craft of

[26] HCA 13/33, fo. 1. [27] PC 2/28, fo. 240.

[28] Alan Roddie, 'Jacob, the Diver', *Mariner's Mirror*, 62 (1976), 258, citing East India Company correspondence.

[29] SP 16/19, fo. 28. [30] HCA 13/52, fo. 460ᵛ. [31] SP 16/365, fos 17ᵛ, 19, 27, 193, 195–7.

[32] HCA 13/244/149.

[33] *A Calendar of Material Relating to Ireland from the High Court of Admiralty 1641–1660*, ed. Elaine Murphy (Dublin, 2011), 18.

[34] Bulstrode Whitelocke, *Memorials of the English Affairs, or, An Historical Account of what Passed from the Beginning of the Reign of King Charles the First, to King Charles the Second his Happy Restoration* (1682), 453.

[35] SP 29/22, fo. 36.

[36] James Derriman, 'The Wreck of the *Albemarle*', *Journal of the Royal Institution of Cornwall*, NS 1 (1992), 140.

[37] SP 16/484, fo. 115ᵛ; *CSP Venice 1640–1642*, 227; *Sad News from the Seas. Being a True Relation of the Losse of that Good Ship called the Merchant Royall* (1641).

'shipwrightry'.[38] 'A good ship is long in making, great pains and costs in rearing and rigging of it,' wrote one early modern observer.[39] Its parts, masts, and tackling had 'more than an hundred several denominations', wrote another. Henry Mainwaring, *The Sea-Mans Dictionary: Or, An Exposition and Demonstration of all the Parts and Things belonging to a Shippe* (1644), listed structures and fittings in alphabetical order. Nathaniel Boteler, *Six Dialogues about Seas-Services* (1685), named these parts from keel to masthead, stem to stern.[40] Thousands of oak trees died for each ship's hull, beams, and planking, and thousands of manhours went into its construction. Shipwreck could reduce this assemblage to debris and kindling. Its capital value and commercial utility became splinters. 'Even now worth this, and now worth nothing,' mused a shipowner in Shakespeare's *Merchant of Venice.*[41]

The development of insurance syndicates spread the risk and mitigated loss, but still left merchants and mariners vulnerable. The English marine insurance business of the Elizabethan era was confused and unorganized but grew in sophistication in the seventeenth century. Coverage was available for the 'perils and dangers of the seas', including 'extreme tempest of shipwreck', with underwriters investing 'of and after the rate of six pounds per cent'.[42] Such provisions were no doubt sensible precautions, but they did not help the Oxford investor Abel Munday, 'who for loss of his goods by seas hanged himself' in September 1612.[43] Nor was Shakespeare's merchant of Venice protected when all his vessels miscarried, costing him his credit, his fortune, and his liberty.[44] The 'treacherous dealing' of the owners of the *Elizabeth* of London were exposed in 1641, after they obtained an insurance certificate for a ship that was already cast away.[45] Moralists urged fortitude in the face of shipwreck adversity. 'You lose one or two now and then, it is nothing but mercy that you have any left to trade or traffic withal,' counselled Daniel Pell in 1659.[46] Shipwrecks were among the hazards of enterprise, prompting reflection upon the inscrutable power of God.

[38] Mun, *Discourse of Trade*, 42; Sutherland, *Ship-Builders Assistant*, 22, 37, 112–38.

[39] Daniel Cawdrey, *A Late Great Shipwrack of Faith* (1655), 26.

[40] Cotton Mather, *The Sailours Companion and Counsellour* (Boston, 1709), 44; Henry Mainwaring, *The Sea-Mans Dictionary: Or, An Exposition and Demonstration of all the Parts and Things Belonging to a Shippe* (1644); Nathaniel Boteler, *Six Dialogues about Seas-Services* (1685), 90–301. See also Edward Hayward, *A Full and Perfect Account of the Size and Lengths of Riggins for all His Majesties Ships and Frigats* (1666).

[41] William Shakespeare, *The Merchant of Venice* (performed *c.*1597), Act I, scene 1.

[42] J. S. Kepler, 'The Operating Potential of London Marine Insurance in the 1570s', *Business History*, 17 (1975), 44–55; Violet Barbour, 'Marine Risks and Insurance in the Seventeenth Century', *Journal of Economic and Business History*, 1 (1929), 561–96; Lucy S. Sutherland, *A London Merchant 1695–1774* (Oxford, 1933), 42–80. Sir Henry Johnson's insurance dealings in the 1670s are recorded in BL, MS Add. 22,184, fo. 56. See also Nicolas Magens, *An Essay on Insurances*, 2 vols (1755); Frank C. Spooner, *Risks at Sea: Amsterdam Insurance and Maritime Europe, 1766–1780* (Cambridge, 1983).

[43] BL, MS Egerton 923, fo. 56; Anthony Wood, *Modius Salium* (Oxford, 1751), 27.

[44] Shakespeare, *Merchant of Venice*, Act III, scene 2.

[45] *Calendar of Material Relating to Ireland from the High Court of Admiralty 1641–1660*, ed. Murphy, 1.

[46] Pell, *Pelagos*, 402.

Levels of Loss

No reliable statistics gauge the extent of loss by shipwreck, but scholars of this topic in the 'age of discovery' consider the level 'high' or even 'staggering'.[47] Shipping to the Indies faced exceptional dangers, with 'a reasonable estimate' of 12–18 per cent lost to the Portuguese in the sixteenth and seventeenth centuries.[48] The wreck rate in Jacobean England's trade to the Indies may have been in the order of 7.5 per cent if Thomas Mun's count of six out of seventy-nine ships 'cast away by the perils of the seas' may be trusted.[49] By the eighteenth century the greatly expanded East India Company lost 3–5 per cent of its ships each year.[50] The Dutch East India Company (VOC) lost 734 ships between 1600 and 1794, an average close to four a year, several on English coastlines.[51] The French East India Company experienced similar levels of distress.[52] England's Admiralty reported thirty-six naval vessels lost between 1688 and 1691, including twelve that foundered or were cast away on England's shores.[53] The most judicious estimate, derived from almost nine thousand Iberian, French, and English voyages of the early modern period, suggests that 'approximately 5 percent of ships putting to sea each year wrecked'.[54] Evidence from the early American Atlantic likewise suggests that '4 to 5 percent of voyages ended in disaster', though the emigrant passages to New England were relatively unscathed.[55] Whether English coastal traffic suffered such loss is undetermined (see Figure 2).

[47] William J. McCarthy, 'Gambling on Empire: The Economic Role of Shipwreck in the Age of Discovery', *International Journal of Maritime History*, 23 (2011), 69–84; Cheryl A. Fury, 'The Work of G. V. Scammell', in Cheryl A. Fury (ed.), *The Social History of English Seamen, 1485–1649* (Woodbridge, 2012), 36.

[48] James Duffy, *Shipwreck and Empire: Being an Account of Portuguese Maritime Disasters in a Century of Decline* (Cambridge, MA, 1955), 63; C. R. Boxer (ed.), *The Tragic History of the Sea 1589–1622: Narratives of the Shipwrecks of the Portuguese East Indiamen* (Cambridge, 1959), 24–7.

[49] Mun, *Discourse of Trade*, 38.

[50] Anthony Farrington, *Catalogue of East India Company Ships' Journals and Logs 1600–1834* (1999); H. V. Bowen, 'The Shipping Losses of the British East India Company, 1755–1813', *International Journal of Maritime History*, 32 (2020), 326.

[51] Karsten Bracker, 'The Lost Ships of the Dutch East India Company—A Cartographic Analysis', https://www.academia.edu/29228296/The_lost_ships_of_the_Dutch_East_India_Company_a_cartographic_analysis (accessed January 2021); www.treasurenet.com.forums/shipwrecks/17237-list-all-653-dutch-voc-shipwrecks-1595-1800-a.html (accessed January 2021); www.vocshipwrecks.nl (accessed January 2021).

[52] Alain Cabantous, *Les Côtes barbares: Pilleurs d'épaves et sociétés littorals en France (1680–1830)* (Paris, 1993), 42. See also Marcello Berti, 'I rischi nella circolazione marittima tra Europa nordica ed Europe mediterranea nel primo trentennio del seicento ed il caso della seconda guerra anglo-olandese (1665–67)' in Simonetta Cavaciochi (ed.), *Ricchezza del Mare Ricchezza del Mare: Secc. XIII–XVIII* (Florence, 2006), 809–39.

[53] Huntington Library, MS Ellesmere 9093.

[54] David D. Hebb, 'Profiting from Misfortune: Corruption and the Admiralty under the Early Stuarts', in Thomas Cogswell, Richard Cust, and Peter Lake (eds), *Politics, Religion and Popularity in Early Stuart Britain: Essays in Honour of Conrad Russell* (Cambridge, 2002), 105.

[55] Amy Mitchell-Cook, *A Sea of Misadventures: Shipwreck and Survival in Early America* (Columbia, SC, 2013), 1, 30; Cressy, *Coming Over*, 144–77.

Figure 2. Claude Lorrain, 'Le Naufrage', *c.*1638–1641. Ailsa Mellon Bruce Fund. Courtesy of the National Gallery of Art, Washington.

The level of distress spiked in times of tempest, like 'the last terrible tempestious windes and weather' of 1613.[56] Another 'tempestuous storm of wind, thunder, and lightning' in 1622 destroyed eight ships, and drowned three hundred men in Devonshire, 'so that it is thought the loss by shipwreck in the west parts of England is forty or fifty thousand pounds'.[57] In the 'Great Storm' of 1703, by one contemporary account, 'the merchantmen that were lost [at Bristol alone] were modestly computed to be worth £100,000'.[58] Eighteenth-century figures suggest that as many as one in thirty voyages (3.3 per cent) went amiss, despite improvements in charts and seamanship.[59] These losses entailed human tragedy

[56] *The Last Terrible Tempestious Windes and Weather: Truly Relating Many Lamentable Ship-Wracks* (1613).

[57] *The Fourth of September: Newes from Sundry Places, both Forraine and Domestique* (1622), 10–12.

[58] *God's Wonders in the Great Deep, or, The Seaman's Danger and Deliverance Exemplified*, 84; Hubert Lamb, *Historic Storms of the North Sea, British Isles and Northwest Europe* (Cambridge, 1991), 4, 21, 55, 59, 72. See also Daniel Defoe, *The Storm: Or, A Collection of the Most Remarkable Casualties and Disasters which Happen'd in the Late Dreadful Tempest, both by Sea and Land* (1704); Daniel Defoe, *An Historical Narrative of the Great and Tremendous Storm which Happened on Nov. 26th, 1703* (1769); Daniel Defoe, *A Tour through the Whole Island of Great Britain*, ed. Pat Rogers (1971), 95, 137–8.

[59] Cathryn Pearce, *Cornish Wrecking 1700–1860: Reality and Popular Myth* (Woodbridge, 2010), 20–1.

as well as economic damage. The price was high for the development of a global economy, but English coastal communities were among its beneficiaries.

Without firm figures for the value of ships, the worth of cargoes, the volume of wrecks, and the scale of loss, it is impossible to gauge the cost of wrecks to the international maritime community. Nor can we estimate the proportion of that wealth transferred to shore-based claimants, except to say it was substantial. Rough estimates suggest that losses to the seventeenth-century English merchant community ran as high as £250,000 a year, with foreign losses significantly higher. Losses in the Channel were said to be 'frequent and lamentable'. Proponents for setting lights on the Goodwin Sands claimed in 1641 that recent wrecks on those banks were 'valued at £400,000, besides the loss of men's lives, which is unvaluable'.[60] These calculations, of course, are speculative, but they point to the cost of commerce in troubled waters. If only a fraction of that wealth could be recovered by salvagers and wreckers, it meant profit for shore-based claimants and bounty to the local economy.

A rough guide to the frequency of maritime catastrophe appears in reports to Restoration-era Secretaries of State. Port officials around the country provided information on the movements of ships, and their distresses. Hardly a month went by without sad news of ships cast away and seamen drowned.[61] Reports from 1667 may be regarded as typical. In February the port office of Dartmouth reported the loss of a hundred-ton Ostend trader, laden with herrings, cast away at Start Point, Devon, with most of her men drowned. In the same month a Dutch vessel with five hundred hogsheads of wine was wrecked in South Wales.[62] In March officials at Dover reported that the packet boat from Ostend went down with about thirty persons. In May seven small vessels were cast away on the Goodwin Sands, 'and several other great ships are missing'. Plymouth officials reported in August the wreck of a ship from Virginia, cast away near Fowey in Cornwall.[63] More distress followed as the weather deteriorated in the autumn. September brought news of a Swansea collier cast away near Minehead, Somerset, 'having lost her main mast and forced ashore by reason of the great storm'. The *Blessing* of Swansea and the *Mary* of Minehead were also lost, their crews 'all foundered in the sea'. In the same month, Harwich officials reported, 'a Hull man with lead and other Hull trade was cast away upon the Whitaker', but 'a fisherman saved all the persons'.[64]

Marine losses mounted in October. In the Bristol Channel near Swansea a ship carrying livestock from Wexford 'was thrown on the shore... amongst the rocks', but 'by providence the mariners and passengers are landed, with most of the

[60] *Charles by the Grace of God... for the Maintenance of Light-Houses at the North and South Forelands* (1637); *The Answers to the Severall Objections, Made against the Lights for the Goodwin Sands* (1641), 1.

[61] SP 29/83, fos 67, 159; SP 29/176, fo. 88; SP 29/178, fo. 12; SP 29/180, fo. 3, and many more.

[62] SP 29/190, fo. 41; SP 29/182, fo. 31.

[63] SP 29/194, fo. 26; SP 29/200, fo. 27; SP 29/213, fo. 95.

[64] SP 29/217, fos 33, 34, 172.

cattle'. The Swansea agent reported three more vessels cast away, with only three mariners saved. In Norfolk a Yarmouth vessel 'was cast away upon the sands of Winterton ... the master and boy was lost, the rest saved by swimming to the shore'. There was 'so much wreck floating in the sea' that observers 'were amazed to see it'. More ships lost that month included five or six cast away near Margate, Kent, and another collier sunk with all hands off Northumberland.[65] October's most spectacular wreck was the *Santo Cristo de Castello*, a Dutch man-of-war under Genoese charter—800 tons, with 130 crew and 40 guns, bound from Amsterdam to Cadiz with £50,000 worth of iron, cloth, and spices—that went down off the Lizard. Authorities at Falmouth and Plymouth rushed to send the news to London.[66]

November 1667 was another rough month. 'Every day brings news of ships cast away', wrote John Carlisle from Dover. A Newcastle collier was lost at Bridlington, a Plymouth ship from Barbados was wrecked in Cornwall, and the *Elizabeth* ketch of Whitby was cast away on the Isle of Wight. Three Ostenders came to grief near Dungeness, and another was wrecked near Pevensey, according to the officer at Rye.[67] A Dutch merchantman was wrecked on the rocks near Falmouth; Thomas Hicks reported, 'it is supposed she might be insured, for she was cast away very carelessly.' Towards the end of the month the Deal agent reported another loss on the Goodwin Sands of an English pink of 100 tons.[68]

The year ended with more wrecks, though perhaps no more than usual. Winterton, Norfolk, saw another collier founder, while a vessel carrying hides and provisions for France went down near St Ives in Cornwall. A small frigate bound for Tangier was wrecked in Mounts Bay, three more ships and crew were lost in the Scillies, and the 130-ton *Peregrine* of Hull went down with only three survivors.[69] The Falmouth agent Thomas Holden reported the indignation of 'a great don bound for Flanders' whose Spanish vessel perished on the Isles of Scilly. Though lucky to survive, the passenger complained of the 'the cruelty of the islanders', who, he said, valued 'the saving of the goods and money [more] than his life'.[70] The legend of 'barbarous' wreckers was by then well advanced.

More than forty wrecks were mentioned in these reports from 1667, not counting those that came to grief in Irish, Scottish, or foreign waters. Only five were identified by name. Some lay beyond reach and beyond help, but most brought material goods ashore. Similar observations in other years record comparable calamities. Communications in 1677, for example, mostly from southern ports, mentioned the casting-away of more than thirty-five vessels, but gave names

[65] SP 29/219, fos 93, 117, 163–4; SP 29/221, fo. 51,

[66] SP 29/219, 115, 161; SP 29/224, fo. 33. For modern exploration, see P. McBride, R. Larn, and R. Davis, 'A Mid-17th Century Merchant Ship Found near Mullion Cove: 3rd Interim Report on the *Santo Christo de Castello*, 1667', *International Journal of Nautical Archaeology*, 4 (1975), 237–52.

[67] SP 29/222, fo. 92; SP 29/223, fos 6, 134, 181, 205.

[68] SP 29/222, fo. 62; SP 29/223, fo. 234.

[69] SP 29/224, fos 11, 97; SP 29/225, fos 18, 156; SP 29/254, fo. 4.

[70] SP 29/225, fo. 159.

to only seven of them. Typical memoranda reported the wreck of 'a Dutch vessel ... very richly laden', a Bordeaux wine ship 'cast away... to the westward of this place', and 'three Canary ships lately lost near us'. Winter storms left 'much wreck' in the water and cast broken boats and barrels on shore.[71] Often we learn no more than that several vessels were lost and that floating debris was seen. The record is inevitably incomplete, but some casualties may be further identified in correspondence of owners and shippers, complaints against wreckers, and proceedings of the Admiralty courts.

Documentation survives of more than 850 named vessels that were wrecked or cast away on English and Welsh shores between 1550 and 1750 (see Appendix). Many more were unidentified or unrecorded. Archaeologists have found the remains of some of them, and others await discovery in the archives or in the sea. Most of those listed in the Appendix were newsworthy or subject to dispute, which is why evidence of their trouble survives. Larger ships, foreign-owned ships, and vessels with high-value cargoes may be over-represented, especially if their owners sought restitution and survivors presented testimony. Ships that were smaller and lightly laden, and wrecks that evaded legal, bureaucratic, or journalistic attention, were less likely to be recorded. Losses of naval vessels are also under-represented, though some, like the *Anne Royal* (1636), the *London* (1665), and the *Gloucester* (1682), were well documented. The true number of wrecks in this period may well have exceeded four thousand. Each one exposed and tested relationships between claimants of the sea and of the land.

With varying degrees of precision, we know the locations where 755 of these ships came to grief. The heavily trafficked coast of the Channel or Narrow Seas from Southampton to the Isle of Thanet saw the greatest number of wrecks (269 or 36 per cent) with Kent's Goodwin Sands, the Sussex cliffs near Seaford, and the Isle of Wight especially lethal. The rocky coasts of the south-west posed different dangers, claiming 263 (35 per cent) including 42 in the Isles of Scilly and 120 in other parts of Cornwall. The banks and beaches of the North Sea from the Thames Estuary to Northumberland had 150 (20 per cent) from this sample. Irish Sea coasts from Cumberland to the Bristol Channel had 73 (almost 10 per cent), including 54 in Wales. Comparable geographical distributions appear in charts of nineteenth-century wrecks, from a time when such casualties exceeded 1,500 a year.[72]

It should not be surprising that early modern England's much-vaunted maritime expansion entailed accidents and loss, which accountants could reckon as the cost of doing business. The concomitant loss of life is incalculable. But the

[71] SP 29/390, fos 121, 155–6, 174, 179, 232, 242, 250, 252, 284; SP 29/391, fos 72, 110, 227, 230–1, 239; SP 29/392, fos 6, 11, 381; SP 29/393, fo. 8; SP 29/397, fos 37, 47, 58, 194, 221, 234, 255–6, 288; SP 29/398, fos 123, 143.

[72] See Appendix; *Wreck Chart of the British Isles for 1859: Compiled from the Board of Trade Register* (1860); 'Wreck Chart of the British Isles for the Year 1873–4', *Lifeboat*, 9/98 (November 1875).

seaman's loss was the landsman's gain, as goods from the world's oceans came ashore. Coastal communities sprang into action whenever a wreck reached their shores, giving succour to survivors, and gathering and redistributing as much material as possible. It was, as the proverb said, an ill wind that blew nobody any good. How that transfer of wealth and goods was accomplished, to whose benefit, and amid what controversy, is discussed in the following chapters.

2
The Perils of the Sea

'The unconscionable and all-devouring sea' ruined cargoes and drowned sailors, a Jacobean treatise reminded readers.[1] Common knowledge from literature and scripture was confirmed by those who went down to the sea in ships. Storms and shipwrecks in the Bible (Jonah, St Paul), in the classics (Homer, Vergil), and in the writings of the Renaissance (Erasmus, Rabelais, Sidney, Shakespeare) were presented as punishments for the hubris of heroes and the sins of sailors. Preachers and moralists used this maritime imagery to warn of the shipwreck of the soul or the shipwreck of the state.

While the master narrative of the age attributed disaster and deliverance to divine providence, more objective reports by merchants and mariners described the actual mishaps of voyaging, extremities of weather, crises of foundering and abandonment, and the deaths and survivals of shipwreck victims. They told of ships being pushed beyond their handling, as mariners were overwhelmed by the fury of the waves, as navigational error, faulty seamanship, and blind misfortune played their parts. Discursive texts and scribal reports told how shipwrecks happened, and how they were understood. Sharing a common vocabulary, they presented a maritime viewpoint to a land-based audience.

One did not need to roam the sea to appreciate its dangers, or to recognize its power to drown or ruin mariners. Snug in a chair in an inland city, miles from salt water, a reader could contemplate the perils of the deep. Accounts of storms and shipwrecks exposed the working of providence, and displayed the fortitude of characters in extreme and hazardous conditions. Leaving analysis of the 'burden of meaning' and 'dramatic potential' of 'allegorical, fictional, and polemical shipwreck texts' to literary scholars, a historian may consider how classic accounts shaped popular perceptions of the myriad perils of the sea. Shipwrecks real, mythical, and metaphorical were part of English cultural consciousness. They were imagined and moralized, as well as experienced and endured, entering the archives and both the pictorial and textual canons (see Figure 3).[2]

[1] *The Last Terrible Tempestious Windes and Weather: Truly Relating Many Lamentable Ship-Wracks* (1613), sig. A4.

[2] Literary analysis includes Hans Blumenberg, *Shipwreck with Spectator: Paradigm of a Metaphor for Existence* (Cambridge, MA, 1997); Margarette Lincoln, 'Shipwreck Narratives of the Eighteenth and Early Nineteenth Century: Indicators of Culture and Identity', *British Journal for Eighteenth-Century Studies*, 20 (1997), 155–72; Bradin Cormack, *A Power to do Justice: Jurisdiction, English Literature, and*

Shipwrecks and the Bounty of the Sea. David Cressy, Oxford University Press. © David Cressy 2022.
DOI: 10.1093/oso/9780192863393.003.0003

Figure 3. Simon Novellanus after Cornelius Cort, 'The Shipwreck', *c.*1595. Rosenwald Collection. Courtesy of the National Gallery of Art, Washington.

Ancient Mariners

The *Holy Bible*, read in every church, familiarized parishioners with maritime distress. Everyone knew, from the 107th Psalm, that 'they that go down to the sea in ships, that do business in great waters, these see the works of the lord, and his wonders in the deep. For he commandeth, and raiseth the stormy wind, which lifteth up the waves thereof. He maketh the storm a calm so that the waves thereof are still.'[3] 'The God of heaven' sent such a storm against the vessel carrying Jonah, 'so that the ship was like to be broken. Then the mariners were afraid, and cried

the Rise of the Common Law, 1509–1625 (Chicago, 2007); Carl Thompson (ed.), *Shipwreck in Art and Literature* (New York, 2014); James V. Morrison, *Shipwrecked: Disaster and Transformation in Homer, Shakespeare, Defoe, and the Modern World* (Ann Arbor, 2014); Brigitte Le Juez and Olga Springer (eds), *Shipwrecks and Island Motifs in Literature and the Arts* (Leiden, 2015); Steve Mentz, *Shipwreck Modernity: Ecologies of Globalization, 1550–1719* (Minneapolis, 2015); Jennifer H. Oliver, *Shipwreck in French Renaissance Writing: The Direful Spectacle* (Oxford, 2019), 13, 21, 144; Steve Mentz, '"We Split!": Shipwreck in Early Modern European History and Culture', in Claire Jowitt, Craig Lambert, and Steve Mentz (eds), *The Routledge Companion to Marine and Maritime Worlds, 1400–1800* (Abingdon and New York, 2020), 580–97.

[3] Psalms, 107: 23–9.

every man unto his god, and cast forth the wares that were in the ship into the sea, to lighten it of them.' Jettisoning cargo was a standard response to life-threatening conditions, but only casting out Jonah would assuage this particular tempest, 'and the sea ceased from her raging'.[4]

The New Testament told of a similar 'tempestuous wind' that overpowered the ship carrying St Paul to Italy. Following conventional practice, Paul's mariners 'used helps, undergirding the ship, and struck sail'. Then, 'exceeding tossed by a tempest... they lightened the ship' and cast out her tackling. Driven by the wind against an unknown land, 'they ran the ship aground, and the forepart stuck fast... but the hinder part was broken with the violence of the waves.' Thankfully, by God's providence, everyone on board 'escaped all safe to land' on 'broken pieces of the ship', and sought the hospitality of the 'barbarous' local inhabitants ('barbarous' in language, not behaviour).[5] Nor was this Paul's only misadventure; as he told the Corinthians, 'thrice I suffered shipwreck, a night and day I have been in the deep... in perils in the sea'.[6] Going down to the sea in ships was evidently a dangerous business, best left to professionals and people who needed to travel.

The Bible reminded readers that ships could be tested to the point of destruction, and their fate was in God's hand. Strenuous efforts to maintain seaworthiness, to secure planking, to lighten loads, and to cut down masts and tackle might reduce the risk of foundering, only if God helped those who helped themselves.

Classical antiquity also bequeathed a literature of storms and shipwrecks. A typical voyage started well, but was beset by hostile circumstances. Monstrous tempests challenged men and ships, as capricious gods bestowed enmity or favour. Heroes suffered and then survived, while their unnamed followers perished. No epic would be complete without such an episode.[7]

Homer's *Odyssey*, Englished by George Chapman in the reign of James I, offers exemplary scenes of wreckage and deliverance. In book five Odysseus tells how his ruined ship was tortured by the sea, 'floating at random, from wave to wave', until he alone clung to debris amid the surf of Nausicaa's island. In book twelve he relates an earlier storm that smashed his ship near the rocks and whirlpools of Scylla and Charybdis: the cables burst, masts and tackle tumbled, crewmen crushed and tossed overboard, and the whole vessel was choking 'with let-in surges'. Only Odysseus escaped, on flotsam of mast and keel, until he washed up on the island of Calypso. Shipwrecks in this savage world began with angry gods, and deliverance depended on more benign divinities.[8]

Virgil's *Aeneid*, composed around 20 BC, offered maritime adversity in abundance. Divine friends and enemies governed the fate of the hero Aeneas, as he voyaged across the Mediterranean, a refugee from the fall of Troy. 'Huge

[4] Jonah, 1: 4–15. [5] Acts, 27: 14–44. [6] 2 Corinthians, 11: 25–6.

[7] H. H. Huxley, 'Storm and Shipwreck in Roman Literature', *Greece and Rome*, 21 (1952), 117–24.

[8] Homer, *Odyssey*, books V, XII; *Homer's Odyssey*, trans. George Chapman (1615), 79–83, 191–3.

blustering winds' broke his fleet, 'and so devoured men, riches, writings, arms', their goods and tackle 'swimming in boisterous floods'. Dashed against the coast of Africa, only seven out of twenty vessels came safe to land. As if this was not ordeal enough, the survivors suffered further shipwreck on their continuing voyage, leaving companions on rocky crags and breaking shoals. Their oars splintered, their helmsman overwhelmed, the Trojans pressed on to their Italian destination, and perhaps, in some legends, as far as the British Isles. Tudor and Stuart translations brought this epic to English readers, with further examples of maritime distress.[9]

One of the lessons of these ancient and biblical texts was that shipwrecked sailors might be saved by divine intervention. Another was that fortune brought some to friendly shores, where even 'barbarians' could exhibit charity and hospitality. These were model messages for seamen and land folk in early modern England.

Renaissance Wrecks

The classic *naufragium* (shipwreck) dialogue of Erasmus (1466–1536), first printed in Latin in 1523 and available in English by 1606, drew on folklore, fables, antiquity, and hagiography, as well, it seems likely, as recent seafarers' stories. Voyaging in northern waters, off the coast of Holland, the mariners of this story meet mountainous seas, too violent to handle. They attempt to lighten ship by tossing goods and possessions overboard, as Paul's shipmates had done off Malta. As conditions worsen, and the winds rage more and more, the master orders the mast to be cut down, and shrouds and sails to be jettisoned. Facing calamity, the passengers pray to be saved, while the mariners undergird the ship with ropes lest it soon split in pieces. The vessel becomes 'noisome and rent, and leaking on every side', as the crew launch the ship's boat, starting a scramble for places, but the boat is overset, with the loss of thirty lives. Those remaining commit themselves to the waves, on whatever flotsam they can find, and a fortunate few are pulled ashore by the hospitable Dutch. There they find 'lodging, fire, meat, apparel, and all necessaries', like Paul's group of survivors, lucky not to land on the shores of more 'cruel and barbarous nations' (perhaps the English).[10]

[9] Virgil, *Aeneid*, books I, V; *The XI Aeneids of Virgil*, trans. John Vicars (1632), 2–7; *The Works of Publius Virgilius Maro*, trans. John Ogilby (1675), second pagination, 1–7, 210–37; Sheldon Brammall, *The English Aeneid: Translations of Virgil 1555–1646* (Edinburgh, 2015). Ovid, Seneca, and Lucan also wrote scenes of storms.

[10] W. B., *Seven Dialogues both Pithie and* Profitable (1606), sigs G–H; Thomas Heywood, *Pleasant Dialogues and Dramas* (1637), 1–15; *Twenty Select Colloquies, out of Erasmus Roterodamus*, ed. Roger l'Estrange (1680), 1–10; *Collected Works of Erasmus: Colloquies*, ed. Craig R. Thompson (Toronto, 1997), 351–67.

Erasmus derives moral messages from his story and uses it to mock priestly superstitions. The *naufragium* colloquy includes a version of the classic lifeboat dilemma, asking who most deserves to be saved: the man of God, the man of law, or the man of labour? It also unfolds the standard phases of a shipwreck narrative, in which a fair voyage turns foul, with ever-increasing distress, until survivors and wreckage are scattered ashore. The tempest tests their fortitude and the firmness of their faith.

François Rabelais (1494–1553) also obtains allegorical mileage from a storm at sea. English Protestant critics interpreted the storm in *Pantagruel* to represent 'the pope's thunderbolts' and 'the cruel persecution that was raised in France', but the author either imagined or had experience of foul marine weather. In the seventeenth-century English translation, as the wind picks up, the master orders preparations: 'Hands upon deck... in with your topsails, lower the fore-sail... brade up close all them sails, strike your top masts... lash your guns fast.' Then

> immediately it blowed a storm, the sea began to roar mountain high... waves breaking upon our ship's quarter, the northwest wind blustered and overblowed; boisterous gusts, dreadful clashings and deadly scuds of wind whistled through our yards, and made our shrouds rattle again. The thunder grumbled so horridly that you would have thought heaven had been tumbling about our ears; at the same time it lightninged, rained, hailed, the sky lost its transparent hue, grew dusky, thick and gloomy... it seemed to us a lively image of the chaos, where fire, air, sea, land, and all the elements were in refractory confusion.

As conditions deteriorate, the vessel begins to founder: 'this wave will sweep us away... the mizzen sail's split, the gallery's washed away, the masts are sprung... the keel is up to the sun... Alas, who shall have this wreck?' The storm exposes the cowardice of the roguish but spineless Panurge, and the greater composure of other characters. In this case the ship finds safety, although voyagers in a later Rabelaisian episode end 'stranded amid shoals'.[11]

John Donne memorialized similar perils, but more dignified behaviour, in his poem 'The Storme', ostensibly about his voyage with the Earl of Essex in 1597, but also a meditation on death. The ship 'shak'd with an ague... our tackling snapping ... our totter'd sails, rags', in a chaos of darkness, rain, lightning, and thunder, but avoided being wrecked. Convincing as description, this was also an adaptation of the familiar storm narrative of the classical literary tradition.[12]

[11] *Pantagruel's Voyage to the Oracle of the Bottle. Being the Fourth and Fifth Books of the Works of Francis Rabelais* (1694), pp. xxxii, 78–81; *The Complete Works of François Rabelais*, ed. Donald M. Frame and Raymond C. La Charité (Berkeley and Los Angeles, 1991), 477–88, 646–7.

[12] *The Poems of John Donne*, ed. Herbert Grierson (1957), 155–7; Clayton D. Lein, 'Donne's "The Storme": The Poem and the Tradition', *English Literary Renaissance*, 4 (1974), 137–63.

Sir Philip Sidney's *Arcadia* predictably includes another ship-killing storm. Who would want romance adventure without one? Set at sea, Sidney's princes meet the inevitable tempest.

> Winds began to speak louder . . . blowing whole storms of hail and rain upon them . . . Then the traitorous sea began to swell in pride against the afflicted navy . . . making mountains of itself, o'er which the tossed and tottering ship should climb, to be straight carried down again to a pit of hellish darkness, with such cruel blows against the sides of the ship . . . that there was left neither power to stay, nor way to escape.

At length 'the tyranny of the wind, and the treason of the sea' drove the vessel onto a rock, 'till she had broken herself in pieces, and as it were tearing out her own bowels to feed the sea's greediness'. The surviving prince, 'brought out of the sea's fury to the land's comfort', arrives on the beach 'much bruised and beaten both with the sea's hard farewell, and the shore's rude welcome'. Of such prose are heroes made.[13]

Simile, metaphor, and allegory made heavy use of the imagery of tempest and shipwreck in Edmund Spenser's *The Faerie Queene.* Beset with other perils, the courteous knight was oppressed 'like as a ship with dreadful storm long toss'd, I Having spent all her masts, and her ground-hold, I Now far from harbour likely to be lost'.[14]

With greater economy, and changing perspective, Shakespeare stages the tempest in the play of that name. As the mariners bestir 'or we run ourselves aground', the passenger Gonzalo swears 'now I would give a thousand furlongs of sea for an acre of barren ground'. Witnessing the disaster from the island shore (or perhaps imagining it), Miranda notes the roar of 'the wild waters . . . The sky, it seems, would pour down stinking pitch, but that the sea, mounting to the welkin's cheek, dashes the fire out.' 'A brave vessel' is 'dashed all to pieces', as the sea swallows 'the good ship . . . and the fraughting souls within her'. 'Full fathom five thy father lies,' sings Ariel to the survivor Ferdinand. The plots of at least five of Shakespeare's plays involve characters who suffer and survive a shipwreck.[15] 'Methought I saw a thousand fearful wracks, ten thousand men that fishes gnaw'd upon,' moans Clarence in *Richard III.*[16]

More derivative, and less convincing, Beaumont and Fletcher's Jacobean comedy *The Sea-Voyage* opens with another ship in danger of 'tempest, thunder and lightning'. The master issues urgent orders, with appropriate nautical jargon:

[13] Sir Philip Sidney, *The Countesse of Pembrokes Arcadia* (1593), fos 65–6.

[14] Edmund Spenser, *The Faerie Queene* (1596), book VI, canto iv.

[15] William Shakespeare, *Tempest* (written *c.*1611), Act 1, scenes 1 and 2. See also *Comedy of Errors, Twelfth Night, Pericles,* and *Winter's Tale,*

[16] *Richard III,* Act 1, scene 4.

'down with the main mast, lay her at hull, farle up all her linens', but a sailor warns, 'she's so deep laden that she'll bulge'. In desperation they move to 'cast over all her lading, she will not swim an hour else', and toss over valuable chests of plate. Like the mariners in Shakespeare's *Tempest*, and in the *Naufragium* of Erasmus, the company is in deep trouble, in a leaking ship, 'her rudder almost spent', her tackling lost, near to death on an unknown shore, where 'they leap from one calamity to another'. The scene teaches nothing about meteorology, nor seamanship, but evokes once more the perils of the deep.[17]

A Poeticall Sea-Piece of 1633, under the patronage if not from the pen of the courtier Endymion Porter, imagines the sea as vexed by 'the stormy fiend', while mariners answered to 'God alone'. The poet conjures waves 'like jaws infernal, mouths of hell, | To swallow whole fleets whole, none left to tell'. In this maelstrom 'the ship's sides crack, the tackle tears like thread, | Some ply the pump, some cry we are all dead'. Shipwreck is inescapable, 'the masts cut down, the goods thrown overboard, | And last themselves, all aid's in vain implored'. Sailors find their 'liquid graves', or struggle against a 'cruel' shore.[18] The vein runs deep, though the language does not soar.

The shipwreck that opens the Restoration entertainment *The Isle of Pines* (1668) is equally generic, beginning with 'a great storm of wind, which continued with such violence for many days'. 'Driven by foul weather', the mariners expect 'suddenly to perish', not knowing whether they would fall 'on flats or rocks'. All are drowned except the narrator, three women, and a negro servant, who make a utopian new England on their imagined desert island.[19]

The most famous account of shipwreck survival, *The Life and Strange Surprizing Adventures of Robinson Crusoe* by Daniel Defoe (1719), includes two scenes of maritime catastrophe with all the classic elements of mountainous seas, an unmanageable ship, and mariners close to despair. The young Robinson's first sea voyage ends with shipwreck off the coast of Norfolk, after a storm so violent that it struck 'terror and amazement in the faces even of the seamen themselves'. In desperation the crew cut away the masts, call all hands to the pumps, and fire guns to summon assistance, before taking to a small boat and watching their ship go down. Eventually the survivors find safety on shore, where fortunately, like St Paul, they are 'used with great humanity'.[20]

Several years later, in the course of a slaving voyage in the south Atlantic, Robinson Crusoe and his companions are called to account for their sins. The ship is caught in a hurricane and loses two crewmen overboard. A second storm throws

[17] Francis Beaumont and John Fletcher, *Fifty Comedies and Tragedies* (1679), 339–41.

[18] *A Poeticall Sea-Piece: Containing in a Spacious Table the Lively Description of a Tempest at Sea, and Shipwrecks* (1633).

[19] Henry Neville, *The Isle of Pines, or, A Late Discovery of a Fourth Island in Terra Australis, Incognita* (1668), 2–3.

[20] Daniel Defoe, *The Life and Strange Surprizing Adventures of Robinson Crusoe* (1719), 10–13.

them against an unknown shore, where their vessel begins to break up on a sandbank. Committing themselves 'to God's mercy and the wild sea', the remaining mariners escape to their longboat, but all but Crusoe are drowned when they were engulfed by 'a raging wave'. Battered by rocks, and half 'strangled in the water', Defoe's hero manages to struggle ashore. This time there are no charitable rescuers, and no question of right to salvage, as the eponymous survivor helps himself to supplies, sustenance, furnishings, and tools.[21]

A generation later the author William Falconer enjoyed great success with his long poem 'The Shipwreck', a sensational and sentimental evocation of the terror of the sea, based on his experiences in the Mediterranean.[22] Falconer's mariners face 'rolling billows' and 'treacherous tides' as they battle seas familiar to Odysseus, Aeneas, and St Paul:

> Companions, binnacle, in floating wreck,
> With compasses and glasses strew'd the deck;
> The mizzen rending, from the bolt-rope flew,
> Torn from the earing to the flutt'ring clue;
> The sides convulsive shook on groaning beams,
> And yawning wide expose the pitchy seams.

And so on, until at last: 'With horrid yaw, along the surge-lash'd strand, | The never-closing jaws of death expand.' One begins to feel salt-soaked, simply by reading.

Shipwrecks of the Soul and State

Preachers and moralists commonly used the metaphor of shipwreck to signify the ruin of a soul or a state. The word conjured scenes of disintegration and despair, as material fittings and finery were reduced to 'a desolate rubbish'.[23] One did not need to have witnessed an actual shipwreck to be moved by the power of the image. A succession of authors across the ages evoked the disaster of 'eternal shipwreck' to address the perils of the human condition.[24]

The Elizabethan cleric Richard Madox imagined mariners 'seashaken with a storm', but safe so long as Christ was on board. Preaching before merchants and

[21] Defoe, *Robinson Crusoe*, 47–52, 57–8.

[22] William Falconer, *The Shipwreck. A Poem. In Three Cantos. By A Sailor* (1762), canto III. There were at least nine editions of this work by 1789. Readers could also marvel at 'true' adventures, such as *Capt. Inglefield's Narrative, Concerning the Loss of His Majesty's Ship the Centaur* (1783), or *A Circumstantial Narrative of the Loss of the Halsewell (East-Indiaman)* (1786).

[23] Daniel Pell, *Pelagos. Nec inter Vivos, nec inter Mortuos, Neither amongst the Living, nor amongst the Dead. Or, An Improvement of the Sea* (1659), 556.

[24] John Brekell, *Euroclydon: Or the Dangers of the Sea* (1744), 38.

mariners at Weymouth in 1581, he prayed to God to 'appease the rage of this tempestuous world, still the storms of the flesh, and rebuke the wicked spirits which seek to bring both body and soul to shipwreck'. Loosed of the anchor of faith, every soul was 'in danger to be eaten up of the sea, and so to make a miserable shipwreck'. The 'seashaken' sailor was the exemplar of trembling humanity.[25]

The downfall of any enterprise—commercial, political, or spiritual—could be couched in this language of wreckage. William Willymat's *Anchor of Faith* (1628), with its cliché nautical title, reminded readers that 'Cain and Judas most fearfully... shipwrecked themselves, to the utter confusion both of body and soul forever'.[26] How dreadful, wrote John Flavell in *A New Compass for Seamen* (1664), that men's 'immortal souls should sink and perish in a storm of God's wrath'.[27] Other ministers mused on 'the rocks of Christian shipwreck', 'the shipwreck of all false churches', and a 'shipwreck of faith occasioned by a fearful wreck of conscience'.[28] John Milton was one of many who likened the crisis that beset Charles I's government to a storm-tossed ship wrecked on dangerous rocks.[29]

Henry Burton, who had seen his share of storms on his passage as a prisoner to the Channel Islands, exhorted a London audience in 1646, 'that you may not be carried with the strong tide of the times by any malignant spirit filling your sails, through many under-water rocks and shelves, endangering not only the splitting of your own vessel, but the total shipwreck of this floating state'.[30] John Turner, preaching under James II, warned of the 'passions and prejudices... which like rocks and shelves, not taken notice of by any sea chart, like moving sands, without any buoys to discover them, would every moment endanger the shipwreck of the state'.[31] Addressing the newly appointed Warden of the Cinque Ports in 1694, James Brome reminded the Earl of Romney that 'a good governor is a skillful ship-master that takes the safest and shortest course, and... so steers as the rocks and

[25] Richard Madox, *A Learned and Godly Sermon... Especially for all Marryners, Captaynes and Passengers, which Travel the Seas* (1581), epistle Bi–Cii^{v}.

[26] William Willymat, *The Anchor of Faith upon which, a Christian Man may Repose in all Manner... of Temptations* (1628), title page.

[27] John Flavell, *A New Compass for Seamen* (1664), 123. See also John Ryther, *Sea-Dangers and Deliverances Improved* (1674), bound and paginated with James Janeway, *Mr James Janeway's Legacy to his Friends: Containing Twenty-Seven Famous Instances of God's Providence in and about Sea-Dangers and Deliverances* (1675), 113, on 'not only the danger of a shipwrecked vessel, and shipwrecked estate, and a shipwrecked body, but a shipwrecked soul'.

[28] John King, *Lectures upon Jonas* (Oxford, 1599); Marco Antonio de Dominis, *The Rockes of Christian Shipwracke: Discovered by the Holy Church of Christ* (1618); John Graunt, *The Shipwrack of all False Churches* (1652); Daniel Cawdrey, *A Late Great Shipwrack of Faith* (1655).

[29] John Milton, *Of Reformation* (1641), 43, 59. For more examples, see David Cressy, *England on Edge: Crisis and Revolution 1640–1642* (Oxford, 2006), 34–5.

[30] Henry Burton, *Conformitie's Deformity: In a Dialogue between Conformity and Conscience* (1646), dedication.

[31] John Turner, *Two Sermons, the First Preached upon January the 29* (1688), 21. Turner's sermons celebrated the queen's conception, and the birth of Prince James. James II himself, as Duke of York, had suffered shipwreck in 1682 aboard the man of war *Gloucester*.

shelves, which might shipwreck the state, be avoided'.[32] Every voyage, every undertaking, was shadowed by shipwreckful potential.[33]

Religious writers floated an endless tide of nautical imagery, aimed as much at shore-dwellers as at sinners at sea. 'Our ship is subject to subversion, if thy holy hand direct us not in merciful providence,' wrote the godly Elizabethan Anthony Anderson, himself a veteran of Irish Sea voyages. In 'this our little ship ... we are environed with these huge roaring seas, horribly raging and breaking in upon us. The winds are vehement, and grow to increase in storms, and our sins be heavy, and Satan seeketh to sink us.' Understanding that tempests were sent to 'punish and prove us', Anderson prayed to God to 'keep whole our masts, provide safety to our sail, hold steady our helm, and be thyself the master of our ship', so that travellers on the voyage of life could reach their desired haven, heaven.[34]

Dozens of writers used similar imagery in the service of evangelical browbeating. Richard Madox imagined

> our sails of heavenly hope, filled with the wind of God's spirit, being directed by the compass of his word ... While Christ is master, although the tide be set on the weather bow, yet the boat shall never be sinking to leeward [or] fall on a wrong coast. And while Christ is pilot, it shall never run upon the flats by mistaking the channel, nor make in against the current by misreckoning the tides.[35]

Every part of a ship, every nautical practice, had its spiritual counterpart. 'The sea is the world, the waves are calamities, the church is the ship, the anchor is hope, the sails are love, the saints are passengers, the haven is heaven, and Christ is our pilot,' wrote the Calvinist William Perkins.[36] 'God's word the compass ... Christ my load star ... the law of God is my pilot,' echoed Henry Mainwaring.[37] 'The word is our compass. Faith is our helm. Hope is our anchor. Charity our sails. Perseverance our ballast. The Holy Spirit our gale,' repeated the Congregationalist Cotton Mather.[38] Over-enchanted by the over-used analogy, some ministers knew not when to reef their sails.

[32] James Brome, *A Sermon Preached in St Maries Church in Dover* (1694), 1–2.

[33] Josiah Blackmore, *Manifest Perdition: Shipwreck Narrative and Disruption of Empire* (Minneapolis, 2002), 1; Jennifer H. Oliver, *Shipwreck in French Renaissance Writing: The Direful Spectacle* (Oxford, 2019), 141.

[34] Anthony Anderson, 'A Form of Prayer for Sea Men and Passengers', appended to *A Godlie Sermon, Preached on Newe Yeers Day* (1576), sig. E1, prayer (not paginated). Anderson himself had sailed to Ireland and back.

[35] Madox, *A Learned and Godly Sermon*, sigs Bi–Cii v.

[36] William Perkins, *The Combat between Christ and the Divell Displayed* (1606), sig. A4.

[37] Henry Mainwaring, *The Sea-Mans Dictionary: Or, An Exposition and Demonstration of all the Parts and Things Belonging to a Shippe* (1644), preface.

[38] Cotton Mather, *The Sailours Companion and Counsellour* (Boston 1709), x, citing the fourth-century bishop Chrystostom.

The Jacobean preacher Robert Wilkinson declared in a wedding sermon at court in 1607 that a woman is 'like a ship', and 'the world is like the sea'. Billows of nautical references follow. The good wife

> sits at the stern, and by discretion as by card and compass shapes her course; her countenance and conversation are ballasted with soberness and gravity; her sails are full of wind . . . she standeth in the shrouds, and casteth out her lead, and when she hath sounded, she telleth . . . of depth and danger. If by default she be grounded, she casteth out her anchors . . . and by winding of herself, she gets afloat again.

And, like a ship, steered 'by the helm or stern, a small piece of wood, so ought the wife . . . be turned and ruled by word of her husband'. Wilkinson warns, however, that,

> of all qualities, a woman must not have one quality of a ship, and that is too much rigging. Oh what a wonder it is, to see a ship under sail, with her tacklings, and her masts, and her tops, and top gallants, with her upper decks, and her nether decks, and so bedecked with her streams, flags, and ensigns . . . but a world of wonders it is to see a woman created in God's image so miscreate oft times and deformed, with . . . her foolish fashions . . . with a ruff like a sail . . . with a feather in her cap like a flag in her top, to tell, I think, which way the wind will blow.[39]

Playing with the genre in the 1650s, Charles Nichols promised readers, 'I will not keep you long upon the deck of an epistle, from entering into the cabins of the treatise', before inviting them to 'taste, feed on, and digest such dry biscuit as this tract affords'. His *Seamans Summons*, once launched, warns of shipwreck, for 'sudden and boisterous storms breathe death in your faces, raking your hopes, as well as rending your cables, digging your grave in the sea'. Tossed by 'tides of lust, and wind[s] of temptation', life's mariners approach 'the coasts of ruin, and rocks of soul-threatening danger'. Only the compass of the word of God, and the pilotage of the Holy Spirit, brings safety, for, without Christ, 'you are amidst rocks and sands', in peril to be cast away.[40] In similar vein, Jeremiah Burroughs described 'a great stormy wind' and its impact on unprepared mariners, 'how suddenly it came, how strong it blew, how it rent their sails, and split their masts, and tore their cables, and burst their anchors'. The message, much repeated, was that 'God is much to be praised . . . who rulest the raging sea and tempestuous

[39] Robert Wilkinson, *The Merchant Royall: A Sermon Preached at White-Hall before the Kings Maiestie* (1607), 5–15.

[40] Charles Nichols, *The Seamans Summons* (1655), epistle dedicatory, 6, 13, 15, 16.

winds'.[41] Many who went down to the sea and sailed in ships knew this to their cost.

Daniel Pell, another minister with maritime experience, likewise compared the 'hazards that mariners do meet withal, in stormy and tempestuous seas', to the hazards facing all wayfaring Christians. Every ship risked 'the severe vengeance of the lord' because of its 'abominable weight of sin' and was 'sure to go to wreck, when the master of her knows not how the sands, the rocks, and the shallows lie, nor how to shape his course into a far country haven', meaning heaven: 'it is a mere wonder that ever any one of them comes back safely home into their harbours.' Pell wrote knowledgeably of desperate leaks, shorn cables, and lost rudders, and evoked the 'difficulty and jeopardy' of mariners in crisis, but his purpose was polemic, not description. The material loss of a merchant venture paled beside the catastrophe of a shipwrecked soul.[42]

These images and analogies had resonance in a land where increasing numbers of readers had familiarity with maritime commerce, or had cousins, sons, or brothers at sea. Countryfolk knew that ships too often perished and that men who drowned full fathom five lacked the comforts of the funeral ritual and a churchyard burial. Landmen bound on voyages customarily wrote their wills before embarking and prayed for safe return. The sea inspired dread as well as devotion. That explains why the partner of an intending ocean traveller might refuse to accompany him, choosing rather to be 'a living wife in England than a dead one in the sea'.[43]

Shipwrecking Storms and Tempests

Early modern mariners did not blame Poseidon or Neptune for the rage of the waves, but were taught to recognize God's power and wrath in every storm. Religious writers represented tempests as displays of providence and occasions for prayer, but seamen were usually too busy in emergencies to do other than attend to the ship. A cry of 'bestir', or 'up every soul nimbly, for God's sake, or we all perish', could have more effect than 'Lord have mercy'.[44] Samuel Page's *Divine Sea-Service* (1616) included 'a prayer to be used in a time of dangers, by storms and tempests at sea', but there is no record of its use.[45] Godly sea-goers were shocked to learn that some mariners thought prayers at sea unlucky and preferred

[41] Jeremiah Burroughs, *A Sea-Mans Direction in Time of Storme* (1640), 32, 33, 71.

[42] Pell, *Pelagos*, 7, 290–1, 398, 427, 531–3, 551.

[43] David Cressy, *Coming Over: Migration and Communication between England and New England in the Seventeenth Century* (Cambridge, 1987), 147.

[44] 'The Journal of Francis Rogers' in *Three Sea Journals of Stuart Times*, ed. Bruce S. Ingram (1936), 144.

[45] Samuel Page, *Divine Sea-Service: Containing Sundry Necessary and Uselfull Forme of Prayer and Thanks-giving for the Helpe of Such as Traveile by Sea* (1616), 7.

to hurl curses at storms. On one rough voyage the Stuart mariner Jeremy Roch observed that a French Catholic passenger 'looked very shittenly to his beads', while a frightened crewman 'turned up the white of his eyes, making an ugly face and dismal cries'.[46] *In extremis*, prayer was all that was left.

The modern shipping forecast reminds radio listeners of continuing meteorological risks. 'Dreadful storms and shipwrecks... are perpetually happening', wrote the former naval chaplain Daniel Pell, who had his share of 'shipwrecking storms and tempests'.[47] Any creative writer, like an ancient mariner, could conjure the elements of impending catastrophe:

> the darkness of the day, the amazement of the lightning, the dreadfulness of the thunder, the clamour of the winds, the cries of the people, the cruelties of the seas, and the infinite contention betwixt life, death, hope, despair, and desolation, like so many massy hammers lie continually beating upon thy heart... in remembrance of God's infinite mercy and power,

offered Gervase Markham.[48] Indebted to literary and biblical sources, this lexicon acquired freshness and immediacy in the words of sea-stricken mariners. The language of literature and divinity hovers behind descriptions of maritime ordeals, even in reports to the Privy Council and testimony before the Admiralty courts.

Directly observed accounts of fatal shipwrecks are few, because dead men tell no tales. Fortunately, however, there were survivors, who told their stories to commissions of enquiry and sometimes elaborated them for the press. Tales of heroic endurance and providential salvation had eager audiences, and sensational accounts sold well. More common were grim reports of tempestuous storms and lamentable loss. The episodes recounted here, gleaned from a variety of sources, describe the stress of weather, its effect on shipping, crises of foundering and abandonment, and efforts to survive and come safely to shore. Shipwrecks rarely happened in calm and clear conditions.

Mariners routinely recalled the 'exceeding tempest', 'the violence of the storm', or 'the force and extremity of foul weather' that made their vessel unmanageable. Despite the best efforts of masters and crew, they faced testing conditions, often at night, when there was 'nothing to be expected but death'. Story after story records the disturbance of the elements, as ships were 'cast away and driven on shore'.[49]

[46] Robert Ralston Cawley, *Unpathed Waters: Studies in the Influence of the Voyagers on Elizabethan Literature* (New York, 1967), 195; 'The Journals of Jeremy Roch', in *Three Sea Journals of Stuart Times*, ed. Ingram, 92. Roman Catholic mariners were said to have prayed to Our Lady of Walsingham.

[47] Pell, *Pelagos*, 398, 533.

[48] Gervase Markham, *A Second Part to the Mothers Blessing: Or a Cure against Misfortunes* (1622), 59–60.

[49] SP 29/250, fo. 219,

Survivors of the *George* of Colchester related how their ship met 'force and extremity of weather... whereby she was overwhelmed and drowned' in 1581.[50] The *Sea Cock*, a 380-ton merchantman, 'good new and strong, and very well furnished', was driven by 'contrary winds and foul foggy weather' to its doom in the Bristol Channel in 1597.[51] A North Sea storm that same year left the naval ship *Roebuck* 'weather-beaten on a lee shore four days and nights', so that 'our foremast, foretopmast, main topmast, and mizzen top went by the board together ...our sails were split and our boat capsized and sunk'.[52] Another North Sea journey in 1613 proved perilous when God 'caused the seas to be outrageous and boisterous, and the waves thereof to be so great, and to arise so high, that many times they were ready to overwhelm the ship'. As the seafarers approached the coast of Norfolk, 'the wind did grow more strong, and the waves greater, and everyone overtaxed with sore labour', as 'the ship began to sink deeper and deeper into the sea'.[53] 'The wind blew so violently that a man could scarce stand on the deck, and the sea wrought over us,' wrote Dawtrey Cooper of another voyage in 1628: 'I never beheld a fleet so tattered in my life.'[54]

Levels of distress spiked in times of great tempest.[55] One 'tempestuous storm of wind, thunder, and lightning' in 1622 destroyed eight ships and drowned three hundred men in Devonshire. 'In divers places besides, were many ships cast away, so that it is thought the loss by shipwreck in the west parts of England is forty of fifty thousand pounds.'[56] Five ships out of Liverpool, carrying 550 men for service in Ireland, were swamped by 'a tempestuous storm' on their second night at sea in March 1625, drowning all but 200 survivors.[57] Another 'great storm' gripped the *Providence* of London in December 1634, so that the crew felt 'great danger of perishing in the sea'. Rough weather 'broke the said ship's foremast and carried away her foresail and foretop sails, main topmast, foremast and rigging, and split her mainsail... her main beam broken, and her second beam cracked', as the ship 'rolled to and fro in the sea'.[58] 'Cross winds and tempestuous weather' in that same winter storm blew the *Hopewell* from one side of the North Sea to the other, so that when the ship grounded upon 'a great shoal upon the larboard bow' the crew had no idea where they were.[59]

[50] HCA 13/24, fo. 165. [51] HCA 13/33, fos 1–3.

[52] Hatfield House, Cecil Papers, vol. 51, fo. 31; Historical Manuscripts Commission, *Calendar of the Manuscripts of... the Marquis of Salisbury, Preserved at Hatfield House*, 24 vols (1883–1976), vii. 208.

[53] *Lamentable Newes, Shewing the Wonderfull Deliverance of Maister Edmond Pet Sayler* (1613), sigs A2–A4.

[54] 'The Journal of Dawtrey Cooper', in Ingram (ed.), *Three Sea Journals of Stuart Times*, 18–19.

[55] *The Last Terrible Tempestious Windes and Weather* (1613); *A Wonderful History of All the Storms, Hurricanes, Earthquakes, etc. That have happen's in England for above 500 years past* (1704); Hubert Lamb, *Historic Storms of the North Sea, British Isles and Northwest Europe* (Cambridge, 1991), 4, 21, 55, 59, 72.

[56] *The Fourth of September: Newes from Sundry Places, both Forraine and Domestique* (1622), 10–12.

[57] SP 16/1, fos 37, 39. [58] HCA 13/51, fos 259^{v}, 260^{v}–261.

[59] HCA 13/51, fos 312–38, 343, 350–8, 385–6.

In 1636 the *Guifte of God* of Hull 'by extremity of stormy weather was driven between two rocks near Newhaven upon the coast of Sussex, where the said ship was beaten to pieces, and all her lading of wines and other goods brake loose out of her, and a great part of them drove on shore'.[60] The *Golden Grape* was wrecked on Chesil Beach, Dorset, in December 1641 amid more 'violent and tempestuous winds and weather'.[61] Report spread that month of 'the casting away of at least forty sail of ships in one place or other upon the coast, to the undoing of many an honest man'.[62] The *Neptune* of London was lucky to reach Limerick in Ireland after two months of torment from contrary winds.[63] More 'extreme tempestuous and stormy weather' forced the *Elephant and Castle* ashore near Bristol in 1642.[64] Another 'violent and most horrible storm of wind at northwest' drove the *St John* of Hamburg onto a North Sea sandbank in November 1653, leaving the mariners 'bewailing their approaching deaths, crying lamentably like children'.[65] Battling the Channel in February 1658, the *Lark* met such extreme winds and snow that the crew cut the main mast and rigging, 'in regard of the extraordinary quantity of ice that was frozen to the ropes'.[66] Other companies faced 'continual storm, very likely to be cast way', before finding refuge or respite.[67] In similar conditions, the mariner Jeremy Roch witnessed the end of the *St Andrew* off Sussex in 1666: 'her old bones were so the shaken she could hardly recover into Rye before she sank.'[68]

A massive storm in September 1671 cut through the coal and fishing fleets of several North Sea nations. A correspondent in Norfolk reported 160 sail missing: 'the sea is so full of wreck on these coasts that those at sea are forced to look out sharp to steer clear of it.'[69] In October 1675 the 130-ton *Florentine* of Plymouth was similarly stricken by 'much bad weather and cross winds', when 'it began to blow so extreme hard that we could scarce hand our sails fast enough'. Edward Barlow recounted 'our great astonishment and fear' when his ship struck a sandbank off the coast of Kent.[70] More 'stress of weather' and occasions of 'dreadful storm and tempest' disabled 'the greatest part of the southern collier fleet' in September 1695, where an observer in Norfolk found 'the whole shore from Blakeney to Lynn was full of vessels aground and wreck'.[71] Report after

[60] HCA 13/52, fo. 319^{v}. [61] HCA 13/244/149. [62] SP 16/486, fo. 171.

[63] *A Calendar of Material Relating to Ireland from the High Court of Admiralty 1641–1660*, ed. Elaine Murphy (Dublin, 2011), 9–10.

[64] Patrick McGrath, 'Merchant Shipping in the Seventeenth Century: The Evidence of the Bristol Deposition Books', *Mariner's Mirror*, 41 (1955), 24,

[65] National Maritime Museum, MS JOD/39 (Memoir of Moses Bathurst).

[66] SP 18/188, fo. 119. For the 'Little Ice Age', see Geoffrey Parker, *Global Crisis: War, Climate Change and Catastrophe in the Seventeenth Century* (London and New Haven, 2013).

[67] British Library, MS Egerton 2533, fo. 474.

[68] 'The Journals of Jeremy Roch', in Ingram (ed.), *Three Sea Journals of Stuart Times*, 60, 92.

[69] SP 29/293, fo. 14.

[70] *Barlow's Journal of his Life at Sea in King's Ships, East & West Indiamen & other Merchantmen from 1659 to 1703*, ed. Basil Lubbock, 2 vols (1934), i. 258–62.

[71] Norfolk Record Office, LEST/Q 37, p. 46 (Lestrange Estate Rolls 1605–1718).

report blamed wreck and near-wreck on unmanageable weather, mountainous waves, frightening storms, or dangerous combinations of miseries.

Most catastrophic of all was the 'Great Storm' of November 1703, which destroyed as many as 300 vessels. Daniel Defoe wrote that 'no storm since the universal deluge was like this, either in its violence or its duration'. Ships from the Severn to the Thames were 'huddled together and drove on shore', grounded, stranded, staved, and wrecked. The storm blew some vessels from Cornwall to the Isle of Wight, and from the mouth of the Thames almost to Norway.[72] Close to 1,200 sailors died when the warships *Mary*, *Northumberland*, *Restoration*, and *Stirling Castle* foundered on the Goodwin Sands.[73] Edward Barlow was at sea in the 270-ton *Fleet Frigate* when hit by this 'violent storm, which all England hath cause to remember'. Lucky to survive, though 'in a dismal condition', Barlow recalled 'swimming by us masts, yards, and sails, and wrecks of ships'.[74] 'Every tide brings fresh wrecks,' the *London Post* reported.[75]

Lost Sailors and Faulty Charts

Handlers of ships in trouble often had few clues to their location when their voyage abruptly ended. Storms tossed ships leagues off course, casting navigation to the winds. A passage from Spain to the Netherlands could end on the coast of Sussex, a ship bound from Ireland for France could wreck in the Bristol Channel, and sailors bound from the Baltic to London could founder on the Goodwin Sands. Wayfinding by night in the midst of a storm was nigh impossible, even with the best of skill and equipment. Though manned by professional sailors, the 800-ton warship *Liberty* was lost in October 1650 on a North Sea sandbank four leagues off Harwich.[76] Great East Indiamen fared just as ill. A homebound Newfoundlander, laden with fish, 'missing the Channel, did put into Bristol', when they were aiming further south for Plymouth or London (see Figure 4).[77]

Every mariner knew that the safest place in a tempest was the open sea. So long as it had sea room, a ship had a chance to survive. 'But if they find themselves near the shore, they look upon their condition as very dangerous... For one ship

[72] Daniel Defoe, *The Storm: Or, A Collection of the Most Remarkable Casualties and Disasters which Happen'd in the Late Dreadful Tempest, both by Sea and Land* (1704), 37, 46, 173–200, 220; Daniel Defoe, *An Historical Narrative of the Great and Tremendous Storm which Happened on Nov. 26th, 1703* (1769); Daniel Defoe, *A Tour through the Whole Island of Great Britain*, ed. Pat Rogers (1971), 95, 137–8; *God's Wonders in the Great Deep*, 80–5. See also Lamb, *Historic Storms of the North Sea*, 4, 21, 55, 59, 72.

[73] Richard and Bridget Larn, *Shipwreck Index of the British Isles*, 7 vols (1995–2005), ii, sect. 6, not paginated.

[74] *Barlow's Journal*, ii. 552–3.

[75] *The London Post, with Intelligence Foreign and Domestick*, 1 December 1703.

[76] SP 18/11, fos 61, 63; SP 25/17, 28.

[77] HCA 13/127, fo. 17^{v}.

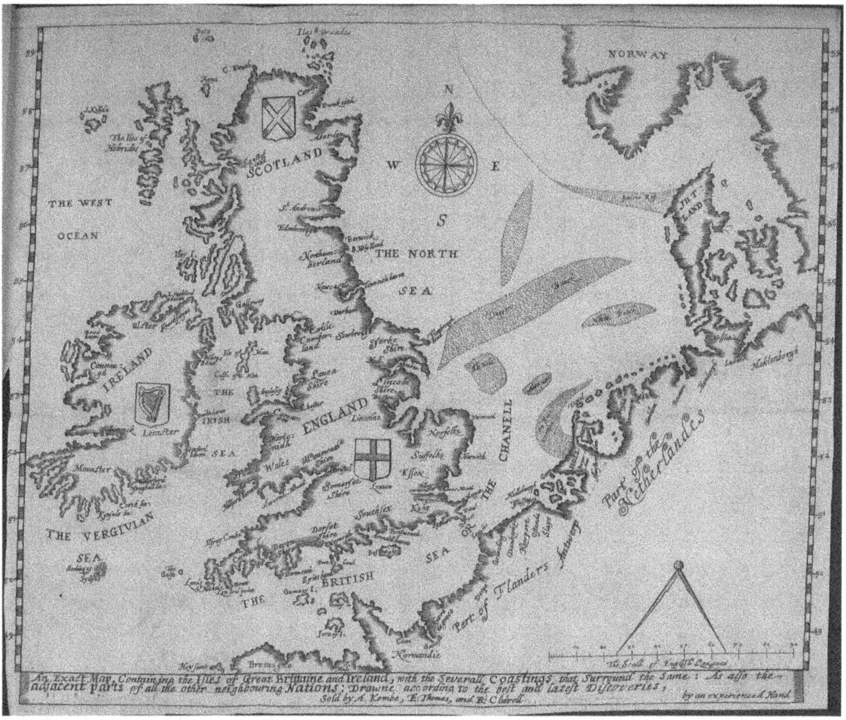

Figure 4. *An Exact Map... with the Severall Coastings*, in Robert Codrington, *His Majesties Propriety, and Dominion on the British Seas* (1665). © The British Library Board, G.18167.

swallowed up in the ocean, many perish upon the coast.'[78] England's fretted coastline challenged sailors with rocks and ledges, sandbanks and shoals, shifting tides, and unpredictable winds, all made worse in violent weather, darkness, or fog.[79] Shipwrecks also begat shipwrecks, as ruins of previous casualties brought vessels into peril; buoys and beacons set by the brethren of Trinity House could mark only a minimum of obstacles in harbours and estuaries.[80]

English coastal waters were notorious for their dangerous weather and unstable conditions. The inhospitable cliffs and headlands of Cornwall and Devon were among 'the wildest, bleakest and most dangerous coastlines imaginable', according to a modern expert.[81] England's Atlantic approaches were especially perilous,

[78] Flavell, *New Compass for Seamen*, 189.

[79] The sandbanks of the outer Thames, from Essex to Kent, are discussed and mapped in Helene Burningham and Jon French, 'Seabed Dynamics in a Large Coastal Embayment: 180 Years of Morphological Change in the Outer Thames Estuary', *Hydrobiologia*, 627 (2011), 105–19. See also William Heather, *The Chart of the Entrances to the River Thames* (1801).

[80] G. G. Harris, *The Trinity House of Deptford 1514–1660* (1969), 158–60. A red buoy with a tin vane marked a wreck in the lower Thames in 1692, *London Gazette*, 17 March 1692.

[81] Larn, *Shipwreck Index of the British Isles*, i, sect. 2, not paginated.

devouring ships by the dozen. It was easy to believe that the rocks of the Isles of Scilly caused 'more shipwrecks than happen perhaps in all the other seas of Europe together', though the mainland had comparable perils.[82] The entire Channel shore from Cornwall to Kent presented multiple hazards of reefs and rocks, rolling shingle, entrapping bays, and forbidding cliffs. A lee shore in a high wind was always a challenging proposition.

Mariners met swirling races and gyres in the sea off Portland, in the area known as 'Deadman's Bay'. The Needles of the Isle of Wight reminded seamen of Scylla and Charybdis. The Goodwin Sands in the narrow seas south of Kent baffled pilots and were reputedly so dangerous 'that not even the timbers of wrecks can be recovered'.[83] Among the maze of ship-killing banks and channels around estuarine Kent and Essex, the Long Sands off Foulness were known as the 'burying grounds'.[84]

Jacobean mariners justly feared the 'sands, shales, shelves, and dangers' of the lower Thames, and were grateful to Trinity House for their markers of hazards. Laden in London in 1604 for a voyage to Ireland, the *Cherubim* 'passed safely through the Fishers' Deep and over the flats, until she came near a sand called the Last', where the expected navigational aids could not be found. According to the mariner Edward Wilson, 'there arose a storm, and by force thereof the anchors came home, and the foresail being set was blown out of the boltropes, and the rudder was stricken away, and so the ship was cast away with her whole lading'. In his view, 'the ship had passed that danger before the storm had come', if only the indicators 'had been there as they ought to have been'.[85]

Norfolk's shifting channels and perilous sands 'over ruled the skill and cunning' of countless navigators.[86] Cromer Bay was so dangerous that seamen knew it as 'the Devil's Throat', along a stretch of shingle beach known as the 'shipwreck coast'. Daniel Defoe found there 'scarce a barn or a shed, or a stable, nay, not the pales of their yards and gardens, not a necessary house, but what was built of old planks, beams, wales and timbers, etc., the wrecks of ships and ruins of mariners' and merchants' fortunes'.[87] Visitors to Waxham, Norfolk, today may see such a mast among the roof beams of the Woodhouse family's Elizabethan barn.[88]

Lethal in an easterly gale, the shallows, banks, and flats from the Humber to the Thames posed fearful navigational obstacles. So threatening was England's east

[82] 'The Travels of Cosmo III, Grand Duke of Tuscany, through England', in *Early Tours in Devon and Cornwall*, ed. Alan Gibson and R. Pearse Chope (Newton Abbot, 1967), 93; Richard Larn, *Cornish Shipwrecks*, iii. *The Isles of Scilly* (New York, 1971).

[83] *CSP Venice 1629–30*, 434.

[84] Larn, *Shipwreck Index of the British Isles*, iii, sect. 1, not paginated.

[85] HCA 13/37, fos 407, 428.

[86] *The Answer of the Masters of the Trinitie-House, to the Special Obiections of the Patentee, for the Keeping of Winterton Lights* (1621), broadsheet.

[87] Defoe, *Tour through the Whole Island*, ed. Rogers, 94.

[88] Caroline Davison and Ronnie Pestell, *Wild Waxham* (Norwich, 2004), 41.

coast that some North Sea mariners avowed that 'they had rather run the hazard of an East India voyage than be obliged to sail all the winter between London and Newcastle'. Atlantic and Mediterranean sailing was no safer.[89]

Experienced seamen understood that some obstructions were unknown, while sands and shoals could change their situation. 'The sea chart', complained one Stuart navigator, 'is so faulty in the very foundation and groundwork... that hereof there may arise so gross error, as may cause the mariner to miss one, two, yea three whole points of the compass'.[90] A compass, in any case, indicated heading, not position. None could know, until the eighteenth century, that charts showed the Isles of Scilly 10–20 miles further north than their true location. Early modern charts misplaced Yarmouth by more than half a degree, an error of 30 miles. Without means to measure longitude, navigators relied on sun sights, dead reckoning, and coastal observation. Crude instruments, opaque skies, and maritime motion compounded the problem.[91] None could understand, before Edmund Halley, that 'the change of the variation of the compass' could mislead coastal sailors 'by near five leagues'.[92] 'More Dutch ships are lost here than any other,' observed an eighteenth-century historian of Dorset, 'which is thought to be owing to an obstinate adherence to their old charts, and not allowing for the true variation of the compass'.[93]

Even skilled navigators faced problems when foul weather 'prevented their taking an observation for ten or eleven days, which... so disconcerted their reckoning' that they knew not where they were.[94] Even with modern navigational aids, such as radar and global positioning, ships still come to grief in treacherous coastal waters.[95] The nautical memoirist Edward Coxere recalled navigational disagreements by 'half a degree, that is thirty miles', that brought one of his vessels onto a Channel sandbank, and 'had the sea run high, we had been all lost.'[96]

[89] J. C., *The Compleat Collier* (1708), 19; Gerassimus D. Pagratis, '"Le fortune di mare": Incidenti della navigazione mercantile nei mari Ionio e Adriatico (1611–1765)', in Simonetta Cavaciocchi (ed), *Ricchezza del Mare: Ricchezza dal Mare: secc. XIII–XVIII* (Prato, 2006), 841–61.

[90] Edward Wright, *Certain Errors in Navigation. Detected and Corrected* (1657), preface. See also Jacob Columne, *The Fierie Sea-Columne, Wherein are Shewed the Seas, and Sea-coasts of the Northern, Eastern, and Western Navigation* (Amsterdam,1640); John Seller, *A Description of the Sands, Shoals, Buoyes, Beacons, Roads, Channels and Sea Marks on the Coast of England* (1671); Greenvile Collins, *Great Britain's Coasting Pilot: The First Part. Being a New and Exact Survey of the Sea-Coast of England* (1693).

[91] *Samuel Pepys's Naval Minutes*, ed. J. R. Tanner (Navy Records Society, 1926), 221, 367; Simon Harris, *Sir Cloudesley Shovell: Stuart Admiral* (Staplehurst, 2001), 384; T. W. Willan, *The English Coasting Trade, 1600–1750* (Manchester, 1938), 21,

[92] Edmond Halley, *An Advertisement Necessary to be Observed in the Navigation Up and Down the Channel of England* (1701), 1.

[93] John Hutchins, *The History and Antiquities of the County of Dorset*, 2 vols (1774), i. 587.

[94] *A Sad and Deplorable but True Account of the Dreadful Hardships, and Sufferings of Capt. John Dean, and his Company, on Board the Nottingham Galley* (1711); *A True Account of the Voyage of the Nottingham Galley* (1711); John Deane, *A Narrative of the Shipwreck of the Nottingham Galley... Revis'd, and Re-Printed* (1730), 1.

[95] Juliet du Boulay, 'Wrecks in the Isles of Scilly', *Mariners Mirror*, 46 (1960), 88–112; Richard Larn et al., *Cornish Shipwrecks*, 3 vols (New York, 1969–71).

[96] Edward Coxere, *Adventures by Sea of Edward Coxere*, ed. E. H. W. Meyerstein (Oxford and New York, 1946), 43.

Naval administrators exonerated the officers of the frigate *Primrose* that was 'cast away nigh the Seven Stones between the Land's End and Scilly' in 1656 because they hit 'a rock not visible or described in any plot that we can find'.[97] Homebound from Asia in January 1666, the crew of the Indiaman *Royal Oak* judged themselves to be west of the Lizard, and 'forty leagues to the leeward of the Island of St Mary's', but after a night of storms the ship became 'enjoined with rocks' on the notorious Bishop and Clerk's pinnacles and 'in a quarter of an hour was split in pieces'.[98] Approaching those same islands in the spring of 1673, Captain John Narborough of the naval vessel *Fairfax* reported, 'we all reckoned ourselves further shot in than we were, and more southerly than we find it to appear', and became 'entangled with rocks called the Bishops and Clerks'.[99] It was on these same rocks that Sir Cloudesley Shovell's fleet shattered in 1707 after the most catastrophic of all navigational miscalculations.[100]

Unskilfulness and Insufficiency

Besides blaming the perennial perils of the sea, dozens of reports of shipwrecks attributed disaster to the arrogance and incompetence of men who were supposed to know better. Experts acknowledged that 'as many ships are lost by ignorance and negligence, as by stress of weather', and that human error could be as dangerous as storms and rocks.[101] The moralist Daniel Pell observed, it was easier 'to lay the blame of your miscarrying in the seas upon the pilot' than 'upon that abominable weight of sin that is in ships'.[102] He might have been thinking of the crew of the *Margaret Constance*, homebound with wine from the Canaries, who sampled too much of their cargo and were wrecked on the Devon coast in fair weather.[103] The *Nathaniel* broke apart on sands off Yarmouth in 1665 with a hundred men on board, 'there being not above ten of the whole number that understood the business of the sea'.[104]

Shipowners engaged local pilots to guide ships through difficult waters, but they did not always give good value. 'It is a wonder how we escaped,' wrote Colonel John Norris, after the ship carrying him along the coast of Suffolk in 1585 was in 'very great peril and hazard to be cast away... by reason of the unskillfulness and

[97] SP 18/138, fo. 265. [98] Bodleian Library, MS Rawlinson A 195, fos 180–180^{v}.

[99] *Journals and Narratives of the Third Dutch War*, ed. R. C. Anderson (Navy Records Society, vol. 86, 1946), 286–7.

[100] James Herbert Cooke, *The Shipwreck of Sir Cloudesley Shovell, on the Scilly Island in 1707* (Society of Antiquaries, 1883); Harris, *Sir Cloudesley Shovell: Stuart Admiral*; Richard Larn (ed.), *'Poor England has lost so many men': The Loss of Queen Anne's Man o' War Association* (St Mary's, Isles of Scilly, 2006).

[101] Collins, *Great Britain's Coasting Pilot*, preface. [102] Pell, *Pelagos*, 555.

[103] HCA 13/57, fos 432–6.

[104] *Newes Published for Satisfaction and Information of the People*, 17 August 1665.

insufficiency of the officers and sailors, especially of the pilot mistaking the channel'.[105] Other ships perished after arguments among mariners whether to weigh or hold anchors, and which course to steer.[106] The pilot of the *Phoenix* of Amsterdam, 'being drunk, went to his cabin to sleep so soon as he came on board' in 1597; on awaking, he insisted that the mariners hoist the foresail, while the master attempted to hold the ship fast with anchors. As the men argued, 'the foresail being hoisted up by commandment of the pilot was blown from the yard by the force of the storm', and 'the ship drove on the rock...and there brake in pieces' near Plymouth.[107] The pilot who attempted to bring the *Sea Cock* of Flushing into a haven in South Wales that same year 'missed the channel, and utterly lost the ship upon the sands, whereby the ship and goods were cast away and utterly lost'.[108]

Another hapless pilot was identified as 'the chief instrument of this misery' when the troopship *Speedwell* foundered in 1624. He too was drunk when he came aboard and at a critical moment 'forced the helmsman to put the helm a port, when it should have been a starboard, and so ran her on the sands'.[109] The master of the *Hopewell*, wrecked on the coast of Essex in 1634, also blamed the pilot, saying, 'he never knew such a man that would undertake a charge, and not know how to perform it', though responsibility was divided between them.[110] The 350-ton trader *William and Anne* was lost in 1634 when the pilot mistook his channel in the dark and drove the ship onto rocks.[111] Elegists for Edward King, the Cambridge scholar drowned off Anglesey in 1637, railed against that 'wretched pilot of the boat, by whose crime a youth of great hope...perished in a rude inglorious death'.[112] The late-Stuart historian of sea laws Alexander Justice noted the gibbeting of 'false and treacherous pilots' in medieval France as a caution to 'succeeding ages'.[113]

Unskilled and inattentive officers and seamen endangered scores of ships. The *Anne Royal* was holed by its own anchor in 1636, 'which pulled out a great part of her keel abaft the mast', causing the man-of-war to sink.[114] 'A falling out' among officers endangered the *Bordeaux*, homebound across the Atlantic in 1647, 'the skipper being altogether unskillful in the art of navigation'.[115] The Mediterranean

[105] SP 84/3, fo. 43.
[106] SP 12/184, fo. 39, 142–7; HCA 13/127, fo. 28; Harris, *Trinity House of Deptford*, 91, 100–10.
[107] HCA 13/32, fos 217–18. [108] HCA 13/33, fo. 2. [109] SP 14/174, fos 81–81^{v}.
[110] HCA 13/51, fo. 326. [111] HCA 13/51, fos 383–4.
[112] J. Karl Franson, 'The Fatal Voyage of Edward King, Milton's Lycidas', *Milton Studies*, 25 1989), 56, citing *Justa Edovardo King Naufrago* (Cambridge, 1638).
[113] Alexander Justice, *A General Treatise of the Dominion of the Sea: And a Compleat Body of the Sea-Laws*, 3rd edn (1724), 153, 156.
[114] *The Autobiography of Phineas Pett*, ed. W. G. Perrin (Navy Records Society, 1918), 163; SP 12/319, fo. 14, for disagreements between the pilot and commander.
[115] See Patrick McGrath, 'Merchant Shipping in the Seventeenth Century: The Evidence of the Bristol Deposition Books', *Mariner's Mirror*, 41 (1955), 23, for 'a falling out' among officers aboard the *Bordeaux* in 1647, 'the skipper being altogether unskillful in the art of navigation'.

trader *Ulysses* was cast away on the Isle of Wight in 1650 'by the carelessness and unskillfulness of the mariners'.[116] The 240-ton *Exchange*, bound for Virginia, fell foul of a Thames estuary sandbank in 1654 when the pilot 'put the helm a port' while the master forced the helm hard a starboard. Charged 'with making a mutiny', the pilot 'did often curse and swear very bitterly', and allegedly wished a 'a plague split her', before that disaster happened.[117]

Reports of this nature often served to assign blame or deflect responsibility. They show how dispute or inattention brought many a prosperous voyage to an end. Officers blamed the pilot of the *Kent* in 1672 for not seeing the waves breaking against a sandbank in broad daylight.[118] The sinking of the man-of-war *Gloucester* in 1682 was likewise attributed to 'the wrong calculation and ignorance of the pilot'.[119] The wreck of the *Nottingham Galley* in the Atlantic in 1710 came after the captain, 'calling out to the steersman to put the helm hard a starboard, was so ill obey'd in the sudden astonishment, as to have the very reverse performed'.[120]

Leaky Vessels

Merchant vessels were artfully constructed to meet the demands of sea service, with an expected life of thirty or more years. English-built vessels were reputedly 'more staunchly timbered' than the cheaper Dutch flyboats and better able to withstand grounding on sandbanks or beaches.[121] But wear and tear, damage, or misfortune affected ships of all nations and caused many of them to leak. 'There is no ship so tight, but that with her labouring in the sea... she will make some water,' observed Henry Mainwaring, and leaks became critical with 'the opening of the seams' and the weakening of the ground-timbers. Cracked spars, parted lines, and torn sails were common experiences. Mariners responded to such occurrences with repairs and patches and relied on pumps to expel inboard water.[122] Too often, however, planks parted, holds flooded, and pumps proved

[116] HCA 13/124, fos 11^{v}, 22. [117] HCA 13/71, fo. 49; HCA 13/127, fos, 27–8.

[118] SP 29/316, fo. 280.

[119] Sir John Dalrymple, *Memoirs of Britain and Ireland*, 2 vols (1773), ii. 68; *The Correspondence of Henry Hyde, Earl of Clarendon and of his Brother Lawrence Hyde, Earl of Rochester*, ed. Samuel Weller Singer, 2 vols (1828), i. 71–3.

[120] Deane, *Narrative of the Shipwreck of the Nottingham Galley*, 2.

[121] Violet Barbour, 'Dutch and English Merchant Shipping in the Seventeenth Century', *Economic History Review*, 2 (1930), 277.

[122] Henry Mainwaring, *The Sea-Mans Dictionary: Or, An Exposition and Demonstration of all the Parts and Things Belonging to a Shippe* (1644), 60–1, 78–9; Phillip F. Reid, 'Something Ventured: Dangers and Risk Mitigation for the Ordinary British Atlantic Merchant Ship, 1600–1800', *Journal of Transport History*, 38 (2017), 196–212, esp. 204. See also Jan Glete, *Navies and Nations: Warships, Navies and Nations in Europe and America, 1500–1860*, 2 vols (Stockholm, 1993), i. 63, on the deterioration of hulls and planking.

inadequate to the task. Other failures of equipment mentioned in shipwreck narratives included rotten cables and lost anchors, detached rudders, and shredded sails, as well as ill-stacked cargo and untethered ordnance. There was 'such difficulty and jeopardy in the seaman's employment', observed Daniel Pell, that any voyage could be his last.[123] Needing new planking, rudder, and half-keel, the leaky *Providence* in 1664 was 'not fit to keep the sea', yet still carried cargo off the coast of Essex.[124] Another vessel, surviving an Atlantic crossing, 'did grow so leaky that she could hardly live in the sea'; carpenters found 'divers of her beams to be broken, and the said ship to be very weak and insufficient for the performance of her intended voyage'.[125] Some ships barely made it home.

When a leak was discovered, John Flavell advised, it was time to 'set the carpenter to search for it and stop it'.[126] 'How nimbly is the sheet lead, or the plug wrapped with canvas, applied', or a 'bag with oakum or rope yarn' sunk over the side, to lodge 'in that porthole of death', remarked Cotton Mather.[127] Mariners knew from experience that it was not that easy.

A London trader off Norfolk in 1613 met waves 'so high . . . they were ready to overwhelm the ship', which 'began to sink deeper and deeper into the sea'. The men at the pumps were 'overtaxed with sore labour', but were unable to save the vessel.[128] Only strenuous pumping prevented the loss of the *George* of London, 'a staunch ship, but she sprang a great leak between the Downs and the Isle of Wight' in 1633.[129] The scuppers of the *Providence* of London flowed with water and wine in 1634, after her cargo shifted and 'divers butts and pipes of wine were staved and run out', but the pumps did their job. Inspection showed her beams to be broken or cracked.[130] Worse fortune afflicted the *Magdalen and Margaret*, already known as a leaky vessel, when 'her caulking washed out of her seams' and 'her ballast washed fore and aft, and her beer swam to and fro in her hold', as a North Sea storm dashed the ship to pieces in 1637.[131]

A lively relation, purportedly the account of a survivor, told how the 700-ton *Merchant Royal*, approaching Land's End in September 1641, 'in stress of foul weather sprung a leak in the bottom of the ship, so that the sailors were forced to tend the pumps day and night', until the pumps stopped working and the vessel had to be abandoned.[132] Moses Bathurst recalled a similar emergency when the

[123] Pell, *Pelagos*, 531.
[124] SP 29/97, fo. 95; SP 29/137, fo. 28; SP 19/136, fo. 68; SP 29/140, fos 164–5.
[125] HCA 13/127, fo. 18. [126] John Flavell, *A New Compass for Seamen* (1664), 161.
[127] Cotton Mather, *The Sailours Companion and Counselllor* (Boston, 1709), 48.
[128] *Lamentable Newes, Shewing the Wonderfull Deliverance of Maister Edmond Pet Sayler* (1613), sigs A2–A4.
[129] *List of Witnesses in the High Court of Admiralty, 1619–49*, ed. G. G. Harris (List and Index Society, 2010), 360.
[130] HCA 13/51, fos 259^{v}, 260^{v}–261. [131] HCA 13/53, fos 317^{v}–318.
[132] *Sad News from the Seas: Being a True Relation of the Losse of that Good Ship called the Merchant Royall* (1641).

St John of Hamburg grounded in November 1653, and the hard sand 'so strained the ship that she became very leaky'. The crew pumped and bailed day and night, eight men to a pump, until the equipment failed, and the ship began to disintegrate.[133] Survivors of the merchantman *Elizabeth* told how densely stacked cargo prevented access to a ship-disabling leak in December 1660. They abandoned their vessel after eight hours of pumping, in a worsening North Sea tempest, the ship 'scarce able to swim'.[134] The *Florentine* of Plymouth had a cargo of fish for the Mediterranean when it foundered in the Channel in December 1675. 'When we pumped our water would smell strong of fish,' wrote Edward Barlow, who saved his journal but lost his clothes when the ship went down.[135] Like Barlow and other professional mariners, the Quaker Edward Coxere experienced 'dangers, difficulties and hardships' at sea, including broken bowsprits, damaged rudders, and leaks. Fatal disaster approached, but thankfully, he recounted, 'providence prevented it'.[136]

Providence took a strange turn when the man-of-war *Gloucester* hit a Norfolk sandbank in May 1682, the rudder broke, and the helmsman was 'killed by the force thereof'. There was no time to pump, 'the sea coming in fast', and the ship went down quickly with most of its company. Memorialists celebrated the 'miraculous delivery' of the Duke of York, who escaped with his pet dog and his strongbox. Few 'Englishmen of respect' were lost, Sir James Dick reported, although the casualty count approached two hundred. Common seamen, 'swimming for their lives, catched all a dead grip of our boat, holding up their heads above water crying help', but Dick and fellow aristocrats diligently loosened their hands, as God set his angels over his royal highness.[137]

In most cases there was time to attempt remedies. A foundering ship might be saved by lightening its load, by throwing 'ponderous' items overboard, by cutting down masts and clearing away tackle, and by judicious manipulation of anchors.[138] It might be possible to undergird a damaged hull with cables and sailcloth, to keep shivering timbers from fatal fracture. These were desperate measures for desperate moments and had been part of maritime wisdom since ancient and biblical times. One of the few actions available to early modern mariners that could not have been used by their classical predecessors was the

[133] National Maritime Museum, MS JOD/39.

[134] SP 29/21, fo. 287; SP 29/23, fo. 14; SP 29/24, fo. 16.

[135] *Barlow's Journal*, i. 258–62.

[136] Coxere, *Adventures by Sea*, 12–13, 38–9, 43–4, 141–6.

[137] Dalrymple, *Memoirs of Britain and Ireland*, ii. 68–72; *Correspondence of Henry Hyde*, i. 71–3. See also Caleb Calle, *On His Royal Highness's Miraculous Delivery and Happy Return* (1682); John Gibbon, *Prince-Protecting Providences* (1682), 5–6.

[138] Pell, *Pelagos*, 290, 427. The jettisoning of cargo was so normal an occurrence in storms that the Jacobean arithmetician John Johnson posed the problem of how much shareholders would lose if 'a certain ship, being in a tempest on the sea was forced to cast overboard so much of her lading as amounted to the sum of 642 pound' (John Johnson, *Iohnsons Arithmatick* (1623), 160).

firing of guns to attract attention, but there is scant evidence that this proved effective. Hundreds of ships were swallowed out of sight, lost on shoals and sands, or beaten to pieces on rocks. The legal perils and prospects of their merchants and mariners, and the claims of coastal countrymen, are discussed in Chapter 3.

3

Wreccum Maris

The Law of 'Wreck of the Sea'

Centuries of legislation, precedent, and practice governed the law of *wreccum maris*, wreck of the sea, which addressed the aftermath of shipwrecks.[1] But understanding, interpretation, and experience of the law varied with situation, circumstance, and levels of knowledge. Though in principle the law applied universally, throughout the kingdom, its treatment at the Inns of Court and the Courts of Westminster did not necessarily match readings by local justices or bailiffs of coastal manors. As Tom Johnson has observed of late medieval England, 'legal categories and discourses were interwoven with social relations and praxes, mentalities and ideologies, and the operation of the economy'.[2] As Bradin Cormack has observed of the early modern period, the law was 'a system of shifting jurisdictional realities', fertile with uncertainties.[3] Lauren Benton and other scholars of 'legal pluralism' have recognized the English legal environment as a mosaic of 'layered and composite' arrangements in overlapping and competing jurisdictions. Problems in dealing with shipwrecks exposed 'unresolved tensions between local authority and imperial oversight' in contests over sovereignty at the edge of dry land.[4] This left much to informal arbitration and negotiation between competing interests.

The law had varied streams and currents, and the law of the sea did not necessarily match the law of the land. Claimants and litigants faced actions in

[1] Valuable studies include Frederick C. Hamil, 'Wreck of the Sea in Medieval England', in A. E. R. Boak (ed.), *University of Michigan Historical Essays* (Ann Arbor, 1937), 1–24; Rose Melikan, 'Shippers, Salvors, and Sovereigns: Competing Interests in the Medieval Law of Shipwreck', *Journal of Legal History*, 11 (1990), 163–82; Graham Dorey, 'Rights to Wreck in Norman Customary Law', *Guernsey Law Journal*, 15 (1993), 63–6; Tom Johnson, 'Medieval Law and Materiality: Shipwrecks, Finders, and Property on the Suffolk Coast, ca. 1380–1410', *American Historical Review*, 120 (2015), 407–32; Susan Raich, 'Wreck of the Sea in Law and Practice in Eleventh- and Twelfth-Century England', in Elizabeth van Houts (ed.), *Anglo-Norman Studies XXXVIII: Proceedings of the Battle Conference 2015* (2016), 141–54; Albrecht Cordes, 'Lex Maritima? Local, Regional and Universal Maritime Law in the Middle Ages', in Wim Blockmans, Mikhail Krom, and Justyna Wubs-Mrozewicz (eds), *The Routledge Handbook of Maritime Trade around Europe 1300–1600: Commercial Networks and Urban Autonomy* (2017), 69–85.

[2] Johnson, 'Medieval Law and Materiality', 407; Tom Johnson, *Law in Common: Legal Cultures in Late-Medieval England* (Oxford, 2020).

[3] Bradin Cormack, *A Power to do Justice: Jurisdiction, English Literature, and the Rise of the Common Law, 1509–1625* (Chicago, 2007), 2.

[4] Lauren Benton, *A Search for Sovereignty: Law and Geography in European Empires, 1400–1900* (Cambridge, 2010), 35; Lauren Benton and Richard J. Ross (eds), *Legal Pluralism and Empires, 1500–1850* (New York, 2013), 4. See also Ken MacMillan, *Sovereignty and Possession in the English New World, 1576–1640* (Cambridge, 2006), and Cormack, *Power to do Justice*.

Shipwrecks and the Bounty of the Sea. David Cressy, Oxford University Press. © David Cressy 2022.
DOI: 10.1093/oso/9780192863393.003.0004

criminal, equity, franchise, seigneurial, or manorial courts, and steered their way through the thickets of statutory law, Admiralty law, common law, customary law, and the law of nations. Different views of legal and illegal activity coexisted, variably construing wrecking as a service, a custom, or a crime. Ambiguities of interpretation and flexibilities in process made legal history into social history, where actions collided with principles, and irregularities flourished. The records of legal proceedings, and associated commentary and correspondence, provide abundant material for a fresh appraisal of the challenges and consequences of maritime misadventures.

Magistrates, crown officials, constables, and commoners could cite the law selectively, or erroneously, to meet their current interests. Lawyers, by profession, disagreed and argued, while popular opinion reflected elements of folklore and tradition. Local legal cultures incorporated forms of 'law-mindedness' that deviated from official positions, reflecting the 'moral economy' and customary experience of the coastal community.[5] Clarity, certainty, and consensus were hard to find.

Shipwrecks dissolved ownership and reassigned property, extinguishing prior possession and establishing new entitlements, as material wealth transitioned from the sea to the shore. Maritime distress turned retrievable cargo and the remnants of wrecked vessels into *res nullius* or *vacantia bona*, the property of no one, until rightful ownership and possession could be determined. The law set forth principles of entitlement and allocation, and procedures for obtaining justice, that did not necessarily command agreement or respect. The tension was perdurable between sea and land, between those who sent goods forth and those who picked them up. A coastal landowner in Spenser's *Faerie Queene* declares:

> That what the sea unto you sent, your own should seem
>
> . . . . .
>
> For what the mighty sea hath once possest
>
> . . . . .
>
> He may dispose by his imperial might,
> As thing at random left, to whom he list.[6]

[5] John Walter, '"Law-Mindedness" Crowds, Courts, and Popular Knowledge of the Law in Early Modern England', in Michael Lobban, Joanne Begiato, and Adrian Green (eds), *Law, Lawyers and Litigants in Early Modern England* (Cambridge, 2019), 164–84; Peter Rushton, 'Local Laws, Local Principles: The Paradoxes of Local Legal Process in Early Modern England', in Lobban, Begiato, and Green (eds), *Law, Lawyers and Litigants*, 185–206. See also E. P. Thompson, 'The Moral Economy of the English Crowd in the Eighteenth Century', *Past & Present*, 50 (1971), 76–136; John G. Rule, 'Wrecking and Coastal Plunder', in Douglas Hay, Peter Linebaugh, John Rule, et al. (eds), *Albion's Fatal Tree: Crime and Society in Eighteenth-Century England* (1975), 168–88; Keith Wrightson, 'Two Concepts of Order: Justices, Constables and Jurymen in Seventeenth-Century England', in John Brewer and John A. Styles (eds), *An Ungovernable People: The English and their Law in the Seventeenth and Eighteenth Centuries* (1980), 21–36.

[6] Edmund Spenser, *The Faerie Queene* (1596), bk V, canto 4. See also John Kelleher, 'The Mysterious Case of the Ship Abandoned off Sark in 1608: The Customary Law Relating to *choses gaives*', in Gordon Dawes (ed.), *Commise 1204: Studies in the History and Law of Continental and Insular Normandy* (St Peter Port, 2005), 171–90.

English law took a more complex view, attempting to adjudicate between shippers, savers, landed proprietors, and royal officials.

In the learned law of medieval and early modern England it was axiomatic that wreck of the sea belonged by prerogative to the crown—that 'wreck being made, the goods that were in the ship being brought to land by the waves, belong to the king'. The same was true of 'royal fishes', such as porpoises, sturgeon, and whales.[7] Kings, however, could assign 'liberty of wreck' to feudal proprietors, corporations, institutions, or individuals, and such privileges became engrained, hereditary, and sometimes contested. By the end of the sixteenth century there were hosts of agencies and jurisdictions claiming rights to wrecks, including the crown, the Duchies of Lancaster and Cornwall, the bishops of Chichester and Durham, admirals, vice admirals, and their deputies, the wardens of the Cinque Ports, and hundreds of lords of manors. The stewards and bailiffs of these claimants were often in dispute about where exactly, on whose beach or headland, within whose precincts or liberties, wreckage came ashore. Survivors of shipwrecks, and the merchants who employed them, had to cope with this complexity if they had any hope of restitution.

Statutes and Cases

Recognizing commercial interests, and modifying a charter of Henry III (1236), Edward I's Statute of Westminster (1275) decreed that should anyone on board survive a shipwreck, 'where a man, a dog, or a cat escape quick out the ship', neither that ship, nor anything within it, should be judged wreck, 'but the goods shall be saved and kept by view of the sheriff, coroner, or king's bailiff... so that if any sue for those goods, and after prove that they were his... within a year and a day, they shall be restored to him without delay; and if not, they shall remain to the king'.[8] This provision contributed a layer of complexity to situations that were already fraught and contested. The escape of a man or beast became a legal test for continuity of ownership, and 'true wreck' was allowed only when all aboard had abandoned their vessel or perished. The law allowed merchants and shippers to lay claim to their goods, but they would not be restored without much wrangling and paying of fees.[9] A statute of Edward III (1354) added the requirement that those who 'saved and kept' shipwrecked goods for the use of their lawful owners should be paid 'convenient for their travail'. The law invited crown agents to work

[7] 'Of the King's Prerogative', *Statutes of the Realm*, i (1235–1377), 226; John Boroughs, *The Soveraignty of the British Seas* (1651), 57, 92, 94; Thomas Madox, *The History and Antiquities of the Exchequer of the Kings of England* (1711), 235; Giles Jacob, *An Appendix to the Modern Justice: Containing the Particular Business of the Quarter Sessions* (1718), 33.

[8] 3 Edward I (1275), *Statutes of the Realm*, i. 28. Later lawyers disagreed whether this statute made new law or was simply a declaration of common law.

[9] Thomas Fuller, *The Historie of the Holy Warre* (Cambridge, 1639), 120.

with seigneurial worthies, representatives of shippers, and 'the best and most sufficient and discreet men' of each county, to manage the business of shipwreck recovery.[10]

These medieval statutes framed the law of *wreccum maris* into the eighteenth century. Tudor and Stuart attorneys added glosses, queries, caveats, and contingencies, as they argued the merits of the civil and common law. Scholarly authors related English practice to the ancient laws of Justinian, the medieval Laws of Oleron, the sea law of Scotland, and the codes of contemporary Europe.[11] Deep learning informed such disquisitions, but they were not necessarily accessible or relevant to coastal country scavengers. People may have heard what the law required, but many nonetheless believed, with Spenser's Artegall, that they could take whatever they could find.

Endless enquiries, suits, claims, and arguments ensued among shippers, sailors, salvors, and droit-holders about the circumstances of shipwreck and whether original ownership persisted. Parties to disputes understood the significance of survival and abandonment—the law of the dog or cat—and used the term 'wreck' with care. Merchants and mariners often said that a ship 'perished' or was 'cast away', was 'driven on shore by stress of weather', or 'fell on the rocks and broke in pieces', rather than admit to it being a 'wreck'. Their vessel might be 'wrecked' because it struck land, but did not become 'such a wreck as gives a forfeiture' if some living thing escaped. *Bona sparsa per naufragium* did not necessarily imply *wreccum maris* if owners could still claim their goods.[12] Those, on the other hand,

[10] 27 Edward III, stat. 2, c. 13 (1354), *Statutes of the Realm*, i. 338.

[11] *John Spelman's Reading on Quo Warranto Delivered in Gray's Inn (Lent 1519)*, ed. J. H. Baker, Selden Society, vol. 113 (1997), 26–42; John Rastell, *The Exposicions of the Termes of the Lawes of England* (1563), fos 115v–116, 271; William Lambarde, *A Perambulation of Kent* (1576), 229; William Welwood, *The Sea-Law of Scotland* (Edinburgh, 1590); William Welwood, *An Abridgement of all Sea-Lawes* (1613); John Selden, *Of the Dominion, or Ownership of the Sea*, trans. Marchamont Nedham (1632), 164–8; Boroughs, *Soveraignty of the British Seas*, 49, 57, 91–9; John Kitchin, *Jurisdictions: Or, The Lawful Authority of Courts Leet* (1651), 24; John Godolphin, *Synēgoros Thalassio: A View of the Admiral Jurisdiction* (1661), 26, 40; Charles Molloy, *De Jure Maritimo et Navali, or, A Treatise of Affairs Maritime, and of Commerce* (1676), 228–9; Guy Miege, *The Ancient Sea-Laws of Oleron, Wisby, and the Hanse-Towns, Still in Force* (1686); Alexander Justice, *A General Treatise of the Dominion and Laws of the Sea* (1705), 391–7; *An Abstract of all such Acts of Parliament, Now in Force, as Relate to the Admiralty, and Navy of England* (1715), 1–2; Giles Jacob, *Lex Mercatoria: Or the Merchant's Companion* (1729), 145–51; Matthew Hale, *A Treatise Relative to the Maritime Law of England* (1787), 37–44. See also 'Observations by Dr Talbot Concerning the King's Prerogative to Wreck of Sea' (1605), BL, MS Lansdowne 132, fo. 104; MS Lansdowne 133, fo. 23; 'Questions to be resolved in touching goods saved out of any ship perished on the sea or seacoast, but the men saved, whereby it is no wreck', SP 12/185, fos 218–20; SP 16/208, fos 153–6; 'The Case of Wreck Goods and Mr Attorney General's Opinion Thereupon' (1702), BL, MS Lansdowne 504/7, fos 12–15. For the law and practice in France, see *Ordonnance de la Marine du Mois d'Aoust 1681* (Paris, 1714), 414–46; Alain Cabantous, *Les Côtes barbares: Pilleurs d'épaves et sociétés littorales en France (1680–1830)* (Paris, 1993); and Francesca Trivellato, '"Amphibious Power": The Law of Wreck, Maritime Customs, and Sovereignty in Richelieu's France', *Law and History Review*, 33 (2015), 915–44.

[12] SP 18/11, fo. 39; John Exton, *The Maritime Dicaeologie, or Sea-Jurisdiction of England* (1656), 153; William Wynne, *The Life of Sir Leoline Jenkins, Judge of the High-Court of Admiralty*, 2 vols (1724), ii. 764; Hale, *Treatise Relative to the Maritime Law of England*, 38.

who sought profit from maritime disaster might describe a vessel as a wreck, 'no living creature being then therein', even when that was not strictly true. Backed by numbers on the beach, an assertive steward could declare, 'I seize upon all', and a crowd could chant 'all is ours', even face to face with protesting survivors. Mariners might argue that they 'saved themselves in their ship's boat', thereby preserving ownership, while salvagers could claim that the act of abandonment made the vessel theirs. Distinction could be drawn between escaping from a foundering ship and coming safe to land.[13] It was popularly believed in Jacobean England that, if six of seven tides washed over a vessel, 'she is wreck', even if her company were saved, though the law said nothing of the sort.[14] Dozens of disputes turned on whether goods were 'unjustly seized' upon false pretence, or whether a 'wreck' could reasonably be claimed and demonstrated. Resolution would show whether appropriated wreckage was spoil and plunder or lawful droit.

Edward I's statute denied true wreck 'if a man, a dog, or a cat escape quick out the ship', but legal wrangling tied this in knots. In one Elizabethan case, mariners who abandoned a ship that was cast away on the Goodwin Sands left behind their dog, tied to a mast, and afterwards, 'finding the dog alive, claimed their goods, and had their ship and goods again'. In a Jacobean case, a crew abandoned a sinking Newcastle collier on the coast of Sussex, carefully 'leaving in her a dog and a cat', and were outraged to find the ship seized as a wreck. When an Ipswich vessel went down with all hands, except for one 'which hanged alive in the tackling until he was fetched down', his survival saved the ship and goods as 'no wreck'. Whether materials were 'good wreck' or not exercised lawyers in London and authorities on every part of the coast.[15] Demonstrating popular knowledge of *wreccum maris*, claimants to derelict vessels commonly reported that such ships had 'neither man, boy, dog or rat', or 'neither man nor cat or any living creature on board'.[16]

The cat that was sole survivor of the tobacco ship *Constance*, lost in 1662, gave the owners a claim on their property.[17] But what if the survivor was a woman? What if a horse, or even a mouse, reached the shore? What about the red deer, a shipment from Prussia, that beached from a Norfolk wreck in 1705? Lawyers stressed vitality as a sign of ownership, but differentiated between creatures that were tame and wild. Against claims 'wherein no one knows to whom the property

[13] PC 2/12, fo. 141; PC 2/38, fo. 457; PC 2/51, fo. 371; HCA 13/32, fo. 112^{v}; HCA 13/70, fos 635–8; HCA 13/72, fos 21^{v}–22; SP 84/161, fos 80–8.

[14] SP 14/121, fo. 104.

[15] SP 11/6, fo. 117; SP 12/185, fos 218–20; SP 14/82, fo. 22; SP 14/87, fo. 8; SP 14/180, fo. 68^{v}; SP 14/184, fos 7, 89; SP 14/215, fos 5–6; SP 16/35, fo. 43; SP 16/208, fos 153^{v}, 159, 159^{v}, etc.

[16] HCA 13/70, fos 659–60.

[17] Rastell, *Exposicions of the Termes of the Lawes*, fos 115^{v}–116; John Cowell and Thomas Manley, *The Interpreter of Words and Terms, Used either in the Common Statute Laws of this Realm* (1701), sub 'Wrecke'; William Blackstone, *Commentaries on the Laws of England*, 11th edn, 4 vols (1791), i. 291–4; iii. 106; Sir Matthew Hale, 'Concerning the Prerogative and Franchise of Wreck', in Stuart A. Moore, *A History of the Foreshore and the Law Relating Thereto*, 3rd edn (1888), 406–9; George F. Steckley, 'The Seventeenth-Century Origins of Modern Salvage Law', *Journal of Legal History*, 35 (2014), 223.

belongs', pets and other domesticated animals, as well as surviving seamen, could serve as proof.[18] The medieval jurist Henry Bracton, whose work was well regarded by Tudor and Stuart lawyers, allowed the survival of a man or dog to prove ownerships of goods from a broken vessel that would otherwise be forfeit to the king.[19] Not satisfied with the capriciousness of such determination, an interregnum reformer called it 'a wicked and unjust law... that if a ship be cast away, and the goods float to land, and neither man, woman, dog nor cat escape alive, the owner shall lose all his goods'.[20] George III's chief justice Lord Mansfield found the medieval test of a surviving dog or cat 'shocking', but recognized it as a device among others for proving ownership and adjudicating claims.[21]

The Admiralty and the Common Law

A related conflict concerned the respective powers of the Admiralty and the other crown courts to deal with these matters. In principle the Admiralty ruled the waves, and the common law governed the shore, but each encroached on the other's domain. Wreckers and salvagers became entangled in technicalities that made the foreshore a zone of dispute. Though John Rule finds the legal position 'clear', and the distinction between salvors and wreckers 'clear-cut', his own work shows the overlap between people working with legitimate claimants and those looking out for themselves.[22]

The statute of Richard II (1392) that declared that 'wreck of the sea shall be tried, determined, discussed, and remedied by the laws of the land, and not before or by the admiral, nor his lieutenant in any wise', would seem to have settled the matter.[23] But Admiralty lawyers remained busy, despite attacks by the common law, and their authority expanded under Elizabeth I and the early Stuarts.[24] The

[18] *John Spelman's Reading on Quo Warranto*, 28, 30, 36; Norfolk Record Office, LEST/Q 37, 49, for the red deer.

[19] Henry de Bracton, *De Legibus et Consuetudinibus Regni Angliae*, ed. G. E. Woodbine, 4 vols, Selden Society (1968–77), ii. 339. Latin editions were published in England in 1569 and 1640.

[20] A. Booth, *Examen Legum Angliae, or, The Laws of England Examined, by Scripture, Antiquity and Reason* (1656), 23.

[21] 'Hamilton and Smyth versus Davis, 1st of June 1771', in *The English Reports Volume XCVIII. King's Bench Division XXVII* (1909), 433–7; William Holdsworth, *A History of English Law*, 17 vols (1903–72), xii. 534; R. H. Helmholz, *Natural Law in Court: A History of Legal Theory in Practice* (Cambridge, MA, 2015), 114–16.

[22] Moore, *History of the Foreshore*, 224–47; *Select Pleas in the Court of Admiralty, Vol. II*, ed. Reginald G. Marsden, Selden Society, vol. 11 (1897), pp. xviii, xxvi; Joanne Mathiasen, 'Some Problems of Admiralty Jurisdiction in the 17th Century', *American Journal of Legal History*, 2 (1958), 215–36; Rule, 'Wrecking and Coastal Plunder', 172, 177; George F. Steckley, 'Merchants and the Admiralty Court during the English Revolution', *American Journal of Legal History*, 22 (1978), 137–75.

[23] 15 Richard II, c. 3, reproduced in W. S., *An Exact Collection of Choice Declarations* (1653), 22; *A Collection of All Such Statutes and Parts of Statutes, as in any Way Relate to the Admiralty* (1742), 9.

[24] W. J. Jones, *The Elizabethan Court of Chancery* (Oxford, 1967), 379–80; Brian P. Levack, *The Civil Lawyers in England 1603–1641: A Political Study* (Oxford, 1973), 74–83.

'Articles Concerning the Admiralty of England' of 1591 confirmed the authority of Lord High Admiral Lord Howard of Effingham over 'goods floating or lying under the water . . . of which there is no possessor or owner, which commonly are called flotsam, jetsam, and lagan'. They also allowed him to 'enquire of those which make wreck of ships or other goods perishing by shipwreck upon the sea, whereof some hath come to the land, or who doth claim to have such wreck, except it be granted him by the king'.[25] These articles enhanced the landward reach of Admiralty jurisdiction, which only grew stronger in the early seventeenth century.

Combating this encroachment, and reciting the Ricardian statute, common lawyers insisted that 'wreck of the sea shall be tried at the common law, because it is cast upon the land'.[26] Sir Edward Coke argued that the Admiralty had no jurisdiction within any English county, and that only the common law would suffice.[27] Resisting Admiralty claims on his Norfolk manors, Sir Hamon Le Strange wrote in 1638 that 'wreck is that which is cast upon the ground or soil, and forsaken by the sea', so 'no admiral can deal with wreck, because it is out of his region or element, which is solely or properly the water'.[28] Another claimant to a wreck protested at an Admiralty enquiry in 1677 that ''twas a thing that the common law was to determine, they had nothing to do with it in this court'.[29] Admiralty judges, of course, disagreed.

Historians used to applaud early modern moves towards the ascendancy of the common law, sometimes endorsing the views of lords of coastal manors that Admiralty claims on their seashore were wholly unfounded. It is now apparent that rivalry long continued between the common lawyers and the civil-law practitioners of the Admiralty, with no clear victory for either side. Sir Henry Marten, the leading civil-law judge of the early Stuart Admiralty, attempted to sidestep the controversy in 1632 by declaring that he too was 'a judge of the common law of England, for he judgeth altogether by the common law and by the ancient customs of the sea and admiralty of England, and useth the civil law only to supplement when the common law and customs fail'.[30] His common-law colleagues were unlikely to have been convinced. Admiralty courts remained active during the Interregnum, though some claimants bypassed them by appealing directly to Oliver Cromwell.[31]

[25] *Articles Concerning the Admiralty of England, and the Iurisdiction Thereof. 21. Julii. Anno Domini. 1591* (1591), articles 6, 23. The articles were reprinted in 1618.

[26] *Reports of Certain Cases Arising in the Severall Courts of Record* (1652), 386.

[27] Sir Edward Coke, *The Fourth Part of the Institutes of the Laws of England: Concerning the Jurisdiction of Courts* (1644), 134–47.

[28] Norfolk Record Office, LEST/Q 37, 45 (Le Strange estate notes, 1605–1718).

[29] Norfolk Record Office, BL/Y2/44.

[30] SP 16/228, fo. 15^{v}. See also SP 16/286, fo. 152, for Marten's assertion in April 1635 that 'there is a legal truth, there is a real truth; the latter perhaps may be known by private credible information, but not the former'.

[31] HCA 13/63–70; SP 18/81, fos 70, 120.

It may be true that 'jurisdictional disputes with the common law courts curtailed Admiralty jurisdiction after the Restoration and reduced the Admiralty's case load', as modern scholarship suggests, but the High Court of Admiralty remained busy throughout the rest of the seventeenth century, and its lawyers more assertive than ever. The 'triumph' of the common law was far from complete.[32]

Admiralty lawyers pushed back against Sir Edward Coke and his allies, claiming that the statute of Richard II did not mean what it seemed to say, and in any case their authority descended from the prerogative of the crown.[33] John Godolphin, publishing in 1661, insisted that the civil-law jurisdiction of the Lord High Admiral 'comprised all matters properly maritime or any way pertaining to navigation', including the tackle, furniture, and lading of ships, and therefore governed 'such as claim wreck to the prejudice of the king or Lord Admiral'.[34] Richard Zouch and John Exton, fellow judges of the civil law, wrote specifically to refute claims that England's 'ports, havens, creeks and coasts' fell outside Admiralty jurisdiction.[35] The Admiralty judge Sir Leoline Jenkins advised Charles II that, when a wreck was in contention, even on land, the Admiralty was 'the proper court for it'. Only the Admiralty could protect 'shattered ships and shipwrecked goods', so that 'the rabble be hindered from meddling, the neighbours from buying, and the landlords from claiming droits and usages warrantable by no law'. A stiffened Admiralty, he argued, would reduce 'the insolencies of the people' and their practices of riot, force, pillage, and spoil. Such matters, he asserted, were 'cognisable' in the Admiralty, though they might also come before King's Bench or Commissions of Oyer and Terminer.[36] Similar arguments continued in the late seventeenth century and beyond, as Admiralty lawyers promoted their courts as quicker and more serviceable than the common law.[37]

[32] Richard J. Blakemore, 'The Legal World of English Sailors, *c*.1575–1729', in Maria Fusaro, Bernard Allaire, Richard Blakemore, and Tijl Vannestre (eds), *Law, Labour, and Empire: Comparative Perspectives on Seafarers, c.1500–1800* (Basingstoke, 2015), 100–20; Richard J. Blakemore, 'Orality and Mutiny: Authority and Speech among Seafarers in Early Modern London', in Thomas V. Cohen and Lesley K. Twomey (eds), *Spoken Word and Social Practice: Orality in Europe (1400–1700)* (Leiden and Boston, 2015), 260. See also George F. Steckley, 'Instance Cases at Admiralty in 1657: A Court "Packed up with Sutors"', *Journal of Legal History*, 7 (1986), 68–83; Steckley, 'Seventeenth-Century Origins of Modern Salvage Law', 209–30; Shavana Musa, 'Victims of Maritime Conflict, Compensation Claims and the Role of the Admiralty Court in the Early Modern Period', *Comparative Legal History*, 5 (2017), 125–41; Gregory Durston, *The Admiralty Sessions, 1536–1834: Maritime Crime and the Silver Oar* (Newcastle, 2017), 41.

[33] Exton, *Maritime Dicaeologie*, 153; Godolphin, *Synēgoros Thalassio*, 26, 44–5; Molloy, *De Jure Maritimo et Navali*, 226–9; Thomas Parker, *The Laws of Shipping and Insurance* (1775), 270; *Select Pleas in the Court of Admiralty*, ed. Marsden, ii. pp. xviii, xxvi; Melikan, 'Shippers, Salvors, and Sovereigns', 176.

[34] Godolphin, *Synēgoros Thalassio*, 26, 41–6.

[35] Richard Zouch, *The Jurisdiction of the Admiralty of England Asserted* (1663), title page, 101; Exton, *Maritime Dicaeologie*, 151–3.

[36] Wynne, *Life of Sir Leoline Jenkins*, ii. 764.

[37] Charles Hedges, *Reasons for Settling Admiralty-Jurisdiction; and Giving Encouragement to Merchants, Owners, Commanders, Masters of Ships, Material-Men and Mariners* (1690), 6, 13–14.

Salvageable materials in the sea were classed as flotsam, jetsam, and lagan, and only became *wreccum maris* when they reached land. Only when 'cast out of the bowels of the sea, and by the waves thereof driven on shore, and upon the reflux thereof left upon the land', could a good wreck be made, and then only if there were no survivors or lawful claimants, at least so some lawbooks insisted.[38] Chief Justice Sir Matthew Hale concurred that 'it is not properly wreck till it be cast upon the shore or land', for 'as long as the goods are floating upon the sea, they are not wreck'.[39] Items in the water, washed by the waves, such as barrels, chests, or spars from a wounded or sinking ship, were flotsam. Goods thrown overboard to lighten a vessel in a storm were jetsam, on their way to becoming flotsam. Lagan were a special category of weighty things, such as ordnance and anchors, that were lost and sunk in the sea, their positions sometimes marked with buoys or other floating indicators. Some coastal residents referred to another category of 'waveson', meaning goods tumbling in the surf. All were contestable when taken up, alongside wreckage that came on shore. Admiralty lawyers laid claim to anything wet, but local custom allowed the gathering of wreckage within the surf and the tidal foreshore.[40] Folklore held that the rights of inhabitants extended 'so far into the seas as they could from the shore discern a Humberkin', which people understood to mean a floating barrel—though the Admiralty judge Sir Henry Marten declared this 'an old idle saying, no man living being able to tell us what such a barrel is'.[41] In some manors the right to a wreck offshore extended as far as a horse could stand, or as far as a man with a long pole could reach, depending on the size of the horse and the length of the pole.[42] Claims to goods found beyond the low-water mark remained contentious into and beyond the nineteenth century.[43]

Lawyers for disputing claimants considered the circumstances of their losing and finding, the actions of mariners and scavengers, and the jurisdictional particulars of their landing. Further complications attached to derelicts—'boats, or other vessels, forsaken, and found empty, without any person in them'—and deodands—items 'instrumental to the death of a man on ship-board', or money

[38] Boroughs, *Soveraignty of the British Seas*, 104; Exton, *Maritime Dicaeologie*, 153.

[39] Hale, *Treatise Relative to the Maritime Law of England*, 37–8, 41.

[40] East Sussex Record Office, SAS/G5/49 (Sir John Gage, 1665); Sir John Constable's case, in George Poulson, *The History and Antiquities of the Seignory of Holderness*, 2 vols (Hull, 1840), i. 89–95, 158–9; Moore, *History of the Foreshore*, 224–33.

[41] SP 16/353, fo. 28; SP 14/11, fo. 72.

[42] SP 14/215, fo. 3^{v}; SP 16/431, fo. 56; Moore, *History of the Foreshore*, 233–41, 247; BL, MS Lansdowne 132, fo. 4; East Sussex Record Office, BH/P/ES/ET/89. One Stuart lawyer mentioned a horse of eighteen hands, and an eighteen-foot spear or lance. Another referred to a horse of fifteen hands, and its rider wielding a half pike.

[43] 'The King (in his Office of Admiralty) v. Forty-Nine Casks of Brandy, January 20, 1836', in *The English Reports Volume CLXVI: Ecclesiastical, Admiralty, and Probate and Divorce VI* (1924), 401–14; Tom Cousins, *Erme Estuary Site Conservation Statement & Management Plan* (Bournemouth, 2018), 'sects 2.4, 5.3, 10.7'.

or jewels found on a washed-up seafarer's body.[44] Bailiffs, stewards, Admiralty men, and manororial-court juries would work to sort this out, even as materials were taken up informally by coastal inhabitants.

Commissions and Consequences

Rather than proceeding through the courts of common law, where they might not find sufficient remedy, merchants and others aggrieved by the plunder of grounded ships could appeal to the Privy Council or the High Court of Admiralty, which might hear the matter directly or refer it to a commission. Parties might also take their case to other bodies such as the Cinque Ports or the Duchy of Lancaster, asking for similar intervention. Mobilizing even heavier legal weaponry, some appellants turned to the equity courts of Chancery, Requests, or Star Chamber. The process turned on petitions and supplications, payments of fees and invocations of patronage, and could cost as much as some of the materials at issue. It was part of the process of negotiation, by which shippers sought restitution, and savers secured composition. Foreign shippers commonly used English partners to appeal on their behalf, and sometimes had help from ambassadors or other diplomatic personnel.[45]

A typical request on behalf of Cuthbert Bricie, 'a poor Scottish man', sought 'remedy of his goods, in whose hands soever they remain', after a shipwreck in Sussex in 1556. Another sought assistance in 1565 for a Portuguese merchant regarding 'certain oils saved from a ship which perished on that coast'.[46] Hundreds of appeals came before the Admiralty for restitution of goods 'which by pretence of a wreck were unjustly seized and carried away', and for 'the recovery of the same goods to the true proprietaries'.[47] Most included a partisan interpretation of the law.

Admiralty judges heard routine business before their courts in London or Southwark, and sent surrogate commissioners and notaries to take testimony in more remote parts of the kingdom. These commissions summoned witnesses on oath, and invited people with wrecked materials in their custody to explain themselves or make restitution. Their proceedings followed civil law, with written interrogatories and depositions like those used in ecclesiastical courts. Writs of assistance required justices, constables, and other officers to aid commissioners in tracing purloined items. Several months could pass before commissions got to

[44] Wynne, *Life of Sir Leoline Jenkins*, i, p. lxxxix.

[45] For cases involving Scotland, SP 59/41, fo. 277; PC 2/21, fo. 124; for Dutch examples, SP 12/534, fo. 10; SP 84/137, fo. 186; SP 84/139, fo. 29; SP 84/163, fo. 4.

[46] PC 2/7, fo. 375; PC 2/9, fo. 166.

[47] PC 2/12, fo. 141. More examples in PC 2/38, fo. 604^{v}; PC 2/51, pp. 279, 371; SP 12/120, fo. 32; SP 12/131, fo. 146.

work, every delay increasing the chance of spoilage or concealment, and allowing prospective deponents to prepare their stories. Opportunities for restitution diminished as goods changed hands, and seafaring witnesses went back to work.[48]

Following the wreck of five ships on the coast of Sussex in 1576, for example, the Admiralty judge Dr David Lewes observed that 'a great quantity' was misappropriated, 'so as the goods extant and certified do amount but to a very small portion in respect of that which came on land'. His commission therefore attempted to locate 'the rest of the said goods which have been embezzled, spoiled, and carried away'.[49] Another commission in Sussex in 1578, regarding a lost cargo of wine and books, similarly empowered its members 'to make diligent search for all such parcels thereof as may be known to have been embezzled by the disorderly access of the country'. If any 'shall refuse to restore so much as shall be proved to have come into their hands', officers were supposed 'to apprehend them, and commit them until they shall have made delivery thereof'.[50]

By employing 'very hard means', their nature unspecified, examiners sent to Devon to recover riches from a wreck near Combe Martin in 1588 managed to recover gold and other goods that the country people had found in the sand. The commissioners reported that they had 'gathered so much of the trash together as we could...from the parties who found it', for 'otherwise the same being dispersed into divers hands amongst poor men it were impossible to recover the same; and much trouble and charge we sustained in the obtaining thereof'.[51] Their business was recovering goods, not punishing wreckers.

Shippers seeking recovery generally knew enough law to argue that vessels were not a 'wreck' if so much as a cat or a dog escaped alive. Their testimony described the circumstances of disaster, and displayed merchants' marks and documents to prove contested titles.[52] Most understood that salvagers expected moieties, droits, and rewards, which the shippers construed as plunder. Medieval law stated that those who 'saved and kept' shipwrecked goods for the use of their lawful owners should be paid 'convenient for their travail'.[53] Allocations varied, but the fishermen who retrieved the shipwrecked armour of Shakespeare's Pericles understood that 'there are certain condolements, certain vails'.[54] Common custom allowed one moiety (a half) 'to him that saves it', though sometimes much less was offered. In Elizabethan Cornwall, according to Richard Carew, wrecks accrued to 'the finders' petty benefit, to whom he that enjoyeth the Admiral's right, by the

[48] Exton, *Maritime Dicaeologie*, 59; Francis Clerke, *The Practice of the Court of Admiralty of England* (1722), 33–7. Records of examinations by commission between 1588 and 1678 are in HCA 13/225–71, none, unfortunately, indexed or calendared.

[49] SP 12/107, fos 212–13. [50] PC 2/12, fos 259, 321. [51] BL, MS Lansdowne 145, fo. 350.

[52] Determination of the ownership of shipwrecked items 'by good marks, and perfect good espiall' is discussed in Edmund Spenser, *Faerie Queen* (1596), bk V, canto 4.

[53] 27 Edward III stat. 2, c. 13 (1354), *Statutes of the Realm*, i. 338; Melikan, 'Shippers, Salvors, and Sovereigns', 176.

[54] William Shakespeare, *Pericles*, Act 2, scene 1.

common custom, alloweth a moiety for his labour'.[55] In early Stuart Dorset, and perhaps elsewhere, salvagers refused to hand over goods that they had found 'unless they may have a full moiety thereof', a demand that shipping agents thought 'unreasonable'.[56] Well-connected salvagers of a Hamburg ship found derelict off the Lizard in 1626 appealed to the royal secretary Sir John Coke that they 'may have the right that in such cases belongeth to them that find wrecks, which is to have the half amongst them', and hoped that a gift of £10 to the secretary's secretary would secure a favourable answer.[57] Admiralty staff advised in 1642 that 'for salvage of ships and goods that is cast away there is no certain rate, but as the vice-admiral and the merchants or masters can agree'.[58]

Officials involved in shipwreck recovery understood that savers needed 'reasonable contentment . . . for otherwise they will be discouraged to go abroad on the like occasion'. But what was 'reasonable' to one party could appear excessive or inadequate to another.[59] According to the civil lawyer William Welwood, it should be left to the 'arbitrement' of the Admiral 'to consider the finder or taker with condign portion, for his travails, charges, and hazard in all circumstances, even with the half at least', with adjustment 'according to the easy or difficult winning and saving of the said goods'.[60] The captain of Cowes Castle on the Isle of Wight restrained scavengers who were making 'spoil' of a wreck in 1633 but promised 'such as would justly take pains for the saving of the goods should be contented and satisfied'. True to his word, he later distributed more than £30 to 'the labourers for saving all the goods and for carrying the goods to Newport'.[61] An interregnum Admiralty lawyer declared that 'something must be allowed to them that have saved and kept them'.[62] Sir Richard Lloyd preferred to compensate salvors according to their level of labour and risk, rather than the worth of the goods they recovered.[63]

Local authorities were supposed to store salvaged materials for a year and a day to safeguard lawful claimants, but some of those same officials were themselves beneficiaries of wrecks. It was their duty, Admiralty judges insisted, 'to cause all that may be found to be inventoried and put in safe condition, to be disposed to such to whom the same shall be due', and to exercise 'true diligence and care' to save wreck materials for their 'right owners'.[64] Perishable materials could be sold, with receipts. Underlings of the Admiralty and the Cinque Ports were supposed to

[55] Hale, *Treatise Relative to the Maritime Law of England*, 41; *The Survey of Cornwall by Richard Carew*, ed. John Chynoueth, Nichols Orme, and Alexandra Walsham, *Devon and Cornwall Record Society*, NS 37 (2004), fos 27^{v}–28.

[56] SP 12/534, fo. 10. [57] SP 16/33, fo. 164.

[58] Wiltshire and Swindon Archives, 865/404. [59] SP 14/127, fo. 169; SP 25/123, fo. 155^{v}.

[60] Welwood, *Abridgement of all Sea Lawes*, 166, 172–3. [61] SP 16/244, fos 36, 38^{v}.

[62] BL, MS Additional 46,501, fo. 236.

[63] Steckley, 'Seventeenth-Century Origins of Modern Salvage Law', 209–30.

[64] SP 12/107, fos 212–3; *Acts of the Privy Council of England, 1542–1631*, ed. J. R. Dasent et al., 45 vols (1890–1964), xxxvii (1619–21), 96.

'take true inventory and note of the burthen of the ship or vessel, anchors, cables, tackle, furniture, loading, and goods', the time and place where they came ashore, and their appraisal 'by four persons at the least, of the most ancient and substantial inhabitants of the place', in the presence of the mayor, bailiff, or other reputable officials.[65] These requirements, if followed, would have aided commissioners, and would have yielded troves of documentation for historians to study. Much, however, was concealed or consumed, and few such schedules and inventories survive.

Admiralty commissions of inquiry usually included locally reputable gentlemen, whose status and authority encouraged cooperation with people involved in wrecking. Sometimes, however, they met resistance. Villagers in Pembrokeshire in 1631 shut their doors and declared they had no business with the commission, or departed before they were fully examined. Behind this recalcitrance, it appears, was rivalry between landowners. One of the commissioners was a Mr Owen, on whose land some of the disputed wreckage arrived, and the reluctant witnesses were clients or kinsmen of his neighbour Henry Lort, who claimed title to the goods for himself.[66] Commissioners in Dorset in January 1642 took depositions from 343 witnesses involved with the goods of the wrecked *Golden Grape*, but did not necessarily hear the truth (see further on this in Chapter 8).[67]

Admiralty authority sometimes met disrespect. Seeking help from a constable in Essex in 1654, the master of the wrecked *John and Ambrose* presented documents authorizing recovery of his goods; but the constable, himself a hoarder of such items, spurned the papers, saying, 'a fly for you and your commission', or words to that effect.[68] Another Essex salvager threw an Admiralty warrant into the fire, saying 'that he cared not a pin for the warrant, nor would he obey the same'.[69] Such expressions of contempt were by no means unique, though grudging deference was more common.

Commissioners sent down to investigate the 'plunder' of the *Speedwell* in Cornwall in 1671 faced fierce resistance from the 'country people'. William Noye of Penzance reported to Sir Jonathan Trelawney in London that the men of Newlyn and Mousehole

> did not appear by our warrants; so...I went there myself to persuade these resolute rustic fellows to come before us; and for my kindness, in the night as I was going home to my house, three or four of them fell upon me, and with clubs did very much beat and abuse me, and endeavour to throw me over a great high cliff, and had a rope with them ready fitted to hang me, and tore all my cloak in pieces.

[65] SP 14/81, fo. 37.
[66] SP 16/182, fos 81, 120–1.
[67] HCA 13/244/149.
[68] HCA 13/70, fo. 47ᵛ.
[69] HCA 13/72, fo. 227ᵛ.

Noye no doubt attracted anger because he was a commissioner for pressing seamen as well as an examiner of wrecks. But it was not only local tinners and fishermen who opposed him. Mr John St Aubyn, a justice of the peace, also 'hindered his majesty's interest' by preventing people from appearing before the commission, 'and received their goods from them'.[70] Without the cooperation of magistrates and commoners, commissioners had little chance of recovering either materials or truth.

Even at the best of times commissioners had problems tracing and recovering merchandize that was scattered in many hands. Witnesses often displayed a remarkable vagueness of memory. Typical were such statements that William Griffin of Lydd 'had seven pieces of Holland, and he hath sold them all to whom he knoweth not', that his neighbour James Riche 'had half a hanging, had sold it to whom he will not tell', and that William Welles of Romney 'saved five tines of wax, delivered one, and sayeth the rest was stolen from him by them of Hythe, he knoweth not who they were'.[71] Deponents elsewhere showed similar selective amnesia. Commissioners in the Cinque Ports in 1593 managed to trace quantities of fabric and other commodities from the *Red Lyon* and the *Golden Lyon*, wrecked the previous year on the Goodwin Sands, after local people confessed to having 'spent, consumed or concealed' them. Employing lawyers, sergeants, bailiffs, and beadles, the commissioners recovered goods to the value of £1,930, and paid out half this sum in rewards. They might have had more success had fewer savers denied detaining goods, pretended 'a privilege', or preferred to deal separately with 'buyers of good value'.[72]

One final problem was that commissions would fall short of expectations. They provided a path for sufferers from shipwreck to recoup some of their losses, but it was not always clear that the return justified the effort. Admiralty commissioners examining a wreck in Elizabethan Devon recorded that their 'charges and bare expenses' exceeded £9, with 'the whole perquisites of the court amounting not above ten pounds . . . the goods received being very bad, of small value and scarce worth the travail'.[73] The early Stuart judge Sir Henry Marten also acknowledged that 'many times all the goods presented at a court, if they were sold, will not defray the charges spent by the judge of the court in gathering them up'.[74] Asked to justify his possession of materials from a wreck in 1583, Sir Edward Mansell declared that 'the charge of carrying or fetching the same anchors and cables would amount to more than the value of the same'.[75] After accounting for losses to the sea, wastage, spoilage, moieties, composition, fees, graft, and fraud, there

[70] SP 29/293, fo. 230; SP 29/303, fo. 52.

[71] Hatfield House, Cecil Papers, vol. 139, fo. 219.

[72] Hatfield House, Cecil Papers, vol. 31, fo. 128. See also PC 2/28, p. 240; SP 16/37, fos 40–3, 72; SP 16/153, fo. 87; SP 16/170, fos 32, 49, for commissions in Norfolk in 1616, Yorkshire in 1626, and Sussex in 1629.

[73] BL, MS Lansdowne 145, fo. 350.

[74] SP 16/208, fo. 298^{v}.

[75] SP 12/169, fo. 24.

may have been little for the investors and investigators to share. Commission processes enabled owners to exercise their rights, but their greatest production was stories.[76]

Crimes and Remedies

It was not clear what law had been broken, what crime committed, when people took wreckage from the shore. Writing about the eighteenth century, John Rule indicates that the appropriation of the cargo and materials of shipwrecked vessels was generally 'illegal', but early modern conditions were more ambiguous.[77] According to Edward I's *capitula itineris*, his instructions to judges, it was a felony for anyone to take 'by wreck of the sea... the goods of any, when the same ought not to be called wreck, nor did belong to them'. It was a crime to declare goods a 'wreck' when they did not meet that criterion, and a crime to misappropriate the property of others.[78] But this 'crime' was not regulated by statute, nor covered by the common law. The only sanction that the Jacobean jurist Ferdinando Pulton could find was that 'whosever layeth hands upon the wreck of the sea, shall be attached by sufficient pledges. The price of the wreck shall be valued and delivered to the town to answer.'[79] There was no sufficient sanction to hold back a determined landed proprietor or a mob.

Admiralty law threatened that, 'if the finder conceal such goods, whether anchors, timber, jewels, dead men with money or jewels about them, etcetera, he not only loseth his just part, but may also be fined at will of the Admiral'.[80] But this was hard to enforce. Those who 'shall meddle with such goods... are holden for robbers', wrote Charles Molloy in the 1670s, although the civil law that he practised had limited means to punish offenders.[81] In practice, scavengers could scour the beaches with impunity, and take whatever they could find, so long as their neighbours condoned their activity. It was widely believed that wreckage was *res nullius*, no man's property, so removing it was no theft; it was also understood that no harm would come to those who handed over shipwrecked goods when so demanded by lawful authorities.

Michael Dalton, the author of the much-reprinted *Country Justice*, conceded that 'the taking and carrying away of such things whereof the owner is unknown, in some cases is no felony'. Only if 'there be owners of them to some purpose... it

[76] Paul Gewirtz, 'Narrative and Rhetoric in the Law', in Peter Brooks and Paul Gewirtz (eds), *Law's Stories: Narrative and Rhetoric in Law* (New Haven, 1996), 2–5.

[77] Rule, 'Wrecking and Coastal Plunder', 169.

[78] *Statutes of the Realm*, i. 237.

[79] Ferdinando Pulton and Sir Anthony Fitzherbert, *De Pace Regis et Regni viz. A Treatise Declaring which be the Great and General Offences of the Realme* (1609), 250. Pulton (1536–1618) incorporated the work of his predecessor Fitzherbert (1470–1538).

[80] Welwood, *Abridgement of all Sea Lawes*, 173.

[81] Molloy, *De Jure Maritimo et Navali*, 226.

is felony to steal such goods'.[82] Such opinions, widely disseminated, gave cover to looters of shipwrecks. The 1697 edition of Dalton's Jacobean handbook repeated that 'the taking away... of wreck of the sea... is not felony', but warned that such takers nonetheless 'shall be punished by fine and imprisonment'.[83] The eighteenth-century jurist Sir William Blackstone explained definitively that, until a statute of 1753 made it a crime, 'larceny... could not at common law be committed of... wreck, till seized by the king or him who hath the franchise: for till such seizure no one hath a determinate property therein'.[84]

Successive regimes made fitful attempts to reform the law on shipwrecks. In 1581 the House of Commons introduced a bill 'against such persons as under colour of claiming right in wrecks do seize the goods of divers persons, having no right thereto'. It got as far as a second reading but died in the crush of business.[85] The next proposal came in 1633, when the Privy Council prepared a proclamation 'for reforming the barbarous custom of riffling and robbing of ships cast away upon the coast'. No text is known of this proclamation, which was never promulgated, but its purpose seems to have been to enhance crown revenues, rather than to safeguard shipowners (see further on this in Chapter 6).[86]

Reformers of the 1650s prepared another bill 'for the preservation of the goods of merchants wrecked or lost either in the sea or upon the shore'. Reacting against 'the violence and unruliness of divers persons living in or near the sea coast', and noting the theft of ships' goods 'by divers ill-disposed persons sometimes secretly but commonly with great violence', these reformers made a proposal that required local officials to supervise wreck sites, and there to 'seize and take into their custody the said goods'. Inhabitants would be obligated to assist these officers and would be granted 'a certain rate' for every pound of value so saved. Disorderly scavengers would be turned into dutiful labourers, and rightful owners would have means to proceed against any who 'did refuse or neglect to execute the duty, power, and authority by this act required' of them. Though well intentioned, the bill was never enacted.[87]

Wreck law remained unchanged after the Restoration, though Sir Leoline Jenkins recommended legislation in 1667 to restrain continuing 'barbarous usages'.[88] Only in Queen Anne's last parliament in 1714 was a new statute passed

[82] Michael Dalton, *The Countrey Iustice, Conteyning the Practise of the Iustices of the Peace* (1618), 236.

[83] Michael Dalton, *The Country Justice* (1697), 373. See also Jacob, *Appendix to the Modern Justice*, 33, repeating that taking away wreck was no felony.

[84] Blackstone, *Commentaries on the Laws of England*, iv. 235; Holdsworth, *History of English Law*, xi. 530.

[85] *Proceedings in the Parliaments of Elizabeth I*, ed. T. E. Hartley, 2 vols (Leicester, 1981), i. 529–30, 540–1; *Commons Journal*, i. 120, 130–1.

[86] SP 16/186, fo. 70; SP 16/189, fo. 40; SP 16/242, fo.4; SP16/248, fo. 53; Steckley, 'Seventeenth-Century Origins of Modern Salvage Law', 212.

[87] Lambeth Palace Library, MS 3475, fos 187–9 (Sir Matthew Hale's notes, *c.*1652).

[88] Wynne, *Life of Sir Leoline Jenkins*, ii. 763.

against ships being 'barbarously plundered... and their cargoes embezzled'. Scavengers now faced fines or imprisonment if they boarded a wreck without permission or impeded the saving of its goods. Any who went so far as to disable a ship that might otherwise be made seaworthy—for example, by removing its rudder or cutting a hole in its side—were 'hereby made guilty of felony'.[89] A private bill introduced in 1737 'for the better preserving ships stranded or forced on shore, and the furniture and cargoes thereof' attempted to stiffen penalties. Among other provisions, it would have made communities collectively responsible for crimes against shipwrecked mariners, and threatened transportation for those who unlawfully took away 'any part of the tackle, furniture, apparel, goods, or cargo of such ship or vessel', but the alteration was not enacted.[90]

Only under George II in 1753 did harsh new legislation threaten imprisonment, transportation, or even death for 'persons who shall steal or detain shipwrecked goods'. Making unauthorized wrecking into a felony, the statute railed against the 'wicked enormities', and 'cruelty, outrage or violence' of those who plundered wreckage, and gave eighteenth-century magistrates weapons that their seventeenth-century predecessors lacked. This law also mandated the death penalty for any who 'shall put out any false light or lights, with intention to bring any ship or vessel into danger', a rumoured practice that was never documented in early modern England.[91] Legislation never stopped predation, however, as demonstrated in both historical and modern accounts. The most prohibitive of legal environments in the second half of the eighteenth century coincided with the peak of wrecking activity in its so-called 'golden age'[92] (see further on this in Chapter 12).

[89] 13 Anne, c. 21.

[90] BL, Harper Collection of Private Bills 1695–1814, no. 32, read 22 July 1737; *Commons Journal*, 22 (1732–7), 685.

[91] 26 George II, c. 19.

[92] Rule, 'Wrecking and Coastal Plunder', 168; Cathryn Pearce, *Cornish Wrecking 1700–1860: Reality and Popular Myth* (Woodbridge, 2010), 123–44, 217–18.

4
The Barbarous Country People

It was sometimes said in early modern England that the violence of the sea was surpassed only by the savagery of its coastal inhabitants. 'The shore more cruel than the sea devours, | For he who claims the wreck cries, all is ours,' trilled a poem of 1633.[1] It was shocking, wrote a later Stuart administrator, that shipwrecked mariners having 'escaped the merciless elements' of the ocean, 'expecting relief from their own countrymen and Christians, should find them more merciless enemies'.[2] Reports accumulated, with much repeating, that shipwrecks occasioned 'rapine' and 'pillage', as the 'barbarous' and 'inhumane' 'savages' of the shoreline made 'spoil' and 'plunder' of cargo and fittings. Victims of shipwreck regularly complained of ill treatment, saying that that their cargoes and furnishings were 'rifled' in 'riotous' manner: their goods were 'spoiled and carried away . . . in disordered sort' by lawless 'thieves and robbers', and 'they that were strongest carried most away'.[3] The plunderers seemed out of control. Following a wreck on the Yorkshire coast in 1626, Viscount Henry Dunbar described 'spoil made by the indigent and barbarous people of the country . . . nigh five hundred of that kind', who 'little regarded' the law.[4] Privy Councillors in 1633 addressed 'the barbarous custom of riffling and robbing of ships cast away upon the coast'.[5] Admiralty lawyers also railed against these 'barbarous usages'.[6] The word 'barbarous' became a casually applied adjective for 'country people', who were 'ready to devour and ruin the whole'.[7]

Historians have been inclined to accept these charges as representations of the activity of wreckers, despite the overblown rhetoric. The impression persists that behaviour on shipwreck beaches was rude and disordered, ruthless and violent, in defiance of law and authority. Some scholars have depicted the swarming and stripping of wrecks as a defiant form of 'crowd behaviour' involving class resistance and redress. The appropriation of wreckage may then be perceived, and even

[1] *A Poeticall Sea-Piece: Containing in a Spacious Table the Lively Description of a Tempest at Sea, and Shipwrecks* (1633).

[2] James Derriman, 'The Wreck of the *Albemarle*', *Journal of the Royal Institution of Cornwall*, NS 1 (1992), 140, with citations from BL, India Office Records, E/1/198 (1708).

[3] PC 2/12, fos 143–4, 259, 321; SP 12/107, fos 122, 21; SP 12/168, fo. 15; SP 16/40, fos 217–19; SP 16/186, fo. 70; SP 16/189, fo. 40; SP 16/242, fo. 4; SP16/248, fo. 53; HCA 13/42, fo. 278^{v}.

[4] SP 16/37, fo. 40.

[5] SP 16/248, fo. 53^{v}; SP 16/258, fo. 156.

[6] William Wynne, *The Life of Sir Leoline Jenkins, Judge of the High-Court of Admiralty*, 2 vols (1724), ii. 763.

[7] SP 29/250, fo. 219; SP 29/293, fo. 230; PC 1/1/50; HCA 49/106, packet C.

Shipwrecks and the Bounty of the Sea. David Cressy, Oxford University Press. © David Cressy 2022.
DOI: 10.1093/oso/9780192863393.003.0005

approved, in terms of the 'moral economy' of the poor.[8] This chapter argues, to the contrary, that the finders and savers of marine wreckage were rarely outrageous, that they generally conformed to community norms, and that salvage involved cooperation between authorities and coastal inhabitants. Accusations of 'plunder' and 'pillage', though persistent, were inflamed, exaggerated, and largely unjustified.

The term 'wrecking', as John Rule recognized, encompassed 'a range of activities from the casual pocketing of articles cast up by the sea to the deliberate luring of vessels ashore; from near beachcombing to open looting'. Not used before the eighteenth century, but too useful for historians to abandon, the word 'wrecking' covers every phase of shipwreck recovery, legitimate or unlicensed, and needs not carry pejorative connotations.[9] Its practitioners were 'wreckers' because they took part in the harvesting or salvaging of material from wrecks. 'Along the shore a crowd of wreckers stand | Ready to seize whatever drives to land,' announced a dramatic entertainment of 1746.[10] Among them, and behind them, were reputable local landowners and officials. Early modern records describe such people as 'savers', and sometimes as 'the barbarous country people'. But no English evidence supports the myth of murderous wreckers drawing ships to their doom.

The canard of wrecker 'barbarity' appears in a variety of sources from the sixteenth century to the present. It features in the writings of clerical and literary moralists, in the work of lawyers and officials, and in the complaints and petitions of merchants and mariners who suffered shipwreck loss. It persists, unfortunately, in popular histories that sensationalize wreckers as murderous and orgiastic.[11] Language used elsewhere to denigrate the 'barbarous' Turks and Indians, or the 'barbarous and cruel' dealings of the papists in Ireland or Spain, was casually applied to such people as the inhabitants of coastal England. 'Barbarous' was an overused adjective, disparaging a class of commoners, and excluding them from the civilized community. Used in classical times to denote outsiders who did not

[8] Interpretations influenced by E. P. Thompson, 'The Moral Economy of the English Crowd in the Eighteenth Century', *Past & Present*, 50 (1971), 76–136, include John Rule, 'Wrecking and Coastal Plunder', in Douglas Hay, Peter Linebaugh, John Rule, et al. (eds), *Albion's Fatal Tree: Crime and Society in Eighteenth-Century England* (1975), 168–88; John Rule, 'Smuggling and Wrecking', in Philip Payton, Alston Kennerley, and Helen Doe (eds), *The Maritime History of Cornwall* (Exeter, 2014), 195–208; and John Styles, '"Our traitorous money makers": The Yorkshire Coiners and the Law, 1760–83', in John Brewer and John Styles (eds), *An Ungovernable People: The English and their Law in the Seventeenth and Eighteenth Centuries* (New Brunswick, 1980), 209–10. Cathryn Pearce, *Cornish Wrecking 1700–1860: Reality and Popular Myth* (Woodbridge, 2010), 153, 165, questions the prevailing 'domination/resistance model'.

[9] Rule, 'Wrecking and Coastal Plunder', 169, 172.

[10] William Hyland, *The Ship-Wreck: A Dramatick Piece* (1746), prologue. The word 'wrecker' appears here sixty years before the earliest usage cited in the *Oxford English Dictionary*.

[11] Bella Bathurst, *The Wreckers: A Story of Killing Seas and Plundered Shipwrecks: From the 18th Century to the Present Day* (New York, 2005). Reviewing Bathurst, *The Wreckers*, Cathryn J. Pearce describes the book as 'an accretion of misinformation... riddled with unsubstantiated assertions and errors' (*International Journal of Maritime History*, 17 (2005), 411–12).

speak Greek, the word came to connote rudeness, vulgarity, and brutality.[12] The harvesting of wrecks, by these lights, occasioned a breakdown in the social order, as civil discipline gave way to greed and violence. Presented with the opportunity of a shipwreck, it is alleged, coastal residents descended into savagery. Such characterizations, I argue, are far from the truth.

Moral Reproach

The litany of disapproval and denigration resounded in literary and religious writings. The Elizabethan lawyer William Lambarde condemned 'the unmerciful covetise' and lack of charity of coastal dwellers, 'showing themselves more careful of their own gain than pitiful of other men's calamities'.[13] The early Stuart historian Thomas Fuller scorned those who 'make advantage of such pitiful accidents, and... strip poor mariners out of those rags of their estates which the mercy and modesty of the waves and winds had left them'.[14] The Sussex minister John Tillinghast, preaching in 1637, berated his own congregation, 'especially of the meaner sort' who 'continue still in their wonted course of barbarism toward the distressed... notwithstanding the many admonitions to the contrary'. Foreign mariners, he reported, 'had rather fall into the hand of Turks and infidels, and should find more courteous usage from them in these cases, than from the English'. It was 'surely a blot and a blemish to so famous an island', as well as offensive to God, that 'our people' should display 'incivility and cruelty towards strangers'.[15] This was a typical pulpit rant by a busy controller, highlighting the cultural distance between his sort and the mob. It was also designed to impress a gentle patron, in this case Lady Margery Gratwick, who, evidence reveals, was not averse herself to receiving shipwrecked goods (see Chapter 9).

Tillinghast used his sermon to contrast the humanity and generosity of the people of Malta, who aided the shipwrecked Christian missionary St Paul, with 'the uncivil carriage and evil behaviour of our neighbours' nearby. According to

[12] Examples include T. S., *A Tragicall Historie of the Troubles and Civile Warres of the Lowe Countries* (1583), title page, on 'the barbarous cruelty and tyrannie of the Spaniard'; Henry Smith, *Gods Arrow against Atheists* (1593), sig. B2^{v}, on the 'barbarous' followers of 'Mahomet'; Richard Knolles, *The Generall Historie of the Turkes* (1603), 1, 2; Edward Waterhouse, *A Declaration of the State of the Colony and Affaires in Virginia* (1622), on the 'barbarous massacre' by the Indians; John Skinner, *A True Relation of the Uniust, Cruell, and Barbarous Proceedings against the English at Amboyna* (1624); *A Late and True Relation from Ireland* (1641), on the 'barbarous and cruel' papists. See also Sir Ferdinando Gorges, *America Painted to the Life: A True History of the Originall Undertakings of the Advancement of Plantations into those Parts* (1658), 17, 26, 108, 182; Samuel Clarke, *A Generall Martyrologie Containing a Collection of al the Greatest Persecutions which have Befallen the Church of Christ* (1660), 361, 380, 389–91; and frequent parliamentary denunciations of the 'barbarous cruelty' of the Cavaliers.

[13] William Lambarde, *A Perambulation of Kent* (1576), 229.

[14] Thomas Fuller, *The Historie of the Holy Warre* (Cambridge, 1639), 120.

[15] John Tillinghast, *Saint Paul's Ship-Wrack in his Voyage to Rome* (1637), epistle dedicatory.

the biblical narrator, 'the barbarous people showed us no little kindness', and, when we departed, 'they laded us with such things as were necessary'. The shoremen of Sussex, by contrast, were 'beast-like' and 'barbarous' in behaviour, apostates to common civility. Paul's rescuers were 'barbarous . . . for their language, not their manners' (not being speakers of Greek), but the phrase transferred readily to 'the barbarous country people' of coastal England.[16]

A similar complaint appears in a long verse tract by George Wither, published in 1628, that denounces the 'wickedness' of shipwreck plunder, 'though it hath not much observed been to be a fault'.[17] What wickedness? How much not observed? The poet answers:

> It is the barbarous usage, wherewith we
> Do entertain those men that shipwrecked be,
> Which here I mean: For, many people have
> Less mercy than the tempest, and the wave.
> That vessel, which the rocks had pity on.
> The cruelty of man doth seize upon;
> And him that is oppressed, quite bereaves
> Of what the quicksand undevoured leaves.

Wither's shipwrecked sailors struggle ashore, only to find

> The neighb'ring people (who in this are far
> More savage, than most barbarous nations are)
> Instead of bringing comfort and relief,
> Add new affliction to their former grief.
> . . .
> Paul did a people ev'n at Malta find,
> (Although a barb'rous island) far more kind.

The shore-dwellers, in this accusation, are not only indifferent to the sufferings of survivors, but may have actively enticed a ship to wreck in order to obtain 'God's gift' or 'God's good . . . what on the shore they find'. The poet reports what

> some people say,
> That, for such mischiefs, they both watch and pray;
> With curses, banning them, who set up lights,
> To guide the seaman in dark stormy nights.

[16] Acts 28: 1–10; Tillinghast, *Saint Paul's Ship-Wrack*, sig. A4, 19; John Brekell, *Euroclydon: Or the Dangers of the Sea* (1744), 48.

[17] George Wither, *Britain's Remembrancer* (1628), fos 214^{v}–216.

This is a comprehensive and characteristic indictment, replete with prejudice, misinformation, and biblical reference, and largely groundless in fact.

More opprobrium flowed from the interregnum cleric William Johnson, who recalled 'the ruins of a shipwreck' in Norfolk and preached against 'the country people enriching themselves with the losses of other men, the worst way of getting in the world'.[18] A Restoration moralizer similarly castigated countrymen who take 'whatever they can rifle from a wreck' and 'do not less hazard their souls than frequently their bodies for the getting of them'.[19] Moral reform and legal action were needed, declared the secretary of the East India Company in 1708, 'to deter all others from the like barbarous and cruel practices'.[20]

The greed of wreckers was the stuff of legend. At Holy Island, on the coast of Northumberland, a Caroline official described

> how the common people there do pray for ships which they see in danger. They all sit down upon their knees, and hold up their hands, and say very devotedly, Lord send her to us . . . They pray, not God to save you . . . but to send you to them by shipwreck, that they may get the spoil of her. And if . . . the ship eschew naufrage, they get up in anger, crying, the Devil stick her, she is away from us.[21]

Similar sentiments were attributed to Cornish chaplains, who asked God, 'not that wrecks should happen, but that if any wreck should happen, Thou wilt guide them into the Scilly Isles for the benefit of the inhabitants'.[22] Reports were repeated of churchgoers, hearing of a shipwreck, who 'ran out from their devotions to the spoil, leaving the parson to preach to the walls', and of parsons too who joined the rush.[23]

Daniel Defoe popularized this legend of predation, criticizing the people of Deal, Kent, who sought 'booty' and 'plunder' from wrecks and never 'concerned themselves for the lives of these miserable creatures', the distressed mariners. This was a canard, for Defoe himself records the mayor of Deal's 'compassion at the distress of the poor creatures' and his efforts that saved five hundred lives.[24] Most

[18] William Johnson, *Deus Nobiscum: Or, A Sermon Preached upon a Great Deliverance at Sea* (1659), 103.

[19] *Lamentable News from Sea; Being a True Relation how a Ship call'd the Cherry, was Lately Cast Away* (1677), 8.

[20] Derriman, 'Wreck of the *Albemarle*', 140.

[21] Gilbert Blakhal, *A Brieffe Narration of the Services Done to Three Noble Ladies* (Spalding Club, Aberdeen, 1844), 159, quoting the words of lieutenant governor Robin Rugg.

[22] Robert Heath, *A Natural and Historical Account of the Islands of Scilly* (1750), 86; John Troutbeck, *A Survey of the Ancient and Present State of the Scilly Islands* (1794), 31; Juliet Du Boulay, 'Wrecks in the Isles of Scilly', *Mariner's Mirror*, 46 (1960), 92–4.

[23] William Smith, *A Full Account of the Late Ship-Wreck of the Ship called The President* (1684), 8; Rule, 'Wreckers and Coastal Plunder', 184.

[24] Daniel Defoe, *The Storm: Or, a Collection of the Most Remarkable Casualties and Disasters which Happen'd in the Late Dreadful Tempest, both by Sea and Land* (1704), 200–2.

notoriously, Defoe described as 'fierce and ravenous' the 'voracious country people' of western Cornwall, where mariners 'find the rocks themselves not more merciless than the people who range about them for their prey'.[25] The eighteenth-century historian of the Isles of Scilly Robert Heath knew better, reprimanding Defoe for his 'false account' of people 'that he never saw, nor could possibly be informed of, in so unfaithful a manner, except by the dictates of his own imagination', but the charge had taken root.[26] Murderous wreckers with treacherous lights have long appeared in popular accounts, despite the efforts of historians to expel them.[27] Tales of this nature had pan-European dissemination, but no more reliable substantiation.[28]

Petitions and Complaints

Examination of the context of accusations of lawless barbarity raises questions about their credibility. Complaints that goods from wrecked ships were 'unjustly seized and carried away . . . in disordered sort' by the 'barbarous' inhabitants of the country often originated with people asserting alternative claims to them. They were expressions of grievance and frustration, not necessarily objective reports. Merchants' factors seeking restitution, and Admiralty sergeants thwarted by local interests, wrote of ships being 'rifled' by 'riotous' wreckers. Charges of 'spoil' sometimes referred to the subsequent distribution of wreckage, after its gathering from the beach. In many cases the words were less description than excuse. Their power evaporates when we ask the historian's question, 'who is saying what to whom, and why?'.

The complaint in 1576 that people came 'in disordered sort . . . with a spoiling intent' and 'made waste' of shipwrecked merchandize in Sussex came from merchants seeking Admiralty writs for assistance and restitution. Their request for 'recompense' to 'the true savers for their industry, labour, and pains', and for 'the spoilers and embezzlers to lose the benefit thereof, and be punished accordingly', posits a distinction between lawful and unlawful wrecking that was hard to maintain in practice.[29] The similar charge in 1578 that goods were unjustly seized 'by pretence of a wreck' and 'embezzled by the disorderly access of the country'

25 Daniel Defoe, *A Tour through the Whole Island of Great Britain*, ed. Pat Rogers (1971), 236.

26 Heath, *Natural and Historical Account of the Islands of Scilly*, 138,

27 Bathurst, *Wreckers*, pp. xv, 125. Cautionary work by historians includes J. G. Pickwell, 'Improbable Legends Surrounding the Shipwreck of Sir Clowdisley Shovell', *Mariner's Mirror*, 59 (1973), 221–3; Geoffrey W. Place, 'Wreckers: The Fate of the *Charming Jenny*', *Mariner's Mirror*, 76 (1990), 167–8; Pearce, *Cornish Wrecking*, 2–3.

28 J. de Courcey Ireland, 'Wreckers', *Mariner's Mirror*, 70 (1984), 44; Henning Henningsen, 'Legends about "Wreckers"', *Mariner's Mirror*, 71 (1985), 215–18; Alain Cabantous, *Les Côtes barbares: Pilleurs d'épaves et sociétés littorals en France (1680–1830)* (Paris, 1993), 236.

29 SP 12/107, fos 122, 212.

came likewise from petitioners who disputed the circumstances in which they lost their ship.[30] The accusation in 1584 that wreckers came 'in riotous sort' with 'ravenous appetites' was part of an action by Sir Edward Mansell against the Earl of Pembroke, each aristocrat claiming rights to *wreccum maris* against the other.[31] Mariners from the shipwrecked *Sea Cock* of Flushing complained in 1597 that 'the country people... made havoc and spoil of all that was saved', but identified those people as tenants and servants of the local landowner Mr Price, who organized the plunder.[32]

The sole survivor of the wrecked collier *Carnation* remarked in 1614 on 'the spoil done by the country people' of Yorkshire but also described how some of those people saved his life by providing him with warmth and shelter. Behaving decently rather than barbarously, the villagers of Saltburn helped the distressed mariner 'in the saving of the goods', until intruders from nearby Redcar 'beat away the watchman... and one robbed another'.[33]

Reports that the owners of the Hamburg merchantman *Ark Noah* were 'grievously impoverished', and their goods 'embezzled and stolen', after the vessel had been wrecked on the Goodwin Sands in 1621, would seem to expose another case of depredation. Yet boatmen from Deal rescued the entire crew and, by their 'industry and pains', saved more than eighty bags of Spanish silver, forty cases of cinnamon, and four bags of pepper, which were moved to Dover Castle for adjudication. 'The master delivered all the goods himself to the savers before he left the ship', and entered into 'reasonable composition' with them, all parties to the transaction being described as 'honest men'.[34] The Deal men, denigrated by Defoe, regularly recovered goods from wrecks off their shore and generally cooperated with the authorities in distributing them.

After another German ship, the *Angel Ratchell*, had perished on the rocks of Sussex in 1622, the owners complained that 'the people in the said part and other residents thereabout were so rude that whatsoever [the crew] saved they took violently from them... as though they had been savage people'. Thomas Elphick, the bailiff of Seaford, cited 'the unruliness of the multitude' when congratulating himself on preserving choice items from this wreck for the Warden of the Cinque Ports. But the bailiff himself appears to have supervised the looting and may have been among its beneficiaries. The German merchants were especially angry that 'Mr Elphick, being a chief man and dwelling there', cheated them of salvage, 'seeing they were strangers and destitute... and made them set their hand to a writing, the contents whereof they know not what it was'.[35]

Viscount Dunbar, who blamed 'the indigent and barbarous people' of Yorkshire for their lawless stripping of a wreck in 1626, was not only disparaging his lowly neighbours but also claiming wrecked goods for himself. As he told the

[30] PC 2/12, fos 143–4, 259, 321. [31] SP 12/168, fo. 15. [32] HCA 13/33, fos 2^{v}, 6.
[33] HCA 13/42, fo. 278^{v}. [34] SP 14/120, fos 27–41. [35] SP 14/127, fos 170, 178.

Duke of Buckingham: 'I am confident she belongs to me, having always had them in that place; if otherwise, I think they belong to your grace.' The grievance that prompted his letter was not that commoners behaved outrageously, but that his rival Sir Matthew Boynton 'seized and conveyed to his house all the principal loading', including a cache of silver dollars.[36]

Complaints accumulated under Charles I of wrecks being 'pillaged by the inhabitants', and their goods carried off 'by force and violence'.[37] The captain of Cowes Castle reported 'a multitude of inhabitants making spoil upon those parcels of goods which the sea cast upon the shore', after a Portuguese prize ship had been wrecked on the Isle of Wight in 1633. The looting stopped, however, as soon as he ordered the scavengers 'to desist from such outrages, and withal to depart'.[38] 'Now all the country comes down, and every man catch what they can, and stave and [de]stroy more than they get,' charged Edward Nuttall after a wreck in Suffolk in 1633. The benefit 'should be absolutely the king's', he assured Secretary Nicholas, now that 'she is held strong in the possession of Sergeant Darcy'.[39] Plans for a proclamation that year against 'the barbarous custom of riffling and robbing of ships' evinced a Caroline distaste for 'barbarous disorder' but were also concerned with royal revenue. Council correspondents complained that 'the rabble of those sea borderers' interfered with 'his majesty's receipts of this nature'[40] (see Chapter 6).

Words such as 'rabble', 'pillage', 'spoil', and 'barbarous' were designed to gain attention. They belonged to a rhetoric of denigration that the propertied class used to distinguish the king's good subjects from the refractory and disordered sort. Members of the elite often railed disparagingly against 'insolent' and 'mutinous' commoners, projecting their own fears and prejudices onto social occurrences. Barbarity was in the eye of the beholder, a word to berate the poor. Like many other parts of discourse, the expressions were not just words but weapons.[41]

The frown of authority could fall on local landowners, as well as their tenants, if they encroached on privileges the king claimed as his own. It was bad enough that locals 'with staves and bills' made off with 'much of the ship's goods' after another ship had been wrecked on the Isle of Wight in 1635; but most galling to the crown was that the looting was performed by servants and tenants of 'Mr Cuttell, who hath some little land thereby... not withstanding they were commanded the contrary in the king's name'.[42] The notoriously corrupt vice admiral Sir James Bagg charged the 'multitude who possessed themselves of the goods' of a prize

[36] SP 16/37, fo. 40. [37] HCA 13/244/149.

[38] SP 16/244, fo. 36. [39] SP 16/252, fo. 26.

[40] SP 16/223, fo. 56; SP 16/248, fo. 53^{v}; SP 16/258, fo. 156; SP 16/327, fo. 33.

[41] J. S. Morrill and J. D. Walter, 'Order and Disorder in the English Revolution', in Anthony Fletcher and John Stevenson (eds), *Order and Disorder in Early Modern England* (Cambridge, 1985), 137; David Cressy, *Charles I and the People of England* (Oxford, 2015), 32–6. See also J. L. Austin, *How to Do Things with Words* (Cambridge, MA,1962), and other works on 'speech act theory'.

[42] SP 16/305, fo. 221; SP 16/311, fo. 41.

galleon that was cast away in Cornwall 1635 with 'barbarous riot and insolence', when he and his Admiralty commissioners proved unable to assert 'his majesty's authority' over local interests. Behind the rhetoric was a dispute between Dutch and Spanish merchants, rivalry between the men of Mousehole and Marazion, and Bagg's own claim to a tenth of the proceeds.[43]

Parties who privileged their own claims to shipwrecks continued to denounce 'the rapine of the country people' who carried off their goods in 'very great disorder and confusion'.[44] Councils continued to register 'complaints that are brought before them of the cruelty and inhumanity of the people . . . inhabiting on the maritime coast'.[45] Oliver Cromwell's Admiralty took note of such 'pagan practices' in 1654, though the principal offender was the lord of the manor.[46]

The Levant merchants of London cranked up the rhetoric when they sought assistance from the government after the loss of the *Aleppo Merchant* near Padstow, Cornwall, late in 1658. They had hopes, they said, 'of redeeming a considerable part of their lading; but through the dishonesty and savage practice of the common people there, they find their expectations disappointed'. When this appeal failed to move the Lord Protector, they petitioned again, alluding not only to 'so unusual and sad a dispensation and disaster befallen them from the hand of God', but also to 'the high aggravation of this their affliction by the rapine and barbarous practices of the rude inhabitants there'. A request for remission of Customs and Excise duties on recovered goods went hand in hand with vilification of the people who brought those goods ashore.[47] Dutch merchants similarly complained in 1660 that 'the country people of the parts adjacent . . . with much tumult and violence' stripped the lading of their ships cast away on the coast of Sussex.[48]

Comparable charges resonated after the Restoration. An irate Spaniard, 'a great don bound for Flanders', 'did much complain of the cruelty of the islanders' after his ship had been wrecked at Scilly in 1667. He was indignant that the salvagers 'left him upon a rock a day or two without fetching him off, though they might safely have done it, valuing the saving of the goods and money [more] than his life'.[49] The 'country people' who plundered the wrecked wine ship *Amity* in 1668 were allegedly 'so barbarous' that the master 'saved not anything considerable', though the crew exaggerated their losses.[50]

Sir William Godolphin and other 'very eminent men' of Cornwall complained in 1671 that the goods of the shipwrecked *Speedwell* were 'plundered' by 'the violence of the country people, who are ready to devour and ruin the whole'. They wrote, in part, to safeguard their own share. The same Sir William protested a few

[43] SP 16/264, fo. 79; SP 16/283, fos 34–4^{v}; SP 16/286, fos 152–152^{v}.
[44] HCA 13/70, fos 636–8; HCA 13/72, fos 21–2. [45] SP 25/97, fo. 129.
[46] SP 18/81, fo. 319. [47] SP 18/200, fos 70, 120. [48] SP 84/163, fos 4–7.
[49] SP 29/225, fo. 159. [50] SP 29/250, fo. 219.

years later 'of his losing the benefit of wrecks' when the brethren of Trinity House proposed building a lighthouse on one of the Isles of Scilly.[51]

Dutch authorities complained of 'barbarous usages' after one of their wine ships was 'distressed... though not cast away' at the Isle of Wight in 1683. Expressing shock that 'a neighbour nation' should be so treated, 'without regard had to the faith of treaties, to the law of nations, nor to the dictates of common humanity', the Secretary of State Sir Leoline Jenkins ordered the island governor 'to rescue these poor men from the violence they labour under, and... to punish those that are guilty of robbing poor people in the extremity of their distress'. Much of this was diplomatic dressing, after the wine had already disappeared into island cellars and taverns. In his former capacity as an Admiralty judge, Jenkins had used similar rhetoric against the 'barbarous usages' of wreckers.[52] Agents for French mariners cast away in Cornwall in 1698 complained of 'pilfering beggars' who 'plundered them of all their goods', though some of those goods were 'saved by the customs house officers'. Reporting this, Secretary of State James Vernon observed that 'if the loss had fallen upon Englishmen I am afraid they must have sat down by it', but government attention was required 'when a sovereign prince [in this case Louis XIV] demands reparation in behalf of his subjects'.[53] 'Barbarous' or not, 'the country people' attracted odium even when engaged in orderly salvage.

The overuse of such words as 'barbarous' to describe the behaviour of wreckers obscures the reality that salvage was a collaborative effort, sometimes guided or directed by men of substance. It was conducted under pressure of time in sometimes-dangerous conditions and was universally disagreeable to parties who had lost their goods. One such casualty, the master of the *Ann* of Portsmouth that 'bilged and broke in pieces' on the Isle of Wight, found the shore 'covered with barbarians' and railed against the 'barbarity of the mob', those 'insolent... ruffians', those 'wreck rogues' and 'inhuman devils', who attacked his lading of citrus fruit and wine. Though much of his cargo slipped out of his hands, at least half of the wine was 'secured by the customhouse and officers of the vice-admiralty there'. The 'wreck rogues' were not so fearsome as might be imagined, for they gave shelter to the sailors who were close to perishing, and one of them helped to retrieve the ship's papers.[54]

When the East Indiaman *Thornton* became 'broken and wrecked' in north Cornwall in 1700, 'great quantities of rich goods were taken and carried away in a very rude and riotous manner' by looters, 'their threatenings so high, and their proceedings so outrageous, that ordinary ministers of justice durst not attempt to suppress them'. Retribution, however, was aimed, not at the Padstow tinners, who provided most of the muscle, but at Captain Charles Bligh, the officer appointed

[51] SP 29/293, fo. 230; SP 44/164, fo. 347.
[52] SP 44/68, fo. 197; Wynne, *Life of Sir Leoline Jenkins*, ii. 763.
[53] SP 44/99, fo. 493.
[54] HCA 49/106, packet C.

'to watch and guard these coasts', who apparently colluded with the wreckers and sailed off with much of the proceeds.[55]

Losses from another East Indiaman, the *Albemarle*, which was wrecked on Cornwall's south coast in 1708, were also exacerbated, so the company charged, by the 'ill designs of the inhumane natives' and 'savage inhabitants', who were 'barbarous' and 'merciless' in their plunder. But close inspection finds that ordinary scavengers worked as much in harness with local worthies and survivors as against them. One of the leading men of Polperro helped to rescue the captain and crew, and gained a gratuity for his service. The bailiffs and stewards of local manors were soon in attendance, along with gentlemen, clergy, and officers of Her Majesty's Customs. The rector of Lansallos allegedly helped to lead 'the furious rabble' that plundered the ship and paid £20 to compound for goods in his possession. The social profile of the wreckers cannot be determined, but it clearly included men of varied substance, status, and occupation. The East India Company wanted offenders punished, but no obvious law had been broken, and no court had grounds to convict.[56]

The hostile and demeaning adjectives so often applied to wreck salvagers reflect distaste for disorder and frustration at loss, but they also served the particular purpose of assigning responsibility and displacing blame. If 'the barbarous country people' were anonymized as a 'mob' or a 'rabble', making 'spoil' and 'havoc' in 'unruly', 'ravenous', and 'riotous' manner, the authorities on the spot could be excused for retreating. If goods were 'rifled' or 'pillaged' by a 'disorderly' assembly, then officers charged with their safekeeping could be exonerated. Gentlemen who appropriated hogsheads of wine and other commodities for themselves could deflect attention to the tenants and labourers who helped to carry them. Individual actions were lost in the crowd. There would be no accounting of lading and loss, no telling whose pockets were lined in the process, amid scenes of savage confusion. Marine insurers would have little to work with but anecdotes.

The labelling of shoreline behaviour as 'cruel', 'inhumane', and 'unjust' also served to dramatize the woes of distressed merchants, to gain support for their grievances. Extravagantly worded complaints were shadings of narrative, ventings of frustration, and spurs to action. Exaggeration was normal. The vocabulary of petitioning involved a thickening of complaint, to achieve desired outcomes: in this case commissions of inquiry and restitution for the recovery of purloined goods.

Inhumane Dealings

Yet another batch of indignation appears in the writings of the High Court of Admiralty judges, who declared the stripping of shipwrecks by 'the rabble'

[55] PC 1/1/50. [56] Derriman, 'Wreck of the *Albemarle*', 128–48.

intolerable. They too promoted the notion of wrecker 'barbarity' and 'inhumanity'. Publishing in 1664, John Exton denounced the 'wicked and mischievous people' responsible for 'such extremities' as the looting of shipwrecked vessels. Both English and foreign merchants, he wrote, 'may have their ships stranded or wrecked and cast away, and have their goods even snatched from them by force, and violence, and carried away, and detained by such as can have neither pretence nor colour for such unjust and inhumane dealings, contrary to the law of nature and nations'.[57] Sir Leoline Jenkins advised Charles II in 1667 that 'the barbarous spoils and rapines used upon the sea coast . . . must be punished',and 'that the rabble be hindered from meddling'.[58] Where ships 'are in distress at sea near the shore, or run aground', wrote Charles Hedges in 1690,

> the country people make a prey of those miserable merchants, and will afford no manner of assistance, but rather contrive all they can that the ship may be cast away, nay many times are so barbarous to kill or drown people making escape to the land, that thereby they might have a pretence of wreck . . . Everyone taketh away what he can get.[59]

The 'rabble', by these lights, was savage and rapacious, just as the shipping agents and moralists alleged.

It would be wrong, however, to accept this rhetoric uncritically. The civil lawyers of the Admiralty practised polemical persuasion, not social observation. Their brief was to resist 'such as claim wreck to the prejudice of the king or Lord Admiral' and to protect 'their majesties' and the Lord Admiral's rights and perquisites' against theft and fraud. They wrote to defend the cognizance, power, and jurisdiction of the Admiralty courts against informal local arrangements and to protect their jurisdiction from the competition of the common law. They gained business from victims of shipwrecks and, not surprisingly, echoed the viewpoints of masters and merchants. Admiralty courts would criticize local lords as well as local labourers who 'seized or possessed themselves of any wrecked goods', but they tangled most often with the claims of manorial proprietors.[60] Their charges of barbarity did not so much describe the scramble for shipwrecked goods as take sides in it. Like other officials and commentators who excoriated coastal countryfolk as 'barbarous', they did not so much demonstrate their charge as assert it.

[57] John Exton, *The Maritime Dicaeologie, or Sea-Jurisdiction of England* (1656), 152.

[58] Wynne, *Life of Sir Leoline Jenkins*, ii. 763–4.

[59] Charles Hedges, *Reasons for Settling Admiralty-Jurisdiction; and Giving Encouragement to Merchants, Owners, Commanders, Masters of Ships, Material-Men and Mariners* (1690), 5–6.

[60] John Godolphin, *Synēgoros Thalassio: A View of the Admiral Jurisdiction* (1661), 46; Exton, *Maritime Dicaeologie*, 152; Hedges, *Reasons for Settling Admiralty-Jurisdiction*, 5; Wynne, *Life of Sir Leoline Jenkins*, i, p. lxxxix.

This is not to say that there was no rough behaviour, no greed or misappropriation, in the rush to retrieve the bounty of the sea; but 'covetise' was not confined to the country people or the poor. The harvest of 'droits' and 'godsends', and the contest over rights to wreck, may have involved intimidation and deception; but evidence of gross transgression is slight. Only by investigating the dealings of manorial proprietors and their tenants, Admiralty droit collectors, and other claimants to shipwrecked goods can the role of 'the country people' be properly contextualized. Only by examination of the detailed statements of participants and witnesses can a reasonable appraisal be made of the fate of broken ships and the 'moral economy' of the people who stripped them.

As subsequent chapters will demonstrate, wreck recovery was generally a cooperative process, involving collaboration between neighbours of varying social status. The common country people did most of the work and absorbed most of the opprobrium, but the profit generally accrued to their masters and betters. As the survivor of one rich wreck in mid-Stuart Cornwall reported, 'a very great part of these goods were salved and taken up by sundry persons... of eminent fortunes'.[61] Viewpoint mattered, so it should not be surprising if seamen who lost their lading spoke of 'pillage', whereas shoremen talked of goods they had 'saved and preserved'. Hostile reports cast coastal commoners as rude and even 'barbarous' plunderers, but depositions reveal the wreckers, for the most part, as dutiful, diligent, and determined, especially when speaking about themselves.

[61] SP 29/22, fo. 36.

5
The Great Profit of the Lords of Manors

The Restoration naval administrator Samuel Pepys noted that 'the great profit of the lords of manors upon the sea coasts lay in wrecks', where they and their tenants 'do most savagely make prey of all shipwrecked persons, goods, and vessels'.[1] Manorial proprietors were indeed among the most aggressive exploiters of *wreccum maris*, but historians have been slow to recognize this.

Cathryn Pearce correctly observes, with regard to wrecking in eighteenth-century Cornwall, that 'the experience of the local lords of the manor in this process has been completely overlooked'.[2] This chapter brings them back into view. Many of the episodes involving shipwrecks illuminate the power that the landed elite exercised within their communities. They also reveal constraints on seigneurial authority under pressure from royal and central government. Landed proprietors gained substantially more from wrecks than their labourers or tenants, though their own rewards were dwarfed by the profits that accrued to the crown.

Manorial jurisdictions have been little studied by early modern historians, but they were by no means antique or irrelevant by the time of the Tudors and Stuarts. To the contrary, as recent research shows, manorial courts remained busily involved in the economic and social life of early modern England and continued so throughout the eighteenth century.[3] Manor courts remained vital in managing community and tenurial relations, especially in country districts, but their governance of 'wreck of the sea' is largely unknown beyond the medieval era.[4]

[1] *Samuel Pepys's Naval Minutes*, ed. J. R. Tanner, Navy Records Society, vol. 60 (1926), 84.

[2] Cathryn Pearce, *Cornish Wrecking 1700–1860: Reality and Popular Myth* (Woodbridge, 2010), 168; Kersti Lust, 'Wrecking Peasants and Salvaging Landlords—Or Vice Versa? Wrecking in the Russian Baltic Provinces of Estland and Livland, 1780–1870', *International Review of Social History*, 62 (2017), 67–93, emphasizes the role of manorial lords in Baltic Imperial Russia.

[3] Keith Wrightson and David Levine, *Poverty and Piety in an English Village: Terling 1525–1700* (New York, 1979), 26–31, 177; J. H. Bettey, 'Manorial Stewards and the Conduct of Manorial Affairs', *Proceedings of the Dorset Natural History and Archeological Society*, 115 (1993), 15–19; Christopher Harrison, 'Manor Courts and the Governance of Tudor England', in Christopher Brooks and Michael Lobban (eds), *Communities and Courts in Britain 1150–1900* (London and Rio Grande, 1997), 43–59; Steve Hindle, 'Persuasion and Protest in the Caddington Common Enclosure Dispute 1635–1639', *Past & Present*, 158 (1998), 37–78, esp. 47–50; Brodie Waddell, 'Governing England through the Manor Courts, 1550-1850', *Historical Journal*, 55 (2012), 279–315; Brodie Waddell, *God, Duty and Community in English Economic Life, 1660–1720* (Woodbridge, 2012), 161; Jonathan Healey, 'The Northern Manor and the Politics of Neighbourhood: Dilston, Northumberland, 1558–1640', *Northern History*, 51 (2014), 221–41.

[4] Rose Melikan, 'Shippers, Salvors, and Sovereigns: Competing Interests in the Medieval Law of Shipwreck', *Journal of Legal History*, 11 (1990), 163–82; Tom Johnson, 'Medieval Law and Materiality: Shipwrecks, Finders, and Property on the Suffolk Coast, ca. 1380–1410', *American Historical Review*, 120 (2015), 407–32.

Shipwrecks and the Bounty of the Sea. David Cressy, Oxford University Press. © David Cressy 2022.
DOI: 10.1093/oso/9780192863393.003.0006

Manorial droits make scant appearance in studies of gentry getting and spending, and most of the manors hitherto studied lay inland.

Eighteen English counties and eight more in Wales had coastlines, and most of their manors with seashores claimed rights to wreck. If a ship was cast away or grounded anywhere on these coasts, it was likely to settle or break apart on a manorial proprietor's land. The rights, dues, and rewards of shipwrecks were among the perquisites of coastal manors and were exercised by their lords, stewards, bailiffs, and tenants. Indeed, wrote the Jacobean civil lawyer William Welwood, 'persons endued with the superiority or signiory of any part of the sea coast do claim all or a part of these things whether cast forth of ships, or otherwise coming on their land'.[5]

Later handbooks reminded lords of manors that a wreck on their land was theirs by prescription, that their bailiffs could seize such goods cast on their shore, and that custom enshrined their entitlement to the best anchor and cable of any vessel that met their soil. Even touching briefly ashore could trigger a claim for 'groundage'.[6] Manorial muniments supplied titles and precedents, while juries of ancients supplied memories. Stewards and tenants would work together to harvest major shipwrecks, while miscellaneous findings, if declared, would be presented in manorial courts. Court rolls recorded the value of such items, the rights by which they were possessed, and sometimes their subsequent disposition.[7]

Manorial lords gained honour and profit from maritime appurtenances and residual feudal incidents, though sometimes at the cost of conflict. Their records yield abundant evidence of competition and negotiation between elite landowners and their neighbours for control of the proceeds of shipwrecks. Arguments abounded about complexities of jurisdiction and privilege as manors changed hands, were leased, joined, forfeited, or subdivided. Investors could purchase wreck rights, along with manorial properties, and might go to law to protect their assets.[8] Physical boundaries and extents could be uncertain and subject to challenge. On whose beach or headland, below whose cliffs, on which side of a wandering stream, did wreckage come ashore? How far beyond the tideline did manorial property extend, and who had rights to materials on the foreshore, or to flotsam in the surf? Who should benefit, at whose expense, if the tide carried wreckage from one lord's land to another's? Whose bailiff, whose tenants, had first pick of the bounty of the sea? The law could rise to every contingency and generated copious documentation.

[5] William Welwood, *An Abridgement of all Sea Lawes* (1613), 171.

[6] William Nelson, *Lex Maneriorum: Or the Law and Customs of England, Relating to Manors and Lords of Manors* (1736), 196–8.

[7] Tom Johnson, *Law in Common: Legal Cultures in Late-Medieval England* (Oxford, 2020), 15.

[8] *John Spelman's Reading on Quo Warranto Delivered in Gray's Inn (Lent 1519)*, ed. J. H. Baker, Selden Society, vol. 113 (1997), 29–42.

Manorial lords faced competition from other powers and agencies, such as the Wardens of the Cinque Ports, the Duchies of Lancaster and Cornwall, the Admiralty, coastal vice admirals, and the crown, within a mosaic of jurisdictions. Claimants needed to show whether their rights derived from documented grants or customary prescription, and whether they had been exercised since time out of mind. They needed enough familiarity with the law to hold their ground or advance their interests, and perhaps to cover transgressions. Jurisdictional disputes called on memory and testimony about the customs and consequences of shipwrecks. Their records reveal lively concern for the opportunities of *wreccum maris*, and for exploitation of its benefits.

Institutional proprietors could be as determined as individual lords to exercise rights to wreck and were just as likely to be involved in disputes. Winchester College, for example, pursued wreck rights, 'and all other casualties and contingencies whatever however by land and water at sea', on the manors it controlled on the Isle of Wight.[9] The Bishop of Chichester had wreck rights within his manorial liberties and claimed profits from other marine mishaps in his diocese.[10] The Bishop of Durham enjoyed 'wreckage of the sea within the county palatine… where no writ of our lady queen runs', so asserted Bishop Barnes in 1584.[11] The dean and chapter of Canterbury resisted challenges by the Warden of the Cinque Ports and claimed right of wreck 'from the Popes Head gate…to Westgate Bay in Birchington, by the right of the manor of Monkton in Thanet'.[12] The crown itself was lord of royal manors, such as Portland, Dorset, and Bishopstone, Sussex, where wreckage frequently came ashore. The monarch had two bodies (corporeal and honorific), but also, in its seigneurial capacity, governed many mansions.

Coastal corporate towns also claimed *wreccum maris* within their liberties, and protected those rights against encroachments by manorial lords, county vice admirals, and other droit gatherers. King's Lynn, Norfolk, for example, claimed a zone of 'sea liberty' where the admiral 'neither can, nor ought, to come'.[13] Yarmouth asserted rights over 'seven leagues' of seashore.[14] Bristol 'refused to give way…pretending that the admiral there had no jurisdiction'.[15] The towns of the Cinque Ports asserted local privileges, which were often overridden by the power of the Lord Warden. The 1616 charter of the Dorset borough of Weymouth and Melcombe Regis specifically allowed it freedom from Admiralty visitations, though aggressive Lord Admirals challenged this privilege.[16] Legal proceedings

[9] Thomas Frederick Kirby, *Annals of Winchester College: From its Foundation* (1892), 26; *The Lisle Letters*, ed. Muriel St Claire Byrne, 6 vols. (London and Chicago, 1981), i. 187.

[10] SP 12/148, fos 78–80; SP 13/e, fo. 3; SP 14/180, fo. 68^{v}; West Sussex Record Office, Ep/1/55/134.

[11] National Maritime Museum, ADL/A/18.

[12] SP 12/195, fo. 186.

[13] Norfolk Record Office, LEST/Q 37, 45.

[14] SP 16/105, fo. 205.

[15] SP 16/139, fo. 79.

[16] M. Oppenheim, 'Maritime History', in *The Victoria History of the County of Dorset*, ii, ed. William Page (1908), 194.

exposed the practicalities of politics and power in competition for the 'benefit' of wreck of the sea.

Manorial proprietors defended their rights with vigour, especially when their appropriation of wreckage was challenged. A particularly rich wreck was likely to stimulate the appetite of competitors, and a treasure ship would quickly attract the government's droit collectors. The early modern gentry were renowned for their litigiousness, but their level of concern in this area has yet to be measured. Dozens of coastal landowners went to law, or appealed for favour, against rival claimants to *wreccum maris*. Friction appears to have been widespread, though rarely as severe as when two Elizabethan gentlemen fought a duel over wreck rights, in which a bystander was killed.[17] Gentle and aristocratic rivals resorted more often to law than to force, although their surrogates sometimes menaced each other and bandied threats. The evidence reveals some of the passions and interests that could be aroused as gentlemen defended their resources and their honour. As Steve Hindle observes in like cases, 'property was not merely a matter of material assets, but more fundamentally a matter of right'.[18] This was made clear by the Jacobean steward of Perranuthnoe, Cornwall, who advised Sir John Trevelyan about wreckage that arrived at his manor, against the claims of a neighbour: '[the matter] now in question is but of small value, but yet the title is of great weight; wherefore I pray your worship to take care of the cause.'[19] *Wreccum maris* represented the proprietor's social and cultural capital as well as his economic advantage.[20] The following tour of the coastline provides examples of manorial claims and beach-side altercations that were echoed more politely in gentle correspondence and the courts.

The Bristol Channel

An unusually violent confrontation developed between supporters of Sir Rhys Mansell and agents of Sir George Herbert after a French vessel laden with raisins, figs, and almonds had been wrecked on the Gower peninsula, on the Welsh side of the Bristol Channel, during Christmastide 1557.[21] Because England and France were at war at this time, the survivors became prisoners, their rights of ownership

[17] William Hughes, *An Exact Abridgement in English of the Cases Reported by Sr Francis More* (1665), 36.

[18] Steve Hindle, *The State and Social Change in Early Modern England, 1550–1640* (Basingstoke and New York, 2002), 80.

[19] Somerset Heritage Centre, DD WO 57/4/8/1, Richard Jeffries to Trevelyan, 14 January 1610.

[20] Helmut K. Anheier, Jürgen Gerhards, and Frank R. Romo, 'Forms of Capital and Social Structure in Cultural Fields: Examining Bourdieu's Social Topography', *American Journal of Sociology*, 100 (1995), 859–903, esp. 862; Simon Gunn, 'Translating Bourdieu: Cultural Capital and the English Middle Class in Historical Perspective', *British Journal of Sociology*, 56 (2005), 49–64.

[21] Glanmor Williams, 'The Affray at Oxwich Castle, 1557', *Gower. Journal of the Gower Society*, 2 (1949), 6–9, citing STAC 2/20/160, STAC 2/24/365, and STAC 4/1/26.

were extinguished, and their goods became subject to seigneurial confiscation. The wreck happened on Mansell's land below Oxwich Castle, and his tenants were first on the scene. 'Such as took it ought to have it', declared Mansell's steward, but neighbouring officials disagreed. Sir George Herbert, vice admiral of Swansea and steward to the Earl of Worcester, claimed superior rights and sent men to secure the wreckage. Mansell's men held the beach and then retreated to the castle, as Herbert's forces arrived on horseback and in strength. Swords were drawn, stones thrown, and insults exchanged, in the course of an affray that brought the parties before Star Chamber. Some of the heat went out of the encounter after one of Mansell's kinswomen died of accidental wounds, but bad blood persisted between the families for several generations.[22]

Sir Edward Mansell, who had witnessed this fracas, protested to the Privy Council that the Earl of Pembroke (Lord Henry Herbert) again sent men 'banded and weaponed . . . in riotous sort . . . with the best part of one hundred in their train' to rifle wreckage from his land after the *Anne Frauncis* of Lynn had been wrecked there in December 1583. The intrusion took place near the boundary of their adjacent manors, where a recent survey had flagged a questionable title. In Sir Edward's view, the earl's property ended 'two or three bowshots more west' than where the ship came to shore. At the time, he said, he did not know 'whether it were wreck, or that any of the people were escaped', alluding to the law on ownership and abandonment. Acting as good lord, Mansell sent his own sons and servants 'to prevent disorders', not to foment them, but menacing behaviour and minor tussles with the Herberts produced 'some controversy of words'. An ordinary landed dispute, which might normally have been settled in Chancery, was here played out with threats of violence on a wreck-strewn Glamorganshire beach.[23]

The matter grew more complicated when the King's Lynn merchant Francis Shaxton claimed ownership of the shipwrecked goods. Mansell's men, he asserted, had 'cut down and spoiled of the timber, plank, and ironwork, which if it might have been preserved, the decayed hull of the ship had yielded £100 or more'. Intervening before the Privy Council on Shaxton's behalf, Pembroke took the opportunity to appear conciliatory and painted his neighbour as greedy and intransigent.[24] Sir Edward Mansell protested that he cared 'much less for the value' than for 'bringing my credit in question'; but the careful inventory he exhibited of ordnance, anchors, and boxes of marmalade saved from the wreck suggests that material concerns also mattered.[25] The dispute moved to Star Chamber, where the Earl of Pembroke prevailed.[26]

[22] SP 12/168, fo. 48. [23] SP 12/168, fos 15–17, 48, 76.

[24] SP 12/169, fos 24–5. For Shaxton's character, see N. J. Williams, 'Francis Shaxton and the Elizabethan Port Books', *English Historical Review*, 66 (1951), 387–95.

[25] SP 12/168, fos 15–17, 48, 76; SP 12/169, fos 24–5.

[26] STAC 5/M12/23 Mansell v. Williams; STAC 5/P35/15 Pembroke v. Maunsell.

Another wreck on the coast of Pembrokeshire in 1630 pitted the landowning Owens of Bosherton against the Lorts of Stackpole, each claiming title within or against the lordship of Castlemartin. Owen's servants and tenants gathered goods on the beach, but Henry Lort, exercising force, sent his bailiffs to retrieve them, 'and they searching for wreck made wreck of some men's own proper goods'. An iron-bound chest with a thousand pounds in money disappeared, allegedly taken, not by the lawless country people, but by Mr Lort, the lord of the manor and sometime sheriff of Pembrokeshire.[27]

Cornwall

To the south and west, the cliffs of Cornwall claimed hundreds of ships, enriching manorial lords and other coastal inhabitants. The Arundells of Lanherne, on the north coast, had a long history of wreck exploitation, involving squabbles with proprietors of other manors, and with the Admiralty and the Duchy of Cornwall. Their opportunities expanded as they acquired more properties, including the lordship of the hundred of Penwith, which encompassed the far west coast. Disputes arose in every generation, with almost every adversary. The hundred jury registered close to £30 worth of wrecked wine, timber, and marine gear between 1565 to 1578, but many items of value stayed off the books. A 100-ton hulk with usable masts and sail was 'kept to Sir John Arundell's use as lord of the franchise', and he also awarded himself an abandoned Portuguese caravel. Barrels of pitch, tar, and wine were dutifully documented, but the lack of valuation attached to findings of nutmeg, cinnamon, and cloves suggests a private appropriation. In 1580 the Privy Council ordered Arundell to deliver to the vice admiral 'certain ordnance and other things taken up out of the sea upon a wreck' within his liberty, but Arundell upheld 'his right and title . . . and therefore desired not to be dispossessed'. To bolster his case, he introduced witnesses with an average age of 82 who remembered wrecks back to the reign of Henry VIII.[28] The Arundells fought suits over wrecks with their Trelawney neighbours of Perranuthnoe well into the reign of James I.[29]

A later Sir John Arundell clashed with the Admiralty, the crown, Prince Charles's council, and lords of half a dozen other manors over proceeds from a wreck at St Ives in 1637. Arundell claimed 'all wreck and admiralty droits whatsoever found in or throughout the hundred of Penwith', while the prince's officers asserted superior rights for the Duchy of Cornwall throughout the county.

[27] SP 16/81, fos 81–81^{v}.

[28] P. A. S. Pool, 'The Penheleg Manuscript', *Journal of the Royal Institution of Cornwall*, NS 3 (1959), 193–200.

[29] Somerset Heritage Centre, DD WO 57/4/8/1.

Both brushed aside the claims of other manorial proprietors. Complainants aired grievances about Arundell's habit of forcing finders to compound in cash, on terms most favourable to himself, for wreckage retrieved within his jurisdictions. When the *Grace of God* of Neath broke up in Cornwall in 1640, with a cargo of Irish hides and tallow, Arundell's man 'claimed the ship for his master as a wreck, and . . . prevented anyone from touching the cargo, till the tide rose and it was too late'.[30] Another episode in the 1680s involved wreckage that came to rest at the mouth of the Gwithian River, where the boundary between Arundell land and the manor of Tehidy was disputed. Opportunities and conflicts of this sort earned the Arundells profit and opprobrium well into the eighteenth century.[31]

On the south side of Cornwall Sir John Killigrew, a kinsman of the Arundells, commanded rights to wrecks on the Lizard peninsula. One wreck on his land in 1619 brought him 'sixteen pieces of Italian velvets, divers parcels of figured taffeta, and much copper wire', items of 'good value', he told Dudley Carleton, 'of which I desire not to be called to account'. Another wreck yielded 'as much silver in bars as amounts to above £3,300 and hopes of much more', though whether he kept it for himself is unknown. Killigrew planned to build a lighthouse at the Lizard, but acknowledged opposition to this service from his tenants. As he told Carleton,

> they affirm I take away God's grace from them. Their English meaning is that they now shall receive no more benefit by shipwreck, for this will prevent it; they have been so long used to reap purchase by the calamity of the ruin of shipping, as they claim it hereditary, and hourly complain on me. Custom breeds strong ills, or good, but I hope they will now husband their land, which their former idle life hath omitted in the assurance of their gain by shipwreck.[32]

The gain, of course, was more his than theirs.

On the Isles of Scilly, 28 miles and more beyond Land's End, the Godolphin family counted the 'benefit of shipwreck' among the 'contingent profits' accruing to their government of the islands. As lease-holders and proprietors, they demanded 'a fifth part, over and above the king's part', of all wreck proceeds from their shores. A parliamentary survey in 1652 rated the annual profit from shipwrecks in the Scillies at £6 13*s.* 4*d.*, though the actual amount was likely to

[30] Historical Manuscripts Commission, *Fourth Report* (1874), 63.

[31] PC 2/13, fo. 253; SP 16/370, fos 36–40; Cornwall Archives and Cornish Studies Service, AR15/1–1108; Pool, 'Penheleg Manuscript', 186–90; Cathryn Pearce, 'The Cornish Arundells and the Right of Wreck: A Case Study of Landlord–Tenant Relations in the Long Eighteenth Century', in Philip Payton, Alston Kennerley, and Helen Doe (eds), *The Maritime History of Cornwall* (Exeter, 2014), 209–17.

[32] SP 14/110, fo. 101; SP 14/115, fo. 4; John Rule, 'Smuggling and Wrecking', in Philip Payton, Alston Kennerley, and Helen Doe (eds.), *The Maritime History of Cornwall* (Exeter, 2014), 204.

have been much higher.[33] When the brethren of Trinity House proposed building a lighthouse in 1680 on the outer island of St Agnes, site of 'the wrecks of several very considerable ships', the current Sir William Godolphin complained 'of his losing the benefit of wrecks, which had its consideration in the rent he pays for the island'. His steward assisted wreck survivors, but also made sure of his salvage rights.[34] Godolphin's tenants were said to be 'clothed and supplied by wrecks sent in by the sea' and their dwellings reinforced by recovered ships' timbers.[35] Scillonians had the reputation of fierce and savage plunderers, but much of their scavenging was done in the service of their lord.

Devon

The south Devon coast between Start Point and Dartmouth was a scene of frequent maritime mishaps, where manorial proprietors 'quietly had and enjoyed diverse and sundry wrecks' brought about 'by reason of great tempests and foul weather'. Edward Ameridith, esquire, the late Elizabethan lord of the manor of Stokenham, was especially litigious in this regard, pursuing simultaneous suits in the Admiralty, the Court of Requests, Chancery, and Star Chamber to secure his rights and to thwart his adversaries. A chain of conveyancing documented his entitlement to 'wreck of the seas within the same manor or lordship' from the time of Henry VIII to his acquisition of Stokenham in 1587.[36]

One of Ameridith's witnesses in a Star Chamber case in 1603 was the 70-year-old yeoman Nicholas Cole, who testified that 'at such time as any wreck or floatage have happened there within the manor or parish' the inhabitants were accustomed 'at their pleasure to repair to the seashores there, and saved as much wreck as they could, and the wreck so being saved was left in the hands of the reeves and other the lord's officers'. On occasion, Cole remembered, 'he hath known to repair for the saving of the said shipwreck above a hundred persons'. It was understood in principle that 'the wrecks there belong unto the lord of the manor'; but, by custom, 'the wreck proving lawful', one moiety went to the lord, and the other 'to such of

[33] Bodleian Library, MS Jones 27*, fo. 17; *The Parliamentary Survey of the Duchy of Cornwall, part II*, ed. Norman J. G. Pounds, Devon and Cornwall Record Society, NS 27 (1984), 148; *Calendar of Treasury Books, 1685–1689*, ed. William A. Shaw (1923), 544; *Calendar of Treasury Books, 1689–1692*, ed. William A. Shaw (1931), 835.

[34] SP 29/359, fo. 33^{v}; SP 44/164, fo. 347; *Samuel Pepys's Naval Minutes*, 202; G. Forrester Matthews, *The Isles of Scilly: A Constitutional, Economic and Social Survey* (1960), 18.

[35] Robert Heath, *A Natural and Historical Account of the Islands of Scilly* (1750), 86; John Troutbeck, *A Survey of the Ancient and Present State of the Scilly Islands* (1794), 31; Juliet Du Boulay, 'Wrecks in the Isles of Scilly', *Mariner's Mirror*, 46 (1960), 92–4; Cathryn Pearce, 'Neglectful or Worse: A Lurid Tale of a Lighthouse Keeper and Wrecking in the Isles of Scilly', *Troze: The Online Journal of the National Maritime Museum of Cornwall*, 1 (2008), 3–15, esp. 5.

[36] STAC 8/46/12; REQ 2/1687/28; also C2/Eliz/A6/50, C2/Eliz/G1/59; Tristram Risdon, *The Chorographical Description or Survey of the County of Devon* (1818), 173–4.

the said inhabitants as have saved the same'. Exploitation of those rights depended upon cooperation with neighbours and tenants that was not always forthcoming.

Neighbouring proprietors mounted competitive salvage operations when the wine ship *Susann* wrecked in the channel between their Devon estates in 1630. John Pollexfen (alias Poulson) of the manor of Mothecombe employed ploughs and oxen over four days to save forty-three pipes of wine, which he refused to yield to authorities. Arthur Ashford, whose land at Wonwell, near Kingston, faced Pollexfen's across the mouth of the river Erme, saved only thirty-two pipes, but ingratiated himself with agents of the Admiralty by providing them with horses and accommodation. Pollexfen and Ashford were both captains of the south Devon trained bands, big men in their district, but relations between them were evidently fraught when shipwrecked wine and manorial honour were concerned.[37]

More harmoniously, though without regard to the ordinary country people who provided the labour, Francis Courtney, esquire, lord of the manor of Powderham, agreed in 1638 with his neighbour Sir Edward Seymour, the vice admiral of Devon, to divide five bags of Spanish money worth £216 4*s.* 6*d.*, lately retrieved from a wreck at the mouth of the river Exe. Courtney 'by right', as 'lord of the wreck', had the 'royalty and privilege of wreck, save only the moiety thererof, which by prescription…doth belong unto the finder and saver'. Seymour, as employer of the finders, gracefully accepted his share. They mutually covenanted to defend each other against claims by any owners or proprietors, 'as well against all others that shall claim to the said moiety, or any part thereof, for finding and salvage', such as the mayor and bailiffs of Dartmouth, the Duchy of Cornwall, or the Lord High Admiral of England.[38] Lawyers for the manor of Powderham a generation later argued that French wines retrieved from a wreck were not imports, and that Charles II's Customs officers had no right to 'seize or meddle with them'.[39] The long continued assertion of such entitlements is demonstrated by the claim in 1993 by the modern lord of the manor of Ermington, Devon, of wreckage due to him by 'his ancient manorial rights'.[40]

Dorset

In coastal Dorset, as elsewhere, the wreck rights of former abbey manors transferred to post-Reformation proprietors. Along the wreck-prone coast of Chesil Beach such rights descended to the Mohuns of Fleet and the Strangeways at

[37] HCA 13/49, fos 10^{v}–11, 24^{v}–35; Thomas Westcote, *A View of Devonshire in MDCXXX*, ed. George Oliver and Pitman Jones (Exeter, 1845), 72.

[38] SP 16/166, fo. 48; Devon Archives, L 1508 M/O/SS/Harbours/25.

[39] Devon Archives, L 1508 M London/Harbours and Rivers/1/2, Q.

[40] Richard Larn and Bridget Larn, *Shipwreck Index of the British Isles*, 7 vols (1995–2005), i, p. x; Tom Cousins, *Erme Estuary Site Conservation Statement & Management Plan* (Bournemouth, 2018).

Abbotsbury, with exemption from Admiralty jurisdiction. The manors of Portland and Wyke Regis fell into royal hands, but James I gave them to Queen Anna. In 1604 she presented her grooms of the Privy Chamber with 'a chest of arrows which is fallen due unto us as wreck cast up by the sea' within those Dorset manors.[41] A dispute between the vice admiral of Dorset and the steward of the royal manor of Portland in 1637, 'touching money taken up on the sands there below the high water mark', brought local inhabitants to testify about the extensions of manorial rights into the sea, where they probed with long poles for shipwrecked materials.[42]

The lords of Abbotsbury and Fleet exercised their manorial privileges when the richly laden *Golden Grape* wrecked on their shores in December 1641.[43] Each sent officers to secure selections of goods. Maximillian Mohun, esquire, took immediate custody of a bolt of silk, a piece of taffeta, a box of letters, and an account book taken from the ship, and set aside more goods including parcels of silver plate that he 'put together upon the beach and preserved'. His men moved barrels of raisins to his house, along with an injured crewman who subsequently died. Sir John Strangeways, a member of parliament for Weymouth and Melcombe Regis, pressed his claims as lord of the manor of Abbotsbury through his agents. One of the salvors found 'certain pieces of eight, amounting to fourteen shillings sterling, which he said was the moiety of certain pieces of eight . . . by him taken up upon the beach within the liberty of Sir John Strangeways, for which he had been so much troubled by the said Sir John's servants'. Others carried booty to Sir John's house in Abbotsbury, either for safekeeping or for his personal profit. Similarly exercising seigneurial privileges, Mr John Jeffries of Wyke Regis took goods from the wreck 'for groundage, because they had put the same on shore, upon his ground'. Survivors of the *Golden Grape* complained of the loss of their goods to the 'people of the country who by force and violence took and carried the same way', but the looting was more systematic than haphazard, and benefited landed proprietors more than commoners on the shore (see Chapter 8).

In the aftermath of this wreck, at a time when the Stuart state was crumbling, Lord Francis Cottington learned that lords of manors were disparaging 'the ancient right and privilege' of the Admiralty. Cottington was vice admiral for Dorset, and a mainstay of the Caroline regime, but had withdrawn to his estate in Wiltshire amid the turmoil of 1641. His deputy John Ellis wrote to him from Weymouth on 24 January 1642 regarding 'the intentions of the servants of many lords of manors adjoining to the sea side . . . not only to claim wrecks of the sea, but to keep admiralty courts, and so to receive and take all droits of Admiralty to themselves'. Among Dorset offenders, the steward of the manor of Burton Bradstock had not only obstructed Admiralty officers in their business but 'hath

41 SP 14/8, fo. 26.
42 SP 14/11, fo. 72; SP 14/215, fo. 3^{v}; SP 16/353, fo. 28; SP 16/431, fo. 56.
43 HCA 13/244/149.

inquired of, seized, and appraised all goods taken up on the sea within or against that manor, and hath charged all the tenants not to deliver any of the goods to me'. The bailiff of the manor of Symondsbury similarly disparaged Admiralty authority, detained wrecked goods, and refused cooperation. These examples 'wrought such an effect', wrote Ellis, 'that now every petty lord . . . do claim to be admirals within their precincts, and charge their tenants to keep all goods by them taken up'.[44]

Sussex

Further east along the Channel in Sussex, manorial tenants at Brighthelmstone (Brighton) had long understood that 'all wrecks or goods washed by the sea on this manor belong to the lord; but if any other find them before the lord's servants, a moiety of the things so found belong to the finder, on his advancing a moiety of that they were valued at'.[45] The lords of the manors near Newhaven and Beachy Head vied with each other, and with the Cinque Ports and the Admiralty, for the frequent harvest of shipwrecks on their coast. One such wreck at Birling in 1563 yielded hogsheads of wine, pieces of iron, and furnishings of ships, whose beneficiaries included Lords Dacre and Abervagenny, Sir Edward Knight, Sir Richard Sackville, and John Thatcher, esquire.[46] The proceeds, as ever, were negotiable, with proletarian labour and seigneurial supervision.

Tenants of Meeching and the royal manor of Bishopstone saved sixty-three pipes of olive oil, thirteen butts of sack, thirteen hogsheads of Gascon claret, and two pipes of white wine, as well as a quantity of cables and sails from wrecks there 1576. Their declared haul was worth at least £800, not counting items that were undervalued or concealed. The Earl of Surrey put in a claim because 'certain parcels have been cast on his land . . . of his manor of Meeching'. The Lord High Admiral said they were his, by the patent of his grant of office. The Bishop of Chichester claimed the goods by prescription, citing precedents of his predecessors. But the queen overrode all, 'in respect of her ancient prerogative'. Even after a portion had been restored to the owners, and the Admiralty had taken its share, the manorial proprietors enjoyed a substantial profit, and their tenants took rewards.[47] Later wrecks in this area generated arguments about where the marsh land of Meeching joined the stone ridge of the main sea, and how far the bounds of

[44] Wiltshire and Swindon History Centre, 865/404, John Ellis, deputy vice admiral to Lord Francis Cottington, vice admiral for Dorset, 24 January 1642.

[45] Thomas W. Horsfield, *The History, Antiquities, and Topography of the County of Sussex*, 2 vols (Lewes, 1835), i. 110.

[46] East Sussex Record Office, AMS 4606/1.

[47] East Sussex Record Office, SAS/A594, SAS/A757.

Bishopstone 'extended to the red cliff end westward' from Seaford beach, across the changing outflow of the Ouse River.[48]

Edward Payne, the leaseholder of the manor at nearby Birling Gate in the parish of East Dean, was early on the scene when a Dutch treasure ship was wrecked on his shore in May 1617. He was able to move '360 bags of coin in pieces or eight' and 'many massy wedges of silver' to his house, as well as ladings of wine, cochineal, and Brazil wood. He may have been within his rights, but he had little clout against more powerful interests. The wardens of the Cinque Ports were ever watchful for their windfall, representatives of the Lord High Admiral also made a claim, while the original shippers wanted their property back. Resolution depended in part on whether this part of the coast beyond Beachy Head lay within the liberties of Seaford or the Cinque Ports, and whether the Dutch merchants had brought their claim to the correct court.[49] None of the records in this case addresses the actual finding and carrying of the goods from the shipwrecked vessel to the shore. Payne was eventually summoned to the Privy Council to answer for his presumption and was briefly committed to the Marshalsea prison.[50]

Disputes of this sort echoed across successive generations, for as long as ships were wrecked and droit holders competed for privilege. After the *Angel Ratchell* had foundered in Sussex in 1622, and officials of the Cinque Ports had moved some of its wines to safety, Mr Elphick of Seaford 'broke open the door and hath taken them out, and converted them to his own use'. 'Mr Hide minister of the town' was also believed to have a chest from the wreck, which the Warden claimed as his due.[51] The gentlemen jurats of Seaford again took command of salvage when the *Rose* of Amsterdam broke up on their beach in 1637, and they negotiated for shares with the Cinque Ports.[52] Hogsheads of wine that washed up near Chichester harbour sparked competition between tenants of a Mr Peckham and agents for the Earl of Arundel, each claiming rights 'as lord of the soil or manor'.[53] The steward for the manor of Littlehampton not only claimed that 'the best anchor and cable were due to my lord of Arundel as groundage', when a Dutch freighter beached there in the 1650s, but laid claim to the entire ship and lading, saying 'I seize upon all' (see Chapter 7).[54]

And so it went. Challenged by the Admiralty in 1665, Sir John Gage reasserted his right to flotsam, jetsam, lagan, 'waveson', and all wreck of the sea on the shores or waters of his six Sussex manors, from 'time beyond the memory of man'.[55] The Earl of Dorset claimed seven and a half pipes of Canary wine that were saved from a wreck on his manor at Seaford in 1690, and was enraged when Customs men at

[48] East Sussex Record Office, SAS/A595, SAS/A596, SAS/A605.
[49] SP 14/2, fo. 244; SP 14/92, fos 64, 241.
[50] SP 14/93, fo. 31.
[51] SP 14/127, fos 193–4, SP 14/128, fo. 73, SP 14/129, fo. 123.
[52] SP 17/D/15.
[53] SP 16/284, fo. 195.
[54] HCA 13/70, fos 635–8, HCA 13/72, fos 21^{v}–22; SP 84/161, fos 80–8.
[55] East Sussex Record Office, SAS/G5/49.

Newhaven seized them for the crown.[56] Newspaper readers could be reassured in 1696, after wine and brandy from a wreck at Rye had been 'seized by the country', with the report that 'the lord of the manor has taken the rest into his possession'.[57] When 'a considerable wreck of wines' came ashore on the coast of Sussex in 1706, the proprietors of the manor of Brighthelmstone took possession and would not yield when the Lord High Admiral of England (Prince George, Duke of Cumberland) laid claim to them. In this case the county assizes determined that the rights of the manor were 'fully established'.[58]

Kent

At the narrowest part of the narrow seas, where the Channel and the North Sea join together, the coast of Kent saw heavy commercial traffic and a stream of profitable wrecks. Lords of coastal manors asserted their rights, but aggressive Wardens of the Cinque Ports exploited every weakness in local title (see Chapter 6). When the lord of the manor of Folkestone attempted to claim a wreck in 1602, for example, and exhibited ancient *quo warrantos* to support his right, agents for the Cinque Ports declared that such documents were easily brought fraudulently, and in any case they needed to show uninterrupted enjoyment of wreck rights for the previous hundred years.[59] Testimony at an Admiralty court at Dover that year about wrecks at 'the Hope at Cliff's End in Thanet... and who enjoyed them' favoured the Lord Warden over the manorial claimant at Minster. These disputes continued into the reign of James I, with the Cinque Ports generally prevailing.[60] In 1619 Richard Broome took possession of an anchor and cable 'for the right of Sir Thomas Pelham, between Hastings and Winchelsea', but officers of the Cinque Ports threatened him with prison.[61] Sir Henry Carey, a later proprietor of Minster in Thanet, claimed royalties of a wreck 'within the low water mark' there in 1620, but was also bested by the Lord Warden.[62] Similarly outmatched was Sir Nicholas Tufton, who introduced a bill in the Exchequer in support of his wreck rights at Dungeness in 1624, but deferred to the Cinque Ports when the Duke of Buckingham intervened on their side.[63] Sir John Hayward, who succeeded Carey as proprietor of Minster, carried on the struggle with considerable frustration and expense. When the rigging, tackle, and sails of a crippled East Indiaman came to rest on his ground in 1628, he withheld them from the vice admiral and would not relinquish his booty 'until it be recovered from him by law'.[64]

[56] *Calendar of Treasury Books 1689–1692*, 841. [57] *Flying Post*, 31 December 1695.
[58] Horsfield, *History, Antiquities, and Topography of the County of Sussex*, i. 111.
[59] SP 12/285, fos 61, 67. [60] SP 12/284, fos 179–83; SP 14/6, fos 89–93; SP 14/90, fo. 161.
[61] SP 14/110, fo. 160. [62] SP 14/116, fo. 32. [63] SP 14/180, fo. 113^{v}; SP 14/181, fo. 85.
[64] SP 16/118, fo. 98.

Admiralty officers during the Interregnum resisted the claims of 'lords of manors who pretend royalty to be granted them by some kings of England'.[65] They were especially hostile to the lord of the manor of Whitstable, Kent, who seized some wrecked planks that had been intended for the navy, and took measures to 'prevent the like pagan practices for the future'.[66]

Clashes of this sort continued for decades. In the 1660s, when the Duke of York was both Warden of the Cinque Ports and Lord High Admiral, his officers enquired 'whether any do usurp or encroach on the Lord Warden's droits or royalties as Admiral? For instance, whether any lords of manors, or others, do challenge to themselves wreck at sea, or other droits of Admiralty, in their manors, without sufficient title in law so to do?'[67] All droits and perquisites were jealously guarded. The warden's officers even came into contention with Queen Catherine of Braganza's surveyor in 1684 over rights to a wreck on her Kentish coastal manors.[68] Also competing with the Cinque Ports, the Finch family of Wye, lords of the manor of Dengemarsh, spent heavily on lawyers to support their own claims to a wreck from the 1680s to the 1720s.[69] The prevailing dynamic in all these conflicts was between manorial lords and competing authorities, not between patricians and dependants, or between merchants and the 'country people'. Lords of Kentish coastal manors faced formidable opposition, but would not back down.

Norfolk

The wreck-rich North Sea coast of Norfolk from Great Yarmouth to Cromer, with its offshore shallows and banks, was an expanse of eroding low cliffs and shingle beaches, overlain with legal demarcations. Traders from the Baltic, Germany, and the Low Countries, as well as colliers from Newcastle, came to grief on these shores. Local topography determined wreck rights, which were most articulated when they were most tested. The manors of Palling and Horsey, leased to the Bacon family, had rights to wreck of the sea 'from a tree called the mark tree between Eccles and Palling, to a cross in Palling, and from the cross to Wynkyll dike, and to a cross called headless cross by the same dike that divided the hundreds of Happing and East and West Flegg'.[70] Challenged by the Admiralty in 1601, the lord of the manor of Eccles claimed 'the benefits of such wrecks' for the previous 328 years.[71] The notorious wreck heritage of the Winterton coast is

[65] SP 18/11, fo. 39; SP 25/123, fo. 159^{v}. [66] SP 18/81, fo. 319.

[67] William Wynne, *The Life of Sir Leoline Jenkins, Judge of the High-Court of Admiralty*, 2 vols (1724), i, p. lxxxviii.

[68] SP 29/359, fo. 107; SP 44/31, fo. 104.

[69] Kent History and Library Centre, NR/LB8/1, U442/L1.

[70] Norfolk Record Office, NAS 1/1/12/Palling/10. [71] BL, MS Lansdowne 145, fo. 132.

still visible in the mast from a stricken vessel spanning the roof of the barn that the Woodhouse family erected at nearby Waxham around 1580.[72]

The wreck of a Scottish vessel at Runton on the north coast of Norfolk on 1577 aggravated a feud between Roger Wyndham, on whose land the ship had come ashore, and Sir Edward Clere of Blickling, 'his mortal enemy'. Wyndham's agents gathered goods to the value of £700 or £800, though other items were 'embezzled by the people of the towns adjoining'. The Scottish owners persuaded the Privy Council to establish a commission of inquiry, and Wyndham became alarmed when Clere was named as a judge.[73] A later Lady Wyndham seized 4,000 deal boards, 400 timber baulks, and 150 masts from a Baltic freighter that was stranded on her ground, and defied anyone else to take them.[74] Wrecks like these gave the severely factionalized Norfolk gentry yet another topic of disagreement.

The Bacon family manors of Stiffkey and Gimingham were sources of opportunity and profit, but they were entangled in legal actions with other landowners, the Admiralty, and the Duchy of Lancaster, which had extensive estates in the area. The recurrence of wrecks on this coastline provided multiple occasions for dispute.[75] Stewards at Stiffkey collected 'eight score bars of iron, two pieces of ordnance, three sacks of wet hops, two hundred clapboards, besides other pieces of broken timber' from a wreck on the sands and salt marsh in 1572. Nathaniel Bacon, mindful of 'what benefit will hereby grow to your lordship', advised his father, Sir Nicholas, 'not to be over hasty in the delivery of the goods to the merchants which claim the property of them'.[76] On another occasion, when the crown attempted to requisition a cargo of wax that had been wrecked in Norfolk in 1582, Sir Edward Clere asked Nathaniel Bacon whether 'it may carry benefit of wreck to you' and advised him 'to discern of such and their dealings, that they which have right may not be defrauded by undue means'.[77]

Similarly protective of his privileges, Sir Nicholas Lestrange of Hunstanton took possession of three hogsheads of wine 'cast upon the sea shore there' in December 1590. Thirteen more hogsheads were 'detained to the use of the lord of the manor', twenty were seized 'to the use of Mr Nathaniel Bacon, esquire', and several more went to other Norfolk gentlemen whose wine stocks were assured for the

[72] Anthony Rossi, 'A Tale of Two Barns: Paston and Waxham', *Transactions of the Ancient Monuments Society*, 56 (2012), 42, 45.

[73] SP 12/120, fos 30, 32.

[74] Norfolk Record Office, BL/Y2/42.

[75] SP 16/290, fos 44–64; SP 16/331, fos 131–61; SP 16/352, fos 115–56, 125; Norfolk Record Office, NAS S2/16/20; Norfolk Record Office, GTN 2/40/35; Norfolk Record Office, BL/Y2/42-4; BL, MS Lansdowne 145, fo. 132; Christobel M. Hoare (ed.), *Records of a Norfolk Village, Being Notes on the History of the Parish of Sidestrand* (Bedford, 1914), 29–32, 37–8. See also Elizabeth M. P. Wells, 'Civil Litigation in the High Court of Admiralty, 1585–1595', in Christopher Brooks and Michael Lobban (eds), *Communities and Courts in Britain 1150–1900* (London and Rio Grande, 1997), 89.

[76] *The Papers of Nathaniel Bacon of Stiffkey*, i. *1556–1577*, ed. A. Hassell Smith and Gillian M. Baker (Norwich, 1979), 48–9.

[77] *The Papers of Nathaniel Bacon of Stiffkey*, ii. *1578–1585*, ed. A. Hassell Smith and Gillian M. Baker (Norwich, 1983), 197, 199–200.

Christmas season. Presentments to the port jury placed valuations on the timbers found upon the shore, but made no appraisal of the wine that went directly to the landowners' cellars.[78]

Claims by the lord of the manor of Gunton in 1631 to 'all wreck of the sea from Cromer to a place called Gonnisburgh' produced a sharp response from the Duchy of Lancaster, whose agents asserted exclusive rights to 'wreck, groundage, anchorage, and other casualties whatsoever happening by sea' in that area.[79] Similarly locked at law with the duchy over boundaries, wreck rights, and customary arrangements, another Sir Nathaniel Bacon declared in 1637 that 'he would not infringe any gentlemen his liberty'. Bacon was one of several suitors arguing about the micro-geopolitics of field boundaries, survey markers, and wreckage that came ashore within the manors of Sidestrand Poning, Gimingham Lancastre, and Stiffkey. Following the example of the Cinque Ports, the agents for the duchy and the crown searched aggressively for flaws in their opponents' titles, hoping to gain by law any bounty that had escaped their grasp on the beach. Their battles were as much about principles and privilege as material advantage and profit.[80]

Some lords of Norfolk manors in the 1650s were willing to farm their wreck rights to investors, preferring a certain annual income to the vagaries of maritime misfortune.[81] Most, however, relied on their stewards and bailiffs to manage *wreccum maris* for their continuing benefit. Agents for the Paston manor at Cromer continued to battle the Duchy of Lancaster and other claimants over wreck rights into the era of the Restoration. The manorial steward John Doughty informed Lady Yarmouth (Rebecca Paston) in 1677 that the duchy's man Sir John Hobart had 'in this business run between the bark and the tree', meaning that he was intrusively busy in the matter.[82]

Proactively, the Norfolk landowner and politician Sir Hamon Lestrange fully briefed himself on the law of shipwreck and its bearing at Heacham, Hunstanton, and Holme, 'all my maritime towns'. His son Sir Nicholas Lestrange reaped the reward of this study in profitable dealing in wrecks. On one occasion in 1692 he locked shipwrecked oil in his barn in defiance of crown officials, 'intending to have tried the case if they persisted in the seizure'. In 1695 Sir Nicholas paid £56 for unclaimed cables, stays, ropes, and masts, and sold them to the shipmasters of Lynn and Lowestoft for £276 18*s.* 7*d.*, a fivefold return on investment. He also

[78] *The Official Papers of Sir Nathaniel Bacon of Stiffkey, Norfolk as Justice of the Peace 1580–1620*, ed. H. W. Saunders, Camden Society, 3rd ser. 26 (1915), 11–12.

[79] Norfolk Record Office, GTN 2/40/35/1.

[80] SP 16/290, fos 44–64; SP 16/331, fos 131–61, SP 16/352, fos 115–56, quote fo. 145; Norfolk Record Office, NAS S2/16/20; Norfolk Record Office, GTN 2/40/35; Hoare (ed.), *Records of a Norfolk Village*, 29–32, 37–8.

[81] Norfolk Record Office, GTN 2/40/35/7 and 8 for Gunton and Gimingham.

[82] Norfolk Record Office, BL/Y2/42–4.

made a quick profit on a hull he bought for £20 and sold to a Mr Blackwell of Lynn for £30.[83]

Yorkshire and the North

Manorial lords, in competition with the High Court of Admiralty, were the principal beneficiaries of shipwreck in Yorkshire, some enduring legal battles in order to secure their droits. *Quo warranto* proceedings initiated in 1575 by the Admiralty against Sir John Constable, lord of the manor of Holderness, challenged his taking of a wreck from the sea. At issue was whether Constable's rights were firmly established, in a manor that had passed through a chain of noble hands, and how far those rights extended from dry soil into salt water. Constable's counsel demonstrated that the right to a wreck was always 'appurtenant to the manor' and that 'he who has the manor has title to the wreck'. Constable's title proved solid, but its extension to the foreshore was more problematic. Who owned and controlled the area 'over which the sea flows and re-flows... between the green-sward and the low-water mark', which was sometimes land and sometimes not? It took four years for Constable to win judgment, on the grounds of case law and custom, that the foreshore was parcel of the manor and that his gathering of wreck there was lawful.[84]

This was not the end of the matter, for another case arose in 1599 regarding the rights of his successor. Challenged again by the Admiralty, lawyers for Sir Henry Constable argued once more that wrecked goods, thrown 'upon the sands then uncovered with water', properly belonged to the manor. Precedent was on their side, but Admiralty jurisdiction demanded respect. For the foreshore, 'when it is ebb it is parcel of the county, and when it is flood belongs to the Admiral'. Flotsam and jetsam were Admiralty perquisites, and the lord's rights on the foreshore consisted only when it was dry. Wreckers and salvagers became entangled in technicalities to the point, as one of Constable's lawyers observed, where 'divers absurdities ensue'.[85]

The dispute flared up again in 1626 in a four-way tussle between Sir Matthew Boynton, the manorial proprietor of Barmston, Lord Henry Dunbar asserting ancestral rights to a wreck in the liberty of Holderness, the vice admiralty court at York, and the ever-watchful Lord High Admiral the Duke of Buckingham. Three

[83] Norfolk Record Office, LEST/Q 37, 46–8 ('Wreck goods bought' and 'Wreck goods delivered', 1695–6).

[84] Sir John Constable's case is discussed in George Poulson, *The History and Antiquities of the Seignory of Holderness*, 2 vols (Hull, 1840), i. 89–95, 158–9; Stuart A. Moore, *A History of the Foreshore and the Law Relating Thereto*, 3rd edn (1888), 224–33; and Bradin Cormack, *A Power to do Justice: Jurisdiction, English Literature, and the Rise of the Common Law, 1509–1625* (Chicago, 2007), 286–7.

[85] Moore, *History of the Foreshore*, 233–41, 247.

crippled ships had come ashore, perhaps under fire from Dunkirk raiders, with cargoes of mixed commodities. Boynton's men were first on the scene and took 'the principal loading' to his house, as well as some five hundred silver dollars and some gold. Also at stake was a lading of wine, some of it 'staved and burst by the sea' but still worth saving. Dunbar wrote ingratiatingly to Buckingham, 'if she be wreck, I am confident she belongs to me, having always had them in that place; if otherwise, I think they belong to your grace'. Buckingham's agents reluctantly judged two of the ships 'no wrecks, for that the companies came alive on shore, which freeth them from being wrecks, and retaineth the property in the owners if they be the king's subjects or friends'. The third, however, apparently a Dunkirker, an enemy privateer, looked more promising, 'to do my lord... service'.[86]

An Admiralty judge at York appointed a commission 'to examine upon oath all such persons as did convey or conceal any part of the goods belonging to the ship' and 'to take into their custody and safe keeping all such goods'. Dunbar wrote again to Buckingham asking for intervention 'in the king's name', to pressure the other parties in the dispute 'to surcease their meddling'. Local, regional, and national authorities were brought to bear on an otherwise unexceptional case of *wreccum maris* touching manorial privileges.[87]

Another jurisdictional mosaic complicated a wreck recovery in the north-east of England. The Bishop of Durham, the Earl of Northumberland, and the Lord Admiral of England all claimed droits, as did the captains of regional castles and the lords of local manors. Wherever the sea brought wrecks ashore, there were gentlemen claiming benefit, coastal residents stripping ladings, and original owners seeking restitution. Early Elizabethan wrecks on the coast of Northumberland, for example, produced rivalries involving English, Dutch, and Scottish merchants; the Earl of Northumberland and his manorial dependants; the keeper of Norham Castle and the governor of Berwick; various border gentlemen; and the inhabitants of Scremerston, Cheswick, Goswick, and other coastal villages (see Chapter 7).

On the other side of England, facing the Irish Sea in Cumberland, the Curwen family, followed by the Penningtons, 'long enjoyed' the coastal manor of Ravensglass, including 'sea wrecks and other maritime profits, which often happen to be very considerable'. A Jacobean Chancery decree confirmed their right to 'the claim of sea-wreck against the lord paramount of the barony of Egremont', which belonged to the Earls of Northumberland. Later in the seventeenth-century Sir William Pennington acquired the adjacent lordship of Drigg, with 'wreck, and flotsam, jetsam, and lagan upon the sea shore cast up within his liberties here, by prescription'.[88]

[86] SP 16/24, fo. 82; SP 16/35, fo. 43. [87] SP 16/37, fos 40–3, 72.

[88] Thomas Denton, *A Perambulation of Cumberland 1687–1688*, Surtees Society, vol. 207 (2003), 80, 83.

Further south in Lancashire members of the Blundell family of Little Crosby were in seemingly endless conflict with Lord Molyneux's stewards over rights to a wreck at wind-blown Ainsdale.[89] 'Stout words' passed between the Earl of Derby's men and the citizens of Liverpool over wreckage in the Mersey inlet of Tranmere Sloyne.[90] Frustrated by his dealings with the Stanleys over wrecks, Sir Richard Houghton appealed to Sir Robert Cecil for protection in 1605, 'having brought myself into a labyrinth where I never intended, I entreat you to take the matter into your own power without further grief to me'.[91] From time to time the entire coastline seemed to be awash with wrecks, keeping the landed elite and their lawyers busy.

*

It may be reasonable to wonder whether the effort was worth the reward. Manor court rolls and account books show local benefits of wrecks from the meagre to the magnificent, as tenants and other savers paid composition to their lords for materials they had found. The lord customarily took a moiety or half the value of each item presented, besides goods moved privily into his possession. Within the liberties of the Cinque Ports, the Warden customarily helped himself to the best anchors and sails, and took a substantial fraction of declared goods from wrecked ships. The rest of the lading, and salvageable ships' furnishings, would be left for negotiation between local landowners, the original merchant owners, and the common coastal people.

Spectacular treasures were infrequent, and invariably attracted the attention of the Admiralty and the crown, but cartloads of consumables found their way into manorial larders and stores unquestioned. While hoping for riches, like the 'sixty ducats and more in rials of plate' that Thomas Denny of Bawdsey, Suffolk, took from his shore in 1581,[92] or the Spanish money occasionally retrieved in the West Country, manorial proprietors were generally content with usable commodities or saleable items that would augment their stores or incomes. Proprietors sometimes acknowledged that 'the goods are but of small value... but the consequence is great', for they signified a system of rights and entitlements as well as material gains.[93] According cultural and honorific advantages, as well financial benefit, these seigneurial privileges sustained Samuel Pepys's observation that 'the great profit of the lords of manors upon the sea coasts lay in wrecks'.[94]

[89] *The Great Diurnal of Nicholas Blundell of Little Crosby, Lancashire: Volume One 1702–1711*, ed. Frank Tyrer and J. J. Bagley, Record Society of Lancashire and Cheshire, vol. 110 (1968), 30.

[90] *Liverpool Town Books*, i. *1550–1571*, ed. J. A. Twemlow (Liverpool, 1918), 160–5.

[91] Historical Manuscripts Commission, *Calendar of the Manuscripts of... the Marquis of Salisbury*, 24 vols (1883–1976), xvii. 602.

[92] HCA 13/24, fo. 163^{v}.

[93] SP 16/139, fo. 79.

[94] *Samuel Pepys's Naval Minutes*, 84.

6

The Lord Admiral's Droits and His Majesty's Profit

Though all rights to shipwrecks in English waters and coastlines belonged, in principle, to the crown, Tudor monarchs gained relatively little by exploiting this prerogative. Most claims were settled locally between landed proprietors and holders of prescriptive rights, in negotiation with merchants, mariners, and the freelance salvors on the beach. Central government took few initiatives and was content to allow subordinates to go about its work. Privileges were to be respected, laws and customs followed, with the crown serving more as a referee than an interested player. Appeals could reach as high as the Privy Council, but Elizabeth I's government was generally reluctant 'to intermeddle in the liberty of noble men that pretend title to the said . . . goods wrecked'.[1] The state was content to adjudicate disputes, making few demands for itself.

A change took place towards the end of the sixteenth century as the crown and its agents recognized *wreccum maris* as a desirable stream of revenue. By the end of the reign of James I the most diligent exploiters of shipwrecks were officials of the Admiralty and other appointees of the state. Their reach grew more demanding during the ascendancy of the Duke of Buckingham in the 1620s and the personal rule of Charles I in the 1630s. While opprobrium attached to 'the barbarous country people', the most vigorous exploiters of shipwrecks were established wielders of power.

Wardens and Admirals

Signs of the shift appeared during the long Admiralty administration of Charles Howard of Effingham, Earl of Nottingham, Lord High Admiral 1585–1619. A statute of Richard II had specifically denied the Admiralty jurisdiction over 'wreck of the sea', but new articles promulgated during war with Spain in 1591 allowed the Lord High Admiral to 'enquire of those which make wreck of ships or other goods perishing by shipwreck upon the sea, whereof some hath come to land'. Nottingham and his successors gained rights to unclaimed flotsam, jetsam,

[1] PC 2/9, fo. 166, with reference to a Portuguese ship wrecked in Sussex in 1565.

Shipwrecks and the Bounty of the Sea. David Cressy, Oxford University Press. © David Cressy 2022.
DOI: 10.1093/oso/9780192863393.003.0007

and lagan, the 'one moiety thereof accruing unto him'.[2] Shipwrecks augmented the already substantial profits that accrued from war and privateering and may have grown in importance as prize income shrank with the Jacobean peace. Beachcombers, wreckers, and the operatives of manorial proprietors would be more strictly scrutinized by seekers of Admiralty droits. Later admirals would expand on these provisions, in vigorous pursuit of profit. In England's Channel Islands 'L'Admiral de Angleterre' clashed with the Royal Court of Guernsey when he pressed such claims in 1613.[3]

The Wardens of the Cinque Ports, crown appointees who governed England's coasts from the mouth of the Thames to the Sussex downs, also quickened their exploitation of wreck rights, in competition with lesser authorities. The Elizabethan William Brooke, Lord Cobham (Warden 1559–97), had ruled with a light hand, instructing his officers with regard to wreck harvesters, 'I would not have you to press them thereunto', but only to record their names.[4] His successors, Henry Brooke, Lord Cobham (Warden 1597–1603), Henry Howard, Earl of Northampton (Warden 1604–14), and Edward Lord Zouch (Warden 1615–25), made more intensive demands, insisting that all 'the benefits of wrecks and findalls' accrued to their office. Legal and antiquarian research reinforced claims by Lord Wardens to ancient rights of 'wreck of the sea at whatsoever coasts and arms of the sea in the ports and members aforesaid adjacent it shall happen to be cast, and all and singular the things which belong and appertain to every such wreck'. Their 'emoluments, commodities, and profits' recognized their contribution to the security of the realm. In this regard, said Lord Zouch's agent, his lordship was 'vigilant not to suffer himself to be abused either in his honour or lawful droits and profits'.[5]

The jurisdiction of the Cinque Ports covered the richest of all wreck zones, including the Goodwin Sands offshore from Deal and Ramsgate, where the Warden claimed Admiralty rights and was watchful for his profits.[6] His lieutenants, sergeants, and droit gatherers policed the beaches of the Forelands, the Downs, and the eastern Channel to 'collect, gather, receive, and seize... all wrecks of sea, and other goods, droits, and duties whatsoever', claiming a third of the value of 'wrecks and findalls at sea' and a moiety or a half of goods that came to

[2] 15 Richard II, c. 3 (1391); *Articles Concerning the Admiralty of England, and the Iurisdiction Thereof. 21. Julii. Anno Domini. 1591* (1591), articles 6 and 23.

[3] *Actes des Etats de L'Ile de Guernsey 1605 à 1651* (St Peter Port, 1851), 32–4. See also John Kelleher, 'The Mysterious Case of the Ship Abandoned off Sark in 1608: The Customary Law Relating to *choses gaives*', in Gordon Dawes (ed.), *Commise 1204: Studies in the History and Law of Continental and Insular Normandy* (St Peter Port, 2005), 171–90.

[4] PC 2/9, fo. 166, with reference to a Portuguese ship wrecked in Sussex in 1565.

[5] SP 12/266, fo. 74; SP 12/284, fos 179, 183; SP 12/285, fo. 61; SP 14/2, fo. 244; SP 14/6, fo. 89; SP 14/215, fo. 7. James I's favourite, Robert Carr, Earl of Somerset, held the wardenship from 1614 to 1615, before being brought down by factional infighting.

[6] SP 14/2, fo. 244; SP 14/89, fos 86, 89, 91; SP 14/92, fos 64, 241; SP 14/93, fo. 31.

land.[7] Some even claimed that the Warden's rights extended over a hundred miles of sea.[8] Droit gatherers from Essex to Sussex engaged in 'trial by law' with lords of manors, and diverted some proceeds to themselves. Owners became more accustomed to the 'fees and duties' required when their vessels suffered shipwreck.[9] Before retrieving 'certain goods and wares lately wrecked' in 1616, merchant claimants had first to satisfy 'all droits, rights, and royalties therein due...as also reasonable composition being agreed upon with the savers of the said goods, and all fees and duties being paid to all the subordinate officers under his lordship', in this case Lord Zouch. One such claimant, Sir Thomas Wynn, rejected the 'unconscionable' terms demanded for the restitution of his sea-stained goods, saying they 'are not worth the money they ask, in the pickle they now be in'.[10]

Like many activities involving money, the resolution of claims over shipwrecks was subject to favouritism, graft, malfeasance, and corruption. Compelling evidence reveals that many of the officials who complained of 'the barbarous country people' were busy lining their own pockets. William Ward, sergeant and 'droit-gatherer general' for the Cinque Ports in 1614, was aggressive in his seizures of wreck goods, and 'embezzleth much of the same to his own use'. He would allegedly persuade salvagers 'to cast commodities into by-corners', then take half himself before making his report. A whistle-blower charged that

> goods are often concealed by his substitutes, who post them from one to another, till the owner thus deluded is driven to go his way desperate... Afterwards at his own time he appoints a day of sharing...commanding the savers to prize the wrecked goods, who must so far undervalue them, as Mr Ward may like the pennyworth... By this means the poor merchant is much wronged, the savers either compelled to be dishonest or to lose their due, and the Lord Warden abused both in his reputation and credit.[11]

Similar charges were brought against John Packnam, the clerk of Dover Castle, who, 'for his fees upon a wreck, he hath combined with the master to defeat the merchant, giving certificate to the master that all the goods perished with the ship, when it hath been justified that the said master hath embezzled divers of them'.[12] Edward Nicholas, secretary to Admiral Buckingham, knew that under-officers, as well as savers, if not well looked unto, 'will embezzle more than the sea

[7] *The Great and Ancient Charter of the Cinque-Ports of our Lord the King, and the Members of the same* (1682), 30; Samuel Jeake, *Charters of the Cinque Ports, Two Ancient Towns, and their Members* (1728), 62; William Boys, *Collections for the History of Sandwich in Kent* (1792), 772; K. M. E. Murray, *The Constitutional History of the Cinque Ports* (Manchester, 1935), 120–38; *A Calendar of the White and Black Books of the Cinque Ports 1432–1955*, ed. Felix Hull (1966), 215, 281; SP 12/266, fo. 74; SP 14/151, fo. 87.

[8] SP 14/185, fo. 12.

[9] SP 14/56, fo. 153; SP 14/75, fos 158–9; SP 14/81, fo. 87; SP 14/87, fo. 106.

[10] SP 14/87, fo. 106; SP 14/89, fo. 136.

[11] SP 14/75, fo. 158.

[12] SP 14/75, fo. 159.

swalloweth'.[13] Other minor officials who profited similarly from wrecks included Francis Brooke, deputy vice admiral for Portsmouth, and his brother John, a navy supply clerk at Southsea, who took possession of goods and gear to which they were not entitled. They made £4 from the sale of a boat, £18 from sails from a Flemish wreck, and varied sums by selling cordage and cloth in Portsmouth.[14] Corruption and collusion were rife, in a culture of greed and kickbacks, but the scale of the abuse is unmeasurable.

Competing with the Warden nationwide was the Lord High Admiral, whose own agents were increasingly diligent on their master's behalf. Clashes occurred in contested jurisdictions like the offshore sandbanks—wet or dry according to movements of the tide—where the Warden and the Admiral each claimed authority. When Lord Zouch's men tried to recover an abandoned Dutch ship in 1616, demanding one-third of its value, they found that one of Admiral Howard's ships 'came likewise thither' and 'set upon the mast of the same ship the mark of the broad arrow, for the Lord Admiral'. On another occasion the men of Deal, Kent, would neither 'stir nor go' to assist in the recovery of a French wine wreck, because 'Sir Francis Howard had set my Lord Admiral's mark on it'.[15] These competitions were simplified from time to time when the wardenship and Admiralty offices were held by the same person.

Admiral Buckingham

When the Marquis of Buckingham became Lord High Admiral in 1619, he waged aggressive campaigns against other coastal franchises to maximize his income from shipwrecks. His chief judge, Sir Henry Marten, assured him that his lordship's honour and his 'share in the profits of the sea' were the sole and central concern of his office. Buckingham's secretary and man of business Edward Nicholas likewise prioritized returns to his lord, though he was willing himself to accept 'a piece of grogram by the next stranger's ship that bring any'.[16] The new Admiral was zealous in monetizing Admiralty rights, pursuing prize goods and wreck profits on every coast while clashing with local traditions and jurisdictions. Admiralty judges held court at Southwark and in the country, pressing claims to all matters maritime, including the tackle, lading, and proceeds of shipwrecks.

Buckingham's Admiralty brushed off competing claims from the Duchy of Cornwall, put heavy pressure on the Cinque Ports, and rolled over less potent authorities. His men made threatening speeches against officers of Lord Zouch, insisting that Kent's Goodwin Sands belonged to the Narrow Seas and were

[13] SP 14/119, fo. 10; SP 14/215, fo. 5.
[14] SP 16/258, fo. 146; SP 16/262, fo. 14.
[15] SP 14/87, fo. 22; SP 14/89, fo. 86.
[16] SP 14/111, fo. 72; SP 14/119, fo. 10; SP 14/181, fo. 84; SP 14/215, fos 5 and *passim*.

entirely subject to the Lord Admiral. Local vice admirals felt pressure to yield profits to 'my Lord Admiral's use', while Buckingham exploited the king's grant 'by letters patent of all pirates' goods'. Even while romping with the king at Newmarket, Buckingham paid attention to his coastal profits.[17]

In July 1624 Buckingham (by this time a duke) promised the ailing Lord Zouch £1,000 down and £500 a year for life for uncontested rights within the jurisdiction of the Cinque Ports, including 'all moneys, places, and casualties whatsoever happening'.[18] He soon acquired the wardenship for himself, and asked Edward Nicholas for a statement of his profits. As Warden as well as High Admiral, Buckingham commanded all coastlines, and demanded annual accounts 'of all the wreck of sea droits and other casualties'. His audits directed gains for his lordship's 'profit and advantage'. When a Hamburg merchantman was wrecked in the Downs in February 1625, Nicholas instructed Sir John Hippisley, the lieutenant of Dover Castle, to 'have a special and superintendent care to see that nothing be therein done to my lord's dishonour or disprofit'. Salvaged goods were to be sold 'for my lord's benefit, in furthering what shall be of his profit', with 'good and profit courtesies' for the officers who arranged the deal. Dividing proceeds from 'preemption' between the lieutenant, the merchant buyers, and himself, Nicholas asked his partners for 'special care that there be nothing done or acted that may in the least manner reflect on my lord, or be the least stain to his honour or disadvantage to his profit', which was reckoned in the range of £10,000.[19] The admiral's instructions to his deputies around the country likewise insisted on 'such profits as are due to his grace' and demanded speedy returns 'for my lord's profit', meaning gain, benefit, and advantage.[20]

These efforts paid handsomely in 1626 when the wreck of a Spanish Netherlander near Dover yielded £30,000, which Hippisley promised 'with all speed [to] make...into ready money' for dispatch to the duke.[21] Privateering activity in the course of war with Spain and France brought even more benefit to the Lord Admiral, who took a tenth of the value of all prizes brought ashore. The best butts of wine and the best chests of sugar were set aside directly for the duke's household consumption. His issue of letters of marque and close attention to privateering proceeds also fattened Buckingham's accounts.[22] Not to miss an

17 SP 14/111, fos 96, 100, 105; SP 14/151, fos 28–9; SP 16/41, fo. 53.

18 SP 14/170, fo. 26; R. G. Marsden, 'Admiralty Droits and Salvage—Gas Float Whitton, No. II', *Law Quarterly Review*, 15 (1899), 358.

19 SP 14/173, fo. 44; SP 14/181, fo. 84; SP 14/185, fo. 12; SP 14/215, fos 6–7.

20 SP 16/41, fo. 53; SP 16/57, fo. 92; SP 16/115, fos 67–77.

21 SP 16/19, fo. 28; SP 16/43, fo. 54.

22 SP 16/40, fo. 5; SP 16/115, *passim*; David D. Hebb, 'Profiting from Misfortune: Corruption and the Admiralty under the Early Stuarts', in Thomas Cogswell, Richard Cust, and Peter Lake (eds), *Politics, Religion and Popularity in Early Stuart Britain: Essays in Honour of Conrad Russell* (Cambridge, 2002), 103–11; John C. Appleby, 'Wars of Plunder and Wars of Profit: English Privateering during the Late Sixteenth and Early Seventeenth Centuries', in David J. Starkey and Morten Hahn-Pedersen (eds), *Bridging Troubled Waters: Conflict and Co-operation in the North Sea Region since 1550* (Esbjerg, 2005), 59–79.

opportunity, Buckingham also engaged the Dutch salvage diver Jacob Johnson to retrieve anchors, ordnance, 'and all manner of commodities lost by shipwreck or other casualties' throughout his jurisdiction.[23] Even posthumously, his administrators sought to collect whatsoever they could from the 'ruins and pieces' of wrecks that the duke had claimed or challenged.[24]

The King's Admiralty

The Duke of Buckingham had made the Admiralty a money pot, and after his assassination in August 1628 the crown took over the apparatus for the 'seizure of... wrecks unto his majesty's use'. The Admiralty was held in commission for the king until 1638, when it was conferred on his son Prince James.[25] Buckingham's secretary Nicholas became Charles I's secretary and ensured that 'his majesty may not receive prejudice in this particular'. The purpose could not be more clear. Pressure mounted against lords of coastal manors who 'pretended' rights to wreck, for, even if the 'the goods are but of small value... the consequence is great, for they will deprive the Admiral of all profits that shall accrue within those places'. There would be little accommodation with any who 'encroach upon his majesty's right of wreck', which had material, financial, and political value.[26] Privateering slowed down as the war came to an end, but shipwrecks remained as profitable as ever, as bankable assets for the crown.

In 1631 the civil lawyer Sir Henry Marten drew up for Secretary Nicholas and the king a comprehensive account of Admiralty jurisdiction, incorporating centuries of precedents and procedures. Filling over three hundred folios, the maritime equivalent of the Book of Orders and other blueprints for Charles I's 'personal rule', it offered a maximalist and expansive account of royal rights. In almost every controversy it privileged 'his majesty's profit and prerogative' over usurping manors and franchises. Marten cited a letter by 'an ancient lawyer of good esteem... concerning some wrongs done by the common law to the Admiral jurisdiction', upheld 'his majesty's regalities belonging unto the same', and cited 'wrongs offered unto his majesty by his subjects in taking from him his wreck of sea and flotsam goods belonging to his crown'. Vigilant scrutiny would be needed against 'stewards of courts baron who have many devices to decay his majesty's right or wreck', in order to secure 'his majesty's profit'.[27]

With Marten's compendium to guide them, officials in the 1630s railed against 'towns and corporations and private lords of manors bordering upon the sea coasts, which do challenge and appropriate to themselves Admiralty jurisdiction

[23] SP 16/4, fo. 87. [24] SP 16/269, fo. 105. [25] PC 2/49, fo. 41.
[26] SP 16/138, fo. 134; SP 16/139, fo. 79; SP 16/186, fo. 70; SP 16/189, fo. 40.
[27] SP 16/208, fos 163–6, 298–300, 318.

and all manner of Admiralty droits and casualties happening within their pretended limits'. Because of such 'encroachments', they said without evidence, 'his majesty's profits by the Admiralty have already almost come to nothing'. There would need to be a crackdown against any who 'take and enjoy to themselves the ... droits and profits naturally and of right belonging to his majesty'. If necessary, the government would initiate *quo warranto* proceedings to restore his majesty's revenue and honour in this regard.[28] Decrying 'impediments from lords of manors and their bailiffs', the civil lawyer Henry Dade (a judge in ecclesiastical courts as well as the Admiralty) declared to Principal Secretary Coke in January 1634 that 'I have always had a desire to advance his majesty's profit arising from shipwrecks'.[29]

The tone and tactics were typical of their time and provenance. 'Everyone is looking to see from what quarter money may be raised,' observed the Venetian ambassador in 1629. 'They are always', he reported a few years later, 'devising ways to supply the ordinary and extraordinary expenses of this crown without summoning parliament'.[30] The exploitation of shipwrecks was part of the project to energize the king's 'mines'—his hidden financial resources—and to maximize royal rights and revenues. It paralleled the raising of money from prerogative dues and fiscal feudalism, from forest fines, purveyance, and fees in distraint of knighthood, though wrecks are not mentioned in Kevin Sharpe's magisterial treatment of such finance in the 1630s.[31]

Highlighting the 'continual sea-harvest of gain and benefit' from England's coasts—an appropriate image of gathering and reaping—Sir John Boroughs, Charles I's Keeper of the Records, insisted on 'the king's sovereign right and power to dispose thereof at his pleasure'. *Wreccum maris*, Boroughs wrote in 1633, was among 'the ancient rights and regalities annexed to their crowns', which monarchs were obliged to protect. Local proprietors who claimed by prescription that their ancestors 'have had wreck there time out of mind' would be reminded that such rights 'did rightfully belong to the king'.[32] This was the context for the planned proclamation in 1633 against the 'the barbarous custom of rifling and robbing of ships', which was as much concerned to maximize royal revenue as to police predation by the poor.[33] Crown officials fixated on the yield of 'his majesty's right of wreck', which some thought might reach £30,000 or £40,000 a year.[34] There was more to be gained by challenging manorial proprietors than by chasing down villagers who had gone off with a few barrels. At no cost to the king, farmers

[28] SP 16/231, fo. 52; SP 16/238, fo. 59; SP 16/239, fo. 2; SP 16/264, fo. 54^{v}; SP 16/277, fo. 207; SP 16/285, fo. 175; SP 16/379, fo. 95.

[29] SP 16/258, fo. 156.

[30] *CSP Venice 1628–9*, 582; *CSP Venice 1632–6*, 196.

[31] Kevin Sharpe, *The Personal Rule of Charles I* (New Haven and London, 1992), 105–30.

[32] John Boroughs, *The Soveraignty of the British Seas* (1651), 1, 57, 94, 98, 104–5, 10; Thomas Madox, *The History and Antiquities of the Exchequer of the Kings of England* (1711), 235.

[33] SP 16/248, fo. 53^{v}.

[34] SP 16/242, fo. 4; SP 16/529, fo. 28; George F. Steckley, 'Seventeenth-Century Origins of Modern Salvage Law', *Journal of Legal History*, 35 (2014), 12.

could be found to follow up Admiralty commissions, to trace and recover goods 'unjustly and fraudulently taken and concealed', with proceeds coming to the crown.[35]

A forthright application of this policy appeared in December 1633 after a laden merchantman was 'wrecked or left as derelict upon the coast near Colchester'. Local boatmen swarmed the ship as usual but faced stiff rebuke from crown officials. The Council commanded the deputy vice admirals and commissioners to use 'all possible diligence and industry' to inquire and search in all jurisdictions, to seize all 'goods, merchandize, lading and furniture belonging to the said ship... for his majesty's use'. There would be no hiding behind privilege or exemption, if his majesty's authority was properly respected.[36]

When a Hamburg treasure ship split on the Isle of Wight in October 1635, spilling chests of bullion into the surf, government agents rushed to secure 'his majesty's interest' therein. 'The country people', predictably, made off with 'driblets' of silver, but only 'small parcels of money and goods' went missing.[37] Efforts with grappling hooks and shovels recovered 16,000 pieces of eight and 73 pounds of silver, which the Admiralty proctor Richard Wynn escorted back to London. The status of this ship as a 'wreck' was disputable, because crewmen survived, and the Hamburg merchants claimed ownership, but England's Admiralty allocated everything to the king. The haul of bullion yielded £6,000 'for his majesty's use' and confirmed Sir Henry Marten's view that the Isle of Wight was 'a place apt enough to be fruitful of such perquisites'.[38]

More wrecks on the Sussex coast in 1637 were jointly managed by the Admiralty and the Cinque Ports, with royal oversight, 'to the end the king may receive the benefit thereof which belongs to his majesty'.[39] Following another south coast wreck that summer, an Admiralty proctor wrote: 'I hope the vice-admiral will manage all for the advantage of the king.'[40] Yet even vice admirals could be sidelined by more direct exploitation. When a wreck in north Cornwall in 1637 yielded 'divers barrels of butter, sack, wool and other goods' of value, Vice Admiral Francis Bassett laid claim to them, quelling competing interest from the bailiff of Sir John Arundell's Penwith hundred. Hearing of this, Prince Charles's council in London reminded Basset that 'all wrecks of sea within the Duchy of Cornwall in the county of Cornwall do belong unto the prince his highness' and instructed him to hand over the goods to duchy officials. Surely he knew, they wrote in a follow-up letter, that 'the office of Lord Admiral of England is now

[35] SP 16/264, fo. 29^{v}; SP 16/268, fo. 1.

[36] SP 16/228, fos 99^{v}–100. The exercise of this commission is documented in HCA 13/50, fos 556–8, 577–577^{v}, 601–4, and HCA 13/52, fos 10–10^{v}.

[37] SP 16/303, fo. 268; SP 16/305, fo. 221.

[38] SP 16/305, fo. 221; SP 16/350, fo. 22; SP 16/353, fo. 76; SP 16/364, fos 57, 75, 105; BL, MS Add. 46,501, fo. 222.

[39] SP 16/364, fo. 4.

[40] SP 16/364, fos 5, 75.

executed by commission in his majesty's own name and for his majesty's own benefit and behoof'.[41] Royal claims to wreck 'for his majesty's profits' were persistent, capacious, and by now unexceptional, an aspect of the expanded power of the state.[42] In March 1638 the king conferred the office of Lord High Admiral, with all contingent profits, on his son Prince James, to be exercised by the Earl of Northumberland during the boy's 'yet tender years'.[43] Threats to good order may have come from so-called barbarous wreckers, but crown profits would be preserved from competing jurisdictions. Predation by royal licence persuaded some coastal residents 'that they had rather trust God with their souls than the Admiral with their goods'.[44] Country people still practised plunder on the beaches, but much of their haul went to agents of the state.

Restoration Bounties

Parliamentary and Interregnum policies await investigation, but after the Restoration, when the Duke of York was both Warden of the Cinque Ports and Lord High Admiral, his officers enquired 'whether any lords of manor, or others, do challenge to themselves wreck at sea, or other droits of admiralty, in their manors, without sufficient title in law so to do'.[45] But the Admiral himself faced challenge when informers charged that goods he had seized belonged instead to the king.[46] Traditional proprietorial claims persisted, while royal officials instructed local agents to inquire 'after the nature of the wreck, and what title his majesty hath to the said ship and goods' and 'to take care that his majesty's interest may be preserved'.[47] Accounts report an annual revenue around £1,800 a year from the Cinque Ports alone in the 1680s.[48] Offices closely controlled by the crown prioritized the needs and interests of the king and channelled funds to Treasury coffers.

Feudal proprietors and coastal lords of manors found comfort in England's common law, but Admiralty lawyers pushed back, wrapping their authority in the prerogative of the crown. John Godolphin argued in 1661 against any 'such as claim wreck to the prejudice of the king or Lord Admiral'.[49] It was an offence 'against the public good of the kingdom', wrote Richard Zouch, for any to claim

[41] SP 16/353, fo. 64; SP 16/362, fo. 126; SP 16/370, fos 36–40. [42] SP 16/379, fo. 95.

[43] PC 2/49, fo. 41. [44] SP 16/327, fo. 33.

[45] William Wynne, *The Life of Sir Leoline Jenkins, Judge of the High-Court of Admiralty*, 2 vols (1724), i, p. lxxxviii; ii. 764.

[46] *Reports of Cases in the Court of Exchequer in the Time of King Charles II*, ed. W. H. Bryson (Tempe, AZ, 2017), 25.

[47] SP 29/414, fo. 67.

[48] Boys, *Collections for the History of Sandwich*, 772; Murray, *Constitutional History of the Cinque Ports*, 120–38.

[49] John Godolphin, *Synēgoros Thalassio: A View of the Admiralty Jurisdiction* (1661), 26, 41–6.

wrecks, 'having no charters nor prescription'.[50] The civil law of the Admiralty, wrote John Exton, 'plainly forbiddeth such as dwell upon or near the shore to take away such goods so wrecked, though stranded, broken, or cast upon ground'. Such items, 'properly called wreck of the sea... belongeth properly to the king, and by his grant unto the Lord High Admiral'.[51] The message was clear, in a barrage of forceful publications, that the crown was watchful of its rights, that courts of Admiralty would govern such matters, and that the state would lay first claim to any bounty of the sea.

Royal revenue from 'wreck of the sea' was piecemeal and unpredictable, but occasionally substantial. Foreign bullion was especially attractive. In 1686 the royal mint took possession of pieces of eight to the value of £3,049 19*s.* 9*d.* 'taken up as wreck in the west', with instructions to pay one moiety thereof to Lord Godolphin, and the rest into the Treasury.[52] James II's regime banked £20,872 from 'wreck of the sea' in 1687, much of it gained from treasure-hunting in the Caribbean, and a further windfall of £4,000 in 1688.[53] When the Genoese vessel *St Anthony*, sailing from Cadiz to Amsterdam, foundered on the Isle of Wight in August 1691, English authorities learned that its cargo included twenty-eight bars of silver intended for Spanish troops in Flanders. The Council asked the island governor to retain 'as many of the said bars of silver as you have now in your custody' and to assist in 'fishing the rest... out of the sea', for delivery to the crown.[54] King William III's share of white wine recovered when the Dutch ship *Paradise* wrecked on the Goodwin Sands in 1697 amounted to £1,425 9*s.* 2*d.*[55]

The maximization of proceeds, however, was no longer the main consideration. The later Stuart state had many more sources of revenue than its predecessors and could afford to allow wreck-goods to serve non-fiscal purposes. Flush with tonnage and poundage, Customs and Excise, hearth tax, poll tax, parliamentary aids, Exchequer debt, and a subsidy from France, the regime of Charles II could be flexible in the exercise of its prerogative. Political favourites might be granted concessions, while friendly foreign powers would be allowed to recover their countrymen's goods. Petitioned by agents and ambassadors, the Council promised 'all reasonable and friendly aid and assistance'. Rather than holding all the 'bullion, packs, pales, trunks, and other merchandize' to which *wreccum maris* might have entitled them, later Stuart governments could be scrupulous in securing their recovery and repatriation.[56] The reciprocal courtesy of maritime

[50] Richard Zouch, *The Jurisdiction of the Admiralty of England Asserted* (1663), 35.
[51] John Exton, *The Maritime Dicaeologie, or Sea-Jurisdiction of England* (1664), 150, 153.
[52] *Calendar of Treasury Books 1685–1689*, ed. William A. Shaw (1923), 1081.
[53] C. D. Chandaman, *The English Public Revenue 1660–1688* (Oxford, 1975), 348–9, 360–1.
[54] SP 44/99, fo. 69.
[55] *Calendar of Treasury Books 1697–1698*, ed. William A. Shaw (1933), 357, 371.
[56] SP 29/288, fo. 1; SP 29/359, fos 39, 106.

neighbours could then be represented as national honour or discretionary goodwill.

After 'a Holland merchantman laden with high-country wines' foundered at the Isle of Wight in February 1681, the Dutch Ambassador remonstrated about 'the barbarous usages' the islanders gave to the shipwrecked crew. Secretary of State Sir Leoline Jenkins told the Isle of Wight governor that it was 'a matter of shame and confusion, as well as of pity and trouble, to see that a neighbour nation, whose alliance the king doth very highly value, is treated in this distress without regard had to the faith of treaties, to the law of nations, nor to the dictates of common humanity'. The king wanted to demonstrate that he had done everything 'to answer his obligations by treaty, and to punish those that are guilty of robbing and spoiling poor people in the extremity of their distress'.[57] In 1683 it was the Swedish envoy's turn to seek favourable treatment. Although Admiralty officials had taken, as was customary, the great anchor and cable from the *Hope* that was wrecked on the Isle of Wight, the Council ordered their return for the benefit of the ship's company, to assist their repatriation.[58] James II in 1686 gave the Dutch salvage rights to their stricken East Indiaman on the Isles of Scilly, 'as a mark of our good will to the States General, and for relief of their subjects in this case'.[59] William III similarly offered 'favour and friendship' when a Genoese ship was wrecked in English waters in 1691, even returning bars of silver to the ship's commander. Neither greed nor altruism was at work in these transactions, which advanced England's diplomatic interests at marginal cost to the treasury, since special considerations applied 'when a foreign prince demands reparation in behalf of his subjects'.[60]

Acts of magnanimity were also acts of power and could be dispensations of patronage. Such considerations may have underlain the Secretary of State's instructions in February 1690 to restore wrecked cargo to Sir John Barker, the lord of the manor of Walton-cum-Trimley, Suffolk, 'that, for the future, he may be permitted quietly to enjoy the benefit of all such wrecks as shall happen within the said manor'. Local proprietors commonly suffered disadvantage in competition with Admiralty droit collectors, but the regime could exercise discretion. In this case Sir John represented the borough of Ipswich, and his vote would be vital in the new parliament assembling in March.[61]

Customs Demands

The expanding power of the state in the later seventeenth century added another layer of authority to the already crowded arena of claimants, as agents of the

[57] SP 44/68, fo. 197. [58] SP 44/56, fo. 69. [59] SP 29/359, fo. 106.
[60] SP 44/99, fos 69, 493. [61] SP 44/97, p. 266.

Customs and Excise demanded duty on goods brought ashore from shipwrecks. Wines and spirits, in particular, were subject to assessment and confiscation, as if their involuntary landing in distress was a form of importation. Salvagers and wreckers resisted with concealment and dissimulation, and occasionally with acts of violence. Protest, subterfuge, and obstruction added to the drama on the shore.

Pressure intensified after the government took direct control of Customs collecting in 1671, replacing inefficient farmers. Rates of £8 per tun on imported French wine and £12 per tun on Spanish wine were confirmed in legislation of 1685. (A tun, the equivalent of two pipes or four hogsheads, carried 210 English gallons, roughly 955 litres.) Total duties and impositions on wine almost trebled between 1660 and 1714, stimulating efforts of avoidance and smuggling.[62] The Restoration lawyer Charles Molloy argued in 1676 that, 'if goods are wrecked on the shore, and the lord having power takes them, he shall not pay custom', but Treasury officials disagreed.[63]

Treasury papers from the late seventeenth century show Customs officers joining a multi-sided contest for wrecked goods along the English coastline. Arriving in the midst of salvage, and wielding the authority of the crown, they subjected cargoes to inspection and seizure, though connivance and corruption were not unknown. Some Customs men complained that they 'were daily threatened with actions by the vice-admirals and lords of manors', who challenged them 'in right of their respective royalties'.[64] One wine dealer in 1677, who was 'at great charge in salving wines in a ship forsaken, driven on shore', protested that dutiable goods were 'all mixed with salt water'.[65] Agents for the manor of Powderham, Devon, objected in 1684 that the state had no right to 'seize or meddle with' wrecked French wines that were 'landed only for preservation' and were held only to protect them from 'the multitude'.[66] The Earl of Dorset became enraged in 1690 when Customs men seized seven and a half pipes of Canary wine from a wreck on his lands in Sussex.[67]

In a four-way tussle between the Admiralty, the Customs, the Treasury, and the Cinque Ports, the collector of Customs at wreck-rich Deal, Kent, forcibly took goods from the sergeant of the Admiralty in 1691, insisting on keeping them until

[62] 1 James II, c. 3; *The Duties at This Present Time on all Merchandize* (1714); Samuel Baldwin, *A Survey of the British Customs: Containing the Rates of Merchandize* (1770); A. D. Francis, *The Wine Trade* (1972), 77; Edward Carson, *The Ancient and Rightful Customs: A History of the English Customs Service* (1972), 43, 48, 56–117; Motoko Hori, 'The Price and Quality of Wine and Conspicuous Consumption in England 1646–1759', *English Historical Review*, 123 (2008), 1457–69.

[63] Charles Molloy, *De Jure Maritimo et Navali, or, A Treatise of Affaires Maritime, and of Commerce* (1676), 230.

[64] BL, MS Lansdowne 504/7, fo. 14ᵛ; *Calendar of Treasury Books 1685–1689*, ed. William A. Shaw (1923), 544; *Calendar of Treasury Papers 1556/7–1696*, ed. Joseph Redington (1868), 515.

[65] *Calendar of Treasury Books 1676–1679*, ed. William A. Shaw (1911), 626.

[66] Devon Archives and Local Studies Service, L 1508 M London/Harbours and Rivers/1/2, Q.

[67] *Calendar of Treasury Books 1689–1692*, ed. William A. Shaw (1931), 841.

duties were paid.[68] The manorial lord Sir Nicholas Le Strange resisted similar efforts in Norfolk in 1692 when the Customs men wanted to 'set the broad arrow' on a vessel of oil that he had saved from a wreck. 'The oil I had lodged in my barn, and refused the keys, intending to have tried the case if they persisted in the seizure', he recorded. Le Strange exercised his influence in London until the Customs men 'waived the point'.[69] Customs commissioners elsewhere complained of 'contrivance' to avoid paying duties on wrecked wines and brandies. The government allowed Customs officials to hold such goods until duties were paid, but manorial droit-holders vehemently objected.[70] The further militarization of Customs enforcement in the eighteenth century added to the bitterness of disputes, in which soldiers and commissioners vied with merchants, landowners, and ordinary wreckers for control of the bounty of the sea.

Wreck harvesters had a bad reputation, but the principal plunderers, it turns out, were not 'the barbarous country people' who were so often blamed, but the government and landed proprietors themselves. The most substantial profiteers were not poor country scavengers, or wreckers, but patricians and officers whose plunder was generally polite. In the hierarchy of appropriation, the state held the greatest power. The 'moral economy' historiography on shipwrecks dwells on looting, insubordination, mob activity, criminality, and class relations, and this remains a model with traction. But a fuller picture requires reference to the seigneurial economy, fiscal feudalism, state formation, and the advantages and abuses of the law.

[68] *Calendar of Treasury Papers 1556/7–1696*, 202.

[69] Norfolk Record Office, LEST/Q 37, 46.

[70] *Calendar of Treasury Books 1685–1689*, 544; BL, MS Lansdowne 504/7, fo. 14^{v}.

7
Shipwreck Tales from Sea and Shore

Buried in local archives, state papers, and the barely catalogued records of the High Court of Admiralty, the reports of inquiries and depositions of witnesses tell compelling stories of the circumstance and aftermath of shipwrecks. Augmented by correspondence and commentary, and the testimony of distressed mariners, they tell how broken vessels came ashore, and how landsmen appropriated the bounty of the sea. Surviving documents illuminate the behaviour and attitudes of salvagers, wreckers, gatherers, and those with whom they dealt. They give voice to countless individuals otherwise lost to history. The question *cui bono*—to whose benefit?—is answered in terms of rights, profits, and material rewards. Reputable village elders recalled precedent, custom, and practices of yore. Others described recent episodes though the eyes of participants and observers. Shipowners and seamen told their stories. Merchants complained of loss. The records are richly detailed on the local topography of shorelines and sandbanks, the demarcations of properties and liberties, the personalities of participants, and the work of wreck recovery. They shed remarkable fresh light on the perils of seafaring and the social dynamics of the water's edge. Those presented here are among the best documented, standing in for many others.

Narratives of shipwrecks, and the statements of people involved in their harvest, open windows into rural coastal communities. They offer a rich trove of evidence, rarely previously considered, that augments observations by social historians about social memory, custom, the landscape, and neighbourly relations. Steve Hindle has emphasized the importance of solidarity and reciprocity within early modern parishes and villages. Andy Wood discerns a 'social electricity... surging up and down the hierarchy', as communities negotiated the stresses of authority and dependence. Both are beholden to Keith Wrightson, whose pioneering work exposed the micropolitics of the parish.[1] Many of these observations apply, and can be tested, in the depositions relating to wrecking.

[1] Steve Hindle, 'A Sense of Place? Becoming and Belonging in the Rural Parish, 1550–1650', in Alexandra Shepard and Phil Withington (eds), *Communities in Early Modern England: Networks, Place, Rhetoric* (Manchester, 2000), 96–114; Andy Wood, *Faith, Hope and Charity: English Neighbourhoods, 1500–1640* (Cambridge, 2020), 101; Keith Wrightson, 'The Politics of the Parish in Early Modern England', in Paul Griffiths, Adam Fox, and Steve Hindle (eds), *The Experience of Authority in Early Modern England* (1996), 10–46; Keith Wrightson, 'Mutualities and Obligations: Changing Relationships in Early Modern England', *Proceedings of the British Academy*, 139 (2006), 157–94.

Shipwrecks and the Bounty of the Sea. David Cressy, Oxford University Press. © David Cressy 2022.
DOI: 10.1093/oso/9780192863393.003.0008

The records exhibit a strong sense of community entitlement, voiced in collective action yet subject to relationships of power and law. A strong sense of place, and a sense of ownership of opportunity appears, for example, in competition between the parishioners of Pevensey and the men of Hastings, and between the tenants of Bishopstone and their counterparts at Meeching. Similar friction between parishioners of Wyke Regis and Abbotsbury, and between the quarrymen of Portland and the fishermen of Fleet, emerged in depositions concerning the *Golden Grape* that wrecked in Dorset in 1641 (see Chapter 8). The coastal workers of Ramsgate, Sandwich, Sandown, and Deal competed for the gifts of the Goodwin Sands. Witnesses recalled a rare outbreak of violence late in Queen Elizabeth's reign, not against shipwrecked mariners but between rival salvagers, when fishermen from Ramsgate bested Sir Edward Wotten's men from Thanet, tumbling one overboard and breaking several heads.[2] There may even have been a festive aspect to wrecking, which is more readily imagined than demonstrated. Shared rewards from moieties and plunder accrued from labour alongside workmates, neighbours, friends, and kin.

Concern for the maintenance of privilege, the restoration of rights, the allocation of proceeds, and observance of the law produced a variety of documentation. Letters and reports tell stories of shipwrecks that might not otherwise be heard. Depositions of witnesses before commissions of inquiry present versions of what participants said they did. Historians who have used comparable records generally recognize them as mediated representations of testimony, rendered in the third person, and sanitized by notaries and scribes.[3] Recollections were often delayed, memories sometimes faulty, and statements not necessarily truthful. Witnesses avoided self-incrimination. While describing where they went, what they carried, and with whom they assembled, shore-based deponents commonly took care to say that they 'saved' particular items rather than took them, that goods were in their 'custody' rather than in their possession, and that they deferred to instructions from landlords, droit collectors, and office holders. Degrees of pilferage and purloining were to be expected, since greed and duplicity never disappeared, but shoremen maintained generally cordial relations with lords of manors, droit holders, and most government officials. Their testimony served more to mend social relations than to sever them. Shipwrecks may have tested the social order but left its architecture intact.

[2] SP 12/284, fos 179–83.

[3] Joanne Bailey, 'Voices in Court: Lawyers' or Litigants'?', *Historical Research*, 74 (2001), 392–408; Frances E. Dolan, *True Relations: Reading, Literature and Evidence in Seventeenth-Century England* (Philadelphia, 2013); Richard J. Blakemore, 'Orality and Mutiny: Authority and Speech among Seafarers in Early Modern London', in Thomas V. Cohen and Lesley K. Twomey (eds), *Spoken Word and Social Practice: Orality in Europe (1400–1700)* (Leiden and Boston, 2015), 254–5, 259, 262, 264; Michael J. Braddick, 'Afterword', in Cohen and Twomey (eds), *Spoken Word and Social Practice*, 446–62; Heather Falvey, 'Relating Early Modern Depositions', in Carl J. Griffin and B. McDonagh (eds), *Remembering Protest in Britain since 1500* (2018), 81–196.

Despite limitations, which apply to many kinds of historical records, the depositions provide our best evidence of coastal, maritime, and inland interactions. Relating these episodes through the words of people involved in them casts the history of shipwreck and shore relations in an entirely fresh light. Their representations pulse with detail and colour. Behind the formalities of exposition one can sense the drama of the scene, the chill of the beach, the crash of waves, the backwash of shingle, the splintering of timber, the cries of the distressed, and competition for advantage. More than a dozen micro narratives, from varied coastlines and communities, expose shipwreck and wreck harvest from the time of Elizabeth I to the age of Charles II. Social history and maritime history converge in these explorations of archival traces.

Northumberland, 1559 and 1565

Hard weather in October 1559 drove the *Bonaventure* of Dieppe ashore on the Northumberland coast, ending its voyage to Scotland. Witnesses reported that the vessel broke apart on the rocks, 'whereby divers of her men were slain and drowned, and also the goods driven chiefly to the seas, and partly on the rocks and sands, where the people of the township adjoining came and did help to save some of the men of the ship, and took of the goods'. The next day Thomas Clavering, esquire, a warlord client of the Earl of Northumberland, 'came thither accompanied with divers borderers under his charge, and seized all those goods that could be found into his custody, as wreck in the right of Norham Castle'. More than two hundred people from parishes just north of Holy Island turned out to assist in salvage. Clavering's men forced local scavengers to turn over their findings—the fruits of his 'liberty'—which he later claimed implausibly 'did not amount above the sum of £44'. The Scottish merchants whose goods went missing said that Thomas Clavering took spoil to the value of £2,400, and they requested a commission to effect restitution.[4]

Strictly, the *Bonaventure* was not 'wreck' if crewmen survived, so the confiscation of its goods was illegal. But Clavering's people claimed that they found the ship 'broken, and the keel cast upward', the mariners apparently perished. Some of the goods were found 'on the sands in different parts of this country for more than a year after, utterly decayed with salt water'. Archibald Graham and other merchants of Edinburgh pressed suit in England's High Court of Admiralty, and Mary Queen of Scots asked her cousin Elizabeth of England to expedite the matter. French diplomacy also stirred the pot. Hearings dragged on for seven

[4] SP 52/5, fo. 62; SP 52/8, fo. 89; SP 52/12, fo. 13; SP 59/6, fo. 197; SP 59/41, fo. 227. Thomas Clavering had given 'manful service' leader in England's recent war with Scotland, commanding a hundred horsemen at Norham Castle: SP 15/8, fo. 100; SP 59/1, fo. 12.

years, with everybody, it seems, hiding something. At one point, backed by the Privy Council, the Admiralty proposed to levy £2,080 against Clavering, later adjusted to £1,200, and, if he failed to pay, 'to cess the whole country of Northumberland'. They even devised a schedule whereby the villages most associated with the wrecking would be charged variable amounts. To hasten collection, they put Clavering and twenty of his followers in prison, but released them a month later for fear of weakening the borderers, 'whose wealth standeth in horses and armour for the defence of the kingdom'. The Earl of Northumberland and the Percy kindred stood by their man and asserted their own rights over shipping. Most of those involved in the spoil were tenants of the earl and enjoyed his effective protection. To task them 'to pay for the small portion they received after the ship was broken up would be the utter decay of these borders', declared Northumberland's allies Sir Thomas Dacre and Valentine Brown. Sir Henry Percy, the earl's brother, further muddied waters by declaring that soldiers of Berwick had spoil of the wreck four hours before the Norham men arrived, and that the governor of Berwick, Sir James Crofts, and Sir Ralph Gray of Ross in Bamburgh had more of the ship's goods than anyone. Thwarted and exhausted, the government gave up trying, the borderers kept their booty, and the Scottish merchants nursed their losses.[5]

The grievances and frustrations resulting from the wreck of the *Bonaventure* remained unresolved when another rich vessel foundered on these shores. The new wreck further strained relations between local proprietors and other claimants, stirring more competition over rights and resources.

On Christmas Eve 1565 walkers on a Northumberland beach found a body. The corpse was badly disfigured, but the remnants of his garments indicated gentle rank. More bodies, and the scattered goods of shipwreck, appeared over the next few days, precipitating a crisis in the political, commercial, and legal affairs of three countries. The Elizabethan statesman William Cecil used all his skill to penetrate its mysteries, to assuage northern magnates, to placate Dutch merchants, and to fend off claims from Mary Queen of Scots. The wreckage, it turned out, was from the *George* of Flushing; the body was that of Francis Yaxley, a former client of Cecil's whom Queen Elizabeth described as 'an evil subject of ours'; the cargo included Catholic books, luxury fabrics and spices, bags of gold for the Scottish queen, a suit of armour for her paramour, and over two thousand tennis balls.[6] As happened so often, a maritime misadventure created problems and opportunities for people on shore.

[5] *CSP Foreign 1559–60*, 141, 256; *CSP Foreign 1561–1562*, 114, 276; SP 12/14, fo. 111; SP 12/17, fos 14–16; SP 52/6, fo. 161; SP 52/12, fos 93, 96, 100, 119, 120, 131; SP 59/5, fos 93, 258; SP 59/6, fos 197–197^{v}; SP 59/7, fo. 77; SP 59/41, fos 227–8.

[6] SP 52/12, fos 13, 42; SP 59/41, fos 227–8; BL, MS Harley 6990, fos 69–70.

The body on the beach was the first indication that a ship had broken in pieces. More bodies and wreckage were discovered over the next few days, and recriminations extended over weeks and months. The sea had thrown up a mystery, which entwined national and international interests with those of regional aristocrats and local scavengers.

Thomas Percy, the Earl of Northumberland (1528–72), as senior lord of the border, claimed *wreccum maris* on this coastline. He sent Secretary Cecil a perfunctory note on 1 February, followed by a 'full discourse' on 3 March, promising to relate 'all the circumstances of the wreck at large, as far forth as I know and can learn by search, enquiry and information'. This is one of the most comprehensive accounts of shipwreck discovery and recovery, yet one wonders how much Northumberland knew, and what he left out. His officers had evidently interviewed witnesses before some kind of commission. By this time the wrecked ship had been identified, the body on the beach had been assigned a name, and multiple claimants had converged on its cargo.

The unfortunate *George* of Flushing, with Adrian Cornelis the master, had left Antwerp on 28 November 1565 bound for Scotland with a rich and controversial lading. It had foundered in a North Sea storm, and shattered on coastal rocks, most likely the Hully Carrs off Seaton Point, 5 miles from Northumberland's Alnwick Castle.[7] There were nine souls on board, including an English gentleman with his servant, but none survived the disaster. The damaged body belonged to Francis Yaxley (1528–65), an English Catholic intriguer who was carrying Spanish money from Pope Pius IV to Mary Queen of Scots. The Scottish queen, not surprisingly, was keen to get it back.

The wreck of a Dutch ship with a Scottish cargo on the English coast created a diplomatic incident that required the skill of Secretary Cecil to handle. News of the mishap prompted Mary Queen of Scots to write on 11 February 1566 to the Earl of Bedford, governor of England's northern garrison at Berwick, about one of her ships that 'by tempest is perished upon the coast' just south of the border late in the preceding year. The ship carried money and goods of great value, bound for her court, and the queen asked for their speedy return. Quick restitution, she said, would be 'equitable and according to justice'.[8] Bedford forwarded this missive to London, where councillors drafted a response. Relations between the two countries in this first decade of Elizabeth I's reign were sisterly but brittle, and Cecil would have to balance dynastic, seigneurial, and confessional concerns, as well as order and justice. The border region was always perilous, and the loyalty of the Percy family was open to question. Shipwrecks in this area were always contentious, with claims and seizures fraught with peril.

[7] William Weaver Tomlinson, *Life in Northumberland during the Sixteenth Century* (1897), 135.
[8] SP 52/12, fo. 13.

Aware of these complexities, Northumberland crafted a careful letter:

> Upon Christmas Eve last after the great storm, a man dead was cast on land, who by divers conjectures and persuasions, gathered by the colour of his hair and double teeth is supposed to be Francis Yaxley, albeit his face was so beat upon the rocks, or otherwise disfigured as no sufficient knowledge could be had of him thereby. This man lying on the sand was first espied by one of my tenants' servants, who called to him a Scottish man, a fellow of his. These two turned him over, what they found about him they will not confess, more than the first man saith, that in one of his pockets he felt a hard thing, what it was he knoweth not, because his companion persuaded him forthwith to depart, and to call for more company, upon promise to divide whatsoever should be found. In that mean-time, the other conveyed what was there, and detaineth the same wholly to himself. This man have I caused to be examined, and put in safe custody, yet nothing will he confess. The country men learning of that wreck, resorted thither, and took up [a variety of goods].

Among their first findings were a barrel of oranges, a firkin of soap, and parcels of pepper, cloves, and ginger; bolts of luxury fabric, including bombazine, taffeta, satin, and twill; three Spanish Morocco skins; a suit of black armour, possibly destined for Scotland's Lord Darnley; and 2,800 tennis balls. The arrival a few weeks later of the Edinburgh merchant James Read, showing marks of ownership of this cargo, added complications to claims already made by the Scottish queen, but Northumberland was confident that no living creature escaped, so the wreck was rightfully his.

Northumberland's account continued:

> Upon Christmas Day at eleven of the clock before noon, certain of my tenants found the little chest, broken in the one end, lying on the rocks, and the tide gone out from it. Out of the broken end of the same appeared red and white cloth, which waved with the wind, and was the cause the same was soever espied. They were four Spanish blankets of those colours, and in the broken end a canvas bag, hanging by one of the plates; which bag, as they say, was torn, and much of the gold that was therein scattered on the rocks and sands. Searching further, they found two little canvas bags tied with a cord, and a white box of wood, wherein was folded in a cloth a chain of gold, with the value of forty pounds as I estimate it; which box one of them took away with him, and is now upon further search confessed and brought to hand. The money and bags they put in a fisher's creel, and one of them bare the same away; which being known to the people resorting thither, they flocked about him that had the money gathered up that was scattered, and had spoiled the whole, if my bailiff had not comed with speed, and with great pain saved the same. There is now comen to my hand and

> possession upon further search the sum of 2,124 crowns, certified in my former letters in several coins, the sum of 5,607 crowns [in reals and crowns of various coinage], whereof I gave in reward to my servant that brought and searched them out forty-five crowns.

The wreck had still more secrets and treasures to reveal:

> Upon the twelfth day of Christmas, certain persons walking to the place where the gold was cast up found there a man dead, with a white beard, seeming to be an old man [now supposed to be Adrian Cornelis, the master of the *George*]; whom one William Greg of Newcastle, tailor, with others searched, and found upon him a great purse full of money as it is supposed, which the said Greg and two of his companions took to themselves. A tenant of mine also found of him a little purse full of gold, which the same Greg with others took from him with force, and divided that was therein amongst a great number that was there present, to some three crowns, to some more, and to some less, to the number of eight score and three crowns, as I am advertised. These crowns, with others gotten in the former spoil, are so dispersed into the hands of an number, and are daily exchanged and put away, as I think it will be unpossible to recover any great part thereof.

Northumberland continued:

> Since, three of the mariners hath been cast up, and after that two more, which was clean consumed saving the bones. The trunk was also cast on land, wherein was found a sleeved cloak of black cloth guarded with velvet, a jerkin and a pair of breeches of English cloth, a shirt, a pillow bere, two pair leather pantoffles, a pair [of] velvet slippers, two pair [of] Spanish leather shoes

and various books, including decrees of the Council of Trent in Latin, an English book called the *Hatchet of Heresies*, a French book, a plat of the siege of Malta, a genealogy of Luther, and others which had gone missing. (*The Hatchet of Heresies*, an English translation of Stanislaw Hozjusz, *De Origine Haeresium Nostri Temporis*, was printed in Antwerp on 10 August 1565. The 'genealogy of Luther' was most likely an English translation of *The Apologie of Fridericus Staphylus*, subtitled 'A Show of the Protestants Pedigree', also printed in Antwerp in 1565. Fresh from the bookstalls, these were apparently part of Yaxley's travelling library, or gifts for fellow Catholics in Scotland.) All these things were Northumberland's to enjoy, he insisted, by 'right' and 'good fortune'. 'The wreck is mine clear by the laws of this realm, and I am not bound to make restitution,' either to the Scottish queen or her agents, or to anyone else. 'My courage serveth me well to defend my right and mine inheritance,' wrote the northern magnate to the Privy Council in

London. Before enjoying the fruits of the wreck, however, the earl would have to retrieve them from the tenants and countrymen who first discovered them on the beach.

Responding to Northumberland's information, Queen Elizabeth, through Secretary Cecil, advised him on 28 March that the Scottish queen expected 'delivery... of a sum of crowns and ducats which she affirmeth were of late by wreck of a ship brought to land, and so come to your possession; to the which she pretendeth a title, for that she sayeth the ship was coming toward her realm with some goods and money.' The letter instructed Northumberland 'not without our direction to write or answer anything to any foreign power' lest he complicate an already-awkward incident. He was to tell the Queen of Scots,

> in humble manner... that you have nothing but that which was found with an Englishman drowned, and... no person on his behalf does prove nor challenge any property therein. Therefore, by the laws of the realm, you hold the same as a just wreck, whereunto you have just title by inheritance, and therefore beseech her to be contented with this answer, being founded upon truth and justice.

This was the letter in which Elizabeth described Yaxley as 'an evil subject of ours'.[9]

The wreck of the *George* of Flushing brought profit to the Earl of Northumberland and his retainers, and reward to some residents of his coastline. Magnate power was maintained, though some of the wealth trickled down to ordinary inhabitants. Were it not for the amount of money involved, and the diplomatic sensitivity of its handling, the documentation would not have been so rich. The Queen of Scots, the Admiralty of England, Elizabeth I's Privy Council, and stakeholders on both sides of the border were still bruised from unresolved dealings over the wreck of the *Bonaventure*, and this new episode brought further complications.

Pevensey 1569 and 1575

A commission in Sussex in 1569, within the Admiralty jurisdiction of the Cinque Ports, asked the vital question, 'were there any man, dog, or any live thing saved?', when a ship carrying olive oil, olives, and 'berries called cushenella' wrecked on Pevensey beach. ('Cushenella' was the notary's version of cochineal, a valuable dyestuff derived from Mexican insects that looked like shrivelled currants when dried. The earliest reference to cochineal in the *Oxford English Dictionary* is 1582.) Depositions survive from seven witnesses, who agreed there were no survivors

[9] SP 52/12, fo. 42.

from the unnamed vessel.[10] No suggestion arises in either questions or answers that the recovery of this cargo was riotous or disorderly. Nothing was plundered, though some of the lading subsequently went amiss. The leading men of the community, the bailiff and jurats, seem to have worked with the Lord Warden's servants to supervise the salvage and to secure its distribution. The commission was mostly concerned to uphold the privileges of Lord Cobham, the Warden of the Cinque Ports, to adjudicate the claims of rival communities, and to ensure that findalls ended up in the proper 'custody and keeping'.

Collective efforts saved 120 'pockets' or pieces of oil, three containers of olives, and several puncheons or pockets of cochineal. Neither the weight nor the value of this haul is specified. Half (a moiety) was taken by the savers, and the other half was carried over the stone beach, above the high-water mark, to be reserved for the Lord Warden. Though guarded overnight by 'certain men of Hastings', this stash began to shrink, as various bags and vessels were carried away. Pilferage was endemic, in this case subsequent to the organized gathering of salvage from the foreshore.

Thomas Lake, one of Lord Cobham's servants, was heard to say that 'it were free for any man dwelling twenty miles hence to have that which he findeth, as freely as any of the town of Pevensey, that leave the one half to the Lord Warden, the other to them that shall so fortune to find it'. Other versions had him allow 'any Scot or stranger coming by chance... to enjoy the findalls and things saved'. These remarks, reported by most of the deponents, alarmed the Pevensey men, since the wreck was on their beach, but it stimulated competition from outsiders. Hastings men, as many as twenty strong, allegedly took a hundred pockets of 'cusshenells' from the ship. A Mr Fyldhedge, a local gentleman, had his men remove two chests of iron, apparently with impunity. Two yeomen of Willingdon, a few miles inland, also went off with oil and cochineal, though whether by purchase, theft, or favour is not clear. The commission was more restorative than punitive, so long as hierarchies of rank and authority were maintained.

Six years later officers of the Duchy of Lancaster examined residents of the duchy's manor at Pevensey about another wreck on the shingle beach near Pevensey.[11] Deponents answered interrogatories about their knowledge of certain goods taken up as wreck, the nature and value of the items they recovered, the names of the people involved, and the authority under which they acted. Twenty-five residents were mentioned by name. John Havell, a 40-year-old yeoman, acknowledged taking up quantities of oil, olives, and berries, 'but to what value the same was this examinant knoweth not'. Havell identified a dozen fellow wreckers among 'a great number of persons, both within the liberty and without,

[10] SP 12/49, fos 152–62. I am grateful to the staff of The National Archives for providing fresh photographs of these depositions.
[11] DL 4/17/57.

but the certain number... he cannot tell'. There were, however, 'a great many more, whose names this examinant now remembreth not'. He himself had a tun of oil (over 200 gallons) from some thirty tuns recovered, 'and sold the same for ten pounds, but what they were worth in value he knoweth not'. The wreckers acted, said Havell, 'according to the authority of their charters, and with others of the Cinque Ports'.

George Wateman, another yeoman, bailiff of the manor of Pevensey, aged 39, confirmed the taking-up of oils, olives, and bags of berries that 'came to the hands of the inhabitants of Pevensey', which were sold 'to the most advantage'. He named sixteen of the people involved. Wateman's own share of the proceeds included four pipes of oil (about 500 gallons), which he sold for £20. Both men signed their depositions with a mark, indicating deficiencies in literacy that by no mean undermined their status or authority. There is no suggestion here of riotous or disorderly behaviour, but rather of a community once again diligently and profitably engaging in salvage from the sea.

Admiralty officials, however, were sceptical that the shoremen's behaviour was benign. A commission established in Sussex in March 1576, following the perishing of several more merchantmen, inquired into claims that 'the inhabitants of that country, and others thither repairing', instead of saving and reserving castaway goods for their rightful owners, as they 'ought in duty to have done, if they had showed their true diligence and care according as became them to do', did rather

> contrary wise and with a spoiling intent and mind... not only disorder themselves in the time of their saving, but since have made waste, spoil, and consuming of part of that which is not yet forthcoming, so as the goods extant and certified do amount but to a very small portion in respect of that which is come on land.[12]

The salvors' proceeds—£10 to John Havell, £20 to George Wateman, and varied sums to others—were substantial amounts at a time when £40 was a handsome year's income.

Bishopstone, 1578

On 24 September 1578 a twenty-ton crayer or flyboat, a small cargo vessel perhaps manned by pirates, was driven ashore by tempest of weather onto marshland near Bishopstone, some 20 miles west of Pevensey along the coast of Sussex. The Privy

[12] SP 12/107, fo. 212.

Council had news of this within the week, and appointed commissioners to investigate reports of embezzlement. There were no aggrieved owners in this case, no petitioning survivors, but the dues and entitlements of finders needed adjudication. Agents for the queen's manor of Bishopstone, next to Seaford, contested claims from the Earl of Surrey's manor of Meeching at Newhaven, both resisted demands from the Bishop of Chichester and the Warden of the Cinque Ports, and all had concerns about 'the disorderly access of the country'. The commissioners took depositions, and reported six weeks later on what was recovered, when, where, and by whom.[13]

Simon Oxeley, aged 40, a yeoman of Newhaven, recalled previous occasions when the men of Meeching waded into the sea to save pipes of oil, which were dragged to safety above the high-water mark. Mark Ockendon of Bishopstone, also a yeoman aged 40, knew 'by the common talk' that the land of the manor extended 'along the stone ridge of the sea to a bank on the west side of the new haven'. The ship came ashore about a furlong east from the haven, but Oxeley was not sure to which manor it belonged. John Lamb, aged 30, a yeoman of Bishopstone, thought 'a parcel of marsh land called Mabbsland [was] accounted to be my Lord of Surrey's land', but the part by the main sea was demesne land of Bishopstone. An ordinary dispute about boundaries and jurisdictions became caught up in an investigation of wrecking.

The men who landed from the ship may have been pirates and 'left the goods and boat there, and fled away'. Richard Penfold of Denton, aged 60, described the damaged vessel as 'a rover, as this examinant supposeth', and thought about fourteen men escaped ashore. The vessel contained about thirteen butts of sack, thirteen or fourteen hogsheads of Gascon claret, two pipes of white wine, and several chests of books. Several shoremen helped 'to stay the said ship upright, and to keep her from falling in the water... thinking that the owners would not have fled, but have come again for the saving of their goods'. Among them, the yeoman John Lamb, aged 33, 'stood by the ship to see her preserved for the queen... to answer the queen if it were due unto her, and they of Bishopstone the other half'. The wine attracted thirsty attention, but coast-dwellers also had an eye for the sails, cables, and anchor. Andrew Drane of Lewes offered forty marks for the abandoned longboat.

The initial report to the Council claimed that John Harris of Bishopstone 'hath conveyed [to his house] one butt of sack, a chest of books, and all the sails of the flyboat, refusing to make restitution thereof'. The commission allowed him to speak for himself. John Harris, yeoman, aged 28, acknowledged taking ten books and a quantity of sack from the wreck, but said he delivered them to the Earl of Surrey's man Sir John Pelham. He also saw his neighbour Richard Hills taking

[13] PC 2/12, fo. 259; East Sussex Record Office, SAS/A596, SAS/A757.

books, 'as many as he could bear', and 'charged him in the queen's name not to carry them away, because he supposed they were in the queen's manor'. Others taking books included a shoemaker of Seaford who made off with some in 'a pack as big as two men could well bear'. The books were not of great value, and were not identified by title, but were evidently worthy of comment. Thomas Harman, the bailiff of Lewes, aged 52, described some of the books in his custody, not by name but by size: 'nine books of a greater scantling, and twenty-five little books of a handbreadth'. Stephen Harris of Bishopstone, aged 40, also had books from the wreck, one of which he bought of a poor man for 2*s*.

The wreck occasioned considerable community discussion about rights and responsibilities. On the night that the ship came ashore the leading men of Meeching and Bishopstone agreed to take half the goods each, 'to be bound to other to keep it safe until it might be known who of right ought to have it'. The next day, however, Surrey's agent Pelham arrived with a Mr Cryer on behalf of Lord Buckhurst and ordered everything to be moved to Lewes.[14] Thomas Daniel, aged 60, the constable of Bishopstone, testified that he watched the goods all night, 'before he went home to take his rest, and before he came again all was gone'.

It was clear that this removal of the goods to Lewes was not uncontested but occasioned much argument and shouting. When the Earl of Surrey's servants attempted to take possession, Mark Ockenden of Bishopstone 'said they should not have it', whereupon Surrey's men called on the sergeant of the Admiralty to arrest him. Sergeant Swift was busy that morning, arresting or threatening to arrest men of both manors. He charged them half a crown each for arrest fees, and another eightpence for bond.

Lewes was a market town, and a seat of county government, so a suitable place to store or sell wrecked goods. Most were transported upriver by barge. Harman the bailiff noted that one of the butts of sack was not full, and was left at Bishopstone, while most of the wine was still in the custody of Pelham and Cryer. Sack, he reported, sold for £12 a tun (210 gallons), and claret at £6 a tun, so the salvaged haul was worth at least £100. A tun of Gascoyne wine and a butt of sack were sold to Felix Sterne of Lewes for £12, 'to pay the poor men that travailed in the saving of the goods'.

While the wine and other findings were being moved to Lewes, scavengers stayed busy at the beach. Thomas Nichols of Newhaven, aged 30, reported that Luke Griston's servants were at the ship, 'and knocked out certain bolts, and set away a windlass which is in Griston's keeping'. The ship fell to pieces on the night after the wreck, 'by reason of nine bolts which were knocked out by Luke Griston's men'. Constable Daniel testified that 'the bolts were stricken out the Friday or Saturday, by whom he knoweth not'. Mark Ockenden agreed that, once the bolts

[14] The Earl of Surrey was Philip Howard (1557–95), later Earl of Arundel. Lord Buckhurst was Thomas Sackville (1536–1608), later Earl of Dorset, who had designs on the Howard estate.

had been removed, 'all the strength of them holding the vessel together was gone, and so at the next flow [it] brake in pieces'.

The wreckers of Bishopstone earned meagre reward for their efforts. £12 were distributed among them, and a half-full butt of sack was theirs for the drinking. Stephen Harris gained an iron-bound chest, a fir chest, and a selection of books. John Harris had books and some wine. Richard Penfold acquired a basket of no value, and a few jars of oil that he was allowed to keep 'for the saving of them'. After the ship had broken up, he took 'a load and a half of wood thereof, little more worth than the travail to fetch it'. Thomas Allen, aged 60, of Newhaven, witnessed these events, 'but meddled not with any of the goods, nor cannot say anything thereof'. The community went about its practised business, as it would continue in years to come.

Goodwin Sands, 1585

On the Feast of Saints Simon and Jude, 28 October 1585, the 150-ton flyboat *Dolphin* of Flushing, laden with oils, Brazil wood, and textiles, grounded on the Goodwin Sands. At least seventeen witnesses testified to their role in the recovery of its goods.[15] The crew of the *Dolphin* escaped in their longboat and came safe to land in Kent. But their vessel remained on the sands and could therefore be considered abandoned. Responding to the emergency, or opportunity, at least six boats set out from Deal and nearby harbours, but whether to save the ship or strip her was a matter to be examined. One question, never fully resolved, was whether the *Dolphin* was doomed and stuck fast, or whether she might have floated with the tide and be made to sail again. Though several miles offshore, so seemingly within the Lord Admiral's maritime jurisdiction, the Goodwins were customarily considered to belong to the liberties or precincts of the Cinque Ports, under the governance of the Lord Warden. Witnesses appeared before the Warden's court in Dover Castle on 8 November to justify their behaviour. Eighteen men made depositions, citing the names of many more (see Figure 5).

Henry Hudson, a sailor of Deal, aged 49, was in one of those boats with six other men, and found four groups of savers already at work when they reached the *Dolphin*. John Coppyn's company from Ramsgate was busy taking down the topsails, while Edward Pascal's crew from Deal 'had the foresail and spritsail'. Hudson described how Pascal 'unreeved the main halyards', and 'George Rands had the mizzen sail', as the vessel was picked apart. Hudson's company gained possession of thirty pieces of Brazil wood, and fifteen or sixteen vessels of oil, as well as a supply of rope, which they stored ashore 'in a little house beside the sea

[15] SP 12/184, fos 26–39. The depositions were taken on 8 and 9 November, within two weeks of the incident.

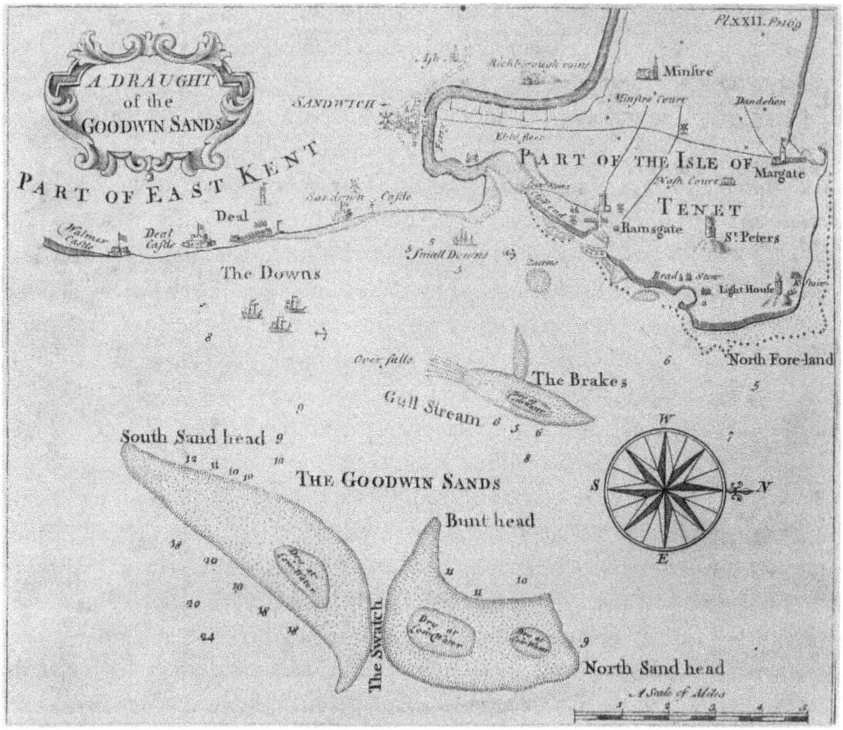

Figure 5. *A Draught of the Goodwin Sands*, c.1750. © Royal Museums Greenwich Images, G216:6/7.

side'. Hudson did not mention it himself, but others reported him making off with the mainsail in his boat.

John Ales of Deal, another sailor, aged about 50, declared that 'he went to save the goods in the ship, and when they came aboard and found no man in her, every man took that which they found, and fell to the spoil'. In his view, shared with several others, 'if the tackling and sails of the ship had not been cut away the ship might have been saved', for after two tides 'he did see her wend'. The systematic stripping of the sailing gear rendered the flyboat unviable and turned a stranding into a wreck.

The salvaging of the cargo went on for several days, through changes of tide, as the sands were exposed and flooded. The Deal men were joined by crews from Ramsgate, Broadstairs, Whitstable, and Walmer—often eight men to a boat—as loads of logwood, pipes of oil, and pieces of cloth were taken ashore, along with the ship's ordnance, provisions, and the personal possessions of the sailors. Most of these goods were lodged in coastal stores and cellars, to await inventory by proper authorities, though some were purloined and concealed. None of the witnesses admitted to hiding any items, though several reported concealment by others.

As the master and crew of the *Dolphin* watched their fortunes ebb away, a court of Admiralty under the civil lawyer Julius Caesar considered the circumstances of the mishap and responsibilities for its cost. A second set of depositions was required from the mariners, to supplement those of the Kentish wreckers.[16] The *Dolphin*, it transpired, had been carrying Spanish and Portuguese goods, which were under wartime embargo, and when the ship put into Plymouth to avoid a storm she was arrested. The Council ordered her to divert to London, and installed a pilot and seven English mariners to guide her there. Whether this pilot was competent, or had ignorantly driven into the Goodwins, was for the court to consider. The Dutch crew, by one account, so much resented being diverted that they would not share food with the English and sailed on 'in violent manner against the will, advice, and expression direction' of the pilot. The unhappiness on board was echoed in statements to the inquiry.

Also at issue was the value of the ship and cargo, for which there were divergent estimates. The Dutch owners put their loss at more than £3,000, while an English merchant declared the ship and tackle 'worth £400 sterling and not above'. Setting much of this aside, Judge Caesar declared that 'whatosever mischance happened thereby either to the said ship or merchandize must be borne by the owners thereof, as *casus fortuitus* which cannot be prevented'. The merchants were the losers, while the Deal men and their neighbours, and the droit collectors of the Cinque Ports, were the beneficiaries. Dozens more wrecks on the Goodwin Sands brought merchants and mariners to grief and distributed their goods across Kent from the Cinque Ports to Canterbury and London.[17]

Stokenham, 1601

The sea at Stokenham, Devon, had long ago cast up 'a ridge of chesil and gravel, called by some Long Sand', a miniature of the dangerous Chesil Beach in Dorset.[18] Interrogatories and depositions in a Star Chamber case in 1603 went into considerable detail about the number and fate of various bags recovered from a shipwreck on this coast two years earlier: of what size, colour, condition, and contents, and whether they were 'full and fast tied'. In dispute was whether one bag, in particular, contained French walnuts, which the finders consumed, or French gold, which they illicitly concealed. Deponents reported that Richard Philips and Hugh Kennaway of Stokenham had scavenged in the forepart of the wreck and came out with 'a great canvas bag containing a bushel and a half in measure', which Philips concealed under his jerkin. Philips at first denied taking any such

[16] SP 12/184, fos 142–8.

[17] SP 12/244, fos 97, 276; SP 12/249, fo. 233; SP 13/F, fo. 1; Hatfield House, Cecil Papers, vol. 21/84.

[18] Tristram Risdon, *The Chorographical Description or Survey of the County of Devon* (1818), 172–3.

bag, but suspicions arose when he took a bag to his neighbour's house in the night-time, asked him to hide it from his wife and family, and offered bribes to keep the matter quiet. Rumour spread that the bag contain bullion, and that the nuts were simply packing. Kennaway sought to disprove this before witnesses when he 'shook out of the bag many French nuts, and parted them amongst the company there'—look, no money! This did not entirely quell suspicion that something of value had been taken, especially when the suspect was able to lend £5 that he was not previously known to possess. Philips insisted he had nothing from the wreck but some nuts, 'which he consumed in his house'.[19]

The ship in question, its name and origin unknown, 'no living creature being then therein', had come ashore on the Long Sand near Torcross, within the parish and manor of Stokenham, on the queen's accession anniversary 17 November 1601. Parishioners and tenants had done their duty, and perhaps exceeded it, in salvaging its 'ordnance, ropes, cables, mast, and other apparel of shipping', as well as French wine, Spanish wool, walnuts, and silver bullion. Inquiries continued into January 1604.

Edward Ameridith, esquire (1532–1606), lord of the manor and a former member of parliament, charged two men of Stokenham—Richard Phillips and Hugh Kennaway—with 'the embezzling and conveying away of wreck', when they allegedly made off with two bags of money and then bribed neighbours to keep the matter quiet. He used Star Chamber to charge his adversaries with riot and unlawful assembly, and with carrying away and concealing material that rightly was Ameridith's to dispose of. Pursuing simultaneous suits in Chancery and the Court of Requests, to advance his interests and to thwart his enemies, Ameridith turned to the prerogative equity courts, he explained, because not knowing 'the certain sum, quantity, quality, and value of that which was in the said bags' that the alleged thieves had taken, he 'hath no remedy by the course of the common laws'.[20] The Quarter Sessions and Assizes, which proceeded by common law and required more specific indictments, could provide him no assistance.

Depositions by John Cole, Richard Dirrant, and Vincent Philips, all husbandmen of Stokenham, each aged 30, gave details about the bag in question. One thought it contained only nuts, another suspected gold and silver, while a third thought that bags had been switched. Margery Weeger, aged 48, the wife of a sailor, recalled Richard Phillips saying 'he was in great trouble with Mr Thomas Ameridith' when he asked her to hide a bag, but she never looked into it. Joan Evans, a maidservant, reported seeing such a bag in Kennaway's hay loft, and he threatened to beat her for coming there. Mary Gyffy, another sailor's wife, was present when Kennaway shook out the bag and its contents. Rumour was rife in all factions. Adversaries testified to their history of 'speech' with the lord of the

[19] STAC 8/46/12. [20] REQ 2/1687/28.

manor and 'the untruths, imperfections, and insufficiencies' of his bill of complaint against them.

Why should such an apparently trivial matter be dealt with in Star Chamber, rather than a manor court, or quietly resolved among neighbours? It seems that this was not only about nuts, or even money, but rather about the rights of manorial lords and the preservation of their status in the community. At issue were the principles and practice of recovery of goods from wrecked ships, the potential profit from such rights or 'droits', and the honour of the gentlemen involved. If the wreck really yielded bullion, half its value could have been shared between the landed proprietor and the crown. But, if substantial treasure had been at stake, not even Edward Ameridith, esquire, was likely to have escaped the predatory attention of the Admiralty. None of this legal posturing, and none of the community dissension it reveals, would be known without the precipitant occasion of a shipwreck.

Goodwin Sands, 1616

Before dawn on 4 January 1616, facing 'extremity of tempest and foul weather', three Dutch merchantmen 'were cast and wrecked upon the Goodwin Sands', the graveyard of hundreds of ships, 6–8 miles off the coast of Kent. The *Abraham* of Hoorn, the *Jonas* of Enkhuizen, and the *Peter* of Amsterdam carried 'merchandize and commodities of great value', which, depending on whose account is deemed credible, were 'utterly spoilt' by greedy predators, or saved 'by the travail and industry of divers persons inhabiting thereabouts'. Complaints and suspicions led to inquiries and commissions that kept agents for the Dutch merchants and the Cinque Ports busy for several months.[21]

The *Abraham* grounded before sunrise, but almost as soon as day dawned there were boats alongside from Deal, with offers of help. So many men swarmed aboard that the Flemish captain 'could not tell what to do, neither bear sway in his own ship'. The Deal men offered to save the cargo in exchange for one-third of its value. The mariners countered by offering 'what four indifferent men would allow them'. The haggling continued as the ship lay in danger, until agreement was marked by a handshake. The Deal men would carry the cargo ashore and submit later to arbitration. The masters of the other vessels made similar arrangements, committing their merchants to compound with the savers.

The crew of the *Jonas* asked some of the Deal boatmen to lay out an anchor, in the hope of winding the ship afloat again, but they refused, bent only on 'spoil'. By working their own anchor, and by casting cargo overboard to lighten the load, the

[21] SP 14/86, fos 3–5, 16, 35, 109, 113, 125, 198–200; SP 14/87, fos 10–10^{v}; SP 14/88, fos 208–10.

Flemings succeeded in dislodging their vessel, but it grounded again on the sands 'in danger of perishing'. Still hoping to save the ship, they cut the main mast, and heaved it overboard, to no avail. This mast, said to be worth £40, with sails and tackling still attached, came ashore at St Margaret's weir, near the white cliffs of Dover, and was cut into pieces by local inhabitants.

While these efforts were in train, each ship was swamped by boatloads of opportunists, offering terms for salvage. Amid the confusion there was no telling what went where or to whom. The Deal men helped themselves to the ships' light ordnance and muskets and offloaded bales of cargo. By Dutch accounts, these rescuers 'pretended to go to save goods, but went to spoil, and cut the merchants' goods most disorderly'. While offering assistance, they did 'cut and break open the merchants' goods . . . to make their prey upon it'.

Within weeks of the incident the Dutch ambassador in London demanded that the goods should be kept safe, so that they be not 'embezzled and purloined away'. Lord Zouch, the Warden of the Cinque Ports, who was also a Privy Councillor, authorized a commission to assuage the merchants, but also to ensure that his own droits were not stinted.

Presentments at an Admiralty court of the Cinque Ports at Dover in March 1616 cited Thomas Stone of Sandwich, mariner, and others of his company 'for striking, beating, and evil entreating of a certain Fleming that had lost his ship on the Goodwin Sands' the previous January. They charged Daniel Brown of Sandwich, Andrew Rand of Deal, John Gillow of Walmer, and others with taking up wrecked goods, 'whereof my lord hath not his part'. Their offence was against the Warden, not the unfortunate Dutch. The savers had allegedly taken as 'pillage' certain parcels of cloves, pepper, cloth, linen, silk, fustian, kersey, skins, and other merchandize that they 'detained and converted to their own use'. Local grocers and dealers bought sacks of spices and hundreds of yards of cloth 'which were parcel of the goods of the aforesaid Flemings'.

The depositions of the shore-dwellers tell a story of enterprise and duty rather than depredation. John and Andrew Rand, fishermen of Deal, presented themselves as salvors, not plunderers, who had courageously assisted mariners in trouble. 'Seeing the ship in such peril', they said, they 'went aboard her, and there abode a whole day and a night'. Their only concern was to help to move the *Jonas* into deeper water, and to get her ready to sail again, as if that task was beyond the Dutch seamen. The next night, however, the storm blew up again, so they 'forsook' the ship to save their lives. 'The weather being extreme, the seas in a rage, the night dark, and having neither light, compass, nor lead, and all hope now in despair', they were lucky to get into Broadstairs. Rather than being punished for taking goods from the wreck, they wanted 'contentment' for their labour, for 'otherwise men will not hereafter adventure to save either ship or goods, but only, as many do, wait upon the wrack and spoil of the merchant'. Whether these remarks were ingenuous may be judged by the information that the deponent

Andrew Rand took twenty-seven pieces of linen from the *Jonas*—tablecloths, diaper napkins, and towels—'of which but twenty he redelivered, and seven he embezzled and retained'. Some would argue that seven out of twenty-seven was a reasonable reward for hazardous salvage.

While this drama was unfolding, yet another ship, the *Phenix* of Dover, was cast away on the Goodwin Sands, to the grief of its owners and to the profit of the Warden of the Cinque Ports.[22] Laden at Middelburg in the Netherlands for a voyage to Drogheda, Ireland, the *Phenix* struck ground 'through the negligence of the master', according to one of the merchants, though the master himself blamed 'foul weather'. The crew escaped to safety and sought assistance from the accomplished salvagers of Kent. But by the time they returned to the sandbank, the ship had already been seized by officers of the Cinque Ports, who found it floating some 4 miles off shore. There followed a legal tussle, which lasted from March to May, to determine whether it was 'a wreck or not', and who had title to its goods.

The Drogheda merchant John Blackney made a list of the lading of the *Phenix*, which came into the custody of the Cinque Ports:

> 20 butts of sack, 26 sacks of hops, 5 bales of madder, 64 firkins of archell [a purple dye-stuff], 3 barrels of white starch, 3 bales of aniseed, one barrel of sugar, 5 puncheons of alum, one chest of pins and certain iron wares, 2 firkins of indico, one chest with some apparel and two pieces of black serge, and other commodities therein, amounting in all to the value of £800 or thereabout.

It was as if a well-stocked grocery had emptied on shore.

Resolution was complicated by the competing jurisdictional claims of the Admiralty and the Cinque Ports, and by tension between the Irish merchants and the English sailing master Robert Fleming, whom they blamed for the mishap. The voices of the salvors are missing from this case, because her cargo was brought ashore by officers of the Cinque Ports, but it generated another set of depositions from ancient mariners of Kent aged 63 to 90, who disputed the Lord High Admiral's claim to wrecks on the Goodwin Sands.

Seaford, 1633

The liberty of Seaford, Sussex, lay at the edge of the jurisdiction of the Cinque Ports, west of the chalk cliffs of Beachy Head, along a dangerous and much-travelled coast. Weather and tides brought streams of wreckage to Seaford's shores, generating disputes among rival claimants. News of a ship driven ashore

[22] SP 14/87, fos 8–19, 106–8; SP 63/234, fos 34, 43.

there in January 1633 reached hundreds of countrymen within hours of the incident.[23] The shepherd John Baker (who made a mark to his deposition, indicating illiteracy) heard about it just before sunset, so 'he put his sheep in fold, and went down to the ship all alone, but at his coming he found the country already come in'. Baker could not identify anybody in the dark, except for Richard Smith, 'whom he knows [more] easily by his voice than by sight'. John Chambers of Seaford (who marked his statement) also went to the ship, 'where he found a hundred men as he conceiveth', including five named neighbours, 'all which he saw taking the main sail from the yard'. Amidst the confusion Chambers saw John Taylor 'beating and striking sundry men, and abusing them and calling out of their names, and scolding at them'. Taylor (apparently the droit gatherer for the liberty) even stuck at him 'with a cudgel, like to fell him, and the next day he saw him strike Mr Chowne, a justice of peace's son, for offering to come into the ship'.

These depositions provided evidence in a suit involving the Warden of the Cinque Ports, the mayor of Hastings, the people of the liberty, and claimants from the wreck. Seaford had originally been a 'limb' of Hastings, but after the reign of Henry VIII its residents asserted 'absolute authority within their own jurisdiction, by their particular charter, and no ways subject to any command' of Hastings. John Baker's visit to the beach ensnared him in complications that he could not have imagined.

The most memorable booty from this unnamed ship in 1633 was a scatter of aristocratic clothing. The attention given to these garments suggests that were possessions of a privileged passenger. Baker made off with

> a scarlet or red cloak lined with stuff like velvet and of a red colour, also a pair of knee tops of cloth lined with red taffeta, also one silk garter, also a piece of cloth lined with black taffeta and fringed with black silk being about a yard square, but for what use he knoweth not, and one glove wrought with silver.

John Chambers did better, taking possession of 'a black velvet doublet, all slashed down the back, and also a fine shirt with three falling bands, with picked laces wrapped in it'. The apprentice John Warren also took a black cloak, a doublet, and breeches from the ship. These were exotic items, not everyday garments, though by no means a full wardrobe. Two weeks later, hearing that these goods were inquired after, and perhaps anticipating reward, the finders turned them in to the house of Mr Hudson, a local gentleman. John Baker found there 'a Frenchman that claimed them, who gave him six shillings for his pains in saving them' (a good sum for a shepherd earning sixpence a day).

The 'Frenchman' turned out to be a M. De la Martinay, a Francophone gentleman of Guernsey. He had appealed to the Lord Warden (Theophilus

[23] SP 16/231, fos 67, 166–7; SP 16/239, fos 30–3.

Howard, Earl of Suffolk), who in turn put pressure on the mayor of Hastings to recover the Guernseyman's goods. When the jurats of Seaford refused to cooperate, the mayor secured a warrant to compel them, identifying the bailiff of Seaford as the 'chiefest delinquent', and the jurat Mr Thomas Elphick as source of 'obstacles' and 'miscarriages'. (Elphick was notorious for his harvest and hoarding of shipwrecked goods, on one occasion having seven pipes of sack in his house, and on another secreting pipes and casks of wines, anchors, cables, and pieces of shipwrecked timber that ought to have been declared.[24]) On this occasion officials demanded restitution of 'all goods and writings', as well as De la Martinay's finery, that came from the distressed ship.

The Essex Sands, 1634

The English merchantman *Hopewell* of London, one of dozens of vessels given that optimistic name, endured a perilous homeward voyage from Russia's White Sea, only to perish on the coast of Essex in December 1634. Months of misery and misfortune ended in wreckage and recrimination. Mariners and investors faced ruin, as local scavengers took possession of their ship's furnishings and cargo. Examinations and commissions of inquiry over the next six months allowed seamen and shore-dwellers to tell their stories. Some witnesses appeared in London, while others were heard locally in Colchester under the authority of the vice admiral of Essex and his deputies.[25] Because the ship came to grief on an offshore sandbank, rather than the land of any manorial lord or proprietor, the Admiralty claimed clear marine jurisdiction.

The *Hopewell* left London in June 1634 with a cargo of codfish and oatmeal, bound for the Muscovy Company's outpost at Archangel, with Thomas Hart as master, and William Wilkinson and John Waites as mates. The passage required breasting the North Sea, then rounding the north cape of Norway, beyond the Arctic Circle, into the Barents Sea, where sailing conditions at the best of times could be unforgiving. In this first stage of the venture the *Hopewell* took on a full cargo of Russian tallow, cordage, fur, silk, hides, and 'other goods of good value' belonging to a consortium of London merchants. The lading included 'beaver wombs', which were the much-prized belly fur of the beasts.[26] Also embarked were

[24] SP 14/127, fo. 193; SP 14/176, fo. 83; Mark Antony Lower and William Durrant Cooper, 'Further Memorials of Seaford', *Sussex Archaeological Collections*, 17 (1865), 148–9, 159.

[25] SP 16/264, fos 60, 62; HCA 13/51, fos 74, 226, 311–38, 342–3, 350–8, 363^{v}–368^{v}, 385–6; HCA 13/52, fos 6^{v}–7, 11, 42^{v}–44, 145^{v}–149; HCA 13/55, fos 334^{v}–335^{v}, 471; HCA 23/11/213 (interrogatories). The vice admiral was Robert Rich, Earl of Essex.

[26] The owners were 'Richard Swift and company, James Frize, William Bladwell, Francis Ashe, Daniel Dobbins, Andrew Cogan, Richard Glover, Thomas Fowell, Jonathan Andrewes, and others', all well-known and well-connected London merchants: Maria Salomon Arel, *English Trade and Adventure to Russia in the Early Modern Era: The Muscovy Company, 1603–1649* (Lanham, 2019), 67–75.

a dozen English traders, seeking a safe journey home before the harsh Russian winter. Supplies for the voyage included three hogsheads of beef, two hogsheads of Russian beer, and quantities of bread and bacon, which may not have been enough for the crowded complement. Local complications delayed departure beyond the end of September.

Friction quickly emerged between the passengers and the crew, setting merchants against mariners. Seamen said that the vessel was overloaded and 'would carry no sail'. Lading had been privileged over victuals. Suspicion arose that the passengers had pilfered supplies, so the officers locked them below decks in the gun room for twenty-four hours to teach them maritime discipline. Mutiny threatened, as the senior mate 'would give others of his company a blow or two with a rope's end... for neglecting the ship', and they in turn threatened 'to pistol Wilkinson and throw him overboard'.[27]

Social dissensions were only exacerbated by the torments of the northern seas. Sailors considered three to five weeks sufficient for a voyage from Archangel to London, but the *Hopewell* battled 'cross winds and tempestuous weather, and... kept at sea eleven weeks'. At last reaching English waters, battered and short of provisions, the crew sent a boat party ashore to Bamburgh Castle, Northumberland, for water, beer, and bread. A few of the passengers stayed there, glad to step on land. The mariners tried to bring the *Hopewell* into Newcastle, but storms and contrary winds tossed them 'over upon the coast of Holland'. The master Thomas Hart by this time was sick, and withdrew to his cabin, where a few days later he was found dead. The mate-cum-supercargo William Wilkinson assumed command, on the grounds that much of the lading was his responsibility. (Wilkinson was a veteran of Archangel voyages and may have been related to shipowners and investors. He had previously quarrelled with Hart, saying he would not be ruled by him.[28])

Renewed storms pushed the *Hopewell* further north, allowing its men no sense of distance or direction. After several dark days they grounded abruptly upon 'a great shoal upon the larboard bow', having no idea of their location, and facing the likelihood of death. After four days of effort, casting anchors, taking in sails, and cutting the main mast, they recovered sea room and were able to make way. The vessel was crippled but still seaworthy and was able to pick up a pilot from a Yarmouth ship it met along the way. As the storm abated, sailors discerned land, but 'could not tell what it was'. Wilkinson argued with the pilot Cranbrook whether to stand off or stand in, but their conversation was cut short when the ship struck ground on a sandbank. Each blamed the other for the disaster. According to the sailor Richard Bewton, Wilkinson told the pilot, 'he never knew such a man that would undertake a charge, and not know how to perform it'; to which Cranbrook responded, weeping, that he 'wished that he had never

[27] HCA 13/51, fo. 365, testimony of Paul Browne, steward aboard the *Hopewell*.
[28] HCA 23/11, nos 145, 213; HCA 13/49, fos 176–176r; HCA 13/51, fo. 74.

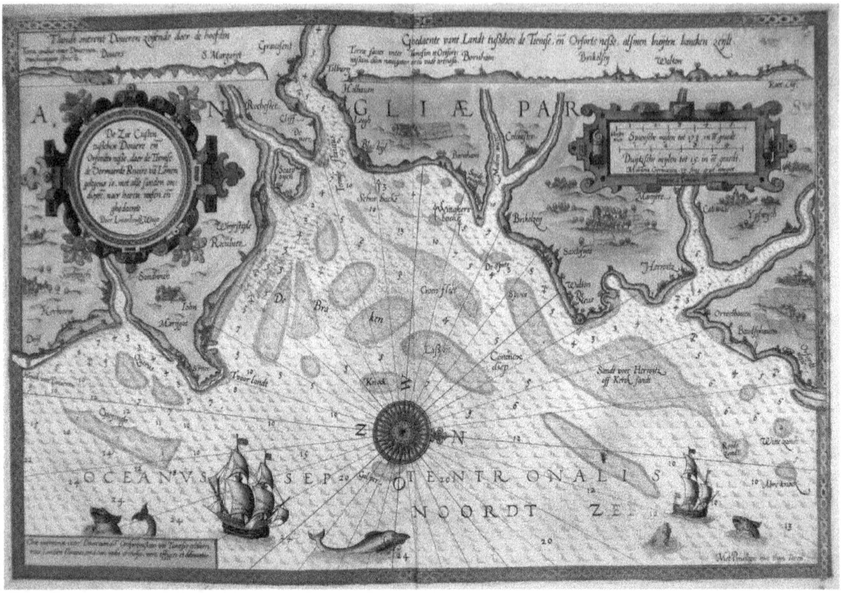

Figure 6. The Essex Sands, from *De Zee Custen tusschen Dovere en Orfordts Ness, daer de Teemse* (Antwerp, 1588). Wikimedia Commons.

come in the *Hopewell,* and had been a pilot in better ships, and was never mistaken before' (see Figure 6).

Stuck fast on a sandbank—the East Barrows near the Spits, within sight of the coast of Essex—the damaged vessel appeared doomed. The depth of water in the hold quickly doubled from eighteen to thirty-six inches. Efforts with pumps and anchors were of no avail, and the crew decided to abandon ship. The mariners readied the longboat and took the passengers aboard, but William Wilkinson locked himself in the master's cabin, saying 'he was minded to stay in his ship' and that 'he would live and die in her.' This was self-interest, not self-sacrifice. He knew that by law abandonment meant forfeiture, whereas the survival of a man, a dog, or a cat aboard a shipwrecked vessel allowed the owners a chance to reclaim their goods. Much would depend upon whether this mishap constituted 'true wreck'. A fight developed as sailors broke down Wilkinson's door and forced him at sword point into the safety of the boat. Witnesses disagreed whether this was a violent confrontation or a charade to protect Wilkinson from accusations of negligence.

Rowing towards land, the survivors hailed a collier, the *Rose* of Woodbridge, and Wilkinson tried to persuade its master to take him back to the ship to save his goods. By this time, however, 'a great fog' had descended, and they were unable to find the stricken vessel. Concluding that it must have sunk, and fearing further mishaps, the crew of the collier set the *Hopewell* men ashore near Bawdsey, Suffolk, at the mouth of the River Debden, and wished them well.

The survivors had escaped with little besides their apparel, perhaps with some coin in their pockets, but at least they were alive, on land, in their native country. Wilkinson made at once for Woodbridge, a few miles up river, where he tried to persuade local officials to help him retrieve his goods. These efforts were thwarted when news arrived that wreckers had already found the ship 'left and forsaken' and claimed it for themselves. Even as Wilkinson negotiated to hire a ketch to conduct salvage, he heard that 'hoys were aboard his ship', ransacking its cargo and fittings. Scavengers from Woodbridge to Wivenhoe were especially quick on the scene. Time was of the essence, for the ship was liable soon to break up.

The *Hopewell* was abandoned on Saturday, 21 December, the shortest day of the year. By the Sunday morning, according to James Major, a sailor of Wivenhoe, Essex, aged 26, there were at least four ketches in attendance, trying to unload the cargo. As he rowed alongside, Major heard the men on board say there was water in the hold, but he saw none. Some of the salvagers thought the ship 'strong and tight enough' to float on the tide but were unable to set it free. The ketch men were joined by 'divers people dwelling at Wivenhoe, Harwich, and other places near unto the place where the said ship was cast away', all busy stripping its furnishings and lading.

Among the salvagers was William Chase, a fisherman of Wivenhoe, aged 38, who told Admiralty examiners that he 'espied a ship lying with her stern towards the flood' on the East Barrows, around mid-afternoon on the Sunday before Christmas. (Perhaps he had spent the morning at church.) He passed a quarter of an hour poking about the wreck, which lay dry on the sand at low tide, and observed that 'all the water was gone from her'. Being of a suspicious mind, and familiar with the ways of the sea, Chase wondered why the *Hopewell* had been 'left and forsaken' in 'fair and calm weather'. In his opinion, 'if... Wilkinson and company had stayed aboard the said ship until the next tide or flood came, they might... have got her off, by laying out an anchor, for that the said ship must needs have floated there at the next tide'. Even without human effort, it seemed to him that the ship had already floated to another place on the sands, perhaps a distance of one and a half miles. The opinion bruited at Wivenhoe, said Chase, was that Wilkinson 'had made his booty or purchase out of the said ship, and therefore had no more care for the preservation of the merchants' goods', in direct contradiction of the story that Wilkinson told.

Witnesses said that the *Hopewell* was potentially salvageable on the Sunday, and the goods on board were dry. By Monday, however, the ship was 'staved' and waterlogged, beyond saving. It was not clear whether the waves or the wreckers were responsible for this deterioration. It was sometimes said that 'the barbarous country people' took axes to the sides of disabled ships, to access their cargo, but no such accusation was made in this case.

William Chase came home to Wivenhoe that Monday night, laden with materials from the wreck, and found William Wilkinson 'looking for goods that were saved'. A watchman was set to guard Chase's ketch, to see that nothing was embezzled, 'but by whose procurement he knows not'. The cargo was later moved to a warehouse controlled by local gentlemen, with Wilkinson paying close attention. Other boatmen gave similar accounts. Wilkinson was said to have urged his company to monitor goods brought ashore, 'but none of them would go with him'.

Another of the salvors was the young sailor Daniel Dudson, who worked in the company of Robert Todd, alias Dodd of East Donyland, to remove bundles of red leather from the *Hopewell* to a storehouse across the river Colne from Wivenhoe. Their haul included tallow, hides, cloth, 'and some other goods', though much 'was spoiled with salt water'. Dudson considered Todd, 'a very honest and just man', who 'did not take the foresaid goods out of the said ship on purpose to steal, embezzle or conceal the same, and so convert then to his own use', but only to hold them until 'the owners and lawful proprietors' made claim.[29] Other salvors gave similar assurances, perhaps believing them to be true.

Representatives of the owners came up from London, and one of them, the merchant Richard Swift, advised Admiralty officials that the goods from the *Hopewell* were 'much dampnified by salt water, and are very perishable, and will suddenly decay unless there be some speedy course taken for the sale and preservation thereof'. Much of the Russian cargo had already disappeared into the commercial hinterland of coastal Essex and Suffolk, while Chase and other salvors sought reward for the items they had recovered. The Muscovy merchants may have had to pay for items that they claimed they already owned. Russian commodities found buyers in an inland arc from Maldon to Harwich, where even the mayor refused cooperation with commissioners because he had wrecked goods in his store.

Pursuing inquiry, in hope of restitution, the investors alleged that 'divers parcels of the goods and lading belonging to the said ship are embezzled and detained by sundry persons, and carried away into towns corporate and jurisdictions which pretend to be exempt from the Admiralty, as the Cinque Ports, Harwich, Colchester, Maldon, the Soken', and other places in Essex, Kent, and Suffolk. They obtained warrants of assistance, authorizing officials 'to inquire and search for, to seize and take into custody... any part of the aforesaid goods, merchandizes, lading or furniture belonging to the said ship... for the use of his majesty or the proprietors to whom it shall appertain'.[30] Witnesses from the ship and the shore had their say about the wreck and its goods. The commissioners, following civil-law procedures, sought to resolve the competing claims of the finders and salvors, merchants and mariners, while Admiralty officials secured

[29] HCA 13/55, fos 334^{v}–335^{v}.

[30] SP 16/264, fos 62, 127^{v}. Proceedings in the suit of Swift *contra* Wilkinson began in the High Court of Admiralty on 28 December 1634; the Essex commission was authorized on 5 May 1635.

shares for themselves and the crown. Recriminations and legal processes went on for five more years, as merchants attempted to retrieve lost value and reconcile their accounts.

Sidestrand, 1636

A long-running dispute over rights to wreck in north Norfolk embroiled the lord of the manor of Sidestrand, his neighbours the Bacons of Stiffkey, and stewards of the Duchy of Lancaster.[31] Sworn at Cromer in September 1636, Christopher Parr, gentleman of Salthouse, aged 70 'or thereabout', recalled the gathering of goods from shipwrecks in the area forty to fifty years earlier. Richard Carr, husbandman of Sidestrand, aged 64, recalled certain material arriving as wreck 'twenty-five years since past', which was 'claimed by the then lord of that manor' but was taken away for the duchy by a deputy of Sir Nathaniel Bacon. Stored with local knowledge, the deponents in this matter had an average age of 59.

Nicholas Beeter, aged 50, yeoman of Paston, Thomas Cutlocke, aged 60, yeoman of North Repps, and Richard Carrr, aged 64, husbandman of Sidestrand, recalled the recovery about 1634 of a certain chest, more than a yard long, that was so heavy that men with horses could scarce drag it up the beach. Thomas Doods, the proprietor of Sidestrand, allegedly 'swore a great oath that never any rogue... should know what was therein, and then causing such as were present to stand further off, he took the goods out of the same chest, and put them up in sacks, and so casting them upon horseback, carried the same himself to his own house', along with other items that he claimed on privilege. The chest was said to contain clothing, jewels, and various personal effects, 'spoiled and rotted' by seawater, but valued at £2–£3. Whether this was true depended on hearsay; and whether Doods was entitled to his harvest depended on resolution of his suits with the duchy.

Thomas Doods gave evidence himself in 1636 about wreckage on the seabanks of his manor. He recited a record of very small gains—pieces of planks and broken timber worth no more than 6*s*., old broken half barrels worth 1*s*. each, and other miscellaneous items of meagre value. On one occasion he bought thirteen deal spars from a man whose name he could not remember, on another he bought ship's timbers for 15*s*. from the owners on the beach. Doods claimed to be scrupulous in determining whether items that came to him were 'wreck' and utterly denied 'collecting and gathering of any wrecks in any secret and private manner, or any plots or practices concerning the same'. Suspicions that he was lying remained unproven. Depositions on Dood's behalf, taken at North

[31] SP 16/290, fos 44–64; SP 16/331, fos 131–61; SP 16/352, fos 115–56; SP 16/355, fos 138–41; Christobel M. Hoare (ed.), *Records of a Norfolk Village, Being Notes on the History of the Parish of Sidestrand* (Bedford, 1914), 29–32, 37–8 where the commission is misdated to 1626.

Walsham the following spring, shed no light on recent shipwrecks, but reasserted the customary manorial privileges of Sidestrand. The Duchy of Lancaster steward Sir John Heydon alleged that Doods did 'disclaim all pretence of right for ever... to the profits and wrecks of sea in Sidestrand', an assertion that Doods denied. The contenders were notables and gentlemen, with humbler neighbours in supporting roles.

Seaford, 1637

The wreck-prone beach of Seaford featured in dozens of contested episodes in the 1630s. Local tradesmen and workmen were accustomed to saving mariners and handling wrecked goods. The lords of the Admiralty, the Wardens of the Cinque Port, local manorial proprietors, and agents for the shippers competed for control of the salvage. Some of the records produced in the course of their inquiries are remarkable for their detail, vitality, and verisimilitude.

John Tillinghast, the rector of Tarring Neville, Sussex, had witnessed the recovery of wreckage near Seaford in 1636 and expressed his displeasure in a printed sermon on the theme of the shipwreck of St Paul. He railed against 'the uncivil carriage and evil behaviour of our neighbours' and reminded his maritime congregation that they, or many of them, shared the same profession with 'those that have perished in these heavy times'. Tillinghast preached charity, against barbarism, and urged his auditors to offer 'kindness to distressed strangers'. It is not sure whether they needed to listen.[32]

On 12 July 1637 yet another rich ship came ashore at Seaford and was immediately attended by a crowd. One of the first reports to reach the Admiralty came express from their agent Thomas Paynter of Shoreham, who had the news from a Dover man that night, and rode to Seaford next morning.[33] The ship appeared 'by all likelihood to be of Hamburg of about 300 tons, which it seems came out of the Straits, and hath met with some enemy'. Pirates, if such they were, had pillaged their prize and 'cut two great holes in the sides of the ship to sink her. But being laden in the hold with oils, it bore the ship and the south winds put her ashore.' No one remained alive, but 'there was a dead man found aboard which showed his head to be shot off, and by him it appeared the ship hath drove long at sea, for he is all putrefied'. The absence of survivors removed all doubts that this was legitimately a 'wreck'.

The mystery vessel

> first grounded far off upon a low water, and Seaford boats went aboard, and brought ashore three bales of raw silk and some remnants of silk grograms. The

[32] John Tillinghast, *Saint Paul's Ship-Wrack in his Voyage to Rome* (1637), epistle dedicatory, 12, 18.
[33] SP 16/364, fo. 6.

> next high water and southeast wind brought the ship to the gravel, whereout is saved in the custody of those of Seaford about a hundred pieces of oils, some tuns, some pipes, and some hogsheads, of which I have particular note, and have seized it to his majesty's use.

Paynter advised the Admiralty that 'the silks and grograms are much sopped, and I fear almost spoiled', though he thought that a silkman might find remedy. The barrels of oil (presumably olive oil) had a mark to signify a merchant's ownership, but Paynter advised: 'I think my Lord Treasurer's warrant might be got to take the goods from them.' His only worry was that, if the salvage remained at Seaford, it would be embezzled.

The Earl of Nottingham, acting as Lord Admiral for the crown, immediately sent orders down to Sussex to secure the ship and goods, 'to the end the king may receive the benefit thereof which belongs to his majesty', though he recognized that 'my Lord Warden of the Cinque Ports' might also claim them.[34] The resulting suits and inquiries generated petitions and depositions that make the 1637 Seaford wreck one of the best documented of its era. Although there was the usual talk of 'pillage', the Seaford salvagers behaved, in their own lights, with exemplary effort and discipline.

Petitioning on behalf of their community on 16 July, the gentlemen Sackville Porter and Thomas Elphick of Seaford related how the vessel, 'so battered and torn that she was in continual danger of sinking', was driven ashore on the rocks of Seaford, 'and there beaten to pieces . . . yet by the great care and pains' of the Seaford men, 'with great peril and danger of many of their lives', they managed to save goods worth £2,000 'or thereabouts'. Now, they asked, 'according to former usage in like cases', for half the value of what they had saved. This was the custom of the Cinque Ports, they said, and, by allowing it, 'others may upon the like occasions be the better encouraged to employ their pains and venture their lives for the saving of such goods as shall be there driven ashore'.[35]

Forty-three men and one woman gave evidence before a commission at Seaford on 22 July about their role in recovering material from the wreck. At least a hundred individuals were named in these statements.[36] Deponents may have been on their best behaviour, in the presence of officials from Dover Castle, though they probably did not share everything they knew. The more they could show they had saved, the greater, perhaps, was their claim to reward. The more they confessed having concealed, and now delivered, the greater, perhaps, was their hope of forgiveness. Most had laboured mightily on the beach to move the lading into the custody of the droit gatherers or reputable gentlemen. The meagre pickings

[34] SP 16/364, fo. 4. [35] SP 16/364, fo. 14.

[36] SP 17/D/15. I am grateful to Christopher Whittick, Amanda Bevan, and the staff of The National Archives for making available photographs of material not included in State Papers Online.

they acknowledged taking for themselves—a piece of the ship, a cartload of wood, a few gallons of oil—contrasted with the hundreds of pounds worth of goods that they helped to recover.

John Hide of Seaford, a tailor aged 36, said that on Wednesday, 12 July, 'about an hour after sun rising, he being on the beach of Seaford, saw a ship in the wash of the shore about a furlong from the land'. He went out in a small boat with two other men and an apprentice, and boarded the ship, where they found 'no living creature'. The vessel was 'full of water, and the goods floating in her, only one broken deck in her, and part of her guns lay in carriages upon the said deck, and the other part lay in the ship, being beat off from their carriages'. Later in the morning the ship was 'driven to shore . . . and by the violence of the sea broke all to pieces' on Seaford beach. 'There appeared to be in her certain vessels of oil, two fardels of raw silk, and some small parcels of grogram.' Hide's associates, and others who followed him, confirmed what he said to be true, although William Bellingham said later that his wife gave Hide 'first notice of the wreck'.

Called again to testify, after other witnesses had spoken, John Hide admitted having 180 skeins of silk and 75 yards of grogram in his custody ('custody' being a more forgiving word than 'possession'). 'One of his maids saved some five gallons of oil' (worth almost 10*s*.), and he had 'another vessel about five gallons in his custody'. Although much of the salvage was in the keeping of the bailiff and gentlemen, various pieces were retained among the neighbours.

John Taylor, aged 42, the vigilant and officious droit gatherer of Seaford, made an early visit to the wreck. He took custody of some of the material that others had saved and turned some over to the bailiff. 'Mr Bailiff', he reported, still had seventeen pieces of eight that were found with clothes in a chest.

Adam Mersh, labourer, worked with a group of ten or more men to save

> thirteen of the largest vessels of oil, whereof eight of them were sent to Mr Elphick senior, as he thinketh, for that they were loaden in his cart, and the other five were carried to Mr Bailiff's house of Seaford, and one except was opened in the presence of Mr Sackville Porter and John Taylor the droit gatherer, wherein was found certain sailor's clothes of little value.

Rumour and observation spread news of findings and concealments.

Richard Dunton, labourer, in company with others, helped to roll 'six vessels of the largest sort oils . . . home to Mr Bailiff's house', and five more to Mr Elphick senior's house, but 'two being left upon the beach he knoweth not what became of'. The next day he helped to save more vessels, and two pieces of cable, 'which was carried to Mr Bailiff's house'. He also acknowledged 'that his wife did save about ten gallons of oil, which is at his house'. Several witnesses admitted to retaining small amount of oil, for domestic rather than commercial purposes. Among them the wife of labourer John Wycarsham 'saved about some eight gallons of oil', and 'he had a vessel rolled to his house, which was half drawn out in the night'.

Henry Payne, labourer, besides helping to move vessels of oil, helped to save a piece of grogram, which was now with Mr Bailiff, but 'how many yards it is he knoweth not'. Peter Glover, labourer, saw Matthew Thomas of Norton carry away oil 'in Mr Bailiff's name... but where he knoweth not'. The labourer Edward Gates reported Nicholas Seaman, Matthew Thomas, and Mr Sackville Porter carting oil away, but 'he knoweth not what became of' the rest, except he rolled one piece to the house of Lady Gratwick, who was patron of the moralizing cleric Tillinghast. Gates said that his wife had two gallons of oil, and he had taken a piece of rope which he sold for 2*s.* 6*d.*

John Jarvis, blacksmith, could account for all thirteen of the pieces of oil that he had saved; six were in Mr Porter's custody, one with Mr Elphick senior, two with Richard Bevis, two in Stephen Bean's custody, one in widow Payne's house, and one with Michael Beck.

The smith William Izack worked as hard as anyone saving oil and cloth and helped to move pieces to the custody of the older Mr Elphick. He was the only deponent to report violence, saying that John Hide and his apprentice tore a piece of grogram out of his arms, 'and that Thomas Hersall did cut and tear, and swore he would have some'. Izack also confessed to taking iron bolts from the ship, 'whereof he sold two for ten pence'.

The only woman to give evidence, Margaret Parry, the wife of the curate of Newhaven, also reported incidents of theft. Assisting in the salvage, 'she had in her hand one piece of silk grogram, and divers being like to defeat her', she sought assistance. She had saved six or seven yards of fabric but 'the residue was all taken from her by persons unknown'. If this was barbarity, it was of the mildest sort.

The gendered nature of these proceedings is inescapable. Wreck recovery was men's work, and so was accounting for it before commissions of inquiry. It involved hammers and hatchets, and haulage with ropes and carts. Yet several deponents mentioned the presence of their wives, who helped on the beach, and went home with modest amounts of cooking oil. Richard Gates's wife had only 'a pail of oil' in her custody, whereas William Bellingham's wife had 'five or six gallons'. She also had 'about half a pound of silk given her by one of the Hides, for that she gave them first notice of the wreck', starting the community scramble for the goods.

The depositions indicate that the men of Seaford and neighbouring Blatchington worked in small companies or 'teams' with neighbours and kinsmen to move materials off the beach. Their occupations reveal them as countrymen, mostly labourers, with a sprinkling of husbandmen, tailors, shoemakers, smiths, and a carpenter. Though this was a coastal community, none of those involved was identified as a sailor or fisherman. In this case, the bounty of the sea arrived on the land and went mostly into the custody of substantial householders. There is limited evidence of a trade in shipwrecked goods, akin to the later commerce of smuggling, though not on a large scale. The tailor John Hide had suspicious amounts of valuable fabric, while Richard Landaye told the commission that 'he heard William Budd say that he sold to a man of Hailsham silk which he bought of Thomas Presse'.

When the commission concluded, the Admiralty court of the Cinque Ports declared that, since 'no living creature escaped alive', everything from the wreck belonged to the Lord Warden. But, in order to allocate dues, and to see 'the savers thereof duly recompensed', an inventory would be made 'of all such oils, goods, merchandizes, with divers pieces of ordnance, anchors, and cables as were the 12th day of July past wrecked within the said liberty'. The declared haul included 69 tuns of oil worth £1,516 3*s.* 4*d.*, 197 yards of silk grogram worth £188 10*s.*, 607 bunches of silk 'much perished by the sea' worth £120, and various ship's furnishing worth £100. The record also showed that John Bean and Richard Elphick of Seaford each still had in their custody a tun of oil worth £22 and that other amounts were distributed around the community. The total value came very close to the £2,000 that the townsmen said they had saved, which was not surprising, since the appraisal was conducted by the petitioners themselves. However, instead of awarding the accustomed moiety, the court declared that the savers would receive only 'a fourth part of the value of the said goods', which still put £500 in their pockets.[37] Nobody knew how much had been embezzled, but the Elphicks and their gentle neighbours did especially well from this episode.

The Seaford drama was not over, for in the autumn details emerged about the identity and circumstances of the vessel heretofore referred to as 'the ship'. It turned out to be the *Rose* of Amsterdam, which had been trading in southern Italy, loading 'clear yellow and pure oil' from Gallipoli near Lecce and 'dry and well-conditioned' silk from Naples. Homebound towards Holland, the *Rose* was attacked near Portland by 'five ships of war of Dunkirk', and 'most of her men were slain'. Eight survivors took to their skiff, and eventually came ashore, so in their view their ship was no 'wreck'. Hearing of developments around Seaford, almost three months later, they hoped to reclaim their goods. One of the Dutch owners matched the marks that Thomas Paynter had copied from the lading. The lawyers would be kept deliciously busy.[38]

Littlehampton, 1654

'I seize upon all,' declared the steward of the Earl of Arundel after the *St Jacob* of Amsterdam ran aground near Littlehampton, Sussex, in October 1654. His

[37] SP 16/365, fos 17^{v}, 19, 27, 193, 195–7.
[38] SP 16/364, fo. 210; SP 16/368, fos 104–13; SP 16/369, fos 228–228^{v}.

intervention turned a mishap into disaster, according to depositions by members of the Dutch crew. The master and mariners of the *St Jacob* gave evidence before the High Court of Admiralty, which was copied and presented to Lord Protector Cromwell. Further testimony came from John Harris, aged 60, a mariner of Rye who tried to assist them.[39]

The *St Jacob* left Portugal on 13 September 1654 for its homeward voyage to the Netherlands. The lading, carefully listed in the depositions, consisted of 264 bales of sumac for the merchants and 22 more on the master's account, 500 rolls of tobacco, 25 chests of sugar, 18 elephant tusks, 5 bales of linen, 4 cases of confitures of sweetmeats, and a miscellany of items consigned by the crew. It was a rich cargo, all lost as 'plunder' and 'spoil' on the beach in Sussex.

While sailing up the Channel on 3 October, the *St Jacob* sprang 'a very great leak' that filled the ship with water, so that they were all 'in great distress and danger to be suddenly swallowed up by the sea'. So 'great and incurable' was the leak, so fast the inrush of water, that crewmen feared that 'every soul should be cast way'. To save themselves and their cargo, the mariners 'made all the sail they could, and did bring the said ship with the lading in her ashore'. They grounded near Littlehampton late at night and immediately sought assistance. An English merchant they met in the haven advised that it was 'too dark and late for getting help', so the master and mariners stayed aboard their ship until the morning. By dawn on 4 October they found 'many of the people and inhabitants of the coast came down to the said ship, endeavouring to plunder her', some trying to climb aboard. At this stage, according to the master, the intending wreckers 'took nothing, saving some lemons, oranges, and things of small consequence', as the Dutchmen held them at bay.

Everything changed with the arrival on the beach of 'a certain person who styled or qualified himself steward to the Earl of Arundel, and empowered to look after wrecks on that coast, as belonging to his lord'. The mariners were relieved to be dealing with someone in authority, and offered 'to pay him, and duty for salvage', even though, as they pointed out, their ship 'was voluntarily there put ashore by means of leaks', the captain and crew remained safe on board, and the cargo lay still in their 'possession and custody'. The master stood 'very respectfully ... with his hat in his hand ... beseeching that he would help', as he pleaded for assistance, while the crowd around the vessel continued to grow.

The English mariner John Harris, acting as intermediary, explained that in such circumstances 'the best anchor and cable were due to my lord of Arundel as groundage'. But the steward, identified as a Mr Howe, responded that 'the whole

[39] HCA 13/70, fos 635–8; HCA 13/72, fos 21^{v}–22; SP 84/161, fos 80–8. The deponents included Albert Lemmerman, merchant of Amsterdam, Arent Marytnsen, the late master of the *St Jacob*, and Henrik Mattysen, the bosun.

ship and lading are due to him, and therefore I seize upon all'. When the steward announced to the assembled crowd

> that she was a wreck, and therefore belonged to the Earl of Arundel, they all cried out that she rather belonged to them, and withal fell in great numbers, and with extraordinary violence aboard, and with all sorts of instruments broke open all the chests and bales, plundering all that was aboard, and afterwards they did cut the masts, and hewed all the ship in pieces, not suffering the master and company to save anything themselves.

All 'tackle, rigging, sails, yards, and all her appurtenances and all her lading and goods' were lost to 'plundering and rifling'. In Harris's account the crowd claimed that these spoils 'were due to them . . . and therewithal fell in a tumultuous furious manner aboard, and fell to pulling, cutting, and hacking, and wholly plundered, took, and carried away all the ship's lading'. One of the mariners testified that

> the coming and speeches of the said Mr Howe were and gave the occasion for the said people so to fall and commit the said spoil and outrage, and that if the said Howe had done his endeavour, and countenanced the master and company, and opposed the said violence, be believeth that same had not been committed, but the said ship and goods, or greater part thereof had been preserved.

In their appeal to the Lord Protector the Dutch owners complained of 'inhumane . . . spoils, depredations, offences, and injuries'. It was outrageous, they said, to treat 'distressed strangers in such a barbarous manner, against all dictates and rules not only of Christianity but humanity'. They, or their agents, employed the full vocabulary of denigration to make their case, though they were more temperate in depositions before the Admiralty. Unspoken, but worth considering, was how English mariners might be treated on Dutch ground if the tables were turned.

Local circumstances might explain how this particular shipwreck got out of hand. Social relations in general were stressed by the turmoil of the revolution, in which deference to rank was challenged. The Arundel estates were especially compromised, first by the absence of the royalist Lord Henry Howard, who had died in 1652, and then by the contested accession of his mentally deficient son Thomas. If the authority of the Arundel steward at Littlehampton was diminished, it may explain why the tenants cheered the wreck for themselves instead of for their lord. It is not clear whether Howe supervised the wrecking or simply allowed it to happen. The owners of the *St Jacob* appealed to the treaty earlier in 1654 that established 'love and friendship' following the recent Anglo-Dutch war, but coastal folk in Sussex may still have thought of the Hollanders as enemies. The complainants did not know 'the names of any of the persons that took away any of the goods', and we do not have the shore-dwellers' side of the story. Admiralty commissioners would do their best, alongside Anglo-Dutch diplomacy, to achieve reconciliation.

The North Sea, 1660

One of the most consequential maritime disasters of the seventeenth century lost much of the historic archive of Scotland to the depths of the North Sea in the winter of 1660. Following the battle of Dunbar in September 1650, when Oliver Cromwell's forces crushed the Scottish army, the state papers, public registers, and historical documents of the crown and kirk of Scotland were confiscated and transported to London. Most remained in the Tower throughout the Interregnum, until repatriation was arranged at the Restoration. In 1651 the archives had been brought south by carts and wagons, but in 1660 they were sent back by ship. One hundred and seven hogsheads, twelve chests, five trunks, and four barrels of papers were loaded aboard the royal frigate *Eagle* in December 1660 for delivery to Edinburgh. This was a huge cargo, of enormous cultural value, which deserved better handling.[40]

The *Eagle* got as far as Yarmouth, where the captain decided that his ship was unstable and that its load needed to be lightened. Anchored in Yarmouth roads, he pressed the merchant ship *Elizabeth* into service, and transferred eighty-five hogsheads of papers to its hold, where they were stacked three deep. This relading was done at sea, in stormy conditions, without the cooperation of the crew of the *Elizabeth*, who had planned a commercial voyage of their own. The two ships were supposed to sail in company, but the *Eagle* lagged behind, for causes unknown.

A few days north from Yarmouth, on 16 December 1660, the *Elizabeth* sprang a leak. Some said that the ship grazed a sandbank in shallow water off Winterton, which may have weakened its timbers. In normal circumstances crewmen could search for such a leak and had the means to stop it. In this case, however, the stacked hogsheads prevented access to the damaged planks. After forty-eight hours of pumping, in a worsening tempest, the crew found their ship awash, and 'scarce able to swim'. 'Finding no relief', a survivor reported, 'at three in the morning, having neither moon nor star, our ship sinking to the overmost orlop, we being nineteen persons were forced to take ourselves to the boat, and to the Lord's mercy'. The *Elizabeth* went down before dawn on 18 December, 18 miles

[40] SP 29/21, fo. 287; SP 29/23, fo. 14; SP 29/24, fo. 16; *The Acts of the Parliaments of Scotland*, vii. AD *MDCLXIMDCLXIX* (Edinburgh, 1820), 65–6; appendix, 2–3, 25–7; David Stevenson, 'The English and the Public Records of Scotland, 1650–1660', in David Stevenson, *Union, Revolution and Religion in 17th-Century Scotland* (Aldershot and Brookfield, VT, 1997), 156–68. I am grateful to Roger Mason for advice on this matter.

out in the North Sea, taking half the archives of Scotland with her. No identifiable wreckage was ever found.

Cold, wet, and dispirited, the crew reached the Scottish coast, 'to the admiration of all the beholders and fishermen'. They landed not far from Dunbar, where Cromwell's victory had started the process that had set the documents on their travels. There would be no wrecking, no salvage, since everything was sunk at sea. Coastal villagers had nothing to find, as only seamen and stories came ashore. The *Eagle* reached Leith two days later, with its share of the records, unaware of the fate of the rest.

A Scottish government inquiry in 1661 attributed the disaster, not to any 'misgovernment' of man, but to 'the violence and furiousness of the waves in so great a storm'. Major Fletcher, the commander of the *Eagle*, justified his transfer of records to the *Elizabeth* by saying that, had he not lightened the load, the frigate too would have perished. John Wemys, the master of the unfortunate merchantman, attributed the loss to the loading of the hogsheads, which prevented repair of the leak. The inquiry agreed that 'he had no hand therein, but the same fell out by accident incident to all who trade at sea'. Instead of bounty for scavengers, there was incalculable loss of Scotland's documentary heritage.

The Isles of Scilly, 1665

The naval administrator Samuel Pepys enjoyed 'a very good dinner' at Trinity House, London, on 15 February 1665, and heard 'an extraordinary discourse of the manner of the loss of the *Royal Oak,* coming home from Bantam, upon the rocks of Scilly; many passages therein being very extraordinary'. He made a note to himself, 'if I can, I will get it in writing'. The record that Pepys obtained was written by 'Mr Daniel', a junior officer of the Indiaman *Royal Oak*, who told a tale of distress and endurance.[41]

Homebound from the spice islands, after a 'fair and healthy' voyage, the crew judged themselves to be west of the Lizard, and 'forty leagues to the leeward of the Island of St Mary's', when the ship was caught in a terrible storm. (The charts were off by 10 miles, and the crew had no way to calculate longitude, even if they had sight of the sun.) After a night of thunder and lightning, blown back and forth, with no clear sense of location, they were before daybreak on 15 January fatefully 'enjoined with rocks'. They had grounded on the notorious Bishop and Clerk's pinnacles, which devoured ships by the dozen. Casting anchors and cutting masts

[41] *The Diary of Samuel Pepys*, ed. Robert Latham and William Matthews, 11 vols (Berkeley and Los Angeles, 1970–83), vi. 36; Bodleian Library, MS Rawlinson A 195, fos 180–180^{v}. A Commission of Inquiry had convened before the High Court of Admiralty on 9 February 1665. The Dutch ambassador reported this loss to the States General on 10 February.

proved no remedy, and there was no time to take to the boats. 'The wind being so violent cast our ship between two rocks, where she in a quarter of an hour was split in pieces.' All was not lost, however, Daniel reports, for

> some of us miraculously got upon the rocks. The day appearing, we found ourselves in a low rock, that could not preserve us from being washed away at high water, so we ventured upon parts of our ship, and got from the rock we first landed on to a higher rock, that praised be God did not flow but sheltered us from the raging waves. Here we sadly beheld one the others, most of us sorely cut and wounded with the sharpness of the rocks, not having meat, drink, or firing to comfort us, and many of us in a manner naked, because the better able to swim. We continued in this sad and lamentable condition from the 18th] in the morning till the 20th in the morning, in which time some of our pepper and several pieces of our ship drove on shore to Scilly, which signified to the inhabitants that there was some ship cast away about their islands. So they looked out, and descried our waft upon the rock where we were preserved. Upon sight thereof the worthy Major Edward Roscarrock, then chief in Scilly, hastened boats to us, which came and took us in, and landed at St Mary's on the 20th day about noon. So it were 52 hours upon the aforesaid rocks, where we endured so much cold that all our legs and hands were so swelled that we could but few of us stand. This is a true relation of our sad passage.

A minister might have told this story differently, stressing the power of prayer and providence, and the wonder-working munificence of God. Daniel's account is strictly professional, for the information of the Admiralty and his East India Company employers; fortitude and enterprise saved marine lives, and rescue came when the islanders became aware of the wreck. He had nothing to say about plunder or salvage, though other reports from the later Stuart period mention harvests of wreckage from Scilly's waters and beaches. One Restoration-era traveller observed that the rocks of the Scillies caused 'more shipwrecks than happen perhaps in all the other seas of Europe together'.[42] The island proprietors, Major Roscarrock's employers, customarily took 'a fifth part, over and above the king's part', of all wreck riches, while the islanders earned wages or reward for assisting in salvage. A Spanish survivor of another wreck there in 1667 complained 'of the cruelty of the islanders', who were more interested in 'the saving of the goods and money than his life'.[43] Daniel's report of January 1666 foreshadows the most notorious shipwreck in the Scillies a generation later, when

[42] 'The Travels of Cosmo III, Grand Duke of Tuscany, through England', in Alan Gibson and R. Pearse Chope (eds), *Early Tours in Devon and Cornwall* (Newton Abbot, 1967), 93.

[43] Bodleian Library, MS Jones 27*, fo. 17; SP 29/225, fo. 159. See also Richard Larn et al., *Cornish Shipwrecks*, iii. *The Isles of Scilly* (New York, 1971).

Sir Cloudesley Shovell's naval flotilla crashed on those same western rocks in October 1707 with the loss of 1,400 lives.[44]

Cakeham, 1676

Among records of wreck inquiry from the later seventeenth century, one set stands out concerning an unnamed French vessel that came to grief on the Sussex coast near Cakeham, West Wittering, in November 1676. The grounding led to the usual scramble for the fittings and lading, in this case commercial quantities of fish. Salvagers came from the villages adjoining Chichester haven, on both sides of the boundary with Hampshire, some with boats, others with horses and carts. Cakeham, the wreck site, was a manor of the Bishop of Chichester, who had *wreccum maris* within his jurisdiction, and the depositions of the vice admiralty court that examined this incident are filed with episcopal records. Fourteen men and one woman gave testimony, naming thirty-seven individuals.[45]

It is evident that some of the Frenchmen survived the mishap (though deponents used the word 'wreck'), for they were able to sell some of their belongings to the salvagers. The records reveal no barbarity or violence, only the usual waterside opportunism of gathering and dealing. Several of the deponents insisted that they had made 'full discharge and satisfaction' of their findings, by making payments to Edward Stanley, esquire, the droit collector for the bishop.

John Clark, gentleman of Westbourne, the salvager with the highest social status, 'went down with his boat to the wreck near Cakeham in Sussex several times, and brought away several parcels of fish for himself and others . . . and also brought away in his boat three sails, whereof one cost him five shillings and another cost him three shillings'. He also acquired some pins of oil, and 'one little gun', for which he paid 2*s.* 6*d.* Other light armaments retrieved from the wreck included a 'murdering' piece and three small muskets.

William Hale, mercer, and George Sherlock, yeoman, worked together to unload fish and also acquired a little boat belonging to the ship, for which they paid 20*s.* The yeoman James Farr went down to the wreck 'four or five times' and used some of the fish to pay a neighbour 'for the loan of his horse'. Richard Bolton, husbandman, 'was down twice with his boats at the wreck where the French vessels were run on shore', and took loads of fish, a hogshead of oil, and 'a little French book'. The oil, he told commissioners, was 'for my Lord Bartlett's use',

[44] James Herbert Cooke, *The Shipwreck of Sir Cloudesley Shovell, on the Scilly Island in 1707* (Society of Antiquaries, 1883); J. G. Pickwell, 'Improbable Legends Surrounding the Shipwreck of Sir Clowdisley Shovell', *Mariners Mirror*, 59 (1973), 221–3; Simon Harris, *Sir Cloudesley Shovell: Stuart Admiral* (Staplehurst, 2001), 333–58; Richard Larn (ed.), *'Poor England has lost so many men': The Loss of Queen Anne's Man o' War Association* (St Mary's, Isles of Scilly, 2006), 21–3.

[45] West Sussex Record Office, Ep/1/55/134.

which he was 'willing to deliver to the proprietor [of] the French vessel, so that he may have a lawful discharge for the same'. Theodore Styler, yeoman of West Thorney, swore he had never been at the wreck, or anywhere near Cakeham, but he nevertheless had oil and boards from the French ship, which he was willing to deliver on demand. The victualler William Sparks of West Wittering allegedly tried to bribe or intimidate the watchmen assigned to guard the wreck, saying that 'if they were gone he would give forty shillings', that 'he could make a great advantage to himself in getting and carrying away the fish and goods belonging to the French vessel, and also declaring to the watchmen that they were fools[if] they did not the like'.

Several deponents spoke of trade on the beach, as cargo and fittings from the ship changed hands. Carters moved wagonloads of Atlantic fish to inland markets, as far away as Arundel and Midhurst in Sussex, Winchester in Hampshire, Farnham in Surrey, and Salisbury in Wiltshire. A variety of beneficiaries gained from this wreck, not least the Bishop of Chichester.

*

These representative episodes illustrate some of the circumstances that brought maritime ventures to grief. They show how ships were lost and how ladings changed hands, along the interface of sea and shore. The *Abraham*, the *Jonas*, and the *Peter* of 1616 were among the many vessels that succumbed to 'extremity of tempest and foul weather'. Ill handling and misfortune added to the torments of the *Hopewell* in 1634. The *Rose* in 1637 was among dozens of ships disabled by pirates and privateers. Leaks forced the *St Jacob* ashore in 1654 and made the *Eagle* unseaworthy in 1660. Narratives like these stand in for scores of voyages that ended ill. Given the frequency of maritime mishaps, of which these are but a sample, the nightmare of 'a thousand fearful wracks' was no exaggeration.

As vignettes or micro-histories, though never completely adequate, these incidents reveal some of the opportunities and complexities that followed early modern shipwrecks. Merchants and mariners suffered—some fatally—while wreckers made free with their goods. Shore-dwellers who were first on the scene were quick to seize advantage and gathered what they could. Under cover of lawful authority, their plunder was recast as salvage. Though urgent, and sometimes chaotic, the harvest was neither barbarous nor savage. Hundreds of countryfolk earned money through the hire of their equipment or labour and shared in the distribution of moieties and rewards. Their names, lives, and activities entered the historical record, where they and their like are generally invisible. Men of property and power gained most, but ordinary people benefited too from the bounty of the sea.

Shoreline communities from Cornwall to Northumberland were mobilized in these moments of peril and opportunity. Further research might yield more about the topography, demography, and social structure of places such as Deal in Kent,

Stokenham in Devon, and the Sussex communities of Bishopstone, Pevensey, and Seaford. Shipwrecks augmented their economies, brought profit to privileged proprietors, and added piecemeal enrichment to households that managed with makeshifts. Participation in wreck recovery is revealed as a social process, embedded in the structures and cultures of each community. The records show yeomen and husbandmen, labourers and artisans, commoners of all sorts, and sometimes their wives and maids, alongside constables, bailiffs, lords of manors, and other notables. Animated by relationships of neighbourliness, authority, and law, wreck harvest brought 'God's gifts' as gain to the country and grief to toilers of the sea.

8
The Bounty of the *Golden Grape*

On the dark winter morning of Saturday, 11 December 1641, the Dutch merchantman *Golden Grape* was driven beyond her handling by 'violent and tempestuous winds and weather', and was wrecked on the south coast of England. Bound from Spain for Le Havre in France with a valuable cargo and a crew of twenty, the ship crashed ashore on Chesil Beach, Dorset, and began to break apart. Seven men drowned in the disaster, and one more crewman died later of his wounds, but twelve bruised mariners struggled ashore, along with unidentified Dutch passengers. As the ship disintegrated, according to the surviving master, everything was lost, 'save only such as were salved by some of the company of the said ship, and by other people of the country who by force and violence took and carried the same away'. It took almost four days for the shattered timbers to disappear. The subsequent inquiry into the salvage and looting of the *Golden Grape* yields one of the most detailed accounts of wreck recovery in early modern history. It exposes some of the micro-historical dramas played out on the shoreline, where communities rallied and competed, where deference met insubordination, and where salvage shaded into theft. More than three hundred depositions before a local Admiralty commission open a remarkable window into the behaviour of English coastal commoners in moments of crisis and opportunity.[1]

The *Golden Grape* was a 'fluyt', a three-masted cargo carrier of some 500 tons burden, built of Baltic timber, perhaps 120 feet long and 24 feet in the beam.[2] Some parish churches were no bigger. Owned by a syndicate based in Amsterdam that included English investors, the vessel had a cosmopolitan crew. This was a normal feature of seventeenth-century commercial shipping, where officers and sailors moved frequently between vessels. At the time of the shipwreck the master, bosun, bosun's mate, gunner, and some of the sailors were English. The rest of the crew were mostly Dutch, though at least one was described as an Irishman. There are hints that friction between the steersman Cornelius van Berkham and the Englishman Thomas Redwood who replaced him as sailing master contributed to the catastrophe, which Redwood attributed to 'extremity of foul weather'.

[1] HCA 13/58, fos 59, 62; HCA 13/244/149. The transcription in Selwyn Williams, *Treasure of the Golden Grape. 11th December 1641. A Chesil Beach Wreck* (Dorchester, 2012), 172–274, has been checked against the originals.

[2] Gerard. J. Tellis and Stav Rosenzweig, 'The *Fluyt* and the Building of the Dutch Empire', in Tellis and Rosenzweig, *How Transformative Innovations Shaped the Rise of Nations* (Cambridge, 2018), 157–76.

Shipwrecks and the Bounty of the Sea. David Cressy, Oxford University Press. © David Cressy 2022.
DOI: 10.1093/oso/9780192863393.003.0009

Like many ships voyaging for profit, the *Golden Grape* carried both declared and undeclared cargoes, as well as goods that mariners traded on their own account. On board, therefore, were formal ladings of freight that were inventoried by their owners, private chests and barrels belonging to individual seamen, and secretly stashed items that were shielded from official scrutiny.

The main cargo loaded at Cadiz included 1,253 barrels of Spanish raisins, 400 jars of olive oil, 16 butts of sherry sack, 3 pipes of red wine known as 'tent', 2 bags of red wool, and some lemons. But, after leaving the port, the *Golden Grape* hove to off the bar of Sanlucar de Barrameda, at the mouth of the Guadelquivar River, to take on a second and more secret cargo. Details are, not surprisingly, murky, but the extra lading was said to include, in addition to forty-three skeins of silk taffeta and two more bags of red wool, a bag containing five hundred gold pistoles, another bag of pistoles and pieces of eight, a peg of silver, a loaf of silver, and uncounted bags of silver plate and pieces of eight. (A Spanish pistole—two escudos or one doubloon—was worth approximately 18*s*. A piece of eight—eight reals or one silver dollar—was worth approximately 4½*s*. in the 1640s.) This undocumented hoard may have been associated with tax evasion, smuggling, or money-laundering. Though Spain and the Dutch Republic were still at war, this did not stop the flow of bullion to the Netherlands. No matter its source and purpose, it made the *Golden Grape* a treasure ship with a lading of great value—at least £10,000 by one estimate.[3] When the raisins, oils, wines, fabrics, and silver were scattered on the Dorset coast—along with the ship's fixtures and fittings and the clothes, shoes, tools, and possessions of the mariners—they became subject to the mercies of salvors and scavengers as well as the protocols of law.

English law provided that 'wreck of the sea'—all goods and furnishings cast fortuitously on English shores—belonged by prerogative to the crown. The extremity of shipwreck extinguished existing rights and created others, as the ownership of property was reassigned. English kings over many generations had granted 'liberty of wreck' to local lords, corporations, Admiralty officials, and other holders of rights or 'droits', so there could be multiple claimants to maritime booty. Enjoyment of the goods and profits of shipwreck depended in part upon the land and jurisdiction where cargo, tackle, and furnishings came ashore, and was frequently contested (see Chapter 3).

Further complications arose from provisions of medieval law, whereby the rights of surviving owners and shippers coexisted with those claiming droits to 'wreck of the sea'. If even one mariner stayed with a stricken ship, the continuity of ownership could be preserved. Provisions of the statute of Edward I were often repeated, that 'where a man, a dog, or a cat escape quick out the ship', neither that ship, nor anything on it, should be judged wreck, but 'the goods shall be saved and

[3] Williams, *Treasure of the Golden Grape*, 81.

kept' for a year and a day for the use of the original owners.[4] Local finders and salvors would be entitled to reward and compensation, but legal process privileged the claims of shipowners and their agents.

The survival of officers and crew meant that the *Golden Grape*, though cast away and broken up, was technically no 'wreck' to be claimed by royal or local droit holders. The Dutch merchants and their agents retained title to their property, and local magistrates were obliged to aid in its protection. Responsible officials were careful not to call the shattered vessel a 'wreck', because of the legal and financial connotations of that word. Rather they referred repeatedly to 'the ship called the *Golden Grape*', even when the ship was broken in pieces. This did not sit well with the hundreds of Dorset coastal dwellers who descended on the beach and, in Thomas Redwood's words, 'by force and violence took and carried away' whatever they could. Nor did it please local droit holders, such as the lords of the manors of Abbotsbury, Fleet, and Wyke Regis, the captain of Portland Castle, the burgesses of Weymouth and Melcombe Regis, and the bailiffs of the vice admiral of Dorset, all of whom claimed shares of wreck profits. Wreck rights on Chesil Beach formed a complicated mosaic, subject to negotiation, while customary and unofficial practices clashed with provisions of the law.

The Channel shores of Dorset were among the plunder coasts of early modern England. The 'long-drawn rattling' undertow of the area known as Deadman's Bay shattered many a vessel and drowned many a mariner. Even as the *Golden Grape* was breaking apart, another ship was seen in difficulty 'driving on shore'. The shelving banks and shifting pebbles of Chesil Beach, also known as Steepstone Beach, were partially separated from inland Dorset by the quieter waters of the narrow Fleet lagoon.[5] The church tower at Wyke Regis, the nearest village to the wreck site, was a navigational landmark in fair weather, and its churchyard a resting place for wreck victims.

Word spread quickly when a shipwreck seemed likely, and opportunists from nearby parishes would gather by the dozens—sometimes by the hundreds—to take possession of salvageable findings. As coastal inhabitants, they were accustomed to helping themselves to the bounty of the sea, while doing their duty to survivors. People of all social classes took part in the scramble, some bringing boats, carts, horses, and tools to secure their best advantage. Most understood their obligations to lawful claimants and expected reward as well as booty from participation in recovery.

[4] 3 Edward I (1275), *Statutes of the Realm*, i. 28.

[5] The usage 'Deadman's Bay' was coined or popularized by the novelist Thomas Hardy. For 'Steepstone Beach', see John Hutchins, *The History and Antiquities of the County of Dorset*, 2 vols (1774), i. 587. The imprint of Williams, *Treasure of the Golden Grape*, is 'Deadman's Bay Publishing'.

Commissioners and Deponents

Within a month of the casting-away of the *Golden Grape* the distressed merchants had secured a commission from the Admiralty for 'finding out to whose hands the goods or any other lading of the ship is come, and preserving of the same'. The commission would be led by the Dorset gentlemen John Arthur and the deputy vice admiral John Ellis, assisted by public notary Francis Cape. The Admiralty proctor David Budd advised Ellis to look to 'his lordship's honour, and the best benefit of the owners, and that must turn to your own best advantage'. Lord Francis Cottington, the courtier vice admiral for Dorset, instructed his deputy to 'be very diligent in examining and proceeding against those of the country who committed those spoils and robberies' and to be sure to 'inform yourself what part there doth belong unto the vice-admiral'. Cottington risked prejudicing the inquiry by declaring, uncalled for: 'I know nothing the whole world more barbarous than that custom of these coasters in the west of England.'[6] His own world had been turned upside down by recent upheavals in London that had forced King Charles to leave his capital.[7] Thus prepared, the commission held sessions of inquiry at Melcombe Regis between 10 January and 28 March 1642. Their task was to retrieve as much as possible of the missing material and to overawe the people who had taken it.

The commission sat for seven days in January, thirteen in February, and two in March, producing 118 folios of testimony from 343 witnesses, and naming a total of 547 individuals. This was a standard commission of inquiry and restitution, unusual only for the quality of its records. Following procedures of civil law, akin to those in ecclesiastical courts, the officials prepared interrogatories and recorded the names, occupations, and residences of deponents, and the testimony they offered. The depositions render, of course, what the clerks chose to record rather then what witnesses actually said, but they nonetheless tell compelling stories. They allow us to approach the wreck from at least three perspectives: from the point of view of the sailors who survived it, through the words of people who scavenged wreckage, and by reference to its subsequent disposition. Participants

6 Wiltshire and Swindon History Centre, 865/404, Budd to Ellis, 6 January 1642; Cottington to Ellis, 9 January 1642. Francis Cottington (1579–1652), Chancellor of the Exchequer, Lord Lieutenant of Dorset, and a member of Charles I's Board of the Admiralty, retired to Fonthill Gifford, Wiltshire, in the political crisis of 1641. John Ellis, an active litigator, served as his deputy vice admiral of Dorset in 1641. John Arthur had a higher local profile as a merchant, shipowner, and churchwarden of Melcombe Regis, becoming Customs collector, captain of Portland Castle, mayor of Weymouth, and vice admiral of Dorset in the 1640s and 1650s. Algernon Percy (1602–68), Earl of Northumberland, served as Lord High Admiral of England from 1638 to 1643.

7 David Cressy, *England on Edge: Crisis and Revolution, 1640–1642* (Oxford, 2006). There had been riots in London in December 1641 following the adoption of the Grand Remonstrance. King Charles and his family left the capital on 10 January after the failed attempt to arrest five members of parliament.

were therefore mobilized twice: first in handling wreck materials, and then in explaining their involvement.

The people named in the *Golden Grape* depositions formed a cross section of Dorset coastal society. They included eighty-four husbandmen and twenty-six yeomen representing farmers of the land, sixty-six sailors and fifty-nine fishermen representing toilers of the sea, plus thirty-two servants and nine labourers, one of them beatifically named Faithful Angel. Thirty-three of those examined were masons, mostly from the stoneworks of the Isle of Portland. The rest were a mixture of tradesmen and craftsmen: bakers, blacksmiths, carpenters, helliers, shoemakers, tailors, thatchers, weavers, and woollen-drapers, plus one each of a brewer, a butcher, a chandler, a joiner, a miller, a roper, a sawyer, a shipwright, and a tanner. These salvors were by no means an undisciplined rabble, but included men of established families, parish leaders, churchwardens, constables, and overseers of the poor.[8] Among figures of authority, just one gentleman, two clerics, a surgeon, and the porter of Portland Castle gave testimony, but other members of the elite were named in the statements of witnesses. Eleven of the deponents were women, and at least twenty-seven other women were mentioned in the handling, hiding, or exchanging of shipwrecked goods. The wreck scene also attracted children, including the son of the fisherman Robert Munday, and the daughter of the husbandman Hugh Browne, who each went home with small caches of raisins.

Most of the wreckers came from the villages of Abbotsbury, Langton Herring, Fleet, Chickerell, and Wyke Regis, adjacent to Chesil Beach, with assistance from men of Weymouth and parishes further inland. Linking the Admiralty records to Dorset Protestation returns shows that 93 per cent of the adult males of Chickerell participated in the wreck of the *Golden Grape*, 75 per cent of the men of Fleet and Langton Herring, 66 per cent of Wyke Regis, 39 per cent of Portisham, and 25 per cent of larger and more distant Abbotsbury.[9] Given the large assembly on the beach, with people coming and going by day and by night, it should not be surprising that some participants remained unidentified. The frequency with which deponents referred to others whose names they 'knoweth not' suggests both anonymity and neighbourliness within a large and fluid crowd.

Pieces of Eight

Shipwrecked sailors, if they were lucky to survive, were likely to be shocked and bedraggled. Wet, cold, and exhausted, they were vulnerable to exploitation and

[8] Deponents included the churchwardens, overseers, and constable of Abbotsbury; an overseer and churchwarden of Chickerell; a churchwarden of Fleet; both churchwardens and overseers of Langton Herring; a churchwarden and overseer of Portisham; an overseer and churchwarden of Portland; an overseer of Wyke Regis; and the constable of Melcombe Regis.

[9] *Dorset Protestation Returns Preserved in the House of Lords*, ed. Edward A. Fry and George S. Fry (1912); Williams, *Treasure of the Golden Grape*, 79–80.

needed wits and energies to cope with their sudden misfortune. Officers would be expected to make contact with local authorities, to protect their owners' interests, and to enlist local manpower for salvage. The crew would need shelter, clothing, food, and perhaps medical attention. Bodies would need to be buried. Foreign seamen would need repatriation. In telling their stories to the inquiry, several crewmen of the *Golden Grape* complained of the 'force and violence' of the 'multitudes' of 'country people living near' who made off with their goods and lading. But they also acknowledged the provision of hospitality and assistance with carriage and storage. Villagers lent horses, tended wounds, supplied labour, and liaised with local authorities. By the time of the inquiry most of the foreigners had left the area, but several English mariners remained to give evidence.

Thomas Redwood of Dover, 'master of the late ship called the *Golden Grape*', did his best to preserve and retrieve the assets in his charge. He managed to secure some of the guns and provisions of the ship and to arrange their safe storage. He enlisted the support of the constable of Weymouth to trace some of the money and plate taken from the ship, successfully gathering 200 pieces of eight from the ship's cook, and 50 more saved by the surgeon. He also acknowledged recovering 'a small gold chain', which he put around his neck. This was but a fragment of the wealth of the *Golden Grape*, but it provided the survivors with a float of liquidity for immediate expenses. Unfortunately, Redwood told the commissioners, 'his bills of loading of all the said goods, his letters of advice, and other letters were all lost at such time as the said ship was cast away', so accounts of its cargo relied on oral testimony. Several weeks would pass before authenticating documents could reach England from Spain or the Netherlands. The gold and silver treasure were never part of the official manifest, and it remained impossible to know how much was lost, embezzled, or purloined.

Cornelius van Berkham of Amsterdam, formerly master but reduced to master's mate of the *Golden Grape*, dutifully assisted in the salvage, and secured the peg of silver and a bag with 525 pieces of eight, which he entrusted to the local alehouse keeper Arthur Grey. Van Berkham also told the inquiry that soon after the ship had been cast away he saw the bosun's mate James Smyth gathering a hatful of gold pistoles, which he put into the pocket of the gunner Robert Coast, then returning aboard for more gold coins, 'which he kept to himself, saying that he would keep something for his own use'. Gunner Coast acknowledged that the bosun's mate had brought out 105 gold pistoles from the wreck, saying 'keep these, and we will divide them between us'.

Smyth himself claimed to have taken instruction from superior officers and to have assisted them in recovering the peg of silver and several bags of gold coins. He was only following instructions from van Berkham and Coast, he said, who told him 'to be silent and to say nothing'. He kept for himself sixteen pieces of eight, 'which he found loose in the steerage', and still had ten pieces of eight and seventeen gold pistoles at the time of the inquiry. The bosun Michael Hatherwick also deposed that he and three others shared 126 pieces of eight, and that he used his portion to pay for clothes and subsistence in Weymouth.

It is clear that those in the know—the crewmen of the *Golden Grape*—prioritized the recovery of the secret bullion over the more mundane cargo of raisins and oil and were somewhat evasive about it. None of the crew could report the value of the silver on board, nor tell to whom it was consigned. Asked repeatedly, they said they 'remembreth not', and denied knowing where most of the money went. Bags of heavy coins could be a lethal encumbrance to mariners scrambling to safety, but also a sore temptation. Crewmen were not averse to syphoning off some for themselves, in compensation for their losses. Few, it seems, had entirely empty pockets, though some reported that they had relinquished their bags of money to 'Mr Strode of Portland [the castle lieutenant], who hath since delivered the same to the vice-admiral', or they had turned them over on request to other lawful authorities. The mariner Richard Rich had to be re-examined a week after his initial testimony about £13 or £14 worth of pieces of eight that 'he had forgotten to express', having delivered them 'to Mary Paine a young woman living in Melcombe Regis to keep for him'. Mysterious amounts simply went missing, or were misappropriated by people on the shore.

Ordered by the master to retrieve money from the ship 'before she was all split', the crewman William Phillis (known as 'little Will') recalled dangerous foraging in the broken cabin of the *Golden Grape*. 'The ship breaking more and more, and this deponent in danger of his life', he put coins in the lining of his hat, and struggled ashore with bags too heavy to carry. 'Being weary and weak', and meeting one Owen Gibbons of Wyke Regis with his horse, he entrusted his load to the villager, 'entreating him to carry it thither for him, which the same Gibbons undertook to do; but to whose house there he carried the same this deponent knoweth not'.

Engaged in this same dangerous recovery, the ship's cook, Thomas Byrd, threw several bags of coins from the shattered vessel, but stopped when 'a countryman in a blue jerkin, whose name he knoweth not', went off with one of the bags. Byrd staggered ashore with two bags on his back, 'but not being able to carry both, he delivered one whole bag to an Irishman, one of the company, who carried the same away, and what he did with it this deponent knoweth not'. Byrd carried the remaining bag all the way to Weymouth, where he delivered two hundred pieces of eight to the master, keeping only for himself enough to buy 'clothes to wear, of which he stood in great want, and which cost him about three pounds'.

Competing with the crewmen, a few villagers with boats were bold enough to board the stricken vessel, attempting to strip it of valuables before it broke completely apart. Several obtained bags of money, which they held onto or hid until pressured by the inquiry. Nicholas Bussell, husbandman of Chickerell, 'being aboard the said ship did there take up and save one bag of Spanish coin, in which he doth conceive there are about two hundred pieces of eight, which he hath in his custody and is ready to deliver'. He asked exception for three pieces that he had used to buy some salvaged wool.

Coming on the scene on the day of the wreck, the fisherman James Gardiner of Wyke Regis gained access to the *Golden Grape*, 'which was then near broken to pieces', and helped himself to raisins. He also took home two rugs and a pillow, and two small Spanish coins, one a teston (worth sixpence), and the other half a piece of eight, which he held at the time of the inquiry. The fisherman Thomas Evans of Abbotsbury likewise gathered raisins and oils and found on the deck 'a little purse of money wherein he conceiveth there were about twenty pieces of foreign coin'. Before he could get it home, however, another gang, 'men of Wyke Regis', took it from him by force. All he had left were two testons, which he was content to turn over to the commissioners.

Yet another fisherman, Daniel Andrews of Wyke Regis, boarded the ship 'with an adze in hand', but 'a wave of the sea came and lighted so violently on his back and bruised him so much, so that he forthwith came away without taking or saving any of the goods or provisions'. All he could grab was 'a shirt, in the sleeve of which there were some letters, and a handkerchief, which he carried to his house and delivered to his wife'. Joan Andrews deposed that, not knowing what to do with these letters (and most likely being illiterate), she showed them to John Hodder of Weymouth, 'who having opened and perused the same redelivered them' to her.

The mason Francis Saveer of Portland was another who went on board the *Golden Grape* and managed to take up 'a short piece of silk that was wrapped about a piece of the ship, and eighteen rows of buttons (which he now delivereth to the vice admiral), two old coats, a jacket, an old shirt, a red waistcoat, and three or four bolts of iron which he hath at home in his custody'. The servant who accompanied him grabbed 'two old jerkins and some old shirts', which Saveer's wife 'threw away so soon as they were brought home'. He did not mention finding any money. The labourer Richard Stradling of Portland also boarded the ship with others 'whose names this deponent knoweth not' and carried out and hid 'certain quantities of wool... but in what place he refuseth to relate'.

Arthur Grey, the alehouse-keeper of Wyke Regis, was among the first to sight the *Golden Grape* as he stood on the beach and watched the seamen come ashore. Some of the survivors asked him 'to help them to some place of succour, for that they were very cold, wet, and faint', and Grey obliged by escorting them across the Fleet to his hostelry. It did not come amiss that they had with them the peg of silver and several bags of money, which they asked his help in carrying. The Dutch steersman carried money into and out of his house, and Grey claimed he 'saw the same no more'. He was agreeable, 'upon command', to deliver the peg of silver to the vice admiral's man, but reserved a hundred pieces of eight to pay for the 'diet, fire, and entertainment' of the company of the *Golden Grape*.

Grey's wife Susanna was also content to have visitors with apparent wealth and resources. There was much coming and going, and moving of bags and chests, during the four days that nine men of the *Golden Grape* lodged in Wyke Regis. Professing an ignorance that was common to so many Dorset witnesses, Susanna Grey alluded to transfers and exchanges of silver 'but by whom she knew not', to places she did not know. One of the crewmen brought in 'a great quantity of coin, about half a peck as she guesseth, which he took away with him again', she 'having no part thereof'. She was sure, however, 'to her best remembrance', that everything from the wreck that had passed through her house had been delivered to the vice admiral, except for 'an old brass kettle and a copper spoon or ladle', and the pieces of eight kept back as a reckoning. The honesty of the alehouse was impugned by at least one crewman, who said that 'Arthur Grey's wife of Wyke Regis, being privy to his hiding of 150 pieces of eight in her garden, had deceived him of 105 pieces thereof, for that when he came afterwards to look for his money there were left only five and forty pieces, the rest being taken away'. As in other rural communities, the alehouse was a social centre, a gathering place, and a site of financial transactions, an appropriate place to distribute goods and concoct stories.[10]

Further testimony to this movement of money came from Owen Gibbons, a sailor of Wyke Regis, who took his horse to aid in the recovery and saw one of the survivors hang 'a long double bag of coin' on the horse's neck. This was the silver that the mariner 'little Will' was too weak to carry. Gibbons believed that this load was added to a chest in the chamber of Arthur Grey's alehouse, 'where more bags of money had been put before'. For their pains, Gibbons and his partner received 'one piece of eight between them', though he also managed to pick up seven barrels of raisins 'and about a peck and a half of loose wet fruit which he also carried home with him'.

Ann Cowrage, a sailor's wife of Wyke Regis, one of many women active on the beach, said that she and a neighbour's servant took turns to carry home a heavy bag of money from the ship, but the last she saw of it was when Richard Gilbert of Portland 'took the said bag and money', promising 'satisfaction for salving the same'. All she had for her trouble was 'twelve pounds of wet raisins of the sun, which she carried home with her, and hath since spent'. Similarly vexed was Agnes Holmes, the wife of a mariner of Weymouth, who gave hospitality to the carpenter of the *Golden Grape* while he was 'very wet and in great distress', and saw her guest transfer pieces of eight from his pockets to a wooden dish before he left without paying for his diet and lodging. The Weymouth surgeon Walter Pyedwell also saw one of the crewmen 'take out of his breeches a bag of money which he did open and tell upon a table', some sixty pieces of eight in total, though what became of

[10] Peter Clark, *The English Alehouse: A Social History, 1200–1830* (1983); Mark Hailwood, *Alehouses and Good Fellowship in Early Modern England* (Woodbridge, 2014).

them 'he cannot say'. Others were more successful in recovering and keeping pieces of eight. The husbandman William Charles claimed to have taken only two pieces of eight from the ship, though another witness believed he had more.

The infusion of specie enlivened the south Dorset economy, at a time when coinage was scarce and most transactions relied on credit. The shortage of cash was especially acute in late 1641, amid the nation's commercial slump, so the windfall was most welcome.[11] The money from the wreck was used for rewards and inducements, as well as more orthodox purposes. For several months local villagers used pieces of eight in routine business, paying tailors' bills and victualling house dues in Spanish coin. John Swettnam, a woollen draper of Melcombe Regis, accepted payment in pieces of eight and offered 'English white money' in exchange for scavenged bullion. Catherine Langar, a widow of Weymouth, collected pieces of eight for the diet and attendance of crewmen who lay at her house. Susan Keat of Abbotsbury exchanged 'seven pieces of Spanish coin . . . for ten or eleven shillings'. Bits and pieces of foreign money still lay scattered on Chesil Beach a week after the wreck, as several deponents reported to the inquiry, and some may be there still.[12]

Men of Authority

Authority was late to appear at the *Golden Grape* wreck site, and local constables were unable to assert much sway. Nobody came forth as a justice of the peace, empowered to impose order. The clergy were studiously absent, though their churches may have been unusually empty on the Sunday after the ship came ashore. Tristram Knapton, rector of Chickerell, acknowledged having seven barrels of raisins and other items brought to his house by parishioners, but took no direct part in the plunder. John Haslewood, rector of Langton Herring, explicitly told the commissioners that 'he was not upon the beach at all after the ship *Golden Grape* was cast away', though his servant was there, and his wife paid 12*s.* for a barrel of raisins. No other minister was mentioned.

Several minor officials from Weymouth and Portland threw their weight about, claiming to be servants of the vice admiral (the distant Lord Francis Cottington and his deputy John Ellis). Their influence over the crowd was limited. John Pope of Weymouth, 'warning himself Mr Vice-admiral's man', persuaded the Abbotsbury baker William Purchas to give up a bolt of silk that he had found, though Purchas was able to sell most of another bolt to 'one of Taunton' for £6 1*s.*

[11] 'Here is no money stirring, all things are at a miserable damp', wrote a neighbour in Hampshire: Historical Manuscripts Commission, *Report on the Manuscripts of the Earl of Egmont*, 2 vols (1905), i, pt 1, 120.

[12] Williams, *Treasure of the Golden Grape*, 157, illustrates gold coins and pieces of eight recovered more recently from Chesil Beach.

'One that names himself William Drake and Mr Vice-admiral's servant' was also able to separate a few straggling scavengers from their loot. (Submitting his account to Vice Admiral Cottington, John Ellis referred to 'your man Drake'.[13]) John Pollard, the constable of Abbbotsbury (a husbandman), acknowledged that he had some wine from the wreck, and some raisins that his children had eaten, but claimed not to have joined the salvors on the beach. James Cornish, the constable of Melcombe Regis (a woollen draper), attempted to retrieve some of the money that his neighbours had from the ship, intending it for the master Thomas Redwood.

The area's commercial elite operated indirectly as conduits for the recovery of plundered goods and were not averse themselves to profiting from wrecks. Mr Fabian Hodder of Weymouth gave lodging to the master of the *Golden Grape* and secured some of the ship's stores and weaponry in his cellar. Though he himself was not called to testify, other witnesses spoke of thirty-two barrels of raisins stored at Hodder's house. Mr John Senior of Weymouth also emerged as a custodian of salvaged items. Besides taking possession of dozens of barrels of raisins, one witness reported, Senior also appropriated a barrel of olives. When Jeffrey Buck, an artisan of Abbotsbury, presented him with 80 pounds of loose wet fruit, Senior gave 20 pounds back to him. Senior likewise allowed the labourer William Critchell to keep 17 pounds of the 117 pounds of raisins he had saved. Even the household of Mr John Arthur, the Admiralty commissioner, was supplied with raisins from the *Golden Grape*.

Landed proprietors in coastal parishes asserted their privilege relating to wrecks. Mr John Jeffries of Wyke Regis reportedly confiscated a jar of oil that one of the salvage crews had recovered, 'for groundage, because they had put the same on shore, upon his ground', took possession of a barrel of raisins with the same justification, and allowed storage of more barrels in his house. Sir John Strangeways, a former sheriff of Dorset and current member of parliament, pressed his claims as lord of the manor of Abbotsbury. One of the salvors, an Abbotsbury fisherman, showed a neighbour 'certain pieces of eight, amounting to fourteen shillings sterling, which he said was the moiety of certain pieces of eight by him taken up upon the beach within the liberty of Sir John Strangeways, for which he had been so much troubled by the said Sir John's servants'. Others helped carry nine barrels of raisins to Sir John's house in Abbotsbury.

Maximillian Mohun (pronounced 'moon'), lord of the manor of Fleet, made similar claims to wrecked goods within his liberty. One of the Portland masons reported that a bolt of silk he had found 'was presently taken from him by Maximillian Mohun of Fleet, esquire'. It was to Mohun that 'a stranger' delivered a box of letters and an account book taken from the ship, evidently thinking him

[13] Wiltshire and Swindon History Centre, 865/404, 'The Account of Mr John Ellis . . . since the 10th of December 1641'.

the appropriate person to take custody of such items. One of the surviving crewmen who was 'very sick' was moved 'to Mr Mohun's house, where he remained until he died'.

Mohun, the only man of rank to depose before the commissioners, acknowledged keeping in his custody 'a piece of taffeta sarsnet which he caused to be dried, about seven or eight barrels of raisins, two of which are broken open, a chest belonging to one of the company of the said ship . . . and other small trifles'. He denied responsibility for the twenty-eight pieces of silk and two parcels of plate that he 'put together upon the beach and preserved', because, he said, they were 'afterwards taken and carried away by some of the inhabitants of Portland'.

Raisins Galore

So much of the *Golden Grape*'s cargo of raisins spilled onto Chesil Beach or was recovered from 'the wash of the sea' that there was a glut of that commodity. Some of the fruit still remained, or was traceable, at the time of the inquiry, but much had been consumed, spoiled, sold, or otherwise disposed of, in ways that witnesses could not then recall. Deponents repeatedly told the commissioners that they could not remember what had happened to the goods they had helped move, or with whom they had shared the labour, as if a collective forgetting had descended upon them. Typical was the statement of the husbandman William Bussell of Chickerell, 'that he hath in his custody three barrels of raisins of the sun which were brought into his house and left there, but by whom this deponent knoweth not'. Regarding another stash of eight barrels, the Weymouth sailor Arthur Gardiner declared that 'he doth not know who put them there or carried them thence'. Most witnesses concluded with the standard assertion, true or not, that they had not now in their own custody, or in the custody of anyone else for their use, 'any other or more of the goods or provisions of or belonging to the said ship'. If they acknowledged still having certain items in their 'custody', it was only to hold them until they were lawfully demanded, and then they would be 'delivered'.

Dozens of scavengers acknowledged taking barrels of raisins, which they claimed were damaged or half empty, and jars of olive oil, some of which had leaked or spoiled. A full barrel of raisins contained about 32 gallons, weighed about 100 pounds, and would need two men to lift it. Oil came in ceramic jars, with capacities of 1–4 gallons, and sometimes in larger wooden barrels. Horses and carts would be valuable assets, though some salvagers brought sacks or jugs, and filled their sleeves, hats, pockets, and aprons with usable or comestible goods. Their testimony allows glimpses of haggling, competition, and theft on the beach, as well as collaboration and concealment.

Mary Smart, the wife of a sailor of Wyke Regis, picked up 'about four pounds of wet raisins of the sun which she put into the boat of one Nicholas Williams to be carried home for her, from whence they were taken but by whom she knoweth not'. Her neighbour Anthony Winter 'took up certain wet raisins, which he put into a bag that he had there with him, and carried home to his children, who have since eaten the same'. The fisherman John Murrey gathered three pecks of raisins out of a barrel that lay on the beach, some of which he took home and consumed, 'and the remainder he hath sold to John King of Melcombe Regis for five shillings', a sum that he was willing to reimburse to the commissioners. (One peck made two gallons.) The wife of Henry Harvest, husbandman, came home with 'about three parts of a peck of wet raisins', but was disappointed to find 'a great deal of gravel and sand amongst them'. Thomas Peck, labourer, gathered 'loose wet raisins, about twelve pounds in weight, which he did put into the sleeves of his coat and carry home with him', along with 'a bundle of wood pieces of the said ship, which he carried home to make firewood'.

A surprising number of barrels allegedly 'fell down in the dirt', and their contents were spoiled, or were taken away and consumed by persons unknown. Such casualties would not be worth counting. When one of the barrels that Morgan Guilliams and his crew were salvaging burst open, they put the raisins 'in linen bags, and in their breeches, and so carried them home upon a horse, where they did divide them between them'. The carpenter Angel Wattes had a similar accident when a barrel of raisins he was carrying fell from his horse and broke in the dirt, though this did not stop him from gathering the residue into a sack. This scavenger's luck continued to run ill, for another bag of fruit he had set aside was stolen from the beach. The Melcombe Regis sailor Simon Wattes also suffered loss when one of the raisin barrels that he had carted to Weymouth 'was emptied by certain women ... and all the fruit carried away'. The rather pathetic gleanings of the fisherman's wife Mary Angel included 'a small quantity of wool in a bag (out of which some others that were there had pulled a great part), which she hath since dried, and doth guess that it weighs about three of four pound', plus 'a jar of oil the greatest part of which was leaked out, and a small quantity of wet fruit that lay loose on the beach'. The fisherman Nicholas Williams of Wyke Regis was similarly unfortunate, having earned two jars of oil for the use of his boat, 'one of which jars is since broken and all the oil leaked out'.

Some of the more enterprising salvors worked in organized 'consortships' of kinsmen, friends, and servants to remove material in bulk. Several arrived on the beach on the afternoon of the wreck, made repeated trips, and worked day and night until the ship was 'broken to pieces and quite carried away'. An informal hierarchy rapidly emerged, based on social authority and the command of equipment, with shipwrecked goods treated as an informal currency. One group used a horse-drawn plough as an improvised vehicle for freight. Others arrived by boat. Partnerships of three or four men were common, with some groups twice that size, hiring or appropriating the equipment they needed, paying for labour with goods from the stricken ship, and engaging other villagers to guard saleable items, to 'keep them safe that they might not be stolen away' by less scrupulous competitors.

While surviving crewmen focused on the specie and bullion, and scores of local villagers helped themselves to oil and raisins, a more narrowly focused group of salvors went after the *Golden Grape*'s cargo of textiles. One such company from the Isle of Portland collected bolts of silk—perhaps twenty-eight, perhaps thirty—most of which 'were shortly delivered to the vice-admiral'. They also harvested 'certain pieces of plate', according to the sailor John Doby, 'but how many there were of them he knoweth not'. None of the Portland men acknowledged finding any silver, though other deponents said that they took some. Eschewing the raisins that floated in abundance, one of this group, the yeoman Jennings Attwooll, also laid hands on 'a flag belonging to the ship, an astrolabe, a cross-staff, and a quadrant, which he hath in his custody'.

A well-organized collective of ten men, several of them surnamed Bishop, Boyt, or Feaver and presumably connected by kin, gathered twenty-two barrels of raisins and twenty-eight jars of oil. They also got hold of three sails from the *Golden Grape*, a great lantern, other ship's furnishings, and 'a small barrel of stinking butter'. Called to account before the inquiry, they affirmed, perhaps ingenuously, that they saved these items only 'for the use of the proprietors' and were 'ready to deliver the same whenever they shall be required'. Their hoard included such useful items as 'a screw to mount a piece of ordnance', 'a compass and a short sword', and 'the oar of a boat'. The Weymouth shoemaker John Pope, who had assisted their effort, was rewarded with a jar and a half of oil, a bundle of wet lemons, 'and about fourteen or sixteen pounds of wet raisins'.

The Weymouth fisherman Walter Bond's team did even better, stripping the ship of its armaments and furnishings. Working cooperatively, and paying for assistance, they took command of cables, hawsers, shrouds, the foremast, the bowsprit, a windlass, a capstan, seventeen round shot, seven pieces of ordnance, two 'murderers' (swivel guns), and two anchors, as well as barrels of raisins and jars of oil. Presumably they claimed some authority for these appropriations. Bond and his partners also made off with five of the eight barrels of raisins that other salvors had left on the beach overnight. A servant left in charge of the raisins reported that 'certain men of Weymouth came thither, and having beaten him did take away the said barrels and carry the same away from him'. These may have been the 'certain men of Weymouth pretending to be the vice-admiral's men' who took all the barrels that another group from Portisham had gathered, 'and what is become of them this deponent knoweth not'.

Another group led by the yeoman Robert Hunt of Wyke Regis saved ten barrels of raisins and, needing a boat to carry them across the Fleet, gave the sailor George Chip two barrels for his trouble. Another local sailor, Thomas Grey, ferried cargo across the Fleet from Chesil Beach to the mainland, taking payment in raisins and shares of proceeds. The yeoman Thomas Bayly deposed that he loaded twenty-six jars of oil into the boat of Nicholas Williams, for him to carry 'over the Fleet unto the mainland', but 'he never saw the said oils nor any part thereof since'. Other sets of barrels went mysteriously missing or were stolen amid the confusion. The evidence hints at inter-village rivalry, as well as pools of collusion, with parishioners generally aiding each other and sabotaging the efforts of outsiders. Later evidence from coastal Dorset describes villagers dividing the beach into search areas, and methodically combing their assigned parts.[14]

Many items changed hands almost immediately, as a result of barter, intimidation, or force. The Wyke Regis husbandman Francis Spratt and two assistants saved seven barrels of raisins, but on their way home 'one William Lovell of Fleet, pretending he had the power from the vice admiral, took four from them, and carried them away'. This same William Lovell reportedly cut open a bag of money he had found in the ship and shared its contents with another enterprising scavenger. Another group from Wyke, led by the fisherman John Andrews, gained possession of eight barrels of raisins, but lost two to a competing group from Portland, one of which was split in pieces, and the other carried away in triumph. Another Abbotsbury man lost his labour when the barrel of raisins he was saving 'was taken from him by the country people'.

Again and again witnesses referred to barrels being carried off or broken, but by whom they did know. Goods went missing or were disposed of, in ways they could not tell. Typical was the statement of Andrew Pitt, yeoman and overseer of Wyke Regis, regarding 'many persons' who handled barrels of raisins, 'but who they were he knoweth not, nor what became of the said fruit'.

The Wreck Economy

Much of the lading of the *Golden Grape* that was retrieved from the beach ended up in the hands of middlemen, dealers, and their customers. Chesil Beach took on the complexion of a three-day country fair, with goods traded to inland markets as far away as Blandford Forum, Sherborne, and Sturminster Newton (each some 25 miles from the wreck site). Some valuable silk went as far as Taunton, more than 40 miles distant, and an enterprising trader from Easter Compton, Gloucestershire, 60 miles from the coast, went home with a barrel of raisins.

John Gilliam, husbandman of Portisham, made the 6-mile trip to Chesil Beach with his cart and two horses, not to scavenge but 'with intent to buy some of the goods that were salved out of the said ship for his money'. He turned a quick profit, selling one barrel of raisins that he earned from cartage for 35*s*. Another deponent reported 'that Thomas Masterman of Upway [5 miles from the wreck

[14] Glanville J. Davies, 'Wreck and Plunder in 18th Century Portland', *Dorset Natural History and Archaeological Society Proceedings*, 103 (1981), 4.

site] did buy at Fleet six barrels of raisins of the sun which he sold and sent unto Sturminster Newton'. Prices were unstable, reflecting supply and demand but also the condition, desirability, and portability of the goods, and the persuasiveness of the sellers. Sir John Miller's man paid 32*s.* for a barrel of raisins for his master.

The fisherman Henry Nosciter of Langton Herring 'bought of a woman of Steepleton (whose name he now remembreth not) one barrel and half of raisins for which he paid her four and twenty shillings, and sold the same again to John White of Sherbourne for forty shillings'. John Angel of Abbotsbury (7 miles along the beach) paid 11*s.* for his raisins, and reselling them 'made nearabout forty shillings of the same'. These were quick and substantial profits for villagers who rarely saw 5*s.* a week.

The mason Richard Baylye of Melcombe Regis got 40*s.* for a barrel of raisins that he sold to 'the wife of Mr John Arthur', one of the gentlemen who would later conduct the commission of inquiry. The husbandman Robert Battin of Waddon sold his barrel of raisins for 30*s.* The thatcher William Symonds of Portisham did not drive so good a bargain, getting only 19*s.* for a full barrel he sold to a blacksmith, who may have traded it for profit further inland. Other deponents mentioned raisins changing hands for more than 30*s.*, down to 12*s.*, 5*s.*, or even 2*s.* a barrel. These lower prices tended to appear several days after the *Golden Grape* had spilled its load, when raisins were a glut on the market, and may have been sold by scavengers with no other use for them.

Among myriad minor trades, the Abbotsbury fisherman William Mallett sold a jar of oil for 6*s.* to 'one whose name he knoweth not', and disposed of loose raisins for twopence the pound. The yeoman's wife Alice Mathews bought a jar of oil for 4*s.*, and sold a pound of wool for 2*s.* 6*s.* 'to a stranger gentleman'. The fisherman John Curters of Wyke Regis, who had two jars of oil for the use of his boat, sold one to 'a stranger' for 3*s.* The labourer Richard Stradling of Portland sold his jar of oil to a neighbour for 4*s.* Alice Mathew, the wife of a soldier of Portland Castle, had wool and oil from the wreck, which she traded for two bushels of wheat worth 10*s.*

These meagre transactions boosted the resources of rural and coastal commoners, adding fruits of the Mediterranean to their country diet, and useful items to their economy of makeshifts. The unexpected bounty of consumables brought Christmas cheer to an otherwise grim season. The winter was cold and dark, while the political establishment was in crisis, but several Dorset families enjoyed extra cash and abundance of raisins. The weaver John Meech of Portisham explicitly stated that the half barrel of raisins he brought home 'he spent in his house in the Christmas time'. The fisherman Thomas Puckett of Abbotsbury was one of several who offered an account of the fruit he had handled, 'save only a small quantity thereof which his children have eaten'.

Besides perishable foodstuffs, the *Golden Grape* yielded a variety of material items that villagers could use or sell. These included the clothing and equipment of the crew, the fixtures and fittings of the ship, and a miscellany of maritime appurtenances. Ralph Lock of Weymouth carried home 'an old junk [cable?] about three fathom in length', which he sold to Peter Joy of Melcombe Regis for 3*s*. Angel Wattes of Melcombe Regis earned 'about four of five pence' for 'some small pieces of iron about four pound weight' that he had carried from the wreck. Other scavengers from Melcombe Regis picked up 'divers pieces of the timber wreck of the said ship, so much as four men were able to carry, which were good for nothing but firewood'.

The sailor Robert Angel of Wyke Regis had 'two old pair of canvas breeches'. William Purchas of Abbotsbury found 'an old pair of breeches with a knife in them'. Others came away with caps, coats, shirts, stockings, a cloak, and varied scraps of clothing that would augment their ordinary apparel. The mason John Eliot of Portland took home a pewter pot, a small silver cup, and a Bible, as well as some clothing and raisins. The sailor Thomas Grey made off with 'a piece of small rope belonging to the ship, two pieces of beef, a piece of leather, and a piece of a plot drawn in paper'. Miscellaneous trophies included a notebook with three quire of paper, two books, three Flemish boxes with salves in them, a small quantity of turpentine, a packet of needles, and 'other small trifles'.

Bits and pieces of marine equipage had value in coastal communities. Major items like sails and masts, ordnance and anchors, had been retrieved by organized teams, and were mostly turned over to the authorities, but rich pickings remained for individual scavengers. The yeoman Andrew Mills took custody of 'a rope about eight fathom in length and about the bigness of this deponent's handwrist'. Another yeoman, Thomas Allen of Fleet, came away with 'a chisel and a hammer, and a hundred and a half of nails'. The yeoman Robert Hunt of Wyke Regis held on to 'some small ropes, a pewter pot, and some broken pieces of timber of the said ship', in addition to the barrels of raisins and jars of oil that were still in his custody at the time of the inquiry. Ralph Bunne of Portland, who had boarded the *Golden Grape* when it first came ashore, took possession of 'a topmast vane which . . . he hath at his house'. Others reported finding and taking a shovel, a musket, a cartridge of powder, navigational instruments, and the contents of seamen's chests. The sailor Richard Doby of the Isle of Portland carried home nineteen lemons and 'a compass belonging to the said ship'. The cobbler Nicholas Gilbert reported saving 'the bolt of a pump and three lemons'. Even latecomers found items worth scavenging. Arriving on the Tuesday, four days after the ship had struck the beach, Thomas Webber, husbandman of Portisham, picked up various pieces of timber, plus 'a great shot, a bottle of wine', some nails, and a spike. The items mentioned were only those declared to the visiting commissioners and may not have represented the full extent of the material recovered.

All over Wyke Regis, Abbotsbury, and the surrounding villages in the early months of 1642 were semi-secret stores of raisins, jars of oil, and odds and ends of salvage, which deponents promised to hand over. Much, as they said, had been sold, consumed, or misappropriated. Some of the more valuable items were stored in cellars or yards, in the hands of Customs or castle officials, or in the custody of responsible gentlemen. Several parishioners of Chickerell entrusted their findings to their minister, Tristram Knapton, who still had charge of seven barrels of raisins and various other goods when the inquiry closed in March. The husbandman Peter Ford still had nine barrels of raisins in store, more than ten weeks after their landing. He told the inquiry that in saving them and carrying them to Abbotsbury 'he hath expended the sum of 48*s.* 8*d.*, which he doth desire may be allowed to him, as also for his pains in saving the same, and then he shall and will be ready to deliver all that he hath'. Another salvager wanted the inquiry to know about 'his coat being much torn in striving to help save the goods of the said ship', as if that entitled him to favourable consideration.

The inventorying and valuing of the goods saved from the *Golden Grape* was handicapped by the vagueness of witness recollections, the likelihood of widespread dissembling, and by the flawed documentation of the lading. The size, variety, and value of the original cargo was never indubitably determined, and no one could say how much was lost in the sea and the surf. Crewmen were evasive about the bullion they carried, and not necessarily truthful about amounts that they had handled or kept. Much of the silver was safe in Portland Castle, but only two hundred of the more than five hundred gold pistoles could be found. Vice Admiral Cottington gained possession of a bag of gold coins, and other officials no doubt took their share.

Salvagers accounted for only 172 of the *Golden Grape*'s 400 jars of olive oil, and only 535 of the 1,253 barrels of raisins.[15] Varying amounts were delivered to the commissioners, but it remains uncertain how much was undeclared, misrepresented, undercounted, or irretrievably lost. If acknowledged salvors were rewarded with their customary moiety, they may have pocketed £500 or more for the recovered cargo. If they received a fraction of the value of the sails, ordnance, and gear they had retrieved, they would have earned several hundred pounds more. If as many as 300 barrels of raisins and 100 jars of oil leaked into the local economy, they could represent an infusion worth some £350. The recovered gear and timbers would have been similarly valued. The number of pieces of eight that escaped restitution remains unknown, but there may have been several hundred in circulation. All told, and conservatively estimated, the wreck of the *Golden Grape* brought the people and officials of south Dorset a windfall exceeding £1,000 at a time when many people made no more than £20 a year. Divided among more than a hundred families, this 'godsend' made nobody rich, but provided welcome relief. The commissioners could never be sure what quantities remained in private hands, despite official restitution. There would always be future wrecks.

[15] Williams, *Treasure of the Golden Grape*, 82.

Wrecking and the Social Order

The *Golden Grape* depositions allow us to make judgements about the legality, propriety, and morality of shoreline conduct and to test again the legend of 'barbarous' depredation. The distressed crewmen claimed that their goods were taken by 'force and violence', but the Dorset evidence shows none of the 'cruelty and inhumanity' or 'barbarous' and 'devilish' practices so often alleged of coastal inhabitants. The Chesil Beach wreckers were practised in their task, determined to take what the sea offered and what the authorities would allow. There were instances of intimidation and theft, as scavengers jostled for advantage, but little of the disorder and insubordination so often associated with grain riots and enclosure protests. There was no lawless frenzy, no rapacious cruelty.

The timing of this episode, amidst a moment of national crisis, seems not to have affected its character. The revolutionary upheavals of 1641 and 1642, which eventuated in civil war, subjected England's social order to extraordinary stress. Traditional gradations of hierarchy and deference appeared to founder amidst a sea of subordination, as customary arrangements of status, rank, and office were tested to their limits.[16] Vice Admiral Cottington was a casualty of this turmoil, but south Dorset was remote from its centre. The villagers who swarmed Chesil Beach in December1641 used social and physical muscle to their best advantage, but behaved with neither savagery nor ruthlessness. They treated the castaway crew with courtesy, and laboured alongside distressed sailors, helping them with shelter, sustenance, and physick. They worked enterprisingly and collaboratively with neighbours and fellows, and generally cooperated with men of higher status and wealth. They deferred, if only sluggishly, to the authority of the vice admiral, local lords of manors, and officials of Portland Castle. They worked within the limits of law and custom, and knew that their scavenging would be tolerated. Their answers to the commissioners early in 1642 may have been evasive and canny, but were not overtly disrespectful. The social order may have been stressed, but it was by no means broken.

Coastal villagers *expected* to profit from shipwrecks, expected to be rewarded for assisting in salvage, and expected to be winked at if they concealed some goods for themselves. Without their work, much less would have been recovered. Authorized salvors and droit holders knew that they depended on the labour of local inhabitants, who would have worked less willingly without due recompense. Mariners and merchants who sought restitution were powerless without the cooperation of shoreline inhabitants; as transients and outsiders, they were no match for deep-rooted networks of locality, community, and kin.

[16] Cressy, *England on Edge*, 347.

When the Admiralty commissioners arrived to investigate the stripping of the *Golden Grape*, the people of the coastal hinterland lined up to give evidence, with appropriate displays of deference and decorum. They tendered partial collaboration to the inquiry, and knew enough to avoid trouble when reminded of their excesses. Many identified neighbours and kinsmen involved in the plunder, but referred to others whose names they 'knew not'. A tactical vagueness was at work. Deponents admitted to salvaging certain items, but remained silent about others. Most offered to 'deliver' their hoard of wreckage, or their pieces of eight, if the authorities so demanded, though often they could not tell what had happened to materials they had handled. A frequent answer to interrogatories was, 'this deponent knoweth not'. This pall of amnesia had elements of 'calculated deference' mixed with dissimulation—characteristic weapons of the weak[17]—but the commissioners were evidently content. The merchant owners gained some compensation, officials and other claimants exercised their droits, while the 'country people' of coastal Dorset took their share.

What mattered most to the authorities was the performance of lawfulness, and the maintenance of hierarchy, with enough doffing of caps and recovery of value to placate competing interests. What mattered to the villagers was the opportunity to stock their larders, barns, and purses from the windfall bounty of the sea. Lord Cottington and his ilk were concerned about barbarity, but there was little on display. The Commission reasserted rules of property and law, while punishing nobody for their violation. It demonstrated a concern for restitution, in accord with the statute of Edward I, without necessarily inconveniencing anybody in Dorset. There would be no prosecutions in this case, and no end to coastal spoil, as political storms in 1642 brought England wreckage of a very different kind.

[17] John Walter, 'Public Transcripts, Popular Agency and the Politics of Subsistence in Early Modern England', in Michael J. Braddick and John Walter (eds), *Negotiating Power in Early Modern Society: Order, Hierarchy and Subordination in Britain and Ireland* (Cambridge, 2001), 131; James C. Scott, *Weapons of the Weak: Everyday Forms of Peasant Resistance* (New Haven, 1985).

9
Mariners in Distress

Classic compendia on shipwrecks remarked on their 'lamentable consequences' and the 'hopeless condition' of those affected by maritime 'calamities'. In the view of one late Hanoverian author, 'shipwreck may be ranked among the greater evils which man can experience. It is never void of danger, frequently of fatal issue, and invariably productive of regret.'[1] This chapter traces some of those consequences for mariners cast roughly ashore.

The English seafaring community swelled from just over 16,000 sailors in 1582 to around 50,000 by the end of the seventeenth century, as commercial and naval shipping expanded. By the mid-eighteenth century some 80,000 men lived by sailing and braving the sea. They came from all coastal counties, and sometimes served in cosmopolitan crews. Many shared common backgrounds with the shoremen they encountered as salvagers and wreckers. Modern scholarship has illuminated their conditions of employment, their hardship and rewards, and their dealings with merchants, family members, and the law. The work of seafaring, as Eleanor Hubbard has recently observed, involved 'fevers, fluxes, accidents, shipwreck, and violence', as well as opportunities for travel and profit.[2]

Little has been written about the local experience of shipwreck, or the mariners' plight as survivors. Much more is known, or imagined, about the fortitude and failings of seaman stranded on distant islands than about their counterparts on the

[1] John Graham Dalyell, *Shipwrecks and Disasters at Sea: Or, Historical Narratives of the Most Noted Calamities and Providential Deliverances which have Resulted from Maritime Enterprise*, 3 vols (Edinburgh, 1812), i, p. xii.

[2] Peter Earle, 'English Sailors, 1570–1775', in Paul van Royen, Jap Bruijn, and Jan Lucassen (eds), *'Those Emblems of Hell'? European Sailors and the Maritime Labour Market, 1570–1870* (St John's, Newfoundland, 1997),73–82; Cheryl A. Fury, *Tides in the Affairs of Men: The Social History of Elizabethan Seamen, 1580–1603* (Westport, CT, and London, 2002); Cheryl A. Fury (ed.), *The Social History of English Seamen, 1485–1649* (Woodbridge, 2012); Richard J. Blakemore, 'The Legal World of English Sailors, *c.*1575–1729', in Maria Fusaro, Bernard Allaire, Richard Blakemore, and Tijl Vannestre (eds), *Law, Labour, and Empire: Comparative Perspectives on Seafarers, c.1500–1800* (Basingstoke, 2015), 100–20; Richard J. Blakemore, 'Orality and Mutiny: Authority and Speech among Seafarers in Early Modern London', in Thomas V. Cohen and Lesley K. Twomey (eds), *Spoken Word and Social Practices: Orality in Europe (1400–1700)* (Leiden and Boston, 2015), 253–79; Richard J. Blakemore, 'Pieces of Eight, Pieces of Eight: Seamen's Earnings and the Venture Economy of Early Modern Seafaring', *Economic History Review*, 70 (2017), 1153–84. See also Beverly Lemire, '"Men of the World": British Mariners, Consumer Practice, and Material Culture in an Era of Global Trade, *c.*1660–1800', *Journal of British Studies*, 54 (2015), 288–319; Eleanor Hubbard, 'Sailors and the Early Modern British Empire: Labor, Nation, and Identity at Sea', *History Compass*, 14 (2016), 348–58; Eleanor Hubbard, *Englishmen at Sea: Labor and the Nation at the Dawn of Empire 1570–1630* (New Haven and London, 2021), 278.

Shipwrecks and the Bounty of the Sea. David Cressy, Oxford University Press. © David Cressy 2022.
DOI: 10.1093/oso/9780192863393.003.0010

coasts of England.[3] The following discussion attends to some of the human costs of shipwrecks, which added to the cost of doing business. It shows that victims who were fortunate to survive were not cruelly treated on shore.

Shipwrecked Sailors

Most victims of maritime disasters drowned. Huge numbers of seamen died when their ships foundered or were wrecked. No reliable statistics are available before the nineteenth century, but incidental evidence indicates a sad congregation of casualties. Report after report confirms that the sea was 'a sepulchre for thousands', that most in peril perished, or that only one or two came alive to land.[4] Dozens, even hundreds, were lost in some disasters, while survivors struggled for breath. Daniel Defoe asserts that six thousand seamen drowned in the 'Great Storm' of 1703, but his figure is purely conjectural.[5] A later estimate by John Wilkinson posits 4,200 drownings annually, but he used this number to support his project for cork life jackets.[6] A British survey in 1812 suggests that 'not less than 5,000 natives of these islands yearly perish at sea', including men lost to accidents and disease.[7] A more modern estimate finds 5 per cent of Bristol's sailors lost each year in the eighteenth century, a figure commensurate with the loss of shipping.[8] Royal National Lifeboat records from a period of greater but safer shipping note 14,457 lives lost from 31,168 wrecks on British coastlines from 1854 to 1874, an average of 723 drowned a year.[9] Dead men, for the most part, tell no tales, but the number washed ashore or lost each year off early modern English coasts could well have reached two thousand. Many died anonymously, like the crew of a wreck at Birling, Sussex, in 1563, 'of what country they were we know not'.[10]

With hope almost lost, as a stricken vessel foundered or fell apart, 'even then, when the seas have seized upon her, and broke her up into an hundred pieces',

[3] Classic accounts relate the wreck of the *Sea Venture* on Bermuda in 1609: William Strachey, 'A True Reportory of the Wrack and Redemption of Sir Thomas Gates', in Samuel Purchas, *Purchas His Pilgrimes... the First Part* (1625), 1734–52; and the ordeal of the *Nottingham Galley* off New England in 1710: John Deane, *A Narrative of the Shipwreck of the Nottingham Galley, etc. First Publish'd in 1711*, 4th edn (1738). These and other dramas are related in Dalyell, *Shipwrecks and Disasters at Sea.*

[4] John Ryther, *Sea-Dangers and Deliverances Improved* (1674), bound and paginated with James Janeway, *Mr James Janeway's Legacy to his Friends: Containing Twenty-Seven Famous Instances of God's Providence in and about Sea-Dangers and Deliverances* (1675), 12.

[5] Daniel Defoe, *The Storm: Or, A Collection of the Most Remarkable Casualties and Disasters which Happen'd in the Late Dreadful Tempest, both by Sea and Land* (1704), 37, 46, 173–200, 220.

[6] John Wilkinson, *Tutamen Nauticum: Or the Seaman's Preservation from Shipwreck, Diseases, and Other Calamities*, 2 vols (1763), sig. a.

[7] Dalyell, *Shipwrecks and Disasters at Sea*, i, p. xiii.

[8] Earle, 'English Sailors, 1570–1775', 87, citing Jonathon Press, *The Merchant Seamen of Bristol, 1747–1789* (Bristol, 1976), 11. Shipwreck was not necessarily the prime cause of such losses.

[9] *Lifeboat*, 9/98 (November 1875).

[10] East Sussex Record Office, AMS 4606/1.

a chance remained to survive.[11] Evacuation to a longboat was standard procedure, but boats were often swamped, smashed, or overloaded. The men of the *Hopewell* of 1634, the *Elizabeth* of 1660, and countless others were lucky to reach land (see Chapter 7). The mariner Edward Barlow recalled his deliverance from the sinking *Florentine* near the Goodwin Sands, as waves 'broke many times into our boat; and we were in more danger of our lives in the boat than whilst we were in the ship, and were forced to keep one of us always throwing out the water as it came in'.[12] Hard rowing and fickle fortune could bring exhausted survivors ashore.

Less fortunate were the passengers and crew of the Holyhead-to-Dublin packet that foundered on the coast of Ireland in December 1670. Twenty-four men attempted escape in the ship's boat, 'which being too heavy sunk her, so they all perished'. On this occasion it proved safer to remain aboard. It was past midnight when 'those that stayed in the ship tied a rope to the middle of a very strong fellow, and he swam and waded ashore... and with much ado made fast the rope, by which twenty-one persons saved themselves, and three more were lost getting to shore by it'. The name of the hero is not given in this report, but the distinguished dead were listed, including Dean Tate, coadjutor to the Bishop of Ossory, and Captain Carteret, brother to Sir George Carteret, the proprietor of New Jersey.[13] The captain, master, and eight or nine men took to their pinnace when the *Kent* foundered on North Sea sands in October 1671, leaving their crewmates aboard. 'They left the ship full of water, her rudder off and her keel broken, and the poor men were with masts and planks making floats to save their lives, if God see it good.' Some reportedly made shore at Cromer, but most were never seen again.[14] Providence made sure that officers and aristocrats of the naval vessel *Gloucester* survived its sinking in 1682, the boats not accommodating the common seamen.[15]

Abandoning a doomed ship was a fateful decision, leaving everything to the mercy of the sea. Sailors would lose their possessions, and proceeds of the voyage, while shippers could forfeit rights to salvage and restitution. Lifeless wrecks and derelicts were prey to any finder. William Wilkinson, in charge of the *Hopewell* that was wrecked on an Essex sandbank in 1634, refused to leave his cabin, and had to be forced into the longboat by sword point.[16] Seven sailors who tried to retrieve gold from the lower deck of the sinking *Royal Merchant* in 1641 'never

[11] Daniel Pell, *Pelagos. Nec inter Vivos, nec inter Mortuos; Neither amongst the Living, nor amongst the Dead. Or, An Improvement of the Sea* (1659), 295.

[12] *Barlow's Journal of his Life at Sea in King's Ships, East & West Indiamen & Other Merchantmen from 1659 to 1703*, ed. Basil Lubbock, 2 vols (1934), i. 258–62.

[13] SP 63/329, fos 256–61.

[14] SP 29/316, fo. 234; SP 29/317, fo. 8.

[15] Sir John Dalrymple, *Memoirs of Britain and Ireland*, 2 vols (1773), ii. 68–72; *The Correspondence of Henry Hyde, Earl of Clarendon and of his Brother Lawrence Hyde, Earl of Rochester*, ed. Samuel Weller Singer, 2 vols (1828), i. 71–3. See also Caleb Calle, *On His Royal Highness's Miraculous Delivery, and Happy Return* (1682); John Gibbon, *Prince-Protecting Providences* (1682), 5–6.

[16] For the *Hopewell*, see Chapter 7.

came up, the ship sunk so fast on them'.[17] A survivor of the *Dolphin* that was wrecked at Land's End in 1670 reported that 'they had £1,000 in money on board, which was the cause of the master lingering in hope to save his money', but the master and five companions drowned.[18]

Escaping with a pocket full of silver might seem sensible, but the weight could drag a body down. The mariners of the *John and Sarah*, wrecked in South Wales in 1702, 'threw themselves overboard; but alas this could not save them, for the boisterous waves, instead of suffering them to creep up the rocks dashed them in pieces against them'. Only one man was found by fishermen 'nine hours after, when the fury of the storm was spent'.[19]

Through the grace of God, or through clutching floating debris, bruised survivors were sometimes rescued, or stumbled ashore alive. Edmund Pet, the sole survivor of a North Sea wreck in 1613, 'by God's help took hold of the main mast', and was rescued after forty-eight hours in the water, 'praised be the name of the lord'.[20] Thomas Ford, the sole survivor of the collier *Carnation* that 'split all in pieces' on the coast of Yorkshire in 1614, 'by God's providence got hold of a piece of the stern, and floated upon it about four hours in the sea until it pleased God to draw the said piece to the shoreward, and he feeling ground left the piece of the stern and waded to the shore, being almost starved to death with the violence of the cold'.[21] Thomas Barnes, shipwrecked off Cornwall in December 1650, was 'the only person by God's mercy miraculously preserved, being cast upon the rock, where for four days and nights he abode in that cold season, and through extremity thereof two of his toes rotted'.[22] Like Odysseus clinging to his mast, Gregory Crow, the sole survivor of a wreck off Kent in 1679, sat on floating timber, 'driving up and down on the sea', until God arranged for his preservation.[23]

God gets less thanks in a junior officer's 'true relation' of the wreck of the Indiaman *Royal Oak* on Scilly's western rocks in January 1666. Remnants of the crew found temporary shelter on one of those rocks after their ship had shattered:

> Here we sadly beheld one the others, most of us sorely cut and wounded with the sharpness of the rocks, not having meat, drink, or firing to comfort us, and many of us in a manner naked, because the better able to swim... It were 52 hours

[17] *Sad News from the Seas: Being a True Relation of the Losse of that Good Ship Called the Merchant Royall* (1641).

[18] SP 29/280, fo. 36.

[19] *God's Wonders in the Great Deep, or, The Seaman's Danger and Deliverance Exemplified* (1710), 12.

[20] *Lamentable Newes, Shewing the Wonderfull Deliverance of Maister Edmond Pet Sayler* (1613), sigs A2–A4.

[21] HCA 13/42, fo. 278.

[22] SP 29/22, fo. 36.

[23] *The Wonderful Preservation of Gregory Crow Being Shipwrackt upon the Coast of Kent* (1679), 2.

> upon the aforesaid rocks, where we endured so much cold that all our legs and hands were so swelled that we could but few of us stand.[24]

'Sea-beaten, bruised, sick, half drowned' sailors were lucky to be alive. Few would be of a mood to follow Gervase Markham's advice from the 1620s: 'if thou hast suffered shipwreck, think not of what thou hast lost,' but reflect instead on sin and salvation.[25] Their battle with the sea was over, as survivors faced the uncertainties of safety on land (see Figure 7).

Ship-Broken Men

After losing their ship, survivors faced the uncertain perils of *terra firma*. Not for them the entertainment that Odysseus received from Nausicaa and Calypso, or 'the wood nymphs' habitation' that succoured Aeneus' 'sea-tired' Trojans. Instead, like the voyagers in Sidney's *Arcadia*, 'much bruised and beaten, both with the sea's hard farewell and the shore's rude welcome', they braced for further

Figure 7. Follower of Claude Joseph Vernet, 'Shipwrecked Sailors', Dulwich Picture Gallery, London, DPG610.

[24] Bodleian Library, MS Rawlinson A 195, fos 180–180^{v}.

[25] Gervase Markham, *A Second Part to the Mothers Blessing: Or a Cure against Misfortunes* (1622), 57, 60.

distress.[26] Their first question, language permitting, may have been a variant of Shakespeare's shipwrecked Viola's: 'what country, friend, is this?' It would be a hard landfall to encounter 'unneighbourly shores' that proved 'more cruel than the sea'.[27] Men who arrived on hostile coasts faced capture or enslavement, but expected better treatment from 'their own countrymen and Christians'.[28] They naturally turned to men of authority—magistrates, constables, local lords, or bailiffs—in the hope of easing their distress.

Ideally, by standards of common humanity, shipwrecked mariners found relief and hospitality of the kind that the people of Malta provided for St Paul. They could hope for the 'lodging, fire, meat, apparel, and all necessaries' that survivors of Erasmus' fictional *Naufragium* enjoyed in Holland.[29] Most would look for repair of their fortunes and means to get home. To their grief, however, some seamen said, their miseries only increased as 'the barbarous country people' plundered their property 'in riotous sort'. Shipwreck exposed mariners to the mercy of a 'rude' and 'disordered' multitude, allegedly given to 'savage practices'. Such claims, I have argued, were rhetorically inflected to express indignation or to gain sympathy, and should be viewed with scepticism (see Chapter 4). They can be further tested against reports of interactions with coastal inhabitants, recovered mainly from State Papers and archives of the High Court of Admiralty.

Hundreds of wreck victims drowned. Beachside scavengers became accustomed to seeing dead bodies, like the corpses washed up in Northumberland in 1565, 'miserably beaten with the seas'.[30] They would be inspected for signs of identity and usable furnishings, then removed for burial. Money found about them might subsidize their funeral expenses.[31] Any jewels taken up belonged in principle to the Lord Admiral, who 'hath the disposition of such goods', but there was no way of monitoring such discoveries.[32] Following a shipwreck off Plymouth in August 1622, one body remained wedged 'for certain days standing upright betwixt two rocks, as though he were alive, and impossible to be got out unless the rocks were

[26] Homer, *Odyssey*, bks V, XII; Virgil, *Aeneid*, bk V; Sir Philip Sidney, *The Countesse of Pembrokes Arcadia* (1593), fos 65–6.

[27] William Shakespeare, *Twelfth Night*, Act 1, scene 2; Charles Nichols, *The Seamans Summons* (1655), 7; *A Poeticall Sea-Piece, Containing in a Spacious Table the Lively Description of a Tempest at Sea, and Shipwrecks* (1633).

[28] James Derriman, 'The Wreck of the *Albemarle*', *Journal of the Royal Institution of Cornwall*, NS 1 (1992), 140, with citations from BL, India Office Records, E/1/198 (1708). For some of the dangers of 'cross-boundary maritime practices', see Daniel Hershenzon, *The Captive Sea: Slavery, Communication, and Commerce in Early Modern Spain and the Mediterranean* (Philadelphia, 2018), 185.

[29] Acts, 27: 14–44; *Collected Works of Erasmus: Colloquies*, ed. Craig R. Thompson (Toronto, 1997), 351–67.

[30] BL, MS Harley 6990, fos 69–70; *Wonderful Preservation of Gregory Crow*, 13.

[31] SP 14/27, fo. 78; SP 16/120, fo. 52; *An Account of the Wrecks 1759–1830 on the North Coast of Cornwall. By John Bray*, ed. A. K. Hamilton Jenkin (Truro, 1975), 13.

[32] SP 16/208, fo. 261.

beaten away'.[33] After another wreck in Pembrokeshire in 1630, observers reported, 'the dead bodies lie stripped naked upon the rocks, and some are unburied and some most lamentably hang yet in quarters upon the rocks'.[34] The parish register of Madron, Cornwall, records the burial in December 1599 of 'John, John, Peter, Peter, and Peter, Frenchmen shipwrakt'. Nearby St Columb Minor records the burial in November 1625 of 'a seafaring man, of a ship cast away . . . at Towan, with three other of his company, they being found and no more'.[35] Searches in other registers may find similar entries.

'Ship-broken men' came ashore battered and bedraggled, traumatized and exhausted. They were lucky to be saved, whether by their own efforts, divine assistance, or the help of shore-dwellers.[36] The mariner Peter Bellingham, who survived the wreck of the *Speedwell* in 1624, 'lost all that ever he had, even his very wearing apparel with the necessities thereunto belonging'.[37] Others cast away in the Irish Sea 'escaped to land with much danger and difficulty' and arrived 'maimed and sorely bruised' on the coast of Anglesey in 1625.[38] One seaman reached land 'almost spent, his flesh sodden with sea water", after clinging to a floating spar.[39] Survivors of a Channel wreck in 1658, though safe, were 'sick, and some not like to live by reason of the extraordinary cold which they took by walking all night upon the sand in their wet clothes'.[40] Some proved strong enough to assist in salvage, though others would labour no more after losing their livelihood. Loyalty to the merchants who paid their wages could attenuate as those wages were imperilled. The very fact of their arrival safe to land complicated legal determination of 'wreck' and made the claims of shoremen to their goods contentious.

Acts of charity by coastal inhabitants offset accusations of barbarity. Salvors often paused their predation to assist surviving mariners. When the mate Thomas Ford stumbled ashore from the wreck of the *Carnation* on the coast of Yorkshire in November 1614, he found beachcombers already at work with hatchets, 'and prayed them for God's sake to help him to a fire'. The villagers found the survivor shelter at a nearby mill and helped him to dry his clothes. The next day he was strong enough to supervise salvage, engaging ten of 'the country people' to recover masts, cables, and anchors for the lawful owners, until intruders from another parish robbed their stash.[41]

[33] *The Fourth of September: Newes from Sundry Places, both Forraine and Domestique* (1622), 11.
[34] SP 16/182, fo. 81^{v}.
[35] *The First Book of the Parish Registers of Madron, in the County of Cornwall*, ed. George Bown Millett (Penzance, 1877), 47; Richard Larn and Bridget Larn, *Shipwreck Index of the British Isles*, 7 vols (1995–2005), i, sect. 2 (not paginated).
[36] William Welwood, *An Abridgement of all Sea Lawes* (1613), 163.
[37] SP 14/175, fo. 119.
[38] *Acts of the Privy Council of England, 1542–1631*, ed. J. R. Dasent et al., 45 vols (1890–1964), xl. 20; SP 16/1, fos 38, 40.
[39] Janeway, *Mr James Janeway's Legacy to his Friends*, 27.
[40] SP 18/179, fo. 54.
[41] HCA 13/42, fo. 278.

Twenty-six of the men of the *Susan* drowned when their ship was wrecked in Devon in February 1630, but two sailors battled the sea. William Spencer, aged 23, 'grew almost past his senses' as he swam towards the shore, and Francis Browne, aged 33, 'grew so weak that he could swim no further', until the gentleman John Pollexfen (alias Poulson) 'ran into the water' and pulled them to safety.[42] The yeoman Nicholas Young of Piddinghoe, Sussex, encountered eight survivors of the *Rose* of Amsterdam in February 1634, 'some of them quite naked, and some of them having only a little covering about their waist, and came like shipwrecked men from the sea'. Acting charitably, he told Admiralty commissioners, he 'did relieve those eight men which came alive on shore with meat, drink, and clothes, and lent them money to carry them home to their own countries'. The bodies of thirty-four less fortunate lay scattered on the beach.[43]

When the hopefully named *Prosperous* shattered in north Cornwall in November 1669, six crewmen drowned, but others were 'wonderfully cast on shore and bruised'. Among the survivors was John Denny, a skinner of Bristol, who appeared to lie dead on the beach, 'covered with some scraw of rubbish'. Mercifully, according to James Janeway, a collector of divine providences, 'an old man looking on the dead people did perceive some life in the said Denny, and the Lord opened his heart that he stripped himself of his own shirt and some clothes, and put on him, and took him from amongst the dead'. No barbarous wrecker he.[44]

Letters between shipowners and officials, concerned with recovery from shipwrecks, more often commend the savers and shoremen than accuse them of cruelty. The owners of the *St Cleere* of Holland, which was lost on the Goodwin Sands in 1617, recognized 'the care and industry of the inhabitants next thereto adjoining', who helped to bring their cargo ashore, even though the landmen then proved reluctant to relinquish it.[45] 'By the merciful protection of the almighty, and with the industrious and painful labour of many men,' the crew of the *Phenix* were 'brought to land, much wet and spoiled', after being 'overthrown' in the sea off Kent in 1618, and they too hoped to recover their merchandize.[46] Even though some goods from the Hamburg merchantman *Ark Noah* were 'embezzled and stolen', after the ship had been 'by misfortune cast away and wrecked' on those same treacherous sands in March 1621, officials of the Cinque Ports commended the 'honest men' of Kent who by their 'industry and pains' saved much of the cargo of cinnamon and pepper. Though the owners complained of being 'grievously impoverished', there was evidence that 'the master delivered all the goods himself to the savers before he left his ship'.[47]

[42] HCA 13/49, fos 34^{v}–35. [43] HCA 13/52, fos 455–455^{v}.
[44] Janeway, *Mr James Janeway's Legacy to his Friends*, 43–4. [45] SP 14/92, fo. 128.
[46] SP 14/104, fo. 188. [47] SP 14/120, fos 27–41.

The merchants and mariners of the *White Swan* of Hamburg, cast away near Beachy Head, Sussex, in July 1624, likewise acknowledged 'the industry and pains . . . of the inhabitants thereabouts abiding' who helped to save their 'tackling, furniture, ordnance, and other goods'. They hoped that the savers would receive 'reasonable satisfaction' for their efforts, 'all fees and droits being paid to the subordinate officers'.[48] Survivors of a Portuguese ship that was wrecked on the Isle of Wight in October 1625 'were almost drowned and like to die with cold' when the inhabitants rescued them, which may have induced them to sign away the residue of their goods.[49] The panic and crisis of shipwreck often made mariners vulnerable to extortion and sharp practice on the beach. Dozens of reports describe how local inhabitants helped wreck victims struggle ashore, before relieving them of their property.[50]

In many cases survivors had no alternative but to negotiate with would-be salvagers. Their representatives often claimed that their men had been cheated by bailiffs or droit collectors who took advantage of their plight. The crew of the *Angel Ratchell* of Hamburg, wrecked at Seaford, Sussex, in 1622, were relieved when 'Mr Elphick, being a chief man and dwelling there', arrived to protect them from the 'rude' country people; but he 'made them set their hands to a writing, the contents whereof they knew not what it was', they being 'strangers, and destitute of help to bring them through the country'.[51] Whether willingly or subject to pressure, masters of other shipwrecked vessels came to terms with local worthies and officials, while individual crewmen trafficked with buyers on shore. Sailors sold cargo and tackle to local victuallers and shopkeepers, and sometimes took part in the plunder themselves. In 1635, for example, John Bagg, a sailor from the *Henry and John* that was lost near Shoeburyness, Essex, sold parcels of diaper to local tradesmen, and joined with other mariners in embezzling fittings from the wreck.[52] In another case that year, the master 'sold such parts of his ship and furniture as could be saved', in order to relieve his crew.[53] Survivors of the *Guifte of God* of Hull sold masts and rigging to support their travel home to Yorkshire from Sussex in 1636.[54] Survivors of the *Golden Grape* used pieces of eight from the ship to pay for clothing, medicine, and accommodation.[55]

Reports accrued of savers and sailors bartering for wreckage and haggling over prices; of crewmen selling lemons 'for their relief'; and of a 'knavish' mariner who 'quitted his ship and sold her whole as she lay', after coming aground in Norfolk.[56] By the time officials arrived at the Lizard to inspect 'a great Dutch ship' that had been cast away there in 1669, they found 'the ship all rifled, and a bargain

[48] SP 14/170, fo. 12. [49] SP 16/523, fo. 19. [50] SP 29/269, fo. 163.
[51] SP 14/127, fo. 178. [52] HCA 13/52, fos 343^{v}, 348^{v}. [53] SP 16/305, fo. 221.
[54] HCA 13/52, fo. 319^{v}. [55] HCA 13/244/149.
[56] HCA 13/24, fo. 165^{v}; HCA 13/33, fo. 3; Norfolk Record Office, LEST/Q 37, 49.

pretended to be made between the master and some of the gentry of the neighbourhood' for its cargo of planks and mast timber.[57] A yeoman of Westbourne, Sussex, bought ropes and other gear from 'one of the men belonging to the French vessels' that had been wrecked nearby in 1676.[58] Similar trades relieved the 'poor men' of the *Unity* of Bergen, cast away off Kent in 1681, who were 'entirely ruined, having nothing for their support but what [the sale of ship's fittings] might afford them'. When the Sergeant of the Admiralty demanded their best anchor and cable as his fee for groundage, the seamen complained that 'very little or nothing would remain for their subsistence'.[59]

Stranded Sailors

Out of their element and stripped of their livelihood, stranded seamen faced destitution. Dependent on charity if they had nothing to sell, they faced new hazards on shore. Foreign survivors would need repatriation, while English sailors would want to get home, or reach a seaport where they might find employment. Local vice admirals had instructions 'to afford them all reasonable and friendly aid and assistance', while not stinting on perquisites and droits.[60] Local worthies offered temporary shelter and negotiated terms of salvage. Commercial and diplomatic agents sometimes intervened to speed up the process. The government of Charles I promised 'courtesy and respect' to seafarers who were 'subject to a prince with whom his majesty is in amity', though that courtesy had limited substance unless they were 'of the better sort'.[61] Survivors of the *Golden Grape* found shelter with local artisans and gentry, and some of the men were still in Dorset a month after their ship had come ashore.[62] It took three months to arrange repatriation for twelve lascars from the East Indiaman *Albemarle*, wrecked in Cornwall in December 1708.[63]

Justices of the peace could issue passes or testimonials for 'any seafaring man suffering shipwreck', asking officials elsewhere 'not to molest or trouble' the unfortunate mariner on his way to his place of birth or employment. Such passes typically identified the traveller by his name and age, and noted when and where he had landed, the name of his ship, and his destination within England.[64] One such pass displayed by a traveller in Jacobean Somerset was suspected to be counterfeit.[65] Lacking a proper pass, one seaman shipwrecked near Liverpool

[57] SP 29/267, fo. 31. [58] West Sussex Record Office, Ep/1/55/134. [59] SP 44/62, fo. 235.

[60] SP 29/359, fos 39, 106. [61] PC 2/35, fo. 233; PC 2/39, fo. 21.

[62] For the *Golden Grape*, see Chapter 8. [63] Derriman, 'Wreck of the *Albemarle*', 139.

[64] Michael Dalton, *The Countrey Iustice, Conteyning the Practise of the Iustices of the Peace* (1618), 99; Giles Jacob, *Lex Mercatoria: Or the Merchant's Companion* (1729), 151.

[65] Somerset Heritage Centre, Q/ST/17/2–4.

had 'no visible way of living', and was later arrested for begging.[66] The poor man 'found wandering' along the coast of Cumberland in 1627, 'being a stranger, and a man of unknown language', was almost certainly an alien mariner. He was passed from constable to constable until he could be examined by officials at Carlisle Castle.[67]

Some distressed seaman stayed long enough in the wreck vicinity to give evidence to commissions of inquiry, or appeared later in London before the High Court of Admiralty. One at least, Richard Rich of the *Golden Grape*, found time to court a young woman of Melcombe Regis, entrusting her with his hoard of pierces of eight. The authorities were more interested in the lost commodities and the ships that carried them than the subsequent histories of the sailors. Mariners in their depositions would tell stories of voyages, claim wages, and give grudging accounts of the wreckers. Most would go to sea again, and some would suffer further shipwreck.

England's shipwreck beaches were difficult for foreigners, and especially 'unneighbourly' for enemy and outlaw mariners. The men of a 'strange ship' driven aground near Liverpool in 1561 could communicate with their rescuers only by gestures, and were surely not the only ones thus handicapped.[68] French, Spanish, Dutch, and Scandinavian mariners also needed interpreters. The crews of pirate ships often abandoned their vessel when forced ashore, because pirates as 'enemies of all mankind' were not entitled to hospitable reception. Fourteen men from a 'rover' that was wrecked at Bishopstone, Sussex, in 1578 'left the goods and boat there and ran away' to avoid prosecution.[69] At least one of the pirates who 'fled away' after another ship was 'spoiled and torn in pieces' in north Devon in 1588 ended up in Exeter gaol.[70] When the Spanish Armada vessel *San Pedro Mayor* was wrecked at Bigbury Bay that October, having circumnavigated the British Isles, more than 140 soldiers and crew were held at Kingsbridge and nearby villages, while the captain and officers of quality were imprisoned at Ilton Castle, the home of Sir William Courtney, on whose land they had come ashore. Because 'they were driven into this realm by chance, and came not of any set purpose', these men were thought to be entitled to 'relief' and lodging. The presence of so many shipwrecked foreigners, some of them sick, posed problems of cost and security until the men could be ransomed, exchanged, or otherwise enlarged. Most

[66] Margaret Spufford, *The Great Reclothing of Rural England: Petty Chapmen and their Ware in the Seventeenth Century* (1984), 25. The seaman was Thomas Broderick, and his wrecked ship was bound for the West Indies.

[67] SP 16/63, fo. 9.

[68] *Liverpool Town Books*, i. *1550–1571*, ed. J. A. Twemlow (Liverpool, 1918), 161.

[69] East Sussex Record Office, SAS/A596, fos 17–22; Mark Hanna, *Pirate Nests and the Rise of the British Empire, 1570–1740* (Chapel Hill, 2015).

[70] BL, Lansdowne MS 145, fo. 350.

went home under a flag of truce in December 1589, but some remained prisoners until 1597. Several died in Devon, 'whereof one was a negro'.[71]

Conventions of reciprocity secured equitable treatment for alien commercial seafarers, but foreigners faced unwelcome complexities if they happened to be wrecked when their countries and England were at war.[72] Interrogation and confinement could follow their coming ashore. When a Dunkirk raider was wrecked on the coast of Lincolnshire in 1626, the crew were brought to London as prisoners before being released.[73] When a French man-of-war ran aground on the Lizard in 1628, the enemy sailors 'forsook her and fled'.[74] The men of a Biscayne ship that was wrecked on the coast of Dorset in January 1629 were 'plundered and stripped' by local inhabitants who considered them Spanish. Among the passengers was the Stuart diplomat Endymion Porter, in Spanish costume, who was imagined to be an enemy alien. Porter took Spanish officers 'of quality' with him to London, while a charitable local gentleman provided clothing and supplies for the rest of the crew. Some of these seamen were stuck in Dorset until March and were eventually repatriated via Portsmouth.[75] Dutch seamen were generally well treated, but faced complexities if they mischanced on English beaches in wartime. The master of a Dutch East Indiaman that grounded at Portland in January 1673 made sure to destroy all papers and letters, and to throw muskets and small arms overboard, before surrendering to Dorset authorities.[76] Foreign merchantmen that were wrecked on later Stuart beaches often secured favourable arrangements for salvage, facilitated by their country's ambassadors or agents.

Civil-war enmities also added to mariners' distress. Six seamen suspected of being Irish rebels were imprisoned at Salcombe, Devon, in 1642 after their *Unity* had been blown off its course from Saint Malo to Cork.[77] A royalist shipwreck survivor in 1650 spent nine months as a prisoner of the Commonwealth after being pulled from the waves near St Michael's Mount, Cornwall.[78] Ransoms and exchanges redeemed others.

These men, and hundreds like them, were understandably bitter at their treatment and loss. Roughly cast from sea to land, they witnessed the end of their ships, the deaths of companions, and the gathering of their goods by salvagers and scavengers. Their lives intersected briefly with those of

[71] SP 12/218, fos 7–9, 32–23; PC 2/15, p. 350; Colin Martin and Geoffrey Parker, *The Spanish Armada* (1988), 201, 205–7. I am grateful to Geoffrey Parker for information on the Spanish side of this episode

[72] See Hershenzon, *Captive Sea*, 134, on negative and positive 'reciprocity'.

[73] *CSP Venice 1625–26*, 596.

[74] SP 16/136, fo. 36.

[75] *CSP Venice 1628–29*, 466, 492–3; PC 2/39, fo. 21; SP 16/131, fos 12, 27; SP 16/132, fo. 85; SP 16/142, fo. 12.

[76] HCA 32/88/27.

[77] *A Calendar of Material Relating to Ireland from the High Court of Admiralty 1641–1660*, ed. Elaine Murphy (Dublin, 2011), 4–6, 11.

[78] SP 29/22, fo. 36.

coastal communities, as marine merchandise, trappings, and fittings became someone else's booty. Bewildered mariners had no cause to love the coves of Cornwall, the sandy beaches of Devon, or the shingle shores of Sussex and East Anglia, but these and other sites of shipwreck saw some of the most critical moments of their lives.

10

Material Bounty Brought Ashore

The wreckage that came ashore from stricken vessels, and passed into the hands of villagers, gentlemen, and officials, varied enormously in content, condition, and worth. Everything consigned for passage at sea, including the equipment and possessions of seamen, was at risk of loss. The transfer could be chaotic, informal, and sometimes illicit, but reports, accounts, and inventories indicate the diversity of items recovered and the values sometimes attached to them. This chapter examines materials that changed hands when shattered ships came ashore and takes stock of the findalls and gatherings that constituted gains from wrecks. Benefiting from recent scholarship on materiality and the 'traffic in things', it emphasizes the weight and heft of goods and gear, their social as well as economic significance, and the effort involved in their handling as they passed across coastal hinterlands.[1]

Goods from the Sea

The nature and meaning of goods changed as people hauled them, valued them, or associated them with exotic locales or privileged status. Their character altered through implication in activities, processes, and events. Materials that were grown, shorn, wrought, packed, and prepared for trade in their places of origin acquired varying commercial value. Commodities by the bale, jar, piece, pocket, or container became merchandize when shippers assigned them for traffic. From cartage or wharfage on land, they became stowage and lading at sea. From objects of commerce, they became goods for consumption. Law and politics redefined some items as contraband. Exotic cargoes—wines from the Continent and the Canaries, fruits of the Mediterranean, spices of Asia and the East—carried resonance of their source. Irish tallow, Newcastle coal, Baltic timber, and Holland cloth all had the whiff of elsewhere. So too did American tobacco and Spanish silver. Provenance

[1] Theoretical considerations are addressed in Frank Trentmann, 'Materiality in the Future of History: Things, Practices, and Policies', *Journal of British Studies*, 48 (2009), 283–307; Ian Cook and Divya P. Tolia-Kelly, 'Material Geographies', in Dan Hicks and Mary C. Beaudry (eds), *The Oxford Handbook of Material Culture Studies* (Oxford, 2010), 99–122; Tom Johnson, 'Medieval Law and Materiality: Shipwrecks, Finders, and Property on the Suffolk Coast, ca. 1380–1410', *American Historical Review*, 120 (2015), 407–32. See also Adrian Green, 'Consumption and Material Culture', in Keith Wrightson (ed.), *A Social History of England, 1500–1750* (Cambridge, 2017), 242–66; Frank Trentmann, *Empire of Things* (New York, 2016).

Shipwrecks and the Bounty of the Sea. David Cressy, Oxford University Press. © David Cressy 2022.
DOI: 10.1093/oso/9780192863393.003.0011

was an element of identity. Goods that were the product of skill and sweat, or the labour of servants or slaves, became the detritus and gatherings of wrecks.

Destined for factors and recipients at journey's end—with bills, manifests, and marks of ownership—every cargo risked the casualties of the voyage. If a ship was in danger of sinking, and its load needed to be lightened, some of that cargo could become jetsam; if flotsam reached the shore, it would be wreckage; when retrieved, it would be salvage or plunder. Goods brought to land represented gain or loss, for local sharing, confiscation, consumption, or resale. Materials lost to the waves might attract the attention of enterprising salvors, perhaps awaiting another age for discovery. Every stage in this chain of mutations adjusted the legal and social standing of materials and their relationship with human agents.

Shipwrecks remade the social meaning of goods and altered their moral, cultural, and economic connotations. The violent curtailment of a voyage transformed ships into wreckage and merchandize into booty, as vessels broke apart and cargoes were dispersed. Ordered loads became disordered spoil. Shipmasters lost control of their lading. Coastal inhabitants picked over maritime debris. The possessions of merchants and mariners became someone else's droits or moieties, booty or plunder. Their legal standing depended on who from the ship survived, and where the material came ashore. Wrecked goods, said some shore-dwellers, were 'godsends' or 'God's grace', to be retrieved and recovered, hauled, stored, hidden, or reported, and perhaps to be traded or used. Seigneurial proprietors regarded them as rights. When investigators asked about wares that were 'bought, sold, given, bartered or exchanged, shared, consumed, broken, spent, concealed, or otherwise done away', they understood the myriad processes whereby possessions changed hands.[2] Every process or transaction altered value and significance.

Shipwrecked materials would not normally multiply the revenues or rescue the fortunes of landed proprietors, but could prove valuable additions to their domestic economy. Exotic spices, French and Spanish wines, and southern fruits and oils were enhancements to a gentleman's table and rare treats for his tenants. Baltic timbers, luxury fabrics, and the miscellany of international ladings added wealth and bulk to the proprietor's stores. To have such items arrive as God's gifts, retrieved from the shore, was surely preferable to paying a provisioner. Wrecked goods, in all their variety, proved welcome augmentations, not only to a plebian economy of makeshifts but also to economies of comfort and abundance. Money from the sea was like manna from heaven for manorial lords and coastal commoners, though not shared evenly between them.

Manorial proprietors, government officials, and ordinary shore folk all became consumers of shipwrecked goods. Theirs was not the consumption of choice and desire, attributed to discriminating shoppers, but rather the consumption of

[2] SP 12/244, fo. 276; SP 14/110, fo. 101.

opportunity. They took what came their way. One month might bring a crippled East Indiaman, laden with trade goods and treasures; next might come a tramp hoy, heavy with hides or fish. 'God's gifts' were indiscriminate and eclectic, and not to go unheeded. They landed unpredictably, to be taken by those best favoured by geography, enterprise, entitlement, and luck. Not quite 'something for nothing', items could be acquired for the cost of their gathering, subject to customary dues, fees, kickbacks, and bribes.

Owners of boats and carts could collect substantial harvests. Poorer villagers did well to come clear with a few jars of oil, a few bushels of fruit, and small loads of salvaged timber. Their gentle landlords and masters were more likely to take prime pickings. The Bacons of Norfolk and the Arundells of Cornwall, for example, stocked their storerooms with wrecked cargoes and took possession of salvageable ships. The Wardens of the Cinque Ports and agents of the Admiralty received their moieties and droits, in cash or in kind, as valuable rewards of office. The crown, as always, registered the most gains, especially when coin and bullion were in view. While commoners performed the labour, and carried the opprobrium, the elite gained honour and status, as well as profit, from the bounty of the sea.

Men of authority—stewards or lords of manors, and Admiralty appointees or Customs men, sometimes backed by soldiers—attended wreck sites to assert their rights. The highest-ranking officials usually took choice of ordnance, sails, anchors, or treasure, before distributing the residue among the commoners on shore. More than mere material objects, worth so much per pound, these items were markers and rewards of official or seigneurial status. Their registers of significance changed again, according to viewpoint and role, as losses to be lamented, gains to be valued, plunder to be excoriated, goods to be liquidated, or property to be stored for a year and a day. Commissioners and inspectors might see shipwrecked goods as materials to be inventoried, or as evidence of embezzlement. Moralists and sensationalists might view them as fruits of mishandling or barbarity. Much of the labour that looked like lawless pillage was in fact performed under contract—oral or implicit—on behalf of manorial lords, vice admiralty officials, or original owners, as finders and savers also looked out for themselves.

Multiple reports mention wreckers descending in swarms, their numbers expanding as information spread. Many worked in gangs or teams, under organized direction, expecting customary rewards as well as shares of the harvest. Some described wading in winter seas, sometimes in the dark, often at risk, to retrieve bobbing, broken wreckage. There was work to be done with hatchets and mallets to break apart casks and timbers. Wreckers at St Nicholas at Wade, Kent, were armed with 'axes, iron crows, iron staves, iron hammers... and long piked staffs' as they broke up a ship in November 1600.[3] Salvors at Bigbury Bay, Devon, in

[3] Kent History and Library Centre, QM/SIq/1.

February1630 were 'enforced... to go into the sea to the middle sometimes' to roll butts of wine to the beach.[4] Wreckers of the *Black Jolly* near Salcombe could work only an hour a day at low tide if the weather was fair, extending their work over weeks.[5] Several of the salvors of the *Golden Grape* were hurt as they went about their work.

Material gain required material equipment. Ropes and tackle, carts and wagons, would be needed to haul findings inshore. Small boats and draught animals helped where necessary. The scene was often one of hurried urgency, to complete the salvage, to extract the maximum, before waves and weather made further recovery impossible. These physical circumstances are part of the story. Minor injuries were not uncommon, and overambitious salvagers sometimes drowned or fell from cliffs. Explaining their actions, and awaiting payment, wreckers often stressed the hardship of their effort, even to the peril of their lives.[6]

Salvagers of a derelict off the coast of Essex in 1633 'sometimes stood up to the knees, sometimes to the waist, and sometimes up to the armpits in water', and laboured with ropes in the December North Sea 'to draw casks and goods and merchandize out of the said ship'. At least one of the savers, Richard Beale of Colchester, 'being much wearied by labouring night and day... his clothes being much wet', took 'a great cold' for his pains. Another lost his boat to a mishap.[7] Beachfront salvagers at Sidestrand, Norfolk, in 1636 struggled with 'a certain chest as wrecked there, the weight thereof was so massy and heavy that [several men] could scarce roll the same to be in safety upon the bank'.[8] Witnesses elsewhere talked of manhandling barrels, stacking wagons, and hauling loads beyond the tideline. Their statements remind us that actions in history did not simply happen but resulted from human labour.

Shipwreck material was well worth collecting, having everyday utility in the economy of coastal environments; pieces of timber, bolts of metal, and yards of cloth were readily pressed into service. Sails and anchors could always be reused. Many items from shipwrecks, however, had exotic qualities, associated more with a gentleman's table than the ordinary country economy. Their circulation gave commoners a glimpse, and perhaps a taste, of the wider world, as cosmopolitan commodities came ashore.[9]

Material from shipwrecks traded from coastal zones to inland markets. As one Elizabethan witness reported after the wreck of a transatlantic trader in Devon, the

[4] HCA 13/49, fo. 35. [5] HCA 13/30, fo. 24v.

[6] Three men drowned in 1698 while retrieving wine and fruit from the *Palmtree* near Falmouth: *Post Boy*, 19–21 July 1698.

[7] HCA 13/50, fos 556–7, 577v, 602. [8] SP 16/331, fo. 153.

[9] Some of the consequences of the cosmopolitan maritime context are explored in Beverly Lemire, *Global Trade and the Transformation of Consumer Cultures: The Material World Remade, c.1500–1820* (Cambridge, 2018), and Lauren Benton and Nathan Perl-Rosenthal (eds), *A World at Sea: Maritime Practices and Global History* (Philadelphia, 2020).

goods 'were dispersed all the country over'.[10] Raisins from the *Golden Grape*, wrecked in Dorset in 1641, reached markets at Sherborne and Taunton. Fish from a wreck at Chichester harbour was sold from Arundel to Salisbury, 40 miles distant. Wine from wrecks on the Goodwin Sands reached vintners and consumers from coastal Kent to London. Such items expanded household stores and dealers' stock, while bringing temporary enrichment to local material lives.

Mixed Cargoes

There is no national register of early modern shipwrecks, nor can a comprehensive account be given of the volume, variety, and value of wreck materials that passed from sea to shore. A crude calculation based on estimates of the volume of traffic, the size and lading of ships, and their likelihood of being cast away puts combined merchant losses to maritime mishaps in the seventeenth century in the range of £250,000 a year (see Chapter 1). The worth of items saved bore scant relation to their original cost, so that only a fraction of the sum lost by merchants came into the hands of coastal inhabitants and shore-based claimants. Much was swallowed by the sea, much ruined, and unknown sums were embezzled or purloined. Droit collectors and commissioners of inquiry were hard pressed to know exactly what had been gathered, what proportion was declared, and how much slipped from sight. Misdirection was endemic, and the record is filled with gaps.

The Admiralty and the Cinque Ports had rules and procedures, not always followed, to record the materials they recovered. To guard against fraud, and to preserve lawful rights, droit gatherers in the Cinque Ports were supposed to inventory the goods that came ashore, in cooperation with local officials.[11] Local vice admirals and commissioners had similar instructions. These requirements, if fulfilled, would have yielded paperwork that future historians could study, but compliance and preservation were erratic. Reports, inventories, certificates, and accounts survive piecemeal, but many are flawed and incomplete. Manor court rolls were similarly supposed to record presentments and valuations of tenants' findings, but these too are often fragmentary and disappointing.

Despite these shortcomings, it is possible to take stock of some of the materials that shipwrecks brought ashore. The following review addresses the heterogeneity of the maritime harvest and catalogues the commodities that transitioned from lading to loot. It is based mainly on State Papers, Admiralty depositions, and manorial records from the mid-sixteenth to the mid-seventeenth centuries.

[10] HCA 13/30, fo. 24. [11] SP 14/81, fo. 37.

An extraordinary mixture of materials was cast up by the sea or wrested from early modern wrecks. Elizabethan episodes exemplify the diversity. Wreck presentments to the Hundred jury of Penwith, Cornwall, between 1565 to 1578 included a great variety of furnishings and fittings, anchors, masts, spars, cables, and other cordage, as well as white, sweet, and Orleans wine, butter, nutmeg, cinnamon, and cloves, barrels of pitch, tar, and flour, a barrel of earthenware dishes, and three pounds of whale spermaceti.[12] The borderers of Northumberland were enriched in 1565 by the misfortunes of the *George* of Flushing, which brought them bolts of bombazine, worsted twill, taffeta, and Moroccan skins, as well as bullion, spices, books, a suit of armour, and several thousand tennis balls.[13] The bailiff of Stiffkey retained 'eight score bars of iron, two pieces of ordnance, three sacks of wet hops, two hundred clapboards, besides other pieces of broken timber' from a wreck on the Norfolk coast in 1572.[14] Later wrecks brought trophies and commodities from Asia, Africa, America, the Baltic, and the Levant.

Sir Edward Mansell's 'true inventory of all such goods as were cast to land' on his Glamorganshire property in 1583 included £12 16*s*. worth of Spanish silver, £3 worth of cloves, £2 worth of marmalade, a silver whistle, a barrel of tar, several empty casks, and three empty chests with their locks broken. Also declared were four pieces of iron ordnance, two anchors, and various cables, masts, sails, and other maritime furnishings. Mansell did not list the barrels of oranges that his tenants and neighbours distributed among themselves.[15] Wreckage recovered at Sir Edward Ameridith's manor of Stokenham, Devon, in the 1580s and 1590s included ships' fittings, skins, tallow, tools, and timbers, as well as sacks of French nuts, bags of Spanish wool, hogsheads of wine, and driblets of coins and jewelry.[16]

Goods brought ashore from the Elizabethan Goodwin Sands included cables, ropes, hawsers, and sails; oils, wines, wax, logwood, textiles, fish, ironware, bell metal, lead, copper plate and wire, brass kettles, candlesticks, tools, books, a flag of linen cloth, and in 1593 two dozen 'bundles or rolls of painted pictures'.[17] Salvagers acknowledged that they had 'spent, consumed, or concealed' various materials from ships that had perished on the sands, but promised to settle their accounts with the Cinque Ports 'at Christ-tide next'. Wagonloads of goods

[12] P. A. S. Pool, 'The Penheleg Manuscript', *Journal of the Royal Institution of Cornwall*, NS 3 (1959), 193–200.

[13] BL, MS Harley 6990, fo. 70.

[14] *The Papers of Nathaniel Bacon of Stiffkey*, i. *1556–1577*, ed. A. Hassell Smith and Gillian M. Baker (Norwich, 1979), 49.

[15] SP 12/168, fos 15–17, 48. A copy of the inventory is in National Library of Wales, Penrice and Margam MS 5278.

[16] *Elizabethan Court Rolls of Stokenham Manor 1560–1602*, ed. W. A. Roberts (Kingsbridge,1984), 105–48; STAC 8/46/12; REQ 2/1687/28.

[17] SP 11/6, fo. 117; SP 12/249, fo. 233; SP 13/F, fo. 1; Hatfield House, Cecil Papers, vol. 21/84.

meanwhile were carted from Kent into London, to be distributed among widening circles of consumption.[18]

Laden in November 1597 Spain for a voyage to the Netherlands, the 350-ton *Sea Cock* of Flushing carried 80 lasts of salt, 150 sacks of Spanish wool, 8 butts of sweet wine, 25 hogsheads of aquavit, 10 pipes of oil, about 25 or 26 hogsheads and 200 small barrels of oil, about 1,000 pounds weight of sarsaparilla, 2 barrels of nails, 500 dozen corks, almost 8,000 horns, a chest of gilt leather, and uncounted baskets of lemons. Passing on the wrong side of Cornwall, the ship 'lost her right course' and 'was cast away and lost all her lading' on the coast of Wales. Though the crew attempted to safeguard their goods, they were no match for the local proprietor and his tenants, who 'made havoc and spoil of all that was saved'. The rich cargo of the *Sea Cock* was God's gift to the local community, to the cost of the merchants of Middleborough.[19]

An expanding economy brought goods of every continent to English shores. Goods recovered from a ship 'all rent in pieces' on the Isle of Wight in 1633 included the usual anchors, cables, hawsers, sails, shrouds, yards, capstan, and navigational instruments; it also yielded four chests of indigo, three hundredweight of sarsaparilla, fourteen hundredweight of Campeche wood, and over four hundred quarters of tobacco.[20] Another new-world wreck on the island in 1635 gave up six barrels of indigo, sixteen bags of Spanish wool, a hundredweight of cochineal, a ton of dye wood, and seven hundred West India hides, all dwarfed in value by the Spanish silver that spilled into the surf.[21] The *Thomas* of London, cast away on the Isle of Wight in 1655 *en route* from Ireland to Dunkirk, carried 150 casks of butter, 80 barrels of beef, 30 casks of pork, 7 casks of tallow, 10 hogsheads of salmon, and 4 packs of feathers, a feast for local scavengers and for the garrison soldiers who attempted to secure possession.[22] The *St Jacob* of Amsterdam, which grounded on the coast of Sussex in 1655, and was stripped by tenants of the Earl of Arundel, contained 264 bales of sumac, 500 rolls of tobacco, 25 chests of sugar, 18 elephant tusks, 5 bales of linen, 4 cases of sweetmeats, 'and some other goods and merchandizes' bound for the Dutch market. The earl's steward declared, 'I seize upon all', and the goods were dispersed across southern England.[23]

Pieces of Ships

Coastal communities supported active and fluid markets for used maritime accoutrements. Sails, cables, and anchors were in constant demand, and many

[18] SP 12/249, fo. 233; SP 13/F, fo. 1; Hatfield House, Cecil Papers, vol. 21/84.
[19] HCA 13/33, fos 1–6, 27–8. [20] SP 16/244, fos 38–38^{v}. [21] SP 16/305, fos 221–2.
[22] *A Calendar of Material Relating to Ireland from the High Court of Admiralty 1641–1660*, ed. Elaine Murphy (Dublin, 2011), 144, from HCA 13/71, fos 246^{v}–247^{v}.
[23] HCA 13/70, fos 635–8; HCA 13/72, fos 21^{v}–22.

other items retrieved from wrecks found immediate use in local fishing and shipping. Navigational instruments and tools had ready buyers. Masts and ship's timbers were easily recycled, if not for other vessels then for purposes of construction. It was well known in Jacobean Cornwall that 'most of the houses near the Lizard are built with the ruins of ships', and similar observations were made on the Isles of Scilly. Touring coastal Norfolk, Daniel Defoe saw structures of all sorts 'built of old planks, beams, wales and timbers, etc., the wrecks of ships and ruins of mariners' and merchants' fortunes'. He may have seen the Elizabethan great barn at Waxham, which features a shipwrecked mast among its framing.[24] Planks and timbers from a carrack that was 'utterly cast away' near Plymouth in 1603 were requisitioned to make platforms and carriages for the fort on St Nicholas island.[25] Wood had myriad uses, and even shivered timbers could be used as fuel.

The records of manorial proprietors and official droit collectors reveal an active traffic in recovered ships' fittings. Finders registered much more than the paltry items listed in late-medieval court rolls, where materials were more often valued in pennies than shillings.[26] 'Presentments of the jury for the Admiralty... within the liberties of Folkstone and Dover' in 1566 listed anchors and cables worth £8, masts worth £2, and variously valued sails, ropes, pumps, and fishing nets.[27] Presentments in Sir John Arundell's hundred at Penwith in the 1560s and 1570s noted pieces of broken ordnance valued up to £2 13*s.* 4*d.*, two anchors each worth 20*s.*, an anchor with a buoy rope 16*s.*, and a piece of anchor 10*s.* Several masts came ashore, or were cut down, worth from 10*s.* to 30*s.*, with shrouds, stays, and netting from 2*s.* 8*d.* to 13*s.* Ships' beams and timbers were valued at 5*s.* to 7*s.* These were notional values, for the record, and may have been much lower than the items' actual worth. Ships cast away on this west Cornish coast more often yielded debris than intact hulls and furnishings, and much may have escaped legal reckoning. Arundell's court registered several sail yards, including one sold for 5*s.* 4*d.* to the vicar at Sennen. Much more valuable, and available for immediate service, an eight-ton pinnace was valued at £7, and a six-ton pinnace at £5. A hulk of 100 tons, with usable masts and sail, was 'kept to Sir John Arundell's use as lord of the franchise', and Arundell also took for himself a derelict Portuguese caravel that his court declined to value.[28]

[24] SP 14/115, fo. 4; Daniel Defoe, *A Tour through the Whole Island of Great Britain*, ed. Pat Rogers (1971), 94, 235–6; John G. Rule, 'Wrecking and Coastal Plunder', in Douglas Hay, Peter Linebaugh, John G. Rule, et al. (eds), *Albion's Fatal Tree: Crime and Society in Eighteenth-Century England* (1975), 171; Anthony Rossi, 'A Tale of Two Barns: Paston and Waxham', *Transactions of the Ancient Monuments Society*, 56 (2012), 42, 45.

[25] Hatfield House, Cecil Papers, vol. 92, fo. 41.

[26] See Johnson, 'Medieval Law and Materiality', 414, 419, 422, and Tom Johnson, 'The Economics of Shipwreck in Late Medieval Suffolk', in James P. Bowen and A. T. Brown (eds), *Custom and Commercialization in English Rural Society: Revisiting Tawney and Postan* (Hatfield, 2016), 122, 125, 127, 130, for items valued in pennies rather than shillings.

[27] SP 12/40, fos 118–27.

[28] Pool, 'Penheleg Manuscript', 193–200.

A wreck at Bishopstone, Sussex, in 1576 left valuable material in the hands of local claimants. Edmund Elphick of Blatchington had a great mast, and his neighbour John French had certain ropes; William Fawkner of Tolton had twelve masts and yards, and a broken anchor; Thomas Allen and Thomas Nichols of Meeching had a ship's boat. The total value of their findings came to £30. While lords and officials argued over jurisdictions, these coastal dwellers had maritime bounty in their possession.[29] Similarly at Stokenham, Devon, the manor court registered a variety of findings: anchors, boats, buckets, cables, casks, chains, chests, masts, and so on. An anchor unclaimed for 366 days was sold for 3*s.* in 1588 'for the use of the lord of the manor'. At nearby Salcombe a capstan from the wrecked *Black Jolly* was sold for 13*s.* 4*d.*[30]

Quick-acting scavengers stripped the sails, cables, and anchors from the *George* of Colchester after the ship 'was overwhelmed and drowned' on an Essex sandbank in September 1580. The crew had gone for help, but when they returned they found themselves dispossessed. The local man William Collins denied having any of their tackle, but then offered to restore anchors and cables in his possession for 20*s.* The aggrieved master of the *George* complained to an Admiralty court that 'they were forced to give him 3*s.* 8*d.* in hand, and promised to pay him 10*s.* more before they could receive the same'. Further information emerged that Collins had taken a foresail from the *George*, 'which he kept to serve his own ketch', as well as various ropes and shrouds.[31] A grounded or abandoned ship was like a sail loft or chandlery, from which wreckers could take what they fancied, subject to later correction. Cables 172 fathoms long (1,032 feet) came ashore from the *Anne Frauncis* in 1583, though their ownership was in dispute.[32] Henry Wyles of Sandwich, Kent, went after the sails and tackle of the *Dolphin* of Flushing in 1585, but discovered them already taken, 'but by whom he knoweth not'.[33]

Seventeenth-century examples show no let-up in appropriation of maritime materials. After the collier *Carnation* of Ipswich had 'split all in pieces' on the Yorkshire coast in November 1614, the surviving officer managed to save £30 worth of ropes and some sails, but lost them to 'the country people', who cut them in pieces and carried them away.[34] In 1616 the fisherman Henry Gillow of Walmer, Kent, found the main topsail of the *Jonas* of Amsterdam, worth £42 when new, which he and others cut in pieces 'and converted to their own use'.[35]

Though wet and torn, a topsail floating in the sea near Brighton in 1624 was appraised at £7, earning half that sum for the fisherman who found it.[36] All the masts and yards of the *St Andrew* were saved in 1634, though several other pieces of the ship were 'good for nought but firewood'.[37] Mariners of the *Guifte of God* of

[29] East Sussex Record Office, SAS/A594, A596, A757.
[30] *Elizabethan Court Rolls of Stokenham Manor*, 144–8; HCA 13/30, fo. 24.
[31] HCA 13/24, fos 165–6. [32] SP 12/168, fo. 17. [33] SP 12/184, fo. 31.
[34] HCA 13/42, fos 278–278^{v}. [35] SP 14/86, fo. 198^{v}. [36] SP 14/173, fo. 129.
[37] SP 16/259, fo. 197.

Hull, which perished near Newhaven, Sussex, in 1636, saved 'all her masts, yards, sails, ropes and rigging, and all things also belonging to the said ship at the time of her casting way', except for 'the great cable and anchor... which was saved but seized for the use of the lord of the soil.' The crew managed to raise £13 18*s*. from the sale of this material, to pay for their diet and homeward travel.[38] A wreck at Seaford in 1637 yielded £100 worth of ship's furnishings.[39] Flags brought ashore included a 'streamer' from the *Anne Frauncis*, 'an ancient' from the *Dolphin* of Flushing, and an ensign from the *Golden Grape*. A Dorset yeoman in 1641 had an astrolabe, a cross-staff, and a quadrant, which could be useful to other mariners. Pieces of the wreck were disposed of at Weymouth and sold further along the coast at Ringstead.[40]

The oyster dredger Peter Lawrence of Great Wakering, Essex, sold two dozen of the copper plates that he took from the *St Jacob* of Danzig when the ship was stranded on a sandbank in 1648.[41] Wreck harvest in later decades included the usual array of cables, stays, ropes, masts, spars, sails, anchors, a pump, and a capstan, as expanding traffic increased the volume of wreckage.[42] Bolts and fasteners could be reused, but nobody in England is known to have shared the belief in seventeenth-century France that 'a nail taken out of a shipwrecked vessel is excellent for the epileptic fits'.[43]

Ordnance

Most commercial ships were armed against pirates, privateers, and foreign foes. Their iron or bronze guns were valuable prizes, often claimed from wrecks for the service of the state. Bronze cannonry typically weighed from 20 to 40 hundredweight (1–2 tons), requiring strenuous haulage. The guns cost around £7 per hundredweight to make and earned some salvors 20*s*. per hundredweight for their recovery.[44]

Shipwrecks put some of this weaponry in private hands, until compensation could be arranged. The manor of Bishopstone, Sussex, retained two falconets

[38] HCA 13/52, fos 319^{v}–320. [39] SP 16/365, fos 17^{v}, 19, 27, 193, 195–7.

[40] Wiltshire and Swindon History Centre, 865/404, Ellis accounts, 1642. For the *Golden Grape* haul, see Chapter 8.

[41] HCA 13/61, fo. 46.

[42] HCA 13/70, fo. 47; HCA 13/72, fo. 13; Norfolk Record Office, LEST/Q 37, 47–8 ('Wreck goods bought' and 'Wreck goods delivered', 1695–6); Christobel M. Hoare, *The History of an East Anglian Soke: Studies in Original Documents* (Bedford, 1918). 352–3.

[43] Bureau d'addresse et de rencontre, *A General Collection of Discourses of the Virtuosi of France* (1664), 294.

[44] Ruth Rhynas Brown, 'The Thundering Cannon: Guns for the English Navy in the 17th Century', in Gert Groenendijk et al. (eds), *A Farewell to Arms: Studies on the History of Arms and Armour* (Delft, 2004), 123–33; Frank L. Fox, 'The *London* of 1656: Her History and Armament', *Journal of the Ordnance Society*, 23 (2011), 15–44.

(light cannon) worth £6 in 1576 until right ownership was resolved.[45] Sir Edward Mansell had four cast-iron pieces from the *Anne Frauncis* in 1583, and some disassembled ordnance.[46] An Admiralty investigation in 1592 heard that 'Roger Chope and William Partridge of Chilston have the eight pieces of ordnance and sundry pieces of cables' from the man-of-war *Black Jolly*, which sank near Salcombe, Devon.[47] Companies of local salvagers made off with the munitions and ordnance of a French man-of-war that wrecked in Cornwall in 1628.[48] After a well-armed Biscayner 'ran aground and went to pieces' on the coast of Dorset in 1629, local gentlemen petitioned for 'the ordnance and powder and musket not disposed of', and asked to keep three or four cannons at Burton Bradstock, 'to guard the place and country from pirates or other incursions'.[49]

In more examples, the Scarborough merchant Timon Thomas ended up with three bronze cannon from the Dunkirk privateer *Fortune*, which was wrecked in Yorkshire in 1632.[50] Servants of an Isle of Wight landowner took two pieces of ordnance from a wreck in 1635, 'notwithstanding they were commanded the contrary in the king's name'.[51] The guns were held for the value of their metal, sold to other mariners, or eventually released to the crown. Organized attempts to recover naval ordnance from sunken warships are discussed in Chapter 11. Shipwrecks also yielded a variety of lesser armaments: calivers, murdering pieces, muskets, and in Dorset in 1604 'a chest of arrows'.[52] Guns from the *Golden Grape* were held in a warehouse at Weymouth before being released to the Admiralty. The captain of Carisbrooke Castle took two pieces of ordnance and a murderer from the *Thomas*, which was wrecked on the Isle of Wight in 1655.[53]

Wine

The English did not make wine, but the middling elite and gentry relished Rhenish wine, and consumed huge amounts of white wine and claret from France, and sweeter wines such as sack and muscadine from Spain, Portugal, and the Canary Islands. London alone landed wine worth £275,000 a year in the first half of the seventeenth century, more than any other imported commodity.[54] Wine arrived in bulk in wooden tuns (210 English gallons, about 955 litres), pipes or butts (105 gallons), hogsheads (52.5 gallons), and barrels (26.25 gallons). Prices varied with desirability and market conditions, with French wines often valued at £6 per tun

45 East Sussex Record Office, SAS/A594. 46 SP 12/168, fo. 17. 47 HCA 13/30, fo. 24.
48 SP 16/136, fo. 36. 49 *CSP Venice 1628–29*, 466; SP 16/140, fo. 47; SP 16/142, fo. 12v.
50 HCA 13/50, fo. 123. 51 SP 16/311, fo. 41.
52 SP 14/8, fo. 26; West Sussex Record Office, EP/1/55/134.
53 *Calendar of Material Relating to Ireland from the High Court of Admiralty 1641–1660*, 144.
54 C. G. A. Clay, *Economic Expansion and Social Change: England 1500–1700*, 2 vols (Cambridge, 1984), ii. 156.

on board, and stronger sack at £12 per tun before the addition of markups, commissions, and duties. Wine retailed in London for £14 or £15 per tun, with drinkers paying 2*d.* to 12*d.* per pint. The provincial gentlewoman Joyce Jeffries paid 6*d.* to 7*d.* per pint of claret, and 8*d.* to 9*d.* per pint for muscadine and sack in the 1640s. The Sussex rector Giles Moore paid a shilling per pint for wine in the early 1660s.[55] Opportunities to evade Excise duties made shipwrecked wine especially susceptible to concealment and dissimulation.[56] The Hastings fishermen who took 20 tuns of wine from a Hamburg vessel wrecked in Sussex in 1652 were allowed to sell it only after paying Excise and Customs.[57]

Prices for Canary wine were erratic. A merchant testified in 1641 that a butt of Canary was worth £9 at lading in the islands, but could be sold in London for £15 or £16. Other dealers valued good Canary from £13 to £18 per pipe, but sold deteriorated wine at less than half that price.[58] Amid shortages of supply in 1677, the price of dockside Canary wine reached £20 per pipe.[59]

Salvage values were especially unstable. A schedule of shipwrecked goods in 1655 listed white wine at £4 1*s.* per tun, and spirits at five times that value.[60] In 1706, in the course of a war in which French goods were embargoed, the steward of the manor of Preston, Sussex, hoped that wine his tenants had taken from the sea would be worth £15 a hogshead at Tunbridge Wells market, 'but if in the meantime a peace be made with France it will be too late'. His mistress Lady Shirley, married to a baron of the Exchequer, asked for shipwrecked wine to be sent up to London, 'so we may drink it, which will end the dispute with the commissioners of the customs'. The steward had faced down 'the mob' who were manhandling the wine, 'offered them half for salvage', and even persuaded them to carry the hogsheads to Brighton.[61]

The wrecks of wine ships drew enthusiastic attention, though salvors were not always honest about what they found and how much they declared. The wine was sometimes described as 'brackish', or 'very salt and nothing worth', while recovered pipes and hogsheads were reported 'but half full'. These may have been fair assessments, but they could also have been excuses for not rendering everything to rightful claimants or to Customs authorities. One finder's hogshead from a wreck at Birling, Sussex, allegedly 'broke falling out of the wain', while another contained only smaller amounts, 'which his folks drank up'.[62] The

[55] HCA 13/70, fo. 425; *The Business and Household Accounts of Joyce Jeffreys, Spinster of Hereford, 1638–1648*, ed. Judith M. Spicksley (Oxford, 2012), 247–87; *The Journal of Giles Moore 1656–1679*, ed. Ruth Bird, Sussex Record Society, vol. 68 (1971), 257.

[56] Edward Carson, *The Ancient and Rightful Customs: A History of the English Customs Service* (1972), 43, 48, 56–117.

[57] SP 25/66, fo. 157.

[58] HCA 13/55, fos 453^{v}–454; HCA 13/56, fo. 389^{v}.

[59] SP 29/390, fo. 77.

[60] HCA 13/127, fo. 25^{v}; A. D. Francis, *The Wine Trade* (1972); Motoko Hori, 'The Price and Quality of Wine and Conspicuous Consumption in England 1646–1759', *English Historical Review*, 123 (2008), 1457–69.

[61] East Sussex Record Office, BH/ES/ET/87–90.

[62] East Sussex Record Office, AMS 4606/1.

breaking-open of kegs on the beach was not unknown, though reports of orgiastic inebriation are most likely exaggerated. Short measures were not surprising in light of ordinary leakage, shipboard pilferage, and negociants' dishonesty.[63]

Rich wrecks brought wine galore, to be shared with inland drinkers. Twenty pounds worth of wine was retrieved near Folkstone in 1566, including a butt of malmsey valued at £3 6*s.* 8*d.*[64] An unnamed ship, believed to be a pirate, 'by tempest spoiled' and wrecked at Hayling Island, Hampshire, in November 1609, carried 27 tuns of claret, 22 of which were bought by the vintner Owen Jennings of Portsmouth before government officials arrived on the scene. Several thousand gallons of French red wine flowed into the Hampshire economy.[65] Agents of the Cinque Ports held 41 pipes of white wine found floating off Dover in February 1622, and recommended that the Lord Warden sell them in London.[66]

Only 75 of the 270 pipes of wine aboard the Canary trader *Susan*, wrecked in Devon, in February 1630, were saved and declared to authorities, and some of these were said to be 'dampnified'. The lifesaving landowner John Pollexfen (alias Poulson) used teams of oxen to save 43 pipes (roughly 4,500 gallons), while his neighbour Arthur Ashford had 32 pipes rolled to his cellar. Ashford collaborated with Admiralty commissioners and accepted £50 for relinquishing his haul, but Pollexfen 'would not accept' their offer. Workers and tenants moved £825 worth of wine, but it cannot be calculated how much stayed in the locality.[67] Salvagers of the *Return* in 1632 recovered 9 butts of French wine but were disappointed to find it 'noisesome and offensive', contaminated by seawater.[68]

Most of the wine and aquavit that the *Guifte of God* was carrying from France perished in the sea when she was wrecked in Sussex in 1636, but an unknown amount 'was stolen and carried away by force by the country people inhabiting thereabouts'.[69] Most of the 56 tuns of French wine lost from the *Mary Rose* in Sussex later that year similarly escaped accounting.[70] Concealment, dissimilation, and short measure were rampant, with varying degrees of collusion among finders, shippers, appraisers, and authorities.

Local gentlemen often kept pipes and hogsheads for themselves. A wreck at Bishopstone, Sussex, in 1578 yielded over £100 worth of wine, snapped up by the gentry, as well as pickings for the poorer folk.[71] When another wine ship was wrecked in Norfolk in 1590, a manorial jury reported that 'three hogsheads were carried to Hunstanton Hall to Sir Nicholas Le Strange's house, by whom we do not know'. More were 'detained to the use of the lord of the manor', 'to the use of

[63] The 'ordinary leakage' of French wine shipped to Ireland in 1643 was 10%–14%, 'depending on the quality of the cask, and wind and weather' (*Calendar of Material Relating to Ireland from the High Court of Admiralty 1641–1660*, 148).

[64] SP 12/40, fo. 118.

[65] Hatfield House, Cecil Papers, vol. 21/430.

[66] SP 14/127, fo. 124.

[67] HCA 13/49, fos 10–11, 34^{v}.

[68] SP 16/215, fo. 54.

[69] HCA 13/52, fo. 319^{v}.

[70] HCA 13/52, fo. 461.

[71] East Sussex Record Office, SAS/A757, SAS/A596.

Mr Nathaniel Bacon esquire', and for the pleasure of other local gentlemen.[72] Registering wrecked wine in the Cinque Ports, an official wrote knowingly to Lord Warden Zouch in 1622 regarding 'your half tun to be laid for your own drinking'.[73] The Duke of Buckingham as Lord Admiral and Warden regularly diverted choice stocks from shipwrecks and prizes to his own household account (see Chapter 6). What was the point of having lordship and droits if you could not occasionally fill your cellars and feast your fellows?

Some wrecks yielded stronger drink, such as the 60 pipes of brandy 'seized by the proprietors of the land where the same came ashore' from a shipwreck in South Wales in 1678, or the brandy divided between 'the country' and the lord of the manor in Sussex in 1695.[74] A sensation-seeking journalist reported that salvagers in Yorkshire were 'surfeited so with wine and brandy' from a wreck in 1679 that 'near half the town . . . lay drunk upon the sands'.[75] Customs men, energetic in pursuit of smugglers, tried to collect revenue from later Stuart wrecks, and faced circles of collusion and obstruction as key commodities were construed as contraband.

Oil

London imported £35,000 worth of oils annually in the reign of Charles I, a sum that quadrupled during the reign of Charles II. Vegetable oil from olives and linseed was augmented by train oil from whales and fish. The oil was primarily used for lighting and lubrication, though large amounts were used in the manufacture of cloth and leather. Culinary uses were relatively limited, though refined households knew salad oils as delicacies.[76] Oil from the Mediterranean came in wooden barrels and smaller ceramic jars. Italian oil in 22-gallon barrels sold for £3 10*s.* to £4 a barrel (rough 3*s.* 4*d.* per gallon) in the mid-Stuart metropolis; Greenland whale oil sold for £20 to £24 per tun (roughly 2*s.* per gallon).[77] Edible sweet oil was more expensive; the provincial gentlewoman Joyce Jeffries paid 5*s.* per pottle (10*s.* per gallon) for salad oil in 1644.[78]

Oil traded informally in the shipwreck economy of south-coast England. Countrymen around Pevensey, Sussex, became brokers of oil after a load landed there in 1569.[79] Some of it may have reached Ticehurst, 20 miles inland, where the Roberts family of gentry paid 16*d.* for a quarter of oil in 1574.[80]

[72] *The Official Papers of Sir Nathaniel Bacon of Stiffkey, Norfolk as Justice of the Peace 1580–1620*, ed. H. W. Saunders, Camden Society, 3rd ser. 26 (1915), 11–12.

[73] SP 14/127, fo. 148.

[74] *London Gazette*, 17–21 January 1678; *Flying Post*, 31 December 1695.

[75] *Domestick Intelligence, or News Both from the City and Country*, 30 December 1679.

[76] Clay, *Economic Expansion and Social Change*, ii. 44, 156.

[77] HCA 13/58, fo. 443; SP 16/85, fo. 74; SP 16/21, fo. 133; SP 16/354, fo. 203.

[78] *Business and Household Accounts of Joyce Jeffreys*, 255.

[79] SP 12/49, fos 154–62.

[80] *Accounts of the Roberts Family of Boarzell, Sussex c.1568–1582*, ed. Robert Tittler, Sussex Record Society, 71 (1979), 136.

Carrying 242 pipes of oil from Spain to the Netherlands, the Dutch ship *Dolphin* was cast away on the Goodwin Sands in 1585. Savers from Kentish havens brought this cargo ashore, to be shared (if declared) with the merchant owners and authorities in the Cinque Ports. John Crawnte of Broadstairs acknowledged saving 15 pipes, but was more reticent about 'one pipe of oil concealed by his company'.[81] Another well-documented wreck at Seaford, Sussex, in 1637 yielded 69 tuns of oil worth £1,516 3*s*. 4*d*. (roughly £22 per tun, £11 per pipe, or 2*s*. per gallon). Besides the amount declared to commissioners, the salvors John Bean and Richard Elphick of Seaford retained a tun of oil each for themselves. Several of the women of the community were allowed to fill buckets of oil for domestic use, as reward for their assistance in the salvage.[82] More shipwrecked oil changed hands in the Isles of Scilly in 1637 when the crew of the *Mary* of Plymouth received 'the greatest butt of oil, about six hogsheads', for their help in recovering cargo from the sunken *Guifte of God*.[83]

Oil from the *Golden Grape* changed hands for 4*s*. to 6*s*. a jar in south Dorset in 1641. Some was traded for labour, or for the hire of equipment. The lord of the manor of Wyke Regis took some by right of groundage. Salvors declared 172 jars of oil of the *Golden Grape*'s lading of 400, the rest being lost or concealed (see Chapter 8). Oil from wrecks in Norfolk in the 1650s changed hands at 20*s*. and 36*s*. a barrel, well below their price in London. Here, too, manorial lords claimed rights, releasing oil and other goods to the finders for a percentage of their appraised value.[84]

Textiles

Much of the traffic around England's coasts carried cloth. English woollens made up a substantial proportion of the nation's exports, while shippers brought in high-value fabrics from the Low Countries, France, Italy, and more distant lands of origin. Saved from the sea, merchant textiles found immediate use in local economies or were traded inland to tailors and dealers. Supervised salvage secured bolts and packs of cloth for their rightful owners, to be released on payment of moieties, droits, rewards, and fees. Some pieces inevitably escaped registration.

The borderers of Northumberland were enriched in 1565 by the misfortunes of the *George* of Flushing, when the luxury fabrics of an Edinburgh merchant arrived on their beaches.[85] Wrecks on the Goodwin Sands in 1592 filled Kentish warehouses with packs of cloth, linen, holland, fustian, napkin, grogram, pieces of tapestry, and embroidered cushions. Commissioners retrieved much from the

[81] SP 12/184, fos 30, 145.
[82] SP 16/365, fos 17^{v}, 19, 27, 193, 195–7.
[83] HCA 13/53, fo. 8^{v}.
[84] Hoare, *History of an East Anglian Soke*, 352–3.
[85] BL, MS Harley 6990, fo. 70.

savers, but some remained in private hands. The men of Deal, they reported, 'had one pack with 38 pieces of brown holland, worth above £200 sterling, and have delivered us 16 pieces amounting to £94'. Other savers declared short measure, 'kept out the best', 'will make no restitution', or sold the cloth secretly to 'buyers of good wealth'. Humble salvors, such as the fishermen John Rogers and Henry Wilson, kept yards of grogram for their share, some of which they sold, and some provided dress material for their wives. Men of Kent from Canterbury to the coast enriched themselves from this windfall, which still left several hundred pounds for distribution to legitimate claimants.[86]

In other examples, the manorial proprietor Sir John Killigrew had 'sixteen pieces of Italian velvets, divers parcels of wrought and figured taffeta, and much copper wire' from a Cornish shipwreck in 1620.[87] White stuffs, Haarlem stuffs, calico, and other draperies came ashore in Colchester in 1633 from a stranded ship off Little Holland.[88] Ten bales of French canvas, four bales of buckram, and a bale of napkins were among textiles brought ashore from the *Henry and John*, which foundered on an Essex sandbank in 1636. Witnesses saw salvagers carrying cloth to the sign of the Lion in Wakering, where some was sold to local housekeepers and tradesmen. Several of the ship's crew took part in this transfer of goods.[89] Sussex tailors likewise gained possession of silk and grogram from distressed shipping.[90] The wreck at Seaford in 1637 yielded 197 yards of silk worth £188 10*s*., and another 607 'bunches' of silk, 'much perished by the sea' but still worth £120.[91] Some of the linen aboard the *Nathaniel* of Guernsey, wrecked in Sussex in 1640, had unfortunately 'taken salt water', and was beginning to 'grow rotten and perish, both in condition and price', so commissioners were told.[92] The vice admiral of Dorset gained possession of some of the silk taffeta from the *Golden Grape* in 1641, but unknown amounts were redistributed and concealed.[93] Bales of silk from the *Peace* of Hoorn, which was wrecked in Cornwall in 1648, emerged at Plymouth markets, where Dutch agents paid 1,100 guilders (close to £100) to recover their merchandize.[94]

The combined value of these informal imports is impossible to calculate. Thousands of yards of cloth changed hands at prices that varied with quality, condition, and demand. Substantial discounts could apply to material derived from wrecks. Normal retail prices for everyday linen averaged 2*s*. per yard in the late sixteenth and early seventeenth centuries. Fine holland sold for 6*s*. a yard under Elizabeth, and 3*s*. to 6*s*. per ell in the reign of Charles I (an ell being one and a quarter yards). Fustian for a doublet cost 2*s*. 6*d*. to 3*s*. 4*d*. a yard in the

[86] SP 12/244, fos 281–6; Hatfield House, Cecil Papers, vol. 21/84. See also Cecil Papers, vol. 139/219, for a similar list of goods saved, declared, delivered, and retained.
[87] SP 14/115, fo. 4. [88] HCA 13/50, fo. 602. [89] HCA 13/52, fos 316–317^{v}, 343^{v}, 348^{v}.
[90] SP 17/D/15, items 1, 5, 6, 23, 25. [91] SP 16/365, fos 17^{v}, 19, 27, 193, 195–7.
[92] HCA 13/55, fo. 581. [93] HCA 13/58, fo. 59. [94] HCA 13/63, fo. 393.

seventeenth century.[95] Luxury fabrics were normally priced beyond the reach of ordinary people, with raw silk at 15*s*. to 30*s*. per pound weight, taffeta and other silks at 10*s*. to 18*s*. per ell, grogram around 19*s*. a yard, and velvet at 20*s*. to 22*s*. per yard. Consumers bought silk lace, ribbon, thread, buttons, and edging, as well as fine silk in many colours by the ounce, the yard, or the ell.[96] A 'piece', 'bale', or 'bunch' of silk had indeterminate dimensions, but a bolt normally measured 32 ell or 40 yards and could be worth £30 to the people who brought it ashore. Retrieved fabric represented money as well as comfort and style.

Clothes from the Sea

Shipwrecks scattered ready-to-wear clothing as well as vendible textiles. They augmented the stock of second-hand clothing, which featured commonly in ordinary people's apparel. The importance of previously worn clothes is made clear in reports of minor crimes and stocklists of travelling chapmen.[97] In remote places like the Isles of Scilly, lacking tailors and haberdashers, there may have been little to wear besides what the sea provided.[98] Coastal scavengers made free with the cast-away raiments of dead mariners and the wardrobes of unfortunate travellers. This wearing apparel was rarely subject to declaration or restitution, unless claimed by a member of the elite. The ordinary clothes of seamen were barely worth mentioning, though valuable gear might appear in inventories. Fine furnishings were more likely to be sold than worn by the finder.

The 1565 wreck in Northumberland yielded 'a sleeved cloak of black cloth guarded with velvet, a jerkin and a pair of breeches of English cloth, a shirt, a pillow bere, two pair leather pantoffles, a pair velvet slippers, [and] two pair Spanish leather shoes', evidently aristocratic accoutrements.[99] A chest of apparel saved from a wreck on the Goodwin Sands in 1592 yielded a silk doublet, a cloak, a pair of breeches, and other items that the finders sold for £3.[100] Three sea mantles, four cloaks, and twelve shirts were among items found on the foreshore of Holderness, Yorkshire, after a shipwreck in 1599.[101] More aristocratic furnishings

[95] Carole Shammas, *The Pre-Industrial Consumer in England America* (Oxford, 1990), 97; *CSPD 1673*, 466; *CSPD 1676–7*, 82; *Business and Household Accounts of Joyce Jeffreys*, 154–237.

[96] Historical Manuscripts Commission, *Calendar of the Manuscripts of... the Marquis of Salisbury*, 24 vols (1883–1976), iv. 574; SP 12/264, fo. 116; SP 16/211, fo. 123; SP 16/427, fo. 201; SP 46/76, fo. 269; SP 46/84, fo. 15; *Accounts of the Roberts Family of Boarzell, Sussex*, 95, 107; *Business and Household Accounts of Joyce Jeffreys*, 156–281.

[97] Margaret Spufford, *The Great Reclothing of Rural England: Petty Chapmen and their Wares in the Seventeenth Century* (1984); Beverly Lemire, 'The Theft of Clothes and Popular Consumerism in Early Modern England', *Journal of Social History*, 24 (1990), 255–76; Green, 'Consumption and Material Culture', 243–4.

[98] Pool, 'Penheleg Manuscript', 186, 187.

[99] BL, MS Harley 6990, fo. 70v.

[100] Hatfield House, Cecil Papers, vol. 21/84; SP 12/244, fo. 287.

[101] Stuart A. Moore, *A History of the Foreshore and the Law Relating Thereto*, 3rd edn (1888), 237.

were found in a chest washed up near Faversham in 1616: in this case a satin doublet and breeches, four Holland shirts and three bands, a pair of silk stockings and garters, velvet boot hosen, four pieces of gold and silver lace, a little dagger, two books, a box of letters, two little doublets for children, and a pair of Holland sheets. Their owner, apparently the courtier-soldier Sir Thomas Wynn, refused to pay the salvage fee demanded because his goods were damaged, so these items became available to countrymen in northern Kent.[102] Other usable findings included three pairs of stockings that Edward Brown of Seaford, Sussex, had from a wreck in 1622, and a leather jerkin and silver ring that Mark Ockendon of Birling most likely removed from a drowned mariner.[103]

Another traveller's chest recovered at Sidestrand, Norfolk, in 1624 contained

> one piece of Scotch flannel, a brass pistol, seven silver rings enamelled, one piece of silver spoon, one small silver piece of outlandish coin, three old shirts, one shirt band, two pair of cuffs, one old cloak turned and not made up, one piece of kersey containing two yards and a half, two pairs of linen stockings, one pair of farsey [perhaps kersey] stockings, one pair of blanket stockings, one old brush, one leather belt, one little small leather case with a little knife, one bodkin and one pair of scissors in it, three old tailors' waistcoats, one pair of breeches, another old brush, one old copper hatband, four pairs of old gloves, three pairs of band-strings, and one pair of brass spurs,

all reportedly damaged by salt water. Thomas Doods, lord of the manor, took possession of these items, and his court baron declared them to be worth £2–3.[104]

More finery from the sea included a scarlet cloak lined with velvet, a pair of knee-tops lined with taffeta, one silk garter, one glove wrought with silver, and various pieces of luxury fabric that the shepherd John Baker of Seaford, Sussex, found on the beach in 1633. Other wreckers squabbled over a black velvet doublet with fashionable slashings, a black cloak, a fine shirt, lace embroidered neckbands, and other pieces of expensive clothing, all apparently the possessions of a Frenchman who was willing to pay to get them back.[105] Scavengers on the same beach in 1637 found ruffled silk stockings, garters, and girdles in a chest from the *Rose* of Amsterdam, as well as 'sailors' clothes of little value'.[106] Coats, shirts, waistcoats, jerkins, and buttons were among the minor treasures of the *Golden Grape* in 1641.

[102] SP 14/89, fos 136–7.

[103] Mark Antony Lower and William Durrant Cooper, 'Further Memorials of Seaford', *Sussex Archaeological Collections*, 17 (1865), 149; East Sussex Record Office, AMS 4606/1.

[104] Christobel M. Hoare (ed.), *Records of a Norfolk Village, Being Notes on the History of the Parish of Sidestrand* (Bedford, 1914), 31, 37.

[105] SP 16/239, fo. 30^v; Lower and Cooper, 'Further Memorials of Seaford', 149–50.

[106] SP 17/D/15, items 1, 5, 6, 23, 25.

Clothes cast ashore from a wreck at Godrevy, Cornwall, in 1686 were of such high quality that they were thought to be Prince James's wardrobe.[107] A chest found on an Essex beach later in the Sturt era contained a gentleman's coats, waistcoats, breeches, leggings, stockings, shoes, gloves, hats, wigs, and a sword. The finder, a labourer of Great Clacton, was indicted for theft by the lord of the manor, who claimed all such wreck as his own.[108] Another wreck on the Isle of Wight provided the countrymen who came aboard with a store of new hats.[109] Later in the Hanoverian period the vagrant memoirist Mary Saxby found an 'opportunity... to get clothed for a trifle' when checks and muslins from a ship wrecked near Sandwich were 'sold cheap'.[110] Though never as valuable as commercial-grade wreckage, seaborne clothing found immediate utility among the coastal poor, providing elements of both covering and fashion.

Culinary Delights

Early modern consumers increasingly enjoyed imported foodstuffs that added add zest and sophistication to their cooking. Coastal inhabitants joined in this development when they handled, and sometimes sampled, comestibles that came from wrecks. Elite households prized high-value spices, grocers carried Ionian currants and 'raisins of the sun', while families of all sorts enjoyed the occasional novelties of oranges and lemons, nuts from France, and sugar from the Caribbean. The opportunities of salvage augmented the diets of ordinary people, brought tastes of the world to country kitchens, and circulated items with social cachet.[111] Wrecks also brought more familiar items, like the 60 pounds of butter that bailiffs of Sir John Arundell seized from a wreck at Zennor, Cornwall, in 1637.[112]

The early modern navigational revolution shifted international trade from the Asian spice road to the world's oceans, and brought pepper, cloves, cinnamon, ginger, nutmeg, and mace to privileged tables. Shipwrecks brought these specialties ashore. Beach scavengers in Northumberland in 1565 shared parcels of cloves, pepper, cinnamon, and ginger, along with a basket of oranges. South-coast wrecks yielded cargoes of citrus and spice. Homebound East Indiamen provided

[107] Cornwall Archives and Cornish Studies Service, AR/15/60.

[108] Essex Record Office, Q/SR 526/7.

[109] *London Post with Intelligence Foreign and Domestick*, 25–28 August 1699.

[110] Mary Saxby, *Memoirs of a Female Vagrant* (1806), 11.

[111] For the importation and adoption of non-European groceries, see Shammas, *Pre-Industrial Consumer in England and America*; Wolfgang Schivelbusch, *Tastes of Paradise: A Social History of Spices, Stimulants, and Intoxicants* (New York, 1992); Jon Stobart, 'Making the Global Local? Overseas Goods in English Rural Shops, *c.*1600–1760', *Business History*, 59 (2017), 1136–53. For the calorific value of early modern diets, see Craig Muldrew, *Food, Energy and the Creation of Industriousness: Work and Material Culture in Agrarian England, 1550–1780* (Cambridge, 2011).

[112] SP 16/370, fo. 38^{v}.

especially rich pickings. The first news of the loss of the *Royal Oak* in the Isles of Scilly in 1665 came when parcels of pepper floated to island shores.[113]

Shipwrecks delivered spices at bargain prices. Wreckers at Dover in 1616 collected 135 pounds of cloves and 47 pounds of pepper, which were locally assessed at £35, roughly half their retail value. Daniel Brown of Sandwich secured 22 pounds of cloves for £5, and was reluctant to give them back. He had them at 4*s*. 6*d*. per pound, whereas inland consumers bought cloves at 7*d*. to 8*d*. per ounce, 9*s*. or 10*s*. per pound.[114] Pepper changed hands in the Cinque Ports at 1*s*. 4*d*. per pound, when country consumers elsewhere paid more than 2*d*. an ounce, around 3*s*. per pound. (These are prices paid by the gentlewoman Joyce Jeffries at Bristol and Worcester in the early 1640s and are comparable to other gentry accounts. Especially valuable were mace at 12*d*. to 14*d*. per ounce or 18*s*. per pound, and nutmeg at 5*d*. per ounce or 6*s*. to 7*s*. per pound. Cinnamon and ginger were cheaper, at 1½*d*. per ounce, or 2*s*. per pound.[115]) The *Rose* of Amsterdam lost 50 tons of almonds and 50 tons of rice when 'she drove on shore' near Newhaven, Sussex, in 1634, and an unknown amount was gathered by scavengers.[116]

Several well-documented wrecks were laden with fruits of the Mediterranean, Malaga raisins, currants from Zante, and citrus from the groves of the south. Dorset villagers accounted for 535 barrels of raisins from the *Golden Grape* in 1641 and traded some of them to inland dealers from 20*s*. to 40*s*. per hundredweight. Other evidence from Admiralty depositions shows raisins selling as cheap as 14*s*. per hundredweight, depending on their quality and condition. Some were quickly consumed, including treats for children, but others were said to be wet or 'dampnified', and tasted of salt water.[117] The wreckers did well, as did dealers, at a time when raisins and currants retailed for 5*d*. to 7*d*. per pound, equivalent to 46*s*. to 65*s*. per hundredweight barrel.[118]

Mariners homebound from the Straits often brought baskets of citrus to sell on the side. These too became pickings for wreckers and scavengers. Some survivors of shipwrecks exchanged oranges and lemons for service or assistance, though others watched helpless as their fruit was taken ashore. Oranges fetched 5*s*. to 6*s*. per hundred in London, lemons 6*s*. to 7*s*., and generally cost more in the Christmas season.[119] Oranges and lemons passed as gifts among the gentry and were prized as remedies for sickness. The Herefordshire gentlewoman Joyce

[113] Bodleian Library, MS Rawlinson A 195, fos 180–180^{v}.

[114] SP 14/86, fos 198–200; SP 14/87, fo. 10; SP 14/88, fo. 209^{v}.

[115] *Business and Household Accounts of Joyce Jeffreys*, 233–50. Lady Margaret Roberts in Elizabethan Sussex paid 8*d*. an ounce for nutmeg, 4*d*. to 5*d*. an ounce for cloves, and 2¼*d*. an ounce for pepper: *Accounts of the Roberts Family of Boarzell, Sussex*, 63–152. The rector of Horsted Keynes, Sussex, paid 1*s*. 3*d*. for a pound of pepper in 1656: *Journal of Giles Moore*, 256.

[116] HCA 13/52, fo. 455.

[117] HCA 13/244/149; HCA 13/39, fo. 12; HCA 12/51, fos 56–9; HCA 13/58, fos 8, 540.

[118] *Business and Household Accounts of Joyce Jeffreys*, 235–71; *Journal of Giles Moore*, 255.

[119] HCA 13/52, fos 267^{v}–268^{v}.

Jeffries paid 9*d.* for six lemons in 1638 as a present for a neighbour on his deathbed. Giles Moore in Sussex paid 2*s.* 2*d.* for a basket of two dozen lemons in 1662.[120] Coastal traders in the reign of Charles II carried oranges and lemons onward from London to ports such as Boston and King's Lynn.[121]

English consumers of the mid-seventeenth century paid 12*d.* to 18*d.* per pound for sugar of varying grades and condition. Sourced mainly in the Caribbean, the commodity was barely known to their Tudor predecessors. The sweetener arrived in loaves and blocks worth 25*s.* to 55*s.*, in chests worth £15 to £25. By this reckoning, the twenty-five chests of sugar removed from the Dutch trader *St Jacob* in 1655 would have been worth at least £300 to Sussex grocers and could be retailed for twice that amount.[122] Shipwreck sugar may have spread the taste among people who might not otherwise have afforded it. Tobacco too, worth 10*s.* to 12*s.* a roll in the 1640s, came ashore from shipwrecks. Tobacco from the shipwrecked *Fortune* in 1653 enriched the deputy vice admirals of Devon and Cornwall.[123] The sale of some 1,500 rolls of American leaf from the *Constance*, wrecked in Wales in 1662, helped to relieve the survivors and reward the salvors.[124] New-world fish from the banks of Newfoundland also arrived in European ships, and these too flooded local markets when the vessels were wrecked. The fish that came ashore at Cakeham in 1676 was probably of Atlantic origin.[125]

Seaborne Wood

At least three kinds of wood came ashore from shipwrecks: ship's timbers, masts and planking that could be reused or recycled; firs, deal board, and other sawn timbers from the Baltic intended for ship construction; and tropical hardwood such as Brazil wood or Campeche wood (*pernambuco* or *haematoxylum*) primarily used to dye linen and leather. All brought gain and opportunity when misfortune led them to land.

After a ship carrying 8,560 fir deals and 40 tons of small wood had run ashore in Northumberland in December 1595, local officials allowed the master 'to sell the same to his most commodity'. Whether this was 'lawful', and how much was 'due

[120] *Business and Household Accounts of Joyce Jeffreys*, 155; *Journal of Giles Moore*, 256.

[121] T. S. Willan, *The English Coasting Trade, 1600–1750* (Manchester, 1938), 204–5.

[122] *Business and Household Accounts of Joyce Jeffreys*, 243–50; *Journal of Giles Moore*, 301. The lading of the *Flora* of Amsterdam in 1646 included thirteen chests of white sugar worth £322, and three chests of muscovado worth £47 10*s.* *Calendar of Material Relating to Ireland from the High Court of Admiralty 1641–1660*, 182; HCA 13/52, fo. 240; HCA 13/70, fos 635–8; HCA 13/72, fos 21v–22; HCA 13/127, fo. 25v.

[123] HCA 13/68, fo. 35.

[124] HCA 13/53, fo. 70; HCA 13/74, fo. 216; *Calendar of Material Relating to Ireland from the High Court of Admiralty 1641–1660*, 167.

[125] West Sussex Record Office, Ep/1/55/134.

to her highness', was for Lord Burghley in London to sort out.[126] Deal boards (sawn softwood) sold at £5 10*s.* to £6 a hundred in late Elizabethan and Jacobean England, so this load was worth close to £500.[127] Similarly valuable was the Swedish ship *Morian*, which split in pieces near Margate in May 1596, losing her lading of 124 masts, 700 deal boards, and 15 tons of fir timber, as well as 7,000 pipe-staves, and 24 oak planks 30 feet long. The wood was destined for French ship-builders at La Rochelle, but instead became 'scattered abroad and taken up by the country thereabouts' in Kent. The master protested, through an interpreter, but most of the goods had changed hands.[128] After another vessel had become derelict off the Essex coast in December 1633, a flotilla of small boats, hoys, and ketches ferried 46 tons of wood to the quays at Colchester, where local Customs officials assessed it as salvage for the king.[129] Savers and salvagers, as well as local carpenters, benefited from losses by the Baltic merchants.

Local records show small-scale transactions as well as substantial investments in wreck-scavenged wood. Thomas Doods of Sidestrand, Norfolk, bought thirteen deal spars in 1632 from a man whose name he could not remember, and sold them for 5*s.* 6*d.* a piece.[130] Another haul of ninety-six deal boards from a Norfolk wreck in 1650 brought £3 in reward to the tenants of Trimmingham.[131] Agents for Lady Wyndham's manor in north Norfolk in 1677 grabbed 4,000 deal boards, 400 timber baulks, and 150 masts from a Baltic freighter that was stranded on her ground. The sea had brought goods worth £300 into her possession, and her ladyship defied the Admiralty or anyone else to challenge for them.[132]

American logwoods also reached English beaches and found ready buyers among dealers and dyers. Protective early modern governments restricted the use of 'the false and deceivable dye called logwood' and prevented it being 'deceitfully imported' and 'secretly dispersed'.[133] Desirable but illicit logwood traded on the English black market, while only limited imports were allowed under licence at high rates of duty. Prices are hard to determine but may have reached £12 or more per ton. Kentish scavengers were no doubt pleased when the *Dolphin* of Flushing, laden with 4 tons of logwood, foundered on the Goodwin Sands in 1585; John Coppyn of Thanet took 102 Brazil logs, and the fisherman Thomas Horsenet of Walmer had 7.[134] Similarly fortunate salvors of the *Black Jolly*, cast away near Salcombe, Devon, in December 1591, brought to land 366 ends of Brazil wood, weighing more than 3½ tons.[135] Wreck commissioners on the Isle of Wight in 1633 recovered 14 hundredweight of Campeche wood, of

[126] Hatfield House, Cecil Papers, vol. 30/12. [127] HCA 13/42, fo. 898.
[128] HCA 13/32, fo. 112^{v}. [129] HCA 13/50, fos 602–4. [130] SP 16/290, fo. 56.
[131] Norfolk Record Office, GTN 2/40/35. [132] Norfolk Record Office, BL/Y2/42.
[133] 39 Elizabeth I, c. 11 (1598); PC 2/31, fo. 407; PC 2/34, fo. 119; SP 14/122, fo. 152; SP 14/127, fo. 160; SP 16/1, fo. 18; SP 16/36, fo. 126; *Stuart Royal Proclamations Volume I: Royal Proclamations of King James I 1603–1625*, ed. Paul L. Hughes and James F. Larkin (Oxford, 1973). 260.
[134] SP 12/168, fos 32, 35; SP 12/184, fo. 39. [135] HCA 13/30, fo. 24.

which 2 hundredweight had been concealed.[136] In 1635 they found 12 hundredweight more of dye wood that had come from the West Indies.[137] Scrupulous merchants knew not to import it, but useful loads came ashore from foreign wrecks and prizes.

Varied Findings

Variably laden argosies cast miscellaneous materials ashore. No list can be complete, but Irish hides, Moroccan skins, and beaver pelts from Russia and America were among noteworthy findings that fell from broken vessels. Cochineal and indigo moved from Sussex beaches to inland dyers. Loads of wax, useful for making candles and essential for sealing documents, were cast ashore in East Anglia in 1582 and were taken up by the bailiffs of Great Yarmouth. On news of this, the Officers of the Greencloth at the court of Queen Elizabeth requisitioned 'ten thousand weight of the best and purest wax, whereof her majesty doth at this present stand in need'. Admiralty commissioners would secure delivery for the crown, paying other claimants the discount price normally used for purveyance.[138] Officials recovered bales of wax worth hundreds of pounds from the *Golden Lyon* and *Red Lyon*, cast away on the Goodwin Sands in December 1592. Three bales carried to John Philpot's house near Dover were mostly traceable, 'except one cake that Wellod's widow got', and others distributed to 'divers of the parish'. Householders and their wives traded cakes of wax for 6*d.* a pound, sometimes making 20*s.* in an evening.[139] The wreck of the *Hopewell* on an Essex sandbank in 1634 yielded 'ten pieces of wax containing 27 hundredweight, one quarter, and thirteen pounds', which changed hands several times before being sold to a chandler in Maldon for £41.[140] It is not known what happened to the two hundred elephants' tusks salvaged at Colchester in 1633, or the eighteen from the *St Jacob* in 1655, but presumably the ivory found ready purchasers.[141]

Several chests or barrels of books came ashore, some damaged by seawater. Most were shipments from the Low Countries or the possessions of mariners and travellers. Books from Catholic Antwerp bound for Catholic Scotland were among the spoils of the *George* of Flushing that was wrecked on the Northumberland coast in 1565. Salvagers retrieved several packs of books from the beach at Bishopstone, Sussex, in 1578.[142] Thomas Denny of Bewdsey, Suffolk, took four or five books from the stricken *Mewe* of Wismere in 1580.[143] More Dutch books

[136] SP 16/244, fo. 38. [137] SP 16/305, fo. 221^{v}.

[138] *The Papers of Nathaniel Bacon of Stiffkey*, ii. *1578–1585*, ed. A. Hassell Smith and Gillian M. Baker (Norwich, 1983), 195–6.

[139] Hatfield House, Cecil Papers, vol. 21/84; SP 12/244, fos 277^{v}–280. [140] HCA 13/55, fo. 471.

[141] HCA 13/50, fo. 602^{v}; HCA 13/70, fo. 635. Elephant ivory became a staple of the Guinea trade.

[142] East Sussex Record Office, SAS/A596, SAS/A757. [143] HCA 13/24, fo.163^{v}.

came from the *St Peter* of Amsterdam, which was cast away in Kent 1592.[144] Illiterate fishermen scavenging a wreck on the Goodwin Sands later that year 'found a truss of canvas wherein were divers books which were in loose papers unbound', but they left all but a few 'as matters nothing worth in their understanding, for that they were so wet'.[145] More appreciative, the vice admiral of Lincoln had 'a barrel of old books' from a wreck on his shores in 1629.[146] Another Dutch ship, the *St Andrew*, gave salvagers ten bundles of Flemish school cards, twelve pairs to the bundle, when it was cast away in Sussex in 1633.[147] French books came ashore from the French vessel wrecked near Chichester harbour in the reign of Charles II.[148]

Twelve trusses or bundles of paper and 290 reams of loose paper, imported from France, were retrieved from the *Henry and John* of Weymouth when that ship 'bilged and became full of water' off Shoeburyness, Essex, in 1636. The stationery was 'much dampnified and spoiled' but still usable, a crewman reported, and 'a good deal of the paper laden in the said ship [was] purloined and taken away by the country people'.[149] A bundle of paper traditionally comprised two reams, a ream had five hundred sheets, and a twentieth of a ream was a quire, which retailed from 4*d.* to 6d., so God's gift, in this instance, was worth close to £100.

Coin and Bullion

All findings paled in value beside the treasure that shipwrecks occasionally brought ashore. Merchants of all nations carried money in their purses, and mariners often toted coins or jewels. East India traders carried specie to underwrite their projects or reward their investors. New World silver passed from Spain to the Netherlands, sometimes illicitly, at risk of wreck on English shores. Shoreline scavengers hoped for 'money, bullion, gold, and silver', and sometimes their wishes were fulfilled. Silver came as plate, currency, cast bars, or rough-shaped pigs or wedges. Wrought silver was worth 5*s.* 8*d.* an ounce, more than £4 10*s.* a pound, in mid-Stuart England. A bar of silver loaded at San Lucar in 1636 was said to be worth £250, and some ships carried dozens.[150] A single piece of eight was worth roughly 4*s.* 6*d.*[151] Tangible, tactile, though useful for nothing but exchange, foreign coins stood out in a rural economy that was chronically starved of cash.[152]

[144] SP 13/F, 1. [145] SP 12/244, fo. 285^{v}. [146] SP 16/152, fo. 78.

[147] SP 16/259, fo. 192. [148] West Sussex Record Office, EP/1/55/134.

[149] HCA 13/52, fos 316–316^{v}, 343^{v}. [150] HCA 13/51, fo. 531; HCA 13/52, fo. 464.

[151] *Business and Household Accounts of Joyce Jeffreys*, 147, 213; *Journal of Giles Moore*, 29. John Ellis in 1642 recorded pieces of eight at 4*s.* 4*d.* a piece, Wiltshire and Swindon History Centre, 865/404.

[152] Craig Muldrew and Stephen King, 'Cash Wages and the Economy of Makeshifts in England, 1650–1800', in Peter Scholliers and Leonard Schwartz (eds), *Experiencing Wages: Social and Cultural Aspects of Wage Forms in Europe since 1500* (New York, 2003), 155–80, esp. 156.

The wreck of the *George* of Flushing in 1565 scattered gold coins on Northumberland beaches. Neighbours found 163 crowns (each worth 5*s.*), according to the Earl of Northumberland, which 'are so dispersed into the hands of an number, and are daily exchanged and put away, as I think it will be unposssible to recover'.[153] The Suffolk gentleman Thomas Denny, reportedly the first to board the Dutch ship *Mewe* after it had been cast aground in 1580, found in the master's cabin a linen bag containing 'sixty ducats and more in rials of plate' that he kept for himself.[154] Beachcombers near Combe Martin, Devon, 'found in the sand certain gold in a purse' from a wreck there in 1588.[155] More Spanish ducats were 'rifled and spoiled at the first landing' of the *San Pedro Mayor* on Devon's south coast later that year.[156] Hoping for similar good fortune, Edward Amerideth, lord of the manor of Stokenham, Devon, convinced himself that his tenants stole a bag of gold from a wreck in 1601, despite their vehement denials.[157] Fifty pounds worth of gold in a pouch tied to a seaman's wrist were allegedly lost to the waves when the bag abraded 'through the continual motion of the dead body' after a shipwreck in Norfolk 1607.[158] Edward Payne of East Dean, Sussex, retrieved a fortune in silver from a wreck on his land in 1617, but had to hand most of it to Admiralty commissioners and merchant claimants.[159] Humberside fishermen found sixty-three pieces of gold about a beached corpse in 1627, much of which they 'divided and spent' before alerting the authorities.[160] A locked chest found by a Cornish cliff in 1633 revealed gold and silver spoons, a silver bowl, a golden chain, and other valuables, but most were lost when the finder, a husbandman, was robbed while trying to sell them at Exeter.[161]

Few wrecks spilled more treasure than the unnamed Hamburg ship that split on the Isle of Wight in October 1635. Supervised salvagers recovered four chests filled with of pieces of eight, 'and afterwards by ladles made for that purpose... and by men's hands digging into the sea sand' retrieved more than four thousand pieces 'in loose monies'. State authorities registered 16,000 pieces of eight and 73 pounds of silver from this wreck, a haul worth close to £6,000. The vast bulk of this fortune was seized for the king, but 'divers pieces of eight were in small parcels and dribblets found and taken up by the country people'. Islanders were also said to have carried off a wedge of silver, which Admiralty commissioners hoped to recover.[162] A few years later Sir Edward Seymour and Francis Courtney, esquire, divided between them Spanish money worth £216, which their men retrieved from a wreck in Devon.[163] Pieces of eight from the *Golden Grape* in 1641 brought unwonted liquidity to the south Dorset economy and paid for tailoring,

[153] BL, MS Harley 6990, fos 69–70. [154] HCA 13/24, fo.163^{v}.
[155] BL, MS Lansdowne 145, fo. 350. [156] SP 12/218, fo. 8.
[157] REQ 2/168/28; STAC 8/46/12. [158] SP 14/27, fo. 78. [159] SP 14/92, fos 64, 241.
[160] SP 16/120, fo. 52. [161] HCA 13/50, fos 262–262^{v}.
[162] SP 16/305, fos 221–2; SP 16/347, fo. 111; SP 16/350, fo. 22; SP 16/353, fo. 76.
[163] Devon Archives and Local Studies Service, L 1508 M/O/SS/Harbours/25.

accommodation, and other services. Vice Admiral John Ellis accounted for four hundred pieces of eight, worth more than £82, while his master Lord Cottington secured a bag of gold pistoles.[164]

Salvagers breaking up the hull of the 60-ton *Anne* of Dartmouth, wrecked near Birling Gap, Sussex, in November 1654, were delighted to find a dozen 'wedges or plates of silver concealed... between the ribs and the planks'. There may have been half a hundredweight of bullion, worth more than £250. After more than a year of legal wrangling, the state determined that this treasure belonged to Oliver Cromwell, the Lord Protector, but that Lady Mary Darcy, the local landed proprietor, should have a third. The *Anne*, it transpired, was formerly the *St Mary* of Saint Malo, perhaps a privateer, which the Commonwealth navy had taken as a prize and sold to a London merchant. Two bars of silver had by this time gone missing, perhaps purloined by seamen in cahoots with 'the country people', whose booty was more than anyone expected.[165]

Shipwrecks and the Economy of Makeshifts

The bounty of shipwreck was capricious, its rewards unpredictable. Nobody could count on getting rich, but coastal inhabitants—the often vilified and usually anonymous 'country people'—became accustomed to gathering materials for gain. Wrecked goods brought a few shillings here, a few pounds there, and sometimes larger windfalls. Collectivities would share in the distribution of moieties and rewards, and individuals would go home with a few sacks of raisins, a jar or two of oil, assortments of maritime debris, and occasional pieces of eight. Such findalls and petty pickings could substantially augment a countryman's earnings, providing treats for a shoreman's children. We read of local tailors supplied with cloth, shoemakers with leather, and grocers freshly stocked with spices and comestibles from the sea. One fortunate finder was able to lend money to his neighbours, which he had not previously been known to possess. Another obtained new sails for his ketch and new cables for his hoy.

The value of the shipwreck harvest may be appreciated by reference to the economic disparities of early modern society. Research by social historians finds that gentlemen who served as witnesses before ecclesiastical courts in the reign of Charles I reported a mean net worth of more than £95, while labourers, the largest and most impoverished group of countrymen, could barely command £2. Reputable craftsmen and tradesmen had an average net worth of £16, with carpenters and clothworkers owning slightly more, and tailors and shoemakers

[164] Wiltshire and Swindon History Centre, 865/404, 'The Account of Mr John Ellis... since the 10th of December 1641'; HCA 13/244/149.

[165] SP 18/95, fos 223–23v; SP 18/102, fos 92–96v; SP 18/127, fo. 32.

somewhat less. Freeholding yeoman were rising in wealth, with a mean net worth of £74, while husbandmen (mostly tenant farmers) were substantially poorer, worth on average £15.[166] These figures may be compared with measures of probated wealth, averaged over the seventeenth century, showing gentlemen worth £329 at death, yeomen £195, husbandmen £80, and labourers £28.[167]

Though gentlemen frequently spent hundreds of pounds in a year, the annual family budget among commoners was barely £40, with most of that reserved for food.[168] A countryman in Elizabethan Sussex earned wages of around 6*d.* a day for threshing, mowing, hedging, and similar work.[169] A seventeenth-century labourer was lucky to earn 1*s.* a day, on days when work was available, and was hard-pressed to make ends meet.[170] Common seamen earned only 20*s.* to 30*s.* a month in the seventeenth century, though some found opportunities to trade on their own account.[171]

Combining these indicators of worth and status with other economic information provides context for occasional gains from shipwreck. For people enmeshed in the economy of makeshifts, scraping by on the edge of privation, the gifts from the sea were veritable 'godsends'. The few shillings gained by selling maritime debris, the money accrued as shares of moieties, and the rewards of labour and plunder, brought bursts of abundance to an otherwise pinched regime. Rare rewards were substantial windfalls, quickly spent. As always, the benefits were stacked by privilege and position, with a rising tide lifting all boats.

[166] Alexandra Shepard and Judith Spicksley, 'Worth, Age, and Social Status in Early Modern England,' *Economic History Review*, 64 (2011), 493–530, tables at 517 and 520. See also Alexandra Shepard, 'Honesty, Worth and Gender in Early Modern England, 1560–1640,' in Henry French and Jonathan Barry (eds), *Identity and Agency in England, 1500–1800* (Basingstoke and New York, 2004), 87–105.

[167] David Cressy, *Literacy and the Social Order: Reading and Writing in Tudor and Stuart England* (Cambridge, 1980), 118–41.

[168] Muldrew, *Food, Energy and the Creation of Industriousness*, 215.

[169] *Accounts of the Roberts Family of Boarzell, Sussex*, 119–21, 129–30.

[170] Muldrew, *Food, Energy and the Creation of Industriousness*, 319.

[171] Richard J. Blakemore, 'Pieces of Eight, Pieces of Eight: Seamen's Earnings and the Venture Economy of Early Modern Seafaring', *Economic History Review*, 70 (2017), 1153–84.

11
Deep Recovery

When a ship foundered offshore, or broke up and sank in open water, loose fittings may have floated as flotsam, but heavy and valuable items commonly sank to the deep. Such wrecks were beyond the reach of shore-based salvagers, even those with horses and long poles. Efforts with hooks and grapnels retrieved some items from the tidal wash, but the loss was otherwise permanent without specialized intervention. Cargoes and accoutrements deteriorated under water. Anchors, ordnance, and bullion stayed where they lay. Ships that sank in harbours, rivers, or shipping channels were hazards to navigation, and needed to be marked if not moved, regardless of the value of their contents.

This chapter tells the story of underwater wreck recovery, from the daring free divers of the sixteenth century employed to locate anchors and cannons, to the enterprising syndicates of the late Stuart period who used breathing apparatus to retrieve silver bullion. It expands the discussion of wrecking from the 'petty pickings' of coastal scavengers to more ambitious harvesting by inventors and investors. Most of this book treats shipwrecks as events or episodes with legal, social, and economic consequences. Here they are also considered as sites, in the archaeological sense, from which maritime bounty could be recovered.

The problem of finding and retrieving wreckage underwater had two principal solutions. One involved deployment of equipment from surface vessels to drag or sweep the wreck zone, to locate and raise desirable items. The other, more dangerous and less common, involved diving beneath the waves, either by breath-hold or with support of some sort of tub or 'engine'. In each case, the hope was that cables could be attached to objects or structures in such a way that they could then be hauled to the surface or moved to shallow water. If ships were not too badly damaged, and not too deeply wedged in rocks, they might be 'weighed' or winched up by cables attached to salvage vessels. Underwater recovery of this sort was complicated and expensive, and mostly relied on funding by the state.

Freelance and speculative salvagers could sometimes find employment with deep-pocketed commercial patrons. The favoured vessel for this kind of work was the hoy, a single-masted coaster with shallow draught, with burden around 60 tons, sometimes working in tandem. William Bourne in *The Treasure for Traveilers* (1578) described how cables, hawsers, and ropes, deployed from a system of ships, hoys, and lighters, could be used to raise even a weighty sunken

Shipwrecks and the Bounty of the Sea. David Cressy, Oxford University Press. © David Cressy 2022.
DOI: 10.1093/oso/9780192863393.003.0012

Figure 8. *Lamentable Newes, Shewing the Wonderfull Deliverance of Maister Edmond Pet Sayler* (1623), title page. © The British Library Board, C.31.e.24.(6).

vessel.[1] The title page of the 1613 pamphlet *Lamentable Newes*, about 'great losses by sea and land', shows two men in a hoy attempting to haul up sunken goods (see Figure 8).[2]

Intrepid Divers

After the Tudor flagship *Mary Rose* had sunk in the Solent in 1545, the Admiralty engaged Venetian specialists to recover her lost guns. One of their workmen, named Jacques Francis by his masters, was a Guinea-born free diver, perhaps a former pearl fisher, who may have been a slave. His name is known because Francis gave evidence in 1548 when some of the contractors were charged with fraud. The accused challenged his testimony on the grounds that 'James Francis is

[1] William Bourne, *A Booke Called the Treasure for Traveilers* (1578), bk 4, 15–16.
[2] *Lamentable Newes, Shewing the Wonderfull Deliverance of Maister Edmond Pet Sayler* (1613).

a morisco born where they are not Christians, and slave to Peter Paulo ... and no credit or faith ought to be given to his sayings'.[3] 'Peter Paulo' was the contractor Piero Paola Corsi, who had gained 'a commission of my Lord Admiral to practice his feat of diving' within the dominions of King Edward VI. Competitors charged that one of Corsi's divers was 'a spy and a sounder of havens to bring in the Frenchmen into the realm', but this could not be proved. Combining diving with grappling, the team used 'two pairs of tongs of iron' to save ingots and ordnance from the *Mathew Barnado*, which was lost off Southampton in 1553.[4]

Already by this time Italian salvagers were experimenting with diving bells, which may have had northern European emulators.[5] The Elizabethan William Bourne credited Venetians and Italians with devising 'some great vessel of metal' that allowed them to 'breathe themselves in the air in the bottom of the sea'. The English, Bourne suggested, could use such a device 'to make their ropes fast unto any sunken ship or vessel', perhaps assisted by the leather diving suit that he also described.[6]

Elizabethan shipwrecks attracted eager salvagers, some employing divers who may have used primitive bells to retain air. A glimpse of this activity appears in correspondence concerning wrecked vessels in Ireland, perhaps stragglers from the Spanish Armada. Sir George Carew described efforts in June 1589 to recover 'three pieces of artillery of brass ... at four and a half fathom of water', where four more guns could be seen. When the cable broke, 'our diver nearly was drowned; but Irish aqua vitae hath such virtue as I hope of his recovery'. Frustrated by lack of success, Carew adds, 'if the diver of Dublin with his instruments were here, I would not doubt to bring good store of artillery from hence'. He concludes his letter by asking for 'an oyster dredger or two, in hope to scrape somewhat out of the seas'. Sir William Fitzwilliam, Elizabeth's Lord Deputy in Ireland, responded that 'the diver of Dublin, if you think he may do good, shall repair to you with all speed'.[7] The Irish Earl of Thomand wrote to Lord Burghley a year later about 'two great pieces each of them weighing twenty-five hundredweight' that he claimed to have recovered from 45 feet of water 'with great charge and labour of drowning'.[8]

Knowledge spread in the early seventeenth century that may have been more theoretical than practical. The German Franz Kessler published designs in 1617 for a *wasserharnish* that allowed a man to work under water, and these were copied and improved. Francis Bacon observed equipment 'employed for working under water on sunken ships' that allowed the diver to replenish his breath, 'and

[3] HCA 13/93, fos 203–4, 275–6. [4] REQ 2/16/28; PC 2/4, fo. 427.

[5] David Whittet Thomson, 'Two Thousand Years under Sea: The Story of the Diving Bell', *American Neptune*, 7 (1947), 261–80; Joseph Eliav, 'Guglielmo's Secret: The Enigma of the First Diving Bell used in Underwater Archaeology', *International Journal for the History of Engineering and Technology*, 85 (2015), 60–9.

[6] William Bourne, *Inventions or Devises: Very Necessary for all Generalles and Captains* (1578), 1819.

[7] Lambeth Palace Library, Carew MS 618, pp. 25, 39. [8] SP 63/155, fo. 53.

then go on with his work'. Bacon also mentioned an invention that could carry men under water, referring to the oar-driven submarine that the Dutchman Cornelius Drebbel demonstrated to James I.[9] The technology could be replicated, but was always dangerous. Underwater expertise could be mobilized only by those with deep financial resources, such as the state itself and the East India Company. But enterprise and ingenuity made possible recovery of the bounty of the sea from beneath its depths as well as from foreshores and beaches.

The most famous operative in early Stuart waters was the Dutchman Jacob Johnson or Janson, known as Jacob the Diver, who developed 'a plain and manifest way of diving deep under water'. The work was hazardous, and required substantial investment, but could yield rewarding profit. Johnson would work for the Admiralty, the East India Company, and consortia of investors, and reckoned to take half the value of whatever he brought up. His business dealings are well documented, but the methods he employed remain mysterious.

By 1624 the Dutchman had contracts to recover anchors and weaponry from the Cinque Ports, the Channel, and the North Sea.[10] He was engaged to search for chests of silver and other sunken treasure. The government employed him 'to do service in recovering sunk ordnance, wrecked goods, and moneys upon his majesty's coasts of England and Ireland'. Johnson demonstrated his skills in 1625 by successfully retrieving forty-three of fifty-nine cannons from the East Indiaman *Moon*, which had gone down near Dover. Confident in his ability, and sure of his worth, he threatened to stop work unless allowed three-quarters of the value of all brass ordnance he recovered.[11] Dutch authorities hoped that he or his team could recover cannons, cordage, and gear from their man-of-war that was lost near Mousehole, Cornwall, early in 1628.[12]

Johnson's commission expired in August 1628 at the death of Lord Admiral Buckingham, but it was quickly renewed for projects off Portsmouth, the Isle of Wight, and the West Country. He now wanted three-quarters of the value of anchors, lead, and iron ordnance brought up, two-thirds of the value of brass (bronze) ordnance, and a third of any silver bullion recovered. He claimed knowledge of 'some wrecked silver that hath lain deep under water by the space of ten years' off the Lizard, and laid plans for its retrieval. This offshore treasure kept its secrets, but success elsewhere was marked by an invoice of May 1629 for 'certain wrecked goods recovered out of the sea near the Isle of Wight by Jacob Johnson the diver', listing 2,360 reales of eight Spanish coin (worth £530), 5 pieces

[9] Franz Kessler, *Unterschiedliche bishero mehrentheils Secreta oder verborgene geheime Künste* (Oppenheim, 1617); Francis Bacon, *Novum Organum* (1620), 330; Thomson, 'Two Thousand Years under Sea', 265–6; Robert F. Marx, *History of Underwater Exploration* (New York, 1990), 31–7.

[10] SP 14/117, fo. 4; SP 14/173, fos 39, 89; SP 14/185, fo. 65.

[11] SP 16/4, fo. 87; SP 16/43, fo. 110; SP 16/142, fo. 12; Alan Roddie, 'Jacob, the Diver', *Mariner's Mirror*, 62 (1976), 253–69.

[12] SP 84/137, fo. 186.

of ordnance, 9 anchors, and 101 pigs of lead.[13] Another record from the Isle of Wight in 1631 notes that 'Jacob the diver' brought up 'one piece of ordnance of iron of twenty hundredweight or thereabout', and about a hundredweight of lead from a site 'outside the Needles at Freshwater'.[14] Johnson clashed with authorities at Dartmouth over rights to fish for wrecks and was last recorded in 1634 petitioning for relief in a thwarted diving operation in Ireland. The locals would not reveal the location of underwater wrecks and prevented him diving 'except he would allow [them] £20 for every brass piece of ordnance he should find and weigh up'.[15]

Other operations relied more on hydraulics and mechanics than on divers to raise sunken objects and to 'weigh' ships. After the warship *Anne Royal* had sunk in the Thames off Tilbury in 1636, the navy entertained competing projects for her salvage, which presented alternative technologies. One group planned to mend the leak and then force out the water, so making the hull 'swim'. John Bulmer, an engineer ('ingeneare'), offered an alternative plan, involving cables, capstans, and anchors to 'wind her upright', 'great casks' to provide buoyancy, and 'four great cables of some twelve inches to be cut into slings, to be fastened to her ports . . . to begin to raise her'. Combining the two plans promised most success. The shipbuilder Phineas Pett, who advised the crown on this project, observed that it 'cost much trouble, great charge, and no small danger to them that travailed about it'.[16] The contractor Bulmer, who spent a quarter of a year dragging the *Anne Royal* to a dock, later claimed authority from Charles I 'to take up any ordnance, ships, or other goods, wrecked or sunk in the seas, within any of his majesty's dominions', having invested 'much study, labour, and expense' in such projects, although he gave no details.[17]

Salvagers employed local knowledge, 'men, boats, cordage, cables, and other necessaries', to raise the Scottish ship *Guift of God* from a rocky ledge in the Isles of Scilly, 'where she was bilged and lay sunk in the sea about six fathoms under water' in 1636. 'Above 200 men' assisted the operation and managed to move the wreck half a ship's length before it slipped back into even deeper water. A second effort with stronger ships was more successful, dragging the *Guift of God* 'about a stone's cast from the shore' into waters barely 4 feet deep at dead low tide. The crew of the *Mary* of Plymouth, who delayed their voyage to Ireland to provide assistance, earned £120 and six hogsheads of oil for six days' work on this project.[18]

[13] SP 16/142, fos 34, 122, 153.
[14] Isle of Wight Record Office, OG/BB/224.
[15] SP 16/148, fo. 164; SP 16/150, fo. 11; SP 167, fo. 66; SP 16/229, fo. 63; SP 16/530, fo. 187; SP 63/254, fo. 438; SP 63/276, fo. 255.
[16] SP 16/319, fos 67–71, 91; *The Autobiography of Phineas Pett*, ed. W. G. Perrin, Navy Records Society (1918), 163.
[17] *To the Right Honourable the Lords, Assembled in the Higher House of Parliament, The Humble Petition of John Bulmer Sea-Captaine* (1641).
[18] HCA 13/53, fos 7^v–8^v.

A remarkable description of underwater apparatus, and its success in raising a sunken ship, appears in the journal of the pioneer leader of colonial New England, John Winthrop. In July 1640 'the *Mary Rose*, a ship of Bristol of about 200 tons... was blown in pieces with her own powder' and sank in Boston harbour. Two years later the ship was

> weighed, and brought to shore by the industry and diligence of one Edward Bendall...he made two great tubs, bigger than a butt [over 100 gallons], very tight, and open at one end, upon which were hanged so many weights as would sink it to the ground (6 hundredweight). It was let down, the diver sitting in it, a cord in his hand to give notice when they should draw him up, and another cord to show when they should remove it from place to place, so he could continue in his tub near half an hour, and fasten ropes to the ordnance, and put the lead, etc. into a net or tub. And when the tub was drawn up, one knocked upon the head of it, and thrust a long pole under water, which the diver laid hold of, and so was drawn up by it; for they might not draw the open end out of water for fear of endangering him.[19]

If such equipment could be improvised and mastered in colonial Boston, its application had potential everywhere. Bendall tried to patent his device and planned to use it for salvage in the Caribbean.[20] The savant John Wilkins caught news of a French improvement in the 1640s 'whereby a man might easily continue under water for six hours together', perhaps with air pumped down by a bellows. 'If it be true, and were commonly known,' wrote Wilkins in 1648, 'it may be of unspeakable benefit for submarine experiments and discoveries'.[21]

Fishing for Guns

England's Interregnum navy of the 1650s and the Restoration Admiralty of the 1660s needed divers and salvagers for their expanded operations. Especially well documented was Robert Willis, whose underwater operations continued intermittently from 1655 to 1666. Willis had lived in Boston, Massachusetts, and may have been associated with the ingenious Edward Bendall and copied his methods. Both men were back in London around 1653, and Bendall may have recommended his former neighbour to the Navy Commissioners; he certainly had business with them in 1655 around the time that Willis was hired. A letter

[19] *The Journal of John Winthrop 1630–1649*, ed. Richard S. Dunn, James Savage, and Laetitia Yeandle (Cambridge, MA, 1996), 331–2, 399–401.

[20] Robert Charles Anderson, *The Great Migration Begins: Immigrants to New England 1620–1633*, i. *A-F* (Boston, 1995), 156.

[21] John Wilkins, *Mathematical Magick* (1648), 186–8.

commending Willis in 1656 observes that 'this poor man is at present necessitated for want of money' and refers to 'his family now in New England, whose livelihood depend much on him'.[22]

Oliver Cromwell's navy tasked Willis with recovering guns and other marine equipment from the *Liberty*, formerly the *Charles*, a 44-gun warship that was lost on a sandbank in the North Sea off Harwich in October 1650. Initial salvage efforts retrieved one gun, but efforts then stalled until March 1655, when the state engaged Willis to find the wreck and to raise her ordnance. The work could be done only at low tide in calm conditions and was repeatedly frustrated by bad weather. Simply locating the offshore wreck posed problems. Locally engaged boatmen were promised 'five pounds, though they find her not, and ten pounds if they find her'. The site would be marked by tethered barrels, which had a tendency to disappear.[23]

A report on 'the business of the *Liberty*' in May 1655 reported success after several days 'with a sweep' of underwater drag lines.

> The ship lieth in fourteen or fifteen foot water at a low water, upon a hard sand, and she lieth upright, and some part of her deck lieth firm, whereon [Willis] saw many shot. He went down into her hold, and here he saw her ballast . . . as great stones, and there he saw a gun; he saw also some cable and a great anchor, whereto he hath put a buoy and buoy rope . . . With much difficulty, by reason of the coldness of the water and his darkness, so low in the ship, [Willis] went down again several times; and he saw two guns more lying near together upon a piece of the ship side which is fallen from the rest of her, and which piece lies flat upon the sand. He finds that she is brake asunder in two or three places; and the timbers in some places stand so high and are so raged with bolts . . . sticking out, that he could not go in some parts of her, being naked, and the place dark, lest he should have spoiled himself therewith. This is all the discovery he could make for the present, he having not those instruments which he useth for that purpose; yet he questions not but many of her guns, if not all, be recoverable.[24]

Those 'instruments' are not specified, but Willis apparently combined free diving with a diving bell or auxiliary air apparatus.

'Robert Willis, diver', spent successive seasons probing this promising wreck, so long, in fact, as the politics changed, that its Commonwealth name *Liberty*

[22] SP 18/132, fo. 53. Robert Willis and his wife Sarah had a daughter in Boston in January 1643 and another by 1653. I am grateful to Robert Anderson of the New England Historic and Genealogical Society for insight into this family and for the suggestion that they may have boarded in a Boston waterfront property belonging to Edward Bendall.

[23] SP 18/11, fo. 61; SP 18/106, fo. 111; SP 25/17, fo. 28.

[24] SP 18/106, fo. 111; SP 18/108, fo. 59. Many of these reports came from Robert Grassingham, the naval shipwright and storekeeper at Harwich.

reverted to the royalist *Charles*. The Navy Commissioners made period payments 'upon account of his wages, and to make engines for his work', and promised the diver 20*s*. for every hundredweight of brass (bronze) that he recovered. In the first season Willis raised a saker (a light cannon) of 18 hundredweight and part of a copper cauldron weighing 3 hundredweight. By 1657 his haul included three more sakers, a brass culverin, and a demi canon, with combined weight of 142 hundredweight. In 1658 he reported: 'I have taken up but one gun more, and two anchors. The gun weighed 26 cwt. [hundredweight] and odd. I have little hope of recovering any more this year, by reason of difficult weather, they being at the present covered with sand.'[25]

Modern divers may recognize some of Willis's frustrations. In August 1655 'the winds have blown so hard southwards and westwards the most part of this summer that the water thereby is thick, and withal the weather so uncertain that he could not go down hardly once in a fortnight; and when he did go down, he found that these winds had covered [the wreck] with sand'. Later in the year the Commissioners observed that 'the providence of God hath this summer past very much frustrated his expectations'. Besides the weather, he had problems with his ship and difficulties with his crew, who were loathe 'to lie day and night among the sands' so far offshore. On one occasion in 1658 he fastened onto a great gun, 'but in the heaving it up, his gear gave way three times'. On another he had to flee from a Flanders man-of-war that fired repeatedly at his hoy.[26]

After an interval, in which his patrons either died or were expelled, Robert Willis gave similar service to Charles II, with similar uneven success. 'Persevering' in August 1662, he 'swept the hatch of the *Charles* and buoyed the place', but the sea was too turbulent to 'lie over her'. A year later he reported 'little profit, although I have had much ado ... I buoyed one gun again, and did intend God willing to weigh her', but bad weather intervened. Although he had 'small benefit' from 'much pains', Willis lived 'every day in hopes of getting more', at least so he told his paymasters.[27] Optimism was part of the name of the game.

Frustrated in that season's work on the *Charles*, Willis wrote an extraordinary letter to his Admiralty sponsor Captain Hicks, dated Harwich, 6 August 1663, which is worth quoting in full:

> I writ you word last week that I had found again the gun which I formerly saw, and this week I had one tide, thinking to make her fast, but could by no means find her, although I brought up brass with an iron tong. I cannot have above two tides in a week to go down, by reason the winds and the sea are so turbulent in

[25] SP 18/115, fo. 109; SP 18/132, fo. 53; SP 16, fos 172–3; SP 18/166, fos 11, 12, 57; SP 18/168, fo. 127; SP 18/170, fo. 22; SP 18/171, fos 24, 50, 137; SP 18/189, fo. 59; SP 46/118, fo. 138.

[26] SP 18/112, fo. 162; SP 18/115, fo. 109, SP 18/191, fo. 187; SP 46/118, fo. 156.

[27] SP 29/58, fo. 97; SP 29/78, fo. 15.

> that place, and the water so thick; and most tides that I have, though the sea be smooth, then so fast as I can get down the sea begin to rise, so the hoy labours and the tub heaves and sets, that I can have no opportunity for that I go for; and by that time I have been up a quarter of an hour the sea is quiet. I am afraid the hand of God or the power of darkness is against me in that place. Yesterday, within an hour after I came out of the water, there came a strange fish and swam around the hoy and setting the water of each side of the hoy and faced us, to all our men's admiration that saw it; it had long grey whiskers five or six inches long at the least, and some say it had long hairs hanging down to the shoulders, but it looked exceeding gasfully [ghastly]. Sir, I have been down many times, and I am afraid I shall have no success in this place. I am greatly distressed, for fear of my master's displeasure, yet if you please to send word how long I shall stay, I will attend my employment with all care and diligence.[28]

Official salvage work on the *Charles* came to an end.

The technology of underwater salvage was further tested following the explosion of the 1,100-ton warship *London* in the lower Thames on 7 March 1665. In service since 1656, the fully equipped *London* was sailing to join the fleet for the recently declared war against the Dutch when the accident occurred. Samuel Pepys heard 'the sad news of the *London*' on the morning of 8 March—that 'a little this side of the buoy of the Nore she suddenly blew up. About 24 men and a woman that were in the round-house and coach saved, the rest, being above 300, drowned, the ship breaking all in pieces, with 80 pieces of brass ordnance. She lies sunk, with her round house above water.'[29] Port officials at Dover reported the same day 'that news flies apace, that that brave ship *London* is blown up but how God knows'. John Carlisle reported that 'I examined a man belonging to a catch which is come into our harbour, that was an eye witness, and about half a league off when the blow was given: nothing left but part of the hull and stern'. 'We are all lamenting the great loss of the *London*,' wrote a Whitehall official on 9 March. The Dutch heard within days that 'the *London*, prepared for vice-admiral Lawson, was blown up while sailing up the river, and only 19 out the crew of 351 saved'.[30]

Minor discrepancies in the number of guns and people lost are not surprising. On board were wives and sweethearts as well as veteran sailors and freshly pressed crew; the full complement of casualties may never be known. Some naval administrators were distressed that the *London* was carrying most of the ensigns, flags, and pennons for the fleet, and now they were hard-pressed to make signals.[31]

[28] SP 29/78, fo. 78, Willis to Hicks, Harwich, 6 August 1663. If they saw a grey seal, they should not have been surprised.

[29] *The Diary of Samuel Pepys*, ed. Robert Latham and William Matthews, 11 vols (Berkeley and Los Angles, 1970–83), vi. 52. Pepys referred on 7 March to the *London* 'manned with 350 or 400 men' (*Samuel Pepys and the Second Dutch War: Pepys's Navy White Book and Brooke House Papers*, Navy Records Society (1995), 111).

[30] SP 29/114, fo. 147; SP 29/114, fo. 195; *CSPD 1664–1665*, 249.

[31] SP 29/117, fos 37, 77.

Modern research confirms that the *London* was heavily armed with seventy-six expensive bronze guns: sixteen demi-cannon, eight 24-pounders, twenty-six culverins, twenty-four demi-culverins, and two minions, with a combined weight of more than 110 tons and a value exceeding £16,000.[32]

Recovering these guns was an urgent matter but a formidably difficult task. Three hundred barrels of gunpowder wrought massive destruction. The *London* was not just sunk but shattered. Early reports speak of her 'breaking all in pieces', with only parts of the hull and stern still visible. Local scavengers would have gone out immediately, and the government would recover what it could.

Two days after the disaster the authorities dispatched 'Robert Willis the diver' to report on 'what guns are to be saved'. Four demi-culverin and two minions were quickly retrieved, but bad weather delayed later efforts.[33] Inspection in the first week of April found 'no more of the wreck than the after timber head on her starboard side, and that was not above two foot above water', though crews were able to secure 'a lazy piece of her main topmast and the main cap'. Lambert Ward, captain of the Wapping-based pink *Sara*, judged the ship all 'blown asunder, as we find by our lead and sounding'. A more thorough survey at low water found wreckage at depths from 3 to 7 fathoms. Ward reported on 11 April that 'within her I find neither deck nor beams nor sides, but about where the mizzen mast stood and abaft it but forward on she is all dispersed abroad'.[34]

The immediate task was to mark this hazard to navigation by setting out warning buoys and by raising a beacon. Lambert Ward took soundings,

> and could not perceive anything that will do any ship harm, not about 30 or 40 foot from the beacon, which is placed [in] the aftermost timber but one; and there I find three fathom water over her; and as for another beacon, it will be needless to send for . . . she is sunk since I came here near two foot.

Ward used small grapnels and a long boathook to probe for wreckage, to little effect. 'I have swept close to her round about her about 20 or 30 fathom . . . but cannot find anything that is worth the writing.'[35]

Better-equipped contractors launched more ambitious operations, though Robert Willis had only a secondary role.[36] Captain William Badily of Deptford secured a vessel and provisions for 'attending the taking up the *London* wreck', and the Navy Commissioners engaged crews 'for the taking up and recovering of

[32] Frank L. Fox, 'The *London* of 1656: Her History and Armament', *Journal of the Ordnance Society*, 23 (2011), 15–44.

[33] WO 7/7, fos 15, 26. I am grateful to Ruth Brown for these references. See also Fox, 'The *London* of 1656', 28.

[34] SP 29/117, fos 22, 157; SP 29/149, fos 123–6.

[35] SP 29/117, fo. 157; SP 29/149, fos 122–36.

[36] Willis is mentioned in Ordnance Office records in March 1666 as due a payment of £50: WO 47/8, fo. 57^{v}. Long retired, he appears in Admiralty records from 1681 to 1683 as 'Robert Willis the diver', a rigger and a shipkeeper along the Thames at Deptford, dying by March 1683: ADM 106/355/39 and 41; ADM 106/365/24.

the ordnance, cables, and anchors belonging to his majesty's ship *London* near Chatham'.[37] The project was beset by bad weather, an uncooperative river, and failures of equipment. In a month and a half of attendance, Lambert Ward's company aboard the *Sara* gathered little more than scrap timber, cables, canvas, and 'a piece of a chain of a pump'. Time and again, their creeper fastened on something 'but could not weigh it', or 'heaved over a strain that we broke our windlass'. Divers are rarely mentioned and would have been hard-pressed to work in the estuary sand and mud. A salvage register from 4 April to 20 May 1665 lists the navy's meagre pickings: On 5 May 'we did get a piece of her lower weal some 22 foot long, with 4 bolts in it, and did get it aboard our ship'. On 15 May 'we fastened to a piece of her bilge and towed it towards Leigh, but could not fetch in . . . so was fain to let it go in eight fathom water.' The salvagers retrieved cordage, some hatch covers, and gun tackle, but no guns.[38]

Meanwhile, perhaps competitively, agents of the Ordnance Office arrived in search of the London's bronze weapons.[39] The Ordnance men sought the use of 'a Harwich hoy which hath a david and a capstall [davit and capstan] which are useful for weighing of guns, etc.' and requested the Navy Commissioners 'to assign her to this office for weighing the *London*'s guns'. This may have been a sister ship of the *Diver* hoy of Harwich that Willis had used in his search for the ordnance of the *Charles*. Primarily used to shuttle naval stores between Deptford and Harwich, the hoy was fitted with cables, blocks, and buckets, and was captained by Giles Bond. On 19 April the Ordnance Office asked for twenty-five men, 'for the more speedy and effective performance of this his majesty's service' in this regard.[40]

The *Harwich* hoy was engaged in the Thames from 8 May until 14 October 1665 'about the weighing of London's guns'. Giles Bond reported to Samuel Pepys on 15 May, 'we have taken up out of the *London* wreck one nine-inch hawser whole and 19 pieces of cable which is about 80 fathom, but no guns at all, the weather being so bad that our divers have been down but three times since . . . she sunk'. [41] The arrival of two large diving bells improved prospects of success, and so did a turn in the weather. Bond asked for six more weeks of victuals and wages in August, 'making use of the present convenient season'. By the time operations ended in the autumn, he had retrieved eighteen pieces of ordnance: four demi cannon, seven culverins, and seven demi-culverins, with a combined weight of more than 30 tons.[42]

[37] SP 29/117, fo. 22, 156; SP 29/119, fo. 93. [38] SP 29/122, fos 18–19.

[39] For rivalry between the Restoration Ordnance Office and the Admiralty, both following orders from the Privy Council and the Secretaries of State, see H. C. Tomlinson, *Guns and Government: The Ordnance Office under the Later Stuarts* (1979), 20, 28, 31–4, 164.

[40] SP 29/110, fo. 100; SP 29/112, fos 21, 67; SP 29/117, fo. 107; SP 29/118, fo. 111.

[41] SP 29/121, fo. 71; SP 29/128, fo. 65; SP 29/268, fos 27, 136.

[42] SP 29/135, fo. 71; Fox, 'The *London* of 1656', 20, 38–9.

The Ordnance Office debenture book 'for the furnishing and fitting out of the late summer fleet', dated 24 September 1667, records payment of £81 16*s.* 10½*d.* to the contractor James Maule 'for one brass 24-pound ordnance by him recovered from the *London* wreck and delivered into his majesty's stores'. The piece weighed 46 hundredweight, 3 quarters, and 2 pounds. Maule's contract discounted this by half, so his payment was based on a weight of 23 hundredweight, 2 quarters, 15 pounds, 'after the rate of £3 10*s.* per cwt.'. Everybody benefited, not least the navy, which acquired refurbished guns at a quarter of their manufactured value. At the prevailing rate of £7 10*s.* per hundredweight, a 24-pounder of the kind that Maule presented could have cost £350.[43] Maule claimed to have perfected 'the art and knowledge of diving and working perfectly with great ease under water in 20–30 or more fathoms deep', and offered that skill to Charles II with some evident success.[44]

There are two more twists in this story of wreck recovery. At some time in the late 1670s the marine engineer William Harrington and a consortium of investors promoted 'a new invention . . . to be wrought without diving, for the weighing or recovering from underwater ships' guns and goods by any accident shipwrecked or lost in harbour or at sea'. They proposed to use this gear to raise guns from the *London*, and to keep half the value of whatever they recovered. Details are obscure, but the experiment evidently proved successful, and Harrington sought payment in February 1680 of £854 5*s.* 'for weighing several guns, amongst which seven of brass and copper out of the old *London* wreck'.[45] At this point the rich City merchant Sir William Prichard entered the story, taking possession of the guns that Harrington had raised, claiming that the Ordnance Office owed him money. Much of Prichard's wealth came from supplying the Ordnance Office with cordage and match, and his technical, financial, and political connections along the river emboldened him in this claim. The dispute was unresolved in the reign of William III, when Treasury minutes in 1695 noted unreconciled accounts 'about the guns taken out of the *London* 17 or 18 years ago'. A total of nine guns may have been raised in the reigns of Charles II and James II, leaving forty-three for the twenty-first century.[46]

In 2005, after three and a half centuries of tidal churn and estuarine traffic, the remains of the *London* were rediscovered. They lie in two zones, adjacent to a

[43] WO 49/102, fo. 24; Ruth Rhynas Brown, 'The Thundering Cannon: Guns for the English Navy in the 17th Century', in Gert Groenendijk et al. (eds), *A Farewell to Arms: Studies on the History of Arms and Armour* (Delft, 2004), 125; Fox, '*London* of 1656', 22. I am grateful to Ruth Brown for supplying images, references, and information.

[44] SP 29/19, fo. 39; SP 29/29, fo. 121.

[45] SP 44/55, fos 110, 158; PC 2/68, fo. 372. Harrington was also employed, unsuccessfully, to search for silver plate lost when the *Gloucester* went down in 1682.

[46] PC 2/69, fos 161, 502; PC 2/73, fos 194, 436; Fox, '*London* of 1656', 29–37; *Calendar of Treasury Papers 1556/7–1696*, ed. Joseph Redington (1868), 365–6; the Calendar mentions four and a half pages of papers, which may shed some light on this matter.

major shipping channel, some 9 fathoms deep at low water. Port of London Authority operations in 1961 had recovered a demi-culverin from the site, and brought up two more guns in 1980, without awareness of their provenance. A commercial diver in 2007 removed five bronze guns from the wreck, declaring two to crown authorities, but fraudulently claiming that the others were found in international waters. (The diver was convicted and imprisoned in 2015, and the guns were repatriated from a collector in Florida in 2017.) In 2008 the site gained designation under the Protection of Wrecks Act (1973), and licensed investigation resumed of its 'rare and well-preserved remains'. Divers subsequently recovered one of the *London*'s gun carriages and a variety of wooden, leather, and metal items, indicative of treasures in the mud. Campaigners associated with the Nautical Archaeological Society launched an initiative in 2019 to 'Save the *London*', and have drawn attention to its possibilities. How their success compares to their seventeenth-century predecessors remains to be seen.[47]

Fishing for Treasure

Scientists, speculators, shipowners, and treasure-hunters of the later seventeenth century competed to perfect and exploit underwater apparatus. Divers and diving gear were in high demand, as the lure of profit stimulated ingenuity. Inventors patented devices for the 'discovery of wrecks and vessels sunk' (1671), for a 'new way of diving and living several hours under the water' (1675), and for equipment 'enabling persons to walk and remain under water three hours with no covering over their heads' (1687), which sounds implausible.[48] Other projectors sought patronage for 'a new sort of engine for diving, never yet used by any, and so made that a person using it may walk up and down of himself, and work on and view any wreck in the sea, and have fresh air to breath in' (1690).[49] Their competitor Francis Smartfoot offered the superior invention of 'a sea crab for working in the sea to fish and take up ships' guns and goods lost or forsaken, and a pair of lungs to be fixed to a man's back for his breathing under water as he swims' (also 1690).[50] Hoping for underwater 'curiosities', Sir Andrew Balfour recommended 'creepers, which the seamen know how to use'.[51] More traffic meant more wrecks,

[47] Fox, '*London* of 1656', 33–7; Daniel Pascoe, 'Forensic Archaeology: Gun Carriages and Bronze Guns from the Wreck of the *London* (1665)', *Journal of the Ordnance Society*, 24 (2017), 43–61; Frank L. Fox, 'The Quex Park 12-Pounder', *Journal of the Ordnance Society*, 25 (2018), 67–8; *Basildon Canvey Southend Echo*, 7 December 2017, https://www.echo-news.co.uk/news/15707555.long-lost-cannons-are-returned-to-southend/ (accessed December 2020).

[48] Thomson, 'Two Thousand Years under Sea', 268–9; Bennet Woodcroft (ed.), *Subject-Matter Index... of Patents of Invention*, 2 vols (1854), i. 239–40; ii. 540–1; *London Gazette*, 1–4 April 1672.

[49] SP 44/235, fo. 215, the petition of John Syrack and Nicholas Finchley.

[50] *Calendar of Treasury Books 1689–1692*, ed. William A. Shaw (1931), 835, 1840.

[51] Andrew Balfour, *Letters to a Friend* (Edinburgh, 1700), 49.

and incentive to recover items of value. Speculators became shareholders in ventures 'for taking up of wrecks out of the seas'.[52]

When the Dutch warship *Anne and Mary* sank near Dartmouth in 1681, England's government allowed the admiralty of Zealand 'to fish for and carry away the tackle, cannon, and whatever things else belonging to the said ship may be recovered... without any trouble or molestation'. This was a mark of goodwill to a neighbouring maritime power, now in amity after recent wars. Again in 1686, when a Dutch East Indiaman was wrecked on the Isles of Scilly, English authorities granted permission for Dutch specialists to 'fish' for 'all that remains of the said ship under water'.[53] The Dutch were experts in matters of this sort, and their equipment and methods would be closely observed.

The most substantial advance in undersea exploration was patented by Edmund Halley and his partners in 1691, and later described in the Transactions of the Royal Society. 'Being engaged in an affair that required the skill of continuing under water,' Halley writes, he devised a method to convey barrels of air down to the diving bell, that allowed men to work 'in nine or ten fathoms of water for above an hour and a half at a time, without any sort of ill consequence'. Halley's system even allowed him 'to keep a candle burning in the bell... notwithstanding the great expence of air requisite to maintain the flame'.[54] Other projectors of the early 1690s promised 'a new engine to carry air into pipes by new-contrived bellows, with plates covered with leather for securing the head and retaining the air' and other inventions 'for taking up wrecks'.[55]

Equipped with increasingly sophisticated apparatus, investors targeted wrecks that were otherwise inaccessible. Plagiarized, fanciful, or ingeniously adapted, their underwater gear opened doors to speculative investment and monopoly contracts. Enterprising treasure-hunters turned their attention to the Americas and the Caribbean, ranging the waters of Hispaniola, the Bahamas, the Bermudas, Jamaica, and by 1692 'all the seas in America' in search of Spanish treasure.[56] None was as successful as the New England mariner William Phips, who, a contemporary pamphlet celebrated, 'will fill our pockets with coin, as well as our ears with astonishment'.[57] Treasure-hunting, then as now, was a secretive business, with much hiding of places, shielding of plans, and embezzlement of loot.

[52] SP 44/235, fos 169, 215, 279, 359, 279; *Flying Post*, 25–8 June 1698; *Daily Courant*, 19 January 1720.

[53] SP 29/359, fos 38^{v}–39, 106; SP 44/56, fo. 71. See also SP 44/204, fo. 51, for a similar arrangement in 1691.

[54] Edmund Halley, 'The Art of Living under Water', *Philosophical Transactions*, 29 (1717), 492–9.

[55] SP 44/235, fo. 359, the petition of John Overing; *Calendar of Treasury Papers 1556/7–1696*, 323.

[56] *Calendar of Treasury Books 1689–1692*, 1721.

[57] *An Exact and Perfect Relation of the Arrival of the Ship the James and Mary Captain Phipps Commander* (1687).

Phips's first expedition to the Bahama Banks in 1683 yielded little profit, but it introduced him to the wreck of a Spanish galleon, north of Hispaniola. Backed by a consortium of investors led by the Duke of Albemarle, Phips undertook to recover 'the hidden treasure of the ocean'. He left England in September 1686 in the 200-ton *James and Mary*, with six divers and a diving tub on board. They reached the Ambroches Bank, now known as Silver Bank, in February 1687, and succeeded in 'taking up the cargo of above forty years wreck in full sea seventeen leagues from any shore in nine fathom water'. Indian free divers worked alongside Anglo-Europeans. Their haul included almost 3 tons of bullion, valued at more than £200,000, of which the crown took a tenth. Albemarle gained £50,000, and Phips earned more than £10,000 and a knighthood.[58] Two more voyages followed, with diminishing returns, as other treasure-hunters scoured the site. Fearful of fraud, the government instructed the Chief Justice of the Bermuda and Summer Islands (Henry Horzdesnell) 'to summon before him all persons concerned in any ship coming from the wreck near Hispaniola', to take security for 'the king's moiety of the treasure recovered'. Some no doubt was hidden, but Horzdesnell dutifully recovered £6,128 for the king, plus twelve bronze cannons.[59] The heirs and executors of some of the investors were still contending for their shares thirty years later.[60]

Sir William Phips, as we may now call him, was not the only English explorer of wrecks in the New World. Philip Ford, the Quaker owner of the *Elizabeth* of London, secured permission in November 1687 to hunt for wrecked treasure 'near the islands and shoals of Bahama', provided a fifth of all proceeds went to the king. The English governors of Jamaica and Barbados were notified of his permit, and officials in London stood ready to receive the loot. Treasury commissioners the following April acknowledged Ford's grant 'for fishing for treasure in the sea within the West Indies', and wondered what progress he had made. 'A very great treasure is supposed to have been taken up . . . yet only small parcels are sent home.' Ford, however, was vindicated when the *Richard and Sarah* arrived from Jamaica with 1,939 ounces of 'silver or Spanish moneys, broken or whole . . . being part of the treasure taken up of the wreck near Hispaniola by the ship *Elizabeth*'. On 10 May 1688 the *Elizabeth* itself reached London with a cargo of silver for the Mint. Ford's crew had given up searching the Bahamas and returned to the proven wreck fields of the Greater Antilles, either competing or collaborating with Phips.

[58] Cyrus H. Karraker, *The Hispaniola Treasure* (Philadelphia, 1934); Peter Earle, *The Wreck of the Almiranta: Sir William Phips and the Hispaniola Treasure* (1979); Peter Earle, *The Treasure of the Concepción: The Wreck of the Almiranta* (New York, 1980).

[59] *Calendar of Treasury Books 1685–1689*, ed. William A. Shaw (1923), 1632, 1651, 1866, 1868–90; *Calendar of Treasury Books 1689–1692*, ed. William A. Shaw (1931), 1112; *Calendar of Treasury Books,1693–1696*, ed. William A. Shaw (1935), 134; C. D. Chandaman, *The English Public Revenue 1660–1688* (Oxford, 1975), 348–9, 360–1.

[60] *Dame Elizabeth Shovell, Widow and Executrix of Sir John Narborough . . . The Appellants Case* (1718).

The Treasury got its share, at least of the amount declared, and Philip Ford more than made his fortune.[61]

The extraordinary success of these ventures led to a scramble of hopeful emulators, and the government demanded a greater portion of the booty. The Duke of Albemarle warned monarchs William and Mary in October 1689 that the crown's insistence on a moiety of all treasure taken up from the seas of America 'has discouraged sloopmen from seeking after new wrecks'. There would be greater incentive, he suggested, if the crown limited its claim to a tenth.[62] A spate of speculation led to the grant of at least a dozen new patents for underwater equipment and exploration between 1689 and 1693.[63]

Some of this expertise was directed to English waters. Philip Ford, who had scoured the Caribbean, secured a seven-year licence in September 1688 for 'all wrecks, jetsam, flotsam, and lagan, goods derelict, riches, bullion and plate, gold, silver coin, guns, copper, brass, iron, and other treasures' that he or his agents could recover from wrecks 'on any of the rocks, shelves, shores, seas or banks upon or near the English coast from the North Foreland to the westward of the Lizard, including the Scilly islands', to which the king was entitled 'in right of the crown, in right of the king's Admiralty, by prerogative royal, or by any right and title whatsoever'. James II was supposed to receive a fifth of everything Ford recovered from these English coasts, and a like fifth was reserved for Lord Sidney Godolphin, the proprietor of the Isles of Scilly. The grant required Ford 'to keep a true and faithful account of all his gettings, and to exhibit the same to the king or Treasury lords'. It also enjoined all admirals, vice admirals, and governors on shore to assist him in his endeavours. The crown evidently expected to profit from these arrangements and believed that Ford could deliver the goods.[64]

Among the first fruits of this venture were some pigs of silver recovered off Cornwall, perhaps from the wreck that Jacob Johnson had sought in the 1620s, or less plausibly from the *Royal Merchant* wreck of 1641. By October 1690 Ford's team had recovered more than 276 pounds of silver (worth perhaps £4,400). The Bishop of Exeter John Trelawney claimed a share of this loot by virtue of his commission as vice admiral, but lawyers demonstrated the priority of Ford's grant and upheld the wreck rights of the crown. Law, ingenuity, enterprise, and sharp dealing brought this booty ashore.[65]

[61] *Calendar of Treasury Books, 1685–1689*, 1632, 1651, 1866, 1868–90; *Publick Occurrences Truly Stated*, 29 May 1688.

[62] *Calendar of Treasury Books 1689–1692*, 274.

[63] Woodcroft (ed.), *Subject-Matter Index... of Patents of Invention*, i. 239–40; ii. 540–1.

[64] *Calendar of Treasury Books, 1685–1689*, 2060–1.

[65] *Calendar of Treasury Books 1689–1692*, 333, 858, 870, 879–80. Ford's men had a pass to return from Cornwall and the Scillies in March 1692: SP 44/342, fo. 191.

Philip Ford seems to have retired, or cashed out, when a new wave of projectors sought licences for wreck recovery in various parts of the king's dominions. Francis Smartfoot, deviser of the 'sea crab', sought rights to the 'the sole use and exercise of the several new inventions' in the same waters Ford had fished, and later claimed diving rights 'in any of his majesty's seas'. He promised the crown one-fifth of everything recovered in depths of 1–10 fathoms, and anything deeper (below 60 feet) he could keep for himself. He needed favourable incentives, he said, because 'preparing the engines and necessaries for working the said invention will be very expensive'.[66] Other projectors sought half the value of royal ships and a tenth of the value of 'all bullion from such wrecks as they should discover and raise'.[67]

Thomas Neale, esquire, who had similar claims in America, expanded his empire to include rights to wrecks off most of England's coastline from Dover to Barnstable and the west coast of Ireland. Whether he could exploit those rights was yet to be seen; in August 1691, despite scant success, Neale was 'still in hopes of a hit'.[68] By 1693 Neale's territory ranged from Havana to Nova Scotia. He was not without rivals, for the Duke of Leinster also had wreck rights throughout the New World.[69] Another consortium in 1693 arranged with Sir John Arundell of Lanherne to search for riches, goods, and chattels in the sea off his Cornish manors with 'crooks, engines or otherwise'.[70]

Later generations of salvagers had choice of more advanced equipment. Early in the reign of George I John Lethbridge (1675–1759) devised an improved 'diving suit', a wooden encasement with sealed holes for the diver's arms, and a four-inch glass viewing port, good for depths down to 10 fathoms. He used it with great success to recover treasure for the Dutch and English East India companies, on one occasion in 1721 bringing up twenty-seven chests of silver, sixty-four iron guns, and other items of value. Collaborators and competitors found plenty of use for their versions of this 'engine', which relied on air retained in the barrel.[71]

Though not crediting the 'very ingenious man' who perfected this 'engine', the under-secretary of state Charles Delafaye promoted the new equipment in 1722 as a means to fish treasure from 'very rich wrecks' in the Spanish dominions. It had already proved its worth in recovering 'twenty thousand pounds sterling, in pigs of silver and pieces of eight, and two thousand pounds in lead and brass guns that were lost in a ship cast away some years ago among the Cape Verde islands'. 'This

[66] *Calendar of Treasury Books 1689–1692*, 835, 1840; *Calendar of Treasury Books 1693–1696*, 996.

[67] *Calendar of Treasury Papers 1556/7–1696*, 323.

[68] SP 44/235, fo. 169; *Calendar of Treasury Books 1689–1692*, 832, 837, 1125, 1315, 1656, 1717; *Calendar of Treasury Books 1693–1696*, 50; SP 44/235, fo. 169.

[69] *Calendar of Treasury Books 1689–1692*, 1125, 1315, 1348–9, 1373, 1697, 1721, 1840; *Calendar of Treasury Books 1693–1696*, 50, 64; *Calendar of Treasury Papers 1556/7–1696*, 398–9.

[70] Cornwall Archives and Cornish Studies Service, AR/15/65.

[71] *Weekly Packet*, 26 March–2 April 1720; Zélide Cowan, 'John Lethbridge, Diver', *History Today*, 28 (December 1978), 825–9.

you may depend on', Delafaye assured Colonel Stanhope, 'that our people have wrought in six fathom water and may do it in twenty, continuing there half an hour at a time, and having the free use of their arms and hands so far as to dig up chests that were buried in the sand. In short, they brought us home the money, which is a sensible demonstration.'[72] Daniel Defoe saw 'several engineers and projectors, some with one sort of diving engine, and some with another', on his tour of Cornwall, and marvelled at the 'strange unprecedented ways' they retrieved riches from wrecks.[73] Other efforts with 'diving engines of an extraordinary sort' proved successful in recovering 'a great treasure of gold and silver, besides anchors, guns, etc.', from a wreck off the north of Scotland.[74]

That underwater apparatus was not always as successful as promised is indicated in Robert Heath's account of attempts 'to discover and weigh the plate of considerable value' from an East Indiaman sunk in the Isles of Scilly in 1743. This may be the most comprehensive account of eighteenth-century diving technology:

> The figure of the diving engine (made up of thick planks, bound together with iron hoops, and headed at the ends) was a tapering vessel, in which the diver was plugged up, with as much air as could be blown into it, with a pair of bellows at his going down. His naked arms went out at a couple of round holes, next the biggest end; being exactly fitted to them, wrapped around with neat's leather, to keep out the water. Lying flat on his face, with his legs buckled down with straps to keep him steady, he looked through a piece of round glass, fixed right before him, in the side of the engine, of about six inches over, and two in thickness. Thus he descended by the force of weights fixed to the under parts of the engine. He carries a life-line in his hand, which he pulls hard upon when he feels too much pressure, or wants to be drawn up. This engine is likewise supported with hoops on the inside, to counter-act the pressure of the water without, in great depths. The biggest end of it, where the diver enters, is made to take off, being fitted with cross bars and screws, to support it when duly fixed. A plug-hole at the upper convexity lets in fresh air when the diver is drawn up; for at being opened, the confined air rushes out. This plug saves the trouble of taking off the head of the engine, to give fresh air at each time of drawing it up.

Unfortunately, on this occasion, 'the tide running strong at bottom, and the sea appearing thick, the diver could not see distinctly through the glass of his engine, so returned without success'.[75]

[72] SP 35/30, fo. 52.

[73] Daniel Defoe, *A Tour thro' the Whole Island of Great Britain*, 2 vols (1724–6), i. 120.

[74] *Stamford Mercury*, 28 June 1716, 1 and 8 November 1722.

[75] Robert Heath, *A Natural and Historical Account of the Islands of Scilly* (1750), 150–4. See also N. D. Falck, *A Philosophical Dissertation on the Diving Vessel* (1775).

Underwater technology would continue to improve, bringing sunken gear within reach of well-financed projectors. Most wreck recovery, however, remained as it had always been: an improvised effort by the shore-based 'country people', limited by how far they could reach, how deep they could wade, and what their equipment could carry. The bounty of the sea remained, for the most part, the material retrievable on land.

12
Eighteenth-Century Wrecking Revisited

The eighteenth century, by some accounts, was the golden age of wrecking, a period when shoreline predation became more common and more contentious. The rewards were enhanced as shipping expanded, with more cargoes to prey upon, but the risks grew greater under the sharpening powers of the Hanoverian state. Approached as arenas of social conflict, exposing proletarian and seigneurial frictions, shipwrecks may be seen as dramatic contests in which the forces of property and propriety were ranged against the moral economy of the poor. The crowd on the beach had numbers, and intangible claims to legitimacy, but the authorities had magistracy, law, and soldiers on their side.[1]

Social historians have understood the shipwreck plunder of this golden age by reference to the sharpening inequities of a proto-industrial economic order. Debate has been shaped by the classic insights of E. P. Thompson, who discerned 'in almost every eighteenth-century crowd action some legitimizing notion' on behalf of 'traditional rights or customs', supported by 'the wider consensus of the community'. Older forms of paternalism lost ground, he finds, as 'the new political economy was disinfested of intrusive moral imperatives'.[2] Expanding this discussion from food riots to coastal plunder, John Rule's influential essay recognizes wrecking as a source 'from which the poor supplemented their meagre living' and emphasizes 'the conflict of custom with legal prohibition'. Involving a redistribution of resources, augmenting 'the makeshift economy of the local populace', wrecker criminality may thereby be construed as a response to poverty and oppression.[3]

More than a generation later, these observations retain their vitality but need modification. While some West Country historians represent wrecking, like smuggling, as 'a legitimate form of livelihood against the increasing intrusion of governmental control and direction', Cathryn Pearce sees a wider range of

[1] John Rule, 'Wrecking and Coastal Plunder', in Douglas Hay, Peter Linebaugh, John G. Rule, et al. (eds), *Albion's Fatal Tree: Crime and Society in Eighteenth-Century England* (1975), 168–88; John Rule, 'Smuggling and Wrecking', in Philip Payton, Alston Kennerley, and Helen Doe (eds), *The Maritime History of Cornwall* (Exeter, 2014), 195–208; John Styles, '"Our traitorous money makers": The Yorkshire Coiners and the Law, 1760–83', in John Brewer and John Styles (eds), *An Ungovernable People: The English and their Law in the Seventeenth and Eighteenth Centuries* (New Brunswick, 1980), 209–10; Cathryn Pearce, *Cornish Wrecking 1700–1860: Reality and Popular Myth* (Woodbridge, 2010).

[2] E. P. Thompson, 'The Moral Economy of the English Crowd in the Eighteenth Century', *Past & Present*, 50 (1971), 76–136, quotes at 78, 90.

[3] Rule, 'Wrecking and Coastal Plunder', 185; Rule, 'Smuggling and Wrecking', 200, 205. See also Styles, '"Our traitorous money makers"', esp. 209–10.

Shipwrecks and the Bounty of the Sea. David Cressy, Oxford University Press. © David Cressy 2022.
DOI: 10.1093/oso/9780192863393.003.0013

complexities involving manorial lords and their neighbours and tenants. 'Wrecking, rather than being condoned by the populace and thus being deemed a social crime, was in fact hotly contested between those who believed in the rights of the lords and those who believed in their personal rights of harvest.' Her analysis finds 'little evidence... to suggest the coercive, dominating relationship between lords and commoners such as that suggested by the bipolar domination/resistance model of E. P. Thompson, James Scott, and Keith Wrightson, at least in regard to wreck and salvage'.[4] Clearly more work is needed, and the social history of the shoreline may look different from a long early modern perspective.

This chapter revisits the history of shipwreck plunder and coastal salvage in the eighteenth century, especially in the neglected period before the 1750s. Considering continuities as well as change, it follows practices of wreck recovery, salvage, and appropriation from the Stuart age through the reign of George II (d. 1760). It relates the fate of shipwrecked vessels to the changing scale of shipping, alterations in social relations, the growing reach of the state, and additions to English law; and it casts doubt on the characterization of wreckers as ungovernable. A new narrative of coastal social relations may emerge from closer study of local episodes. As in the seventeenth century, the outraged rhetoric of some writers misrepresents the collaborative nature and customary acceptance of shoreline retrieval, in which wreckers found common cause with some of their masters and betters. Wreckers, like smugglers, could be found in cahoots with local officials, and were known to drink and socialize with each other.[5]

The Shipwreck Environment

The expansion of naval and commercial shipping, which accelerated under the later Stuarts, continued into the eighteenth century, though with some hesitations as well as spurts. By one count, almost certainly too short, the Anglo-British merchant fleet grew from 1,642 vessels (66,827 tons) in 1582 to 3,281 vessels (261,222 tons) in 1701, to 7,215 vessels in 1755 (473,328 tons), reaching 10,053 vessels (1,134,531 tons) by 1790, with a combined value of well over £3 million. Naval strength expanded from 36 ships (25,000 tons) in 1590, to 177 (196,200 tons) in 1700, to 220 vessels (276,200 tons) by 1750. Ships became bigger as well as more numerous, the average tonnage of the merchant fleet growing from 40.7 in 1582, to 79.6 in 1701, to 112.9 in 1790. Merchantmen of 500 tons, and some twice that amount, were not uncommon. Even if these figures need revision, they

[4] Pearce, *Cornish Wrecking*, 31, 163, 165.

[5] David Chen Smith, 'Fair Trade and the Political Economy of Brandy Smuggling in Early Eighteenth-Century Britain', *Past & Present*, 251 (May 2021), 75–111. Customs officers in Suffolk, assigned to prevent smuggling, were alleged in 1732 to frequent 'the taverns and merchant houses as though they winked at the running of goods' (CUST 97/7 (a reference I owe to Nicholas Rogers)).

indicate an expansion of marine traffic that was likely to yield a commensurate increase in wrecks.[6] The carrying capacity of Europe's combined merchant fleet grew from just over a million tons around 1670 to almost three and half million tons by the 1780s, though the growth was not so linear as some graphs suggest.[7] A useful measure of maritime activity, which takes account of disruptions caused by foreign wars, records 361 clearances from English ports in 1686, 245 in 1697, 290 in 1710, 426 in 1715, 694 in 1751, and 888 in 1772.[8] Figures for the total value of imports provide another suggestive indicator, rising from £5.8 million in 1699–1701, to £6.8 million in 1722–4, £8.2 million in 1752–4, and jumping to £12.7 million by 1772–4.[9] All of these goods arrived by sea. Whatever percentage of this material washed up on beaches would have a substantial impact on informal coastal economies. The numbers of known and named wrecks on English shores varied from year to year, but figures for the 1740s were twice as high as in any previous decade.[10]

Coastal dwellers in every era have gathered and redistributed the shipwrecked bounty of the sea. Opportunity and obligation were always in tension, and arguments over beached goods were as old as seafaring. Rights, droits, duties, and rewards had long been negotiable, under the canopy of custom and law. Shipwrecked sailors, owners of ships, merchants, landholders, crown officials, and local residents squabbled and cooperated to varying degrees in the retrieval and disposal of ladings and fittings. This would continue into the modern era, subject to developments in morality, manners, policing, and law.

Social changes over the course of the early modern era may have led to increased separation between groups and classes, with consequences for the conduct of salvage. Members of the elite appear to have distanced themselves from community rituals, their baptisms becoming more private, their marriages more clandestine, and their funerals more select.[11] Disparities in wealth and education sharpened cultural differences, eroding bonds of neighbourly mutuality. Changes in material circumstances, and developments in taste, left fewer customs in common. It remains somewhat speculative to what degree rural society

[6] Abbot Payson Usher, 'The Growth of English Shipping 1572–1922', *Quarterly Journal of Economics*, 42 (1928), 467; Jan Glete, *Navies and Nations: Warships, Navies and Nations in Europe and America, 1500–1860*, 2 vols (Stockholm, 1993), ii. 549–54. Ralph Davis, *The Rise of the English Shipping Industry in the Seventeenth and Eighteenth Centuries* (1962), 26, finds 323,000 tons of English-owned shipping in 1702, 473,000 tons in 1755, and 1,055,000 tons in 1788.

[7] Richard W. Unger, 'The Tonnage of Europe's Merchant Fleets, 1300–1800', in Richard W. Unger (ed.), *Ships and Shipping in the North Sea and Atlantic, 1400–1800* (Aldershot and Brookfield, VT, 1997), 247–61; Richard W. Unger (ed.), *Shipping and Economic Growth, 1350–1850* (Leiden, 2011), 5.

[8] Davis, *The Rise of the English Shipping Industry*, 24–5.

[9] Ralph Davis, 'English Foreign Trade, 1700–1774', *Economic History Review*, NS 15 (1962), 298–303, esp. 300.

[10] See Appendix, 'Two Centuries of Shipwrecks'.

[11] David Cressy, *Birth, Marriage and Death: Ritual, Religion and the Life Cycle in Tudor and Stuart England* (Oxford, 1997), 188–94, 332–5, 446–9.

in the eighteenth century was more fractured or more polarized than before, but there are signs that the world of labour and the world of politeness drew further apart as gentry and commoners kept to their kind. By the eighteenth century the deference due to rank and hierarchy was perhaps less readily assured, the customary obligations of gentility less generously supplied.[12]

This fraying of the social fabric may have affected how coastal communities responded to the opportunities of shipwreck. Lords of manors and their stewards, local droit collectors, deputy vice admirals, and others who commanded respect had traditionally intervened to manage the recovery of wreckage and to regulate rewards. Their involvement did not end in the eighteenth century, but may have lessened as other agents took command. Did discipline collapse, did social equilibrium become unbalanced, when familiar local figures were less visible or less trusted? Did wrecking become more disorderly, more disreputable, when the authority of leading men of coastal communities was superseded by operatives of the ruling regime?

The eighteenth-century state was bigger, more intrusive, and more efficient than ever, becoming more successful in extracting money from consumers and importers. The army and navy grew to meet the needs of a globalized imperial power. The overall size of the government bureaucracy trebled from the 1680s to the 1720s, with the Excise department outpacing other agencies. The Customs department, which collected duties on imported goods, grew rapidly from its reorganization in 1671, with 1,313 full-time employees by 1690, and 1,839 by 1708, as well as large numbers on temporary assignment. Beginning in the reign of James II, Customs commissioners made regular circuits of coastal inspection, checking performance in the field.[13] Their searchers and collectors became 'receivers of wrecks'—a new presence on the beach—demanding duties on goods brought ashore. Resented as 'clogs on trade', and sometimes susceptible to corruption, Customs officials made it their business to secure grounded vessels, to assess shipwrecked cargoes, and to prevent local people from looting. Sometimes backed by military force, they made intrusive demands that generated animosity from area inhabitants as well as proceeds for the state. Formerly a monitor of revenue and commerce, the Customs became the lead agency for control of the foreshore. Its aggressive attempts at enforcement raised the stakes and the temperature of local disputes, and provoked collisions with lords of manors, traditional droit collectors, and the 'country people'. Wreckers and

[12] Paul Langford, *A Polite and Commercial People: England 1727–1783* (Oxford, 1992), esp. ch. 2, 'The Progress of Politeness', 59–121; Keith Wrightson, 'The Politics of the Parish in Early Modern England', in Paul Griffiths, Adam Fox, and Steve Hindle (eds), *The Experience of Authority in Early Modern England* (New York, 1996), 10–46, esp. 33 on 'the hostile redefinition of behaviour previously tolerated or even applauded'.

[13] John Brewer, *The Sinews of Power: War, Money and the English State, 1688–1783* (New York, 1989), 66–8, 94, 215.

smugglers—sometimes the same people—vented their anger in acts of harassment and intimidation that some polite observers construed as 'barbarous'.[14]

Barbarous Shores

I have argued in an earlier chapter that accusations of 'spoil' and 'rapine' against the 'barbarous country people' are generally crude exaggerations that historians should treat with caution. Such language was adopted for rhetorical purposes to denigrate plebian disorder and to express sympathy for shipwreck victims. The words were used without precision, and often without justification, to distance the commentator from perceived unsavoury practices. The vocabulary became routinized and unreflective, as if wreckers by definition were 'barbarous' (see Chapter 4).

The outrages of 'the barbarous country people' seem only to have grown more common and more desperate, if outraged commentary is to be trusted. Reports of shipwreck plunder in the reign of Queen Anne described beaches 'covered with barbarians', where 'inhuman devils carried away all that was worth the carrying' (regarding the wreck of the *Ann* on the Isle of Wight in 1704).[15] Officers of the East India Company reported scenes of 'rapine and violence' with 'barbarous and cruel practices... against the common reason of all mankind' (regarding the loss of the *Albemarle* in Cornwall in 1708).[16] Attempts to save goods from the *Anna and Helena* that grounded in Devon in 1738 were said to have been hindered by 'the barbarity of the mob', who grew 'desperate', 'outrageous', and 'ungovernable'.[17] Other reports evoked scenes of 'riot, violence, and barbarity', amid 'the monstrous barbarity practiced by those savages', the wreckers.[18] Closer examination will determine whether such epithets were justified (see Figure 9).

Representatives of the news media, parliament, and the church were hostile to practices of wrecking. Daniel Defoe's notorious depiction of the 'strange, bloody, and cruel dealings' of the wreckers of the Isles of Scilly found echoes in popular journalism about 'the unheard of barbarities practis'd on shipwreck'd mariners'.[19] The *Daily Journal*, the *Whitehall Journal*, and other newspapers taught metropolitan readers about Cornish 'savages', 'coast harpies', and 'land monsters, who

[14] Edward Carson, *The Ancient and Rightful Customs: A History of the English Customs Service* (1972), 43, 48, 53, 58, 109–17.

[15] HCA 49/106, packet *C*.

[16] James Derriman, 'The Wreck of the *Albemarle*', *Journal of the Royal Institution of Cornwall*, NS 1 (1992), 128–48, with citations from India Office Records E/1/198.

[17] Devon Archives and Local Studies Service, QS/4/1738/Easter/NO/1–5, QS/4/1738/Easter/EX/1–5.

[18] John Hutchins, *The History and Antiquities of the County of Dorset*, 2 vols (1774), i. 546; 'The Lanisley Letters: to Lt General Onslow from George Borlase, his Agent at Penzance, 1750–53', ed. Thomas Cornish, *Journal of the Royal Institution of Cornwall*, 6 (1880), 374–9.

[19] Daniel Defoe, *A Tour through the Whole Island of Great Britain*, ed. Pat Rogers (1971), 236; *Stamford Mercury*, 13 January 1737.

Figure 9. George Morland, *Wreckers*, *c.*1790. Southampton City Art Gallery/ Bridgeman Images.

live upon sea storms'.[20] An outraged writer in Sussex described the plunder of the *Content*, which was wrecked one Monday in 1746:

> Wretches, like an infection, soon spread across the beach, from five years of age to eighty, with small hooks fixed to long poles, which they use to pull planks, etc., on shore . . . This sport, which they term a God's blessing, continued till Thursday . . . Such are the common people by the sea side, that the Lord have mercy on the unfortunate.[21]

The *Remembrancer* in March 1749 editorialized against the 'savages' in maritime districts, 'who in tempestuous nights hang out false colours, purposely to mislead such ships as happen to be within ken, and to avail themselves of the wreck, which they impiously miscall as deodand'.[22] This was journalistic invention, for no such deception is otherwise documented. The only credit allowed to English coastal inhabitants was that their cruelties were not so outrageous as those of the Irish.

[20] *Daily Journal*, 27 November 1721; *Whitehall Journal*, 2 April 1723.

[21] *London Evening Post*, 1–3 July 1746.

[22] *Remembrancer*, 27 May 1749. See also *General Advertiser*, 26 February 1749, *Old England*, 3 March 1750, for more on the 'inhuman' wreckers.

Other eighteenth-century writers dramatized the exploits of wreckers and may have invented the word. 'Wreckers' first appear in print in the *London Evening Post* in January 1746, following the foundering of the *Two Batchelors* in Sussex, when 'the greatest part of the cargo was plundered and carried off by the wreckers of this coast'.[23] William Hyland's dramatic entertainment of 1746, *The Ship-Wreck*, also employed the term 'wrecker', more than forty years before its first usage recorded in the *Oxford English Dictionary* (1789 for a vessel employed in wreck recovery, and 1820 for a person engaged in that process). Extending over forty pages, Hyland's piece presents the wreckers as opportunistic scoundrels, but also as practised and well-prepared members of their community: 'Along the shore a crowd of wreckers stand | ready to seize whatever drives to land.' With names like Jack Lookout and Tom Plunder, the wreckers take command of 'fortune's store'. The author represents himself as a Sussex farmer, familiar with 'the transactions which happen at shipwrecks', among people both above and below his own station. He describes orderly and well-equipped predation: 'Lads, have you got all things in readiness? Are our wagons, harness, yoke, chains, pullies, and all our gear ready, where it may be had at a minute's notice, in case any poor unfortunate ship fall on shore?' The villagers sing with gratitude for 'those blessings that it hath pleased fortune to send amongst us'. The accident of shipwreck is providential, with no suggestion that 'the shatter'd vessel' was brought ashore by anything but natural catastrophe.[24]

Hyland's wreckers know their duty, and their place in the social order, 'not only in the saving the best anchor and cable, and goods, for our lord of the manor, but also in saving of merchants' goods and poor men's lives'. They know their law, as well as how to thwart it. Aware that some people see them as 'sea poachers', and regard their business as 'havoc', one wrecker declares, 'we ought to be well paid' for our service. When the king's men (Customs officers and constables) arrive on the scene, the countryfolk lend dutiful assistance, while some continue their pillage. When an officer tells a woman to set down the goods she is carrying, she replies: ''tis a grievous thing that men should have no more conscience but to take from the poor what it hath pleased the Lord to send them.' The moral economy of the coastline is evoked in the assertion that 'the bustle people make about wreck goods, which they call pilfering if a man bears anything off, that is no more than to rob a thief'. One of the wreckers anticipates the arrival of 'a commission in our county, about this cursed shipwreck; so that we shall all be obliged to swear, and if to the truth, we are undone'. All are agreed, however, in

[23] *London Evening Post*, 16–18 January 1746.

[24] William Hyland, *The Ship-Wreck: A Dramatick Piece* (1746), prologue, 3, 8, 11. William Hyland of Willingdon, Sussex, yeoman, made his will in 1757 and died in 1769: East Sussex Record Office, PBT/1/1/60/202. For a literary depiction of maritime distress, see the much-reprinted poem by William Falconer, *The Shipwreck. A Poem. In Three Cantos. By A Sailor* (1762). Set in the Aegean, this is a tale of a 'trembling ship' awaiting a 'fatal wave', finally shattering on another 'cruel shore'.

protecting their bounty from inlanders: 'why should we suffer people to come out of the country to a shipwreck, the right of which only belongs to us who live on the coast?'[25] Similar sentiments, less artful, emerge from depositions.

Daniel Defoe, in more benign mood, described the practice of 'going a shoring' whereby the country people swarmed the sands after storms 'to see if the sea had cast up anything of value'.[26] A later eighteenth-century pamphlet satirized this 'custom' of 'going a wrecking' as 'rare sport', as if it were no more harmful than maypole dancing. While one fictitious neighbour calls wrecking 'crying sin', another reckons it 'lawful to open my door whenever fortune knocks at it'. Even the pious countryman Trueman goes 'a wrecking', though more to safeguard valuables, he says, than to steal them for himself.[27]

New Laws

Medieval laws, unchanged before the eighteenth century, set forth principles governing *wreccum maris*, but these were subject to endless argument, shading, and interpretation (see Chapter 3). Wreckage that fell on English shores belonged by prerogative to the crown, who could assign certain rights to agencies like the Admiralty and the Cinque Ports, and to local corporations and landed proprietors. The interests of shippers were protected, especially when there were survivors, and the law promised recompense for the people who assisted in salvage. Handbooks of maritime law and guides for local justices set forth these customary procedures.[28] Commissions of inquiry investigated contentious episodes, but few sanctions were available against illicit spoilers or plunderers.

Reformers since the sixteenth century had sought tougher remedies 'against such persons as under colour of claiming right in wrecks do seize the goods of divers persons, having no right thereto'.[29] A Cornish member of parliament introduced a bill in 1694 'to prevent the great spoils and abuses committed upon wrecks', but this, like its predecessors, was lost in committee.[30] Pressure

[25] Hyland, *Ship-Wreck*, 8, 11, 32, 35, 39, 41.

[26] Daniel Defoe, *A Tour thro' the Whole Island of Great Britain*, 2 vols (1724–6), i. 120.

[27] *The Wreck* (*c.*1796), 3, 7.

[28] The statutes of 3 Edward I (1275) and 27 Edward III stat. 2, c. 13 (1354), were well known through such compilations as *The Statutes at Large*, 3 vols (1706), and *An Abstract of all such Acts of Parliament, now in Force, as Relate to the Admiralty and Navy of England* (1715). See also Francis Clerke, *The Practice of the Court of Admiralty of England* (1722); Mathew Hale, *A Treatise Relative to the Maritime Law of England* (1787), 37–44; Giles Jacob, *Lex Mercatoria: Or the Merchant's Companion* (1729), 145–51; and Christopher Robinson, *Reports of Cases Argued and Determined in the High Court of Admiralty* (1799), 46–9.

[29] *Proceedings in the Parliaments of Elizabeth I*, ed. T. E. Hartley, 2 vols (Leicester, 1981), i. 529–30, 540–1; *Journal of the House of Commons*, 10 vols (1802), i. 120, 130–1; Lambeth Palace Library, MS 3475, fos 187–9 (Sir Mathew Hale's notes, *c.*1652).

[30] *Commons Journal*, 11 (1694), 69.

built after the stripping of the *Albemarle* in 1708, when the East India Company complained of the difficulty of prosecuting wreckers and sponsored a bill 'to prevent the embezzlement of goods and merchandizes cast away upon or near the coast of Great Britain'.[31]

Only in 1714 was a new law enacted 'for the preserving of all such ships and goods thereof which shall happen to be forced on shore or stranded upon the coast of this kingdom'. Addressing complaints by merchants that their ships had been 'barbarously plundered... and their cargoes embezzled', Queen Anne's statute turned activities of previously questionable legitimacy into crimes. Anyone who now boarded any wrecked vessel without permission, or impeded the saving of its goods, faced fines or imprisonment. Anyone who went so far as to disable a ship that might otherwise be made seaworthy, by cutting a hole in its side or stealing its pump, was 'hereby made guilty of felony' and could face the gallows. Other provisions of the Act attended to the management of salvage, empowering justices of the peace, Customs officers, and constables 'to call together as many men as shall be thought necessary to the assistance and for the preservation of such ship or vessel so in distress', and to adjudicate 'the quantum... or gratuities to be paid to the several persons acting or being employed in the salvage of the said ship'. The stripping of wrecks and the saving of cargo would henceforth be better governed, turning unregulated rogue wreckers into disciplined agents of retrieval, or else criminals. The statute was supposed to be read aloud in coastal parish churches four times a year.[32]

The new law privileged the shipping community, provided remedy against egregious excesses, and established Customs officers in local positions of power. It did not address the interests of lords of manors, however, or other claimants who customarily profited from shipwrecks on their coasts. Nor did it make it easier to prosecute savers who took wrecked goods into their custody but failed to turn them over to the authorities. 'Our legislative power is probably ignorant, that such barbarities are committed in England,' opined a contributor to the *Universal Journal* in 1724, who commended 'that excellent law lately passed in Holland, which makes it death for anyone to go aboard a wrecked vessel, unless his assistance be desired'.[33] Maintaining pressure, a correspondent from South Devon in 1735 related the 'barbarity' and 'hellish work' of plunder on yet another wreck, avowing: 'I am filled with the utmost resentment to see such execrable crimes pass unpunished, and heartily wish our legislature would think of some method to bring the abandoned wretches to justice, which at present is not easily to be done.' The *Weekly Miscellany* hoped that the 'barbarous' and 'detestable' practices of the inhabitants of the sea coast 'will soon meet with the animadversion

[31] Derriman, 'Wreck of the *Albemarle*', 132–3, 145. [32] 13 Anne, c. 21.

[33] *Universal Journal*, 12 February 1724. The Dutch law was also commended in *The Weekly Journal, or Saturday's Post*, 18 January 1724.

of the legislature'. The *Daily Post* reported petitions 'for remedy of this common evil' and hoped it would soon be made 'felony without benefit of clergy'.[34]

Responding to the challenge, the merchant lobby in parliament drafted a bill in 1737 'for the better preserving ships stranded or forced on shore, and the furniture and cargoes thereof'. Among other provisions, it would have made communities collectively responsible for crimes against shipwrecked mariners, with fines of £20 or treble the value for anyone converting ships' goods to their own use. Anyone who unlawfully took away 'any part of the tackle, furniture, apparel, goods, or cargo of such ship or vessel' would face transportation as a felon. Provincial journalists approved this 'alteration proposed to be made in the laws of flotsam and jetsam, on account of the unheard of barbarities practis'd on shipwreck'd mariners', but the change was not enacted.[35]

The effectiveness of existing legislation depended upon the willingness of magistrates to prosecute and the readiness of juries to convict. Neither could be assured. Nobody was surprised, on the rare occasion when 'plundering of a wreck' reached the courts, that defendants should be found not guilty. John Woodford, 'the principal in a riot committed at a late wreck in the Isle of Wight', was fined £50 at the Winchester assizes in March 1721, but the judge reduced this to 5 guineas 'out of compassion to his family'.[36] John Vivian, acquitted at the Exeter assizes in 1739 for his role in wrecking in south Devon, was subsequently imprisoned for riot, not plunder, and had to find sureties for his good behaviour.[37] 'Discretionary justice' allowed many of the people engaged in wrecking to avoid severe punishment.[38]

The metropolitan press continued to stir animosity against the coastal 'country people' and campaigned for tougher laws. Generic accounts of murderous inhumanity were repeated, usually without particulars. Reporting the burning of a shipload of brandy in 1749, a Cornish correspondent expressed hope that 'our legislature will take such monstrous abuses and execrable villainy into their speedy consideration'.[39] The legislature deigned not to respond.

Established law remained toothless against 'persons who shall steal or detain shipwrecked goods', allowing 'many wicked enormities' to continue, until strict legislation in 1753 outlawed the 'plundering and destroying vessels in distress'. Pilferage of items 'of small value' could be prosecuted as petty larceny, provided no 'cruelty, outrage or violence' was involved. But otherwise any who 'shall plunder, steal, take away or destroy any goods or merchandize, or

[34] *Whitehall Evening Post*, 2 December 1735; *St James Evening Post*, 2 December 1735; *Weekly Miscellany*, 18 December 1736; *Daily Post*, 17 February 1736.

[35] BL, Harper Collection of Private Bills, 1695–1814, no. 32, read 22 July 1737; *Commons Journal*, 22 (1732–37), 685. *Stamford Mercury*, 13 January 1737.

[36] ADM 1/3670, fo. 184. I am grateful to Nicholas Rogers for this reference.

[37] *Daily Gazetteer*, 30 August 1739. See also nn. 62–5.

[38] Pearce, *Cornish Wrecking*, 132–4, 138–40.

[39] *General Advertiser*, 26 February 1749; *Old England*, 23 December 1749.

other effects, from or belonging to any ship or vessel ... which shall be wrecked, lost, stranded or cast on shore in any part of his majesty's dominions', or 'shall beat or wound' or 'obstruct the escape of any person' from such a vessel, would henceforth be guilty of a felony deserving death. The new law also provided for the search and recovery of goods that had been taken and concealed, and threatened defiant offenders with imprisonment for six months or fines treble the value of whatever they had unlawfully detained. This statute of 1753 was supported by the 'merchants, traders, and insurers of London' and gave later Hanoverian magistrates weapons that their predecessors had lacked, should they choose to deploy them.[40]

Preaching in his Dorset coastal parish in 1753, on the promulgation of this statute, the reverend Thomas Francklyn vented 'indignation at the barbarity of others, who are ever ... ready to devour the shatter'd fragments of a shipweck'd vessel'. 'Custom and practice', he warned, may have countenanced the 'barbarous and inhuman' exploitation of the sufferings of others, but offenders now risked the gibbet if they did not cease 'their odious practice of plundering'. Wreckers now imperilled both 'their necks and souls' if they continued their detestable practices. Nor did Francklyn spare the 'better sort of people', who 'ought to be ashamed to send their servants and teams upon the strand, to steal and carry off other men's property'. 'Rich plunderers', he recognized, were as guilty as poor tenants, for 'exorbitant' and 'merciless' dealing resided 'in all ranks of men'. 'Halters and gibbets are calculated for the daring and the thoughtless, but they work powerfully on *all* complexions ... Woe to him that buildeth his house with blood, and his roofs with iniquity.' Moralizing rebukes of this sort had been preached a century earlier, but the threat now was hanging as well as damnation.[41] But the plunder of shipwrecks did not cease.

According to George Borlase, the gentleman steward of Lanisley, Cornwall, the new law 'does not sufficiently provide against the monstrous barbarity practiced by those savages upon the poor sufferers' of shipwrecks. His fear that the legislation of 1753 was not 'an effectual remedy' seemed justified within months, in his report of a wreck near Helston, 'that notwithstanding the late act, there is much occasion for soldiers here as ever'.[42]

[40] 26 Geo II, c. 19; *Commons Journal*, 26 (1753), 532, 589, 625, 670, 732, 818.

[41] Thomas Francklyn, *Serious Advice and Fair Warning To all the live upon the Sea-Coast of England and Wales* (1756), pp. iv–v, viii, 11, 12, 15, 42–3, 56. Francklyn was vicar of Fleet and rector of Langton-Herring, adjacent to Chesil Beach. See also two tracts from the early nineteenth century: G. C. Smith, *The Wreckers: Or, A Tour of Benevolence* (1818); and Robert Eden, *An Address to Depredators & Wreckers on the Sea Coast* (1840). Smith was a minister at Penzance, Cornwall; Eden was rector of Leigh, Essex, adjacent to the Thames.

[42] 'Lanisley Letters', 378–9.

Customs versus customs

The reports of regional collectors of Customs provide a body of evidence about wrecking unique to the eighteenth century. Empowered to collect duties on imported goods, whether those materials were brought ashore in the normal course of commerce or accidentally spilled on beaches, the officers of the Customs strove to maximize returns. It was not their business to assert the privileges of the seigneurie, or to secure the best anchors and cables for Admiralty droit holders, but rather to raise revenue for the crown. Their reports to the Board of Customs, which survive in great numbers from the reigns of George I and II, include accounts of rescue and salvage, and confrontations with lawless wreckers, as well as their efforts to combat smuggling. Their tone is often recriminatory and apologetic, especially when lawless countrymen got the upper hand.[43] Newspapers gave coverage to some of these episodes, sometimes with sensationalist embellishment. Other accounts may be retrieved from contemporary narratives and from manuscripts in The National Archives. Some of the sums at stake may be inferred from figures for brandy imports in the range of 4,000 tuns (over a million gallons), dutiable at £30 or more per tun.[44]

When a French vessel laden with wine and brandy ran ashore at Sully, south of Cardiff, in 1712, the Customs officers performed their duty and claimed the cargo. Facing them, 'the country folk assembled with guns and pistols, and endeavoured to take the brandy, whereupon . . . the Comptroller of Cardiff went with some officers and some dependants of the lady of the manor of Sully, and dispersed the mob'. A few years later another 'mob', several hundred strong, swarmed the wrecked tobacco ship *Pye*, thwarting the interests of 'the merchants and the revenue'.[45] In Dorset the Customs officers at Weymouth failed to recover cargo from the *Jesus Maria Joseph* in 1716, because, they explained, the mob 'beat, hounded, and resisted us in the salvage'. Nor were the stonecutters of Portland their only foe, for local gentry, like Mr Weld of West Lulworth, opposed the Customs with vigour and persistence. The mob was often leavened with gentle components.[46]

When the *St Peter* of Amsterdam, a vessel of 170 tons laden with brandy and other dutiable goods from France, crashed against the rocks of the Lizard, just after dark on 14 November 1722, a few men scrambled to safety, but the officers

[43] See especially CUST 59 for Weymouth from 1716, CUST 64 for Exeter from 1743, and CUST 97 for Great Yarmouth from 1684. Pearce, *Cornish Wrecking*, makes effective use of CUST 68 for Penzance and Scilly from 1738. See also William J. Ashworth, *Customs and Excise: Trade, Production, and Consumption in England, 1640–1845* (Oxford, 2003), 165–205.

[44] Smith, 'Fair Trade and the Political Economy of Brandy Smuggling', 76, 84–5. French brandy was assessed at £35 5*s*. 6*d*. per tun, but so-called Flemish brandy at only £3 17*s*., before reforms in 1733.

[45] *Cardiff Records*, ed. John Hobson Mathews, 6 vols (Cardiff, 1898–1911), ii. 375, 383.

[46] Glanville J. Davies, 'Wreck and Plunder in 18th Century Portland', *Dorset Natural History and Archaeological Society Proceedings*, 103 (1981), 1–4.

'lay all night' and 'tarried on board till the ship was dry'. Their survival and continued possession should have protected them from wreckers, but the master soon had cause to complain of 'misusage'. On the morning following the mishap, 'the country came down in order to plunder our ship', but were held back by the arrival of Mr George Robinson, a former sheriff of Cornwall. Robinson's men guarded the ship for twenty-four hours, before allowing themselves to be overrun. As 'the country people' were rifling the ship the next evening, they set it ablaze, and continued their plunder, though some of the brandy was evidently preserved. Belatedly, the collector of Customs at Penzance arrived on the scene, backed by soldiers, and placed the wreckage under quarantine. According to the master, in a complaint taken up by the Dutch envoy in London, the Customs men then confiscated the remaining barrels and extortionately 'demanded of the captain . . . more money than the goods which were saved would answer'. The Dutchmen sought 'satisfaction', not only against the Cornish incendiaries, but also against 'the several men of substance that were concerned in the plundering [of their] ship'. The unruliness of the wreckers in this case was matched by the greed of government officials.[47]

London's *Daily Gazetteer* reported the fate of the *William* of Hamburg, with goods worth more than £30,000, which was cast away on sands near Orford, Suffolk, in October 1735. The master and three passengers drowned, but others clung to the shrouds or managed to escape in their longboat.

> The Customs-house officers of this place, with the deputy vice-admiral, came on board the wreck with their boat, and did all in their power to prevent the fishermen and other small vessels, which flocked about her immediately, from plundering the cargo; but being overpowered, some linen was got out of her by the persons in those vessels, which has been since secured. The sails, rigging, etc., were taken quite away. The Aldeburgh officers and some dragoons coming to the Orford officers' assistance, the rest of the cargo was preserved from plundering, and, 'tis hoped, will be saved for the benefit of the proprietors.[48]

Yet another outrage occurred in 1736 at Seaford, Sussex, a frequent scene of shipwreck, after another *St Peter* of Amsterdam was cast away with the loss of all her crew. The cargo included thirty to forty thousand Spanish crowns, most of which were secured by the Customs supervisor at Newhaven, who sent half a ton of silver up to London. That still left spoil for 'the country people', who, the *Daily Journal* reported, 'plundered many thousands of pieces of eight, carrying them off by horse-loads, and loading themselves till the very skirts of their clothes broke

[47] SP 44/124, pp. 83–6.
[48] *Daily Gazetteer*, 10 October 1735; repr. in *Weekly Miscellany*, 11 October 1735.

down with the weight of silver'.[49] Time and again the press reported on wrecks—that 'the Custom-house and Lord Warden's officers used their utmost endeavours to save what they could for the proprietors, but were prevented by the numbers of inhuman wretches that came down upon them'.[50]

Though sometimes supported by as many as fifty soldiers, in their search for dutiable materials, the Customs officers sparred repeatedly with 'the country people' who descended 'according to their brutish custom'. Some lords of manors cooperated with the king's officers, but others conspired to outwit them. Customs men in Cornwall did their best to secure material from the *Vigilantia* of Hamburg, which was wrecked in Mounts Bay in November 1738, but complained that local officials refused to assist them. When they searched for the wine taken from the stricken *Lady Lucy* in 1739, they found four casks in the possession of Thomas Whitford, the minister of Cury, near the Lizard. When the *Whale* was cast away on the Scottish border, Sir John Home of Manderston seized everything, 'as having a special right, of several hundred years standing, to all wrecks within that bound'.[51]

Perhaps informed by Customs House letters, John Troutbeck, the eighteenth-century historian of the Isles of Scilly, described clashes between Customs men and wreck-salvers in the reign of George II. Late in December 1739 the *St Joseph* of Dunkirk, laden with brandy, was lost near Samson island, but the crew and sixty large barrels were saved. The islanders of Tresco took ten barrels 'to their share for the salvage', dividing the contents of three of them and securing the rest in a cellar. Five months later, in May 1740, when the Customs officers attempted to transfer this stash to his majesty's warehouse, they found that local men had broken open the cellar and divided the brandy among themselves. The officers made a search and found 'a great quantity of brandy in small casks and other vessels, which they seized', but before they could transfer it to St Mary's 'they were threatened and obstructed by a mob, who followed them from house to house, swearing they would lose their lives, rather than suffer the brandy to be carried off... The officers, being few in number, and having no arms, were obliged to quit the seizure for the security of their lives.' A short while later these same Tresco men 'came violently upon the Collector' while he was assisting with another stranded cargo, 'and would have destroyed a great part, had they not been repelled'. According to Troutbeck, the leaders of this outrage were prosecuted, one being fined £40, and the rest pardoned on promise 'never to do the like again', though relevant judicial records cannot now be found.[52]

[49] *Daily Journal*, 25 December 1736; *London Tatler*, 25 December 1736.

[50] *Daily Gazetteer*, 10 November 1740.

[51] *London Evening Post*, 6–8 April 1738; *Daily Post*, 8 May 1738; *Daily Gazetteer*, 31 August 1738; Richard Larn and Bridget Larn, *Shipwreck Index of the British Isles*, 7 vols (1995–2005), i, sect. 4, not paginated.

[52] John Troutbeck, *A Survey of the Ancient and Present State of the Scilly Islands* (1794), 204.

Promises to end the practice held little weight. In the winter of 1740, when wrecks on the Isles of Scilly yielded 9,000 gallons of brandy, 'the natives cellared 3,000 gallons, on which the duty was £750, and claimed it as their salvage, one third being the custom of the islands'. The Customs collector was indignant that 'they were supported by Mr Thomas Smith, who is deputy steward to my Lord Godolphin in these islands, and governs them as he pleases'.[53] In 1748 the Customs collector and surveyor in Cornwall attended the wreck of the Dutch wine ship *Jonge Alcida*, 'but to no purpose; the violence and barbarity of the country people was such that they could not save one cask, and ran a hazard to their lives in the attempt'. In the following year, when the *Two Friends* wrecked near Plymouth, Customs men watched helplessly 'a vast number of people, some with axes, and others with hatchets, horse and short crooks, breaking to pieces and carrying away everything'.[54] Some people later reminisced about outwitting or suborning the revenue men to secure the alcohol for themselves.[55]

Shipwreck Episodes

Maritime mishaps led frequently to shoreline dramas, as distressed survivors, state officials, local gentry, and 'the country people' competed for control of the goods. The fates of ships and cargoes, and the exploits of the people who plundered them, became well known to readers of the English press. Many of the accounts of shipwrecks were recast as morality tales with religious or polemical weighting. The following selection of episodes adds detail to the history of eighteenth-century wrecking, and exposes the voice, identity, and social range of participants.

The London *Evening Post* of 9–12 December 1710 reported that

> the *Gardner Galley* of Bristol, being stranded near Pendennis in Cornwall, and in hazard, most of the foremast men left her, and the country people came down to plunder her as a wreck. The captain and officers, having called the magistrates of the town to their assistance, endeavoured to keep off the mob, who proving obstinate, fired upon them with powder to frighten them. But that not taking effect, they fired some small shot, by which they killed and wounded several, and preserved the ship. By the help of the townsmen, part of the loading was taken out, and the ship set ashore; so that 'tis hoped both she and cargo will be saved.'[56]

[53] Larn and Larn, *Shipwreck Index*, i, sect. 3, not paginated.

[54] Larn and Larn, *Shipwreck Index*, i, sect. 4, not paginated; Pearce, *Cornish Wrecking*, 90, 124, 126.

[55] *An Account of Wrecks 1759–1830—on the North Coast of Cornwall: By John Bray*, ed. A. K. Hamilton Jenkin (Truro, 1975), 11–12.

[56] *Evening Post*, 9–12 December 1710.

'The townsmen' were evidently more reputable than 'the country people', while armed agents of magistracy overawed 'the mob'.

Competing newspapers published accounts of the loss of the *Royal Anne* at the Lizard in November 1721. Some merely reported that the warship was cast away in Cornwall, and that all but three men were drowned. Casualties were said to have numbered 207, 222, or 'about 300', including Lord Belhaven, identified by his diamond ring, and twenty-four 'other gentlemen'.[57] Accounts of survivors appeared within a week, describing both the voyage of the *Royal Anne* and its aftermath. Bad weather and bad seamanship were blamed for the disaster. Lord Belhaven and Captain Willis had disagreed about when and where to sail, but their 'fatal mistake' was confusing the Lizard Point with Land's End. The officers were astonished when, between two and three of the morning on 10 November, their ship was dashed to pieces among rocks.

Newspapers offered hack accounts of 'the country people who, always after wrecks, come down to the seaside for booty'. The *Flying Post* told readers that the wreckers of the *Royal Anne* buried the dead who had money or jewels about them, 'but let those who have nothing in their pockets drive with the tide'.[58] The *Daily Journal* carried news 'that upon the first notice of the above misfortune, the people of the sea coast ran out of the churches, armed with their hatchets, etc., to the sea side in quest of plunder'. The veracity of these reports is untested, but the wreck did not occur on a Sunday, when parishioners were supposedly at worship.[59] The three survivors told the Board of Admiralty how they clung to a rock, 'not above musket shot from the mainland', and were eventually saved by boatmen who 'came to fish for what they could get'.[60] 'When daylight appeared they saw a sight full of melancholy, that was the Cornish savages at the sea shore, rifling the bodies of their dead brethren, who instead of sending off their boats to carry them to land, continued their depredations till three in the afternoon, when they vouchsafed to set them ashore.'[61] There are no reports from the Cornish point of view. Naval wrecks of this sort left an inordinate number of bodies to bury and offered fewer lucrative godsends for salvors. Within days the government sent a frigate from Plymouth 'to cruise upon the wreck, to prevent the country's plunder, and to take up such stores and things of value that can be saved, and likewise the dead bodies they shall find floating'.[62] A month later the *Whitehall Evening Post* reported that two ships had gone to the Lizard 'with a new-invented diving engine, to fish upon the wreck of the *Royal Anne*', and by the following summer twenty

[57] *Applebee's Original Weekly Journal*, 25 November 1721; *Evening Post*, 25–8 November 1721; *Post Boy*, 28 November 1721.

[58] *The Flying Post, or the Post-Master*, 18 November 1721.

[59] *Daily Journal*, 20 November 1721.

[60] *Daily Courant*, 29 November 1721, repeated in *London Gazette*, 28 November–2 December 1721, and *Post Boy*, 30 November 1721.

[61] *Daily Journal*, 27 November 1721; *Post Boy*, 28 November 1721.

[62] *Weekly Journal or British Gazetteer*, 25 November 1721.

guns had been recovered.[63] Newspapers routinely wrote of 'the country people who came with axes and other weapons to plunder', but in 1732 a reporter at Bridgewater observed of another wreck in Somerset: 'the lord of the manor is very busy about her, and is so forward as to send hither for carpenters to rip her up.'[64]

John Troutbeck noted memorable shipwrecks in the Isles of Scilly in the reign of George II, recording that, in 1730, 'a vessel from the Canary Islands, laden with wine, was lost upon the island of Rosevean', an uninhabited outcrop among Scilly's western rocks.

> Some fishermen went to his assistance, and got some of the men off, but the captain would not quit the vessel, on account of a large quantity of money being on board. The weather became worse, so he and one man got upon the island, where they were saved by lashing themselves to a rock; they remained in this situation three days before they could be got off.[65]

In October 1736 the *Triumph*, bound from Jamaica to London with a cargo of sugar, indigo, dye wood, 'and other valuable articles', was likewise 'dashed in pieces against the rocks' of St Mary's. The captain, carpenter, boatswain, and other crewmen drowned, but several who stayed on board were providentially saved.

> Some were lost by endeavouring to secure part of the money, others were preserved with bags of it brought ashore, and others were bruised to pieces among the rocks...The rich furniture was saved by the islanders...with a considerable quantity of money, which was divided among the salvers, though the then commanding officer [of the island garrison] took a proper share of it into his possession...The accident was said to be owing to the ill conduct of the crew, intoxicating themselves with rum at coming into their soundings, and the thick weather.[66]

Four more wrecks stand out for the richness of their records, further illuminating dealings among mariners, officials, and the people on shore.

The *Anna and Helena*, Devon 1738

Early on the morning of 21 March 1738 the Dutch freighter *Anna and Helena*, homebound from Bordeaux, became stranded on Thurleston Sand in Bigbury Bay,

[63] *Whitehall Evening Post*, 30 December 1721; *Post Boy*, 18 August 1722.

[64] *The County Journal, or The Craftsman*, 6 February 1731; *The Flying Post, or The Post-Master*, 21 September 1732.

[65] Troutbeck, *Survey*, 202.

[66] Troutbeck, *Survey*, 202–3.

Devon, on the lee shore where many previous ships had bilged, and was promptly plundered. Customs officers who arrived after noon found that

> some part of the cargo of the said ship, and her cables, anchors, and sails, had been saved for the use of the proprietors by the assistance of some of the neighbouring gentlemen, but that the mob was by that time grown very rude and ungovernable, and several hundred of them with axes, hatches, crows of iron, and other destructive instruments and edge tools had entered into the body of the said ship, and cut her stern post, and also several holes in the deck and sides of the said ship, and by that means rendered her incapable of sea service.

The mariners and the Customs men secured a dozen hogsheads of wine, and a few more salvageable items, but were insulted, jostled, and outmatched by the wreckers. Much of the cargo of wine, brandy, indigo, prunes, and coffee went missing, which, in the opinion of the Customs men, 'might have been saved if it had not been for the barbarity of the mob'.[67]

Within a month the government began proceedings against 'the persons concerned in plundering the cargo' of the *Anna and Helena* and assured the Dutch envoy of their best endeavours. The Customs collector at Dartmouth advised the Commissioner in London that 'it will be a work of time, the people being unwilling to inform against their neighbours, almost the whole country for fifteen or twenty miles round being concerned therein'. He nonetheless identified Thomas Hingston of Kingsbridge, shopkeeper; William Robertson of Kingsbridge, shipwright; Richard Wakeman of Kingsbridge, shopkeeper; John Shepherd of Thurlestone, yeoman; Edward Langman of Thurlestone, yeoman; and John Guyst of Churchstow, hellier—all men of reputable status—as 'very active and assisting in plundering and carrying off part of the cargo'. The Dartmouth searcher added the names of Peter Hardy, Thomas Wakeman, Nicholas Prettysons, and Roger Moore of Thurlestone, labourers, who took a sail, which they cut up and divided amongst themselves; and William Hingston of Thurlestone and Sydrach Lewis of South Huish, sailors, among the rioters. The Customs searcher at Salcombe further identified Daniel Weymouth of Malborough, yeoman; William Harridan, Thomas Moore the younger, John Staning, and John Steeve of Malborough, husbandmen; and Abraham Dowst and John Nettle of South Huish, labourers, as active in the plunder. Mr John Roope of Horswell, 'a gentleman of good estate' who saw the whole transaction, also secured warrants 'against Arthur Luckcraft and John Vivian, labourers, who first stopped and embezzled the first hogshead of wine the mob took... and knocked in one of the heads, and huzzaed and encouraged the mob to come and divide it, though forbid by Mr Roope and others'. Vivian further incriminated himself by striking Roope's horse and

[67] SP 36/45/2, fos 52–5.

threatening the gentleman with an axe.[68] The government thus had the names of twenty-one men who could be charged with felonies under common law or the statute of 1714, and more were added as examinations proceeded. Most were respectable artisans or workmen, and few paid a price for their involvement.

The state's case was not helped, however, by the bailiff of the manor of Thurlestone, James Adams, who claimed 'all wrecks that shall be driven on shore or found in or upon the said royalties, and to seize and preserve the same' for his lord, Sir William Courtney. Adams too had gone down to the *Anna and Helena*, to offer assistance and to collect fees of groundage, and particularly identified the shipwright William Robertson as helpful in securing the cargo, and one who did no injury and took no plunder. Only later 'a great number of people came in an outrageous manner', and plundered or destroyed the lading. Nor was conviction assured when several witnesses declared themselves 'some distance from the place where the ship was stranded', and thereby 'prevented from seeing and taking notice of any of the rioters and plunderers'.[69]

Political and diplomatic pressure quickened the inquiry, which led to examinations at the Exeter Quarter Sessions in April 1738. The Dutch envoy had appealed to the Secretary of State, and then to King George himself, to seek compensation for the owners, justice against the perpetrators, and assurance of assistance in future like circumstances. Lords Harrington and Walpole demanded a full and prompt account of the proceedings, which may be why these Quarter Sessions files are duplicated in State Papers.[70]

Witnesses retold their stories before the court, adding details and naming additional offenders. Adrian Wagnaer, the master of the *Anna and Helena*, related, through an interpreter, how his ship was driven ashore, how he asked local gentlemen for help, and how their efforts were overwhelmed by a riotous mob 'to the number of about two or three thousand' (a gross exaggeration). Especially outrageous were John Lishions, shoemaker, and his brother Thomas Lishions, labourer, both of South Milton, who assaulted Wagnaer on his own deck with staves taken from his cargo, 'and so barbarously beat him over the back and sides that he at present retains the marks thereof'. Others who attacked him, or were forward in robbing his ship, included James Jarvis of South Huish; Isaac Jarvis the younger of South Huish, tailor; John Trenick of Malborough; and Andrew Couch of Thurlestone, victualler. Further accusations of violence were levelled against John Freeman of Ringmoor, labourer, who allegedly struck the head of a Customs man who tried to stop him carrying off a case of brandy.

[68] SP 36/45/2, fos 46–56.

[69] SP 36/45/2, fo. 8; Devon Archives and Local Studies Service, QS/4/1738/Easter/EX/4.

[70] Devon Archives and Local Studies Service, QS/4/1738/Easter/NO/1–5, QS/4/1738/Easter/EX/1–5; SP 36/45/2.

The landowner John Roope, of Horswell in the nearby parish of South Milton, recalled his effort to preserve the cargo, and the violence he suffered from determined wreckers. When he tried to prevent the mob from carting away wine, he said, John Vivian of Churchstow, 'with a large axe came forward', and struck Roope's horse 'a violent blow on the nose'. Vivian then menaced Roope with the axe, and threatened that if he 'moved one step forward towards him he would murder him, or used words to that effect'. This was felonious assault, made more shocking to the Hanoverian elite by the insolence of a labourer berating a mounted gentleman. Arthur Luckcraft, another labourer of South Huish, supported Vivian's action and encouraged the mob in their plunder.

Peter Elliot, the Customs searcher from Dartmouth, gave information that corroborated Roope's account. Vivian's violent defiance, the liberating of the wine, and the opening of the first hogshead emboldened the crowd, and quickened their spoil and rapine. Elliot's testimony was only slightly undercut by his report that, being 'entrusted to look after the goods saved for the proprietor in a cellar some distance from the wreck, he was unable to prevent further looting'. His colleague William Sanders, master of the Customs boat at Tor Cross, similarly reported efforts to prevent plunder, 'but to no purpose'. He himself was 'insulted and struck in the execution of his duty by one John Nettle of South Huish, who was then carrying a bag of prunes'.

The magistrates of Devon had ample testimony of damage to this stricken vessel, violence against mariners, obstruction of Customs men, assaults against gentlemen, and the lawless carrying-away of shipwrecked cargo. Information, however, did not necessarily lead to indictments, and indictments did not guarantee conviction. Of more than a score of named wreckers, only John Vivian, who had threated John Roope with an axe, and Philip Davies, not previously identified, were referred for trial at the assizes. The *London Evening Post* reported in February 1739 that these two 'ringleaders in plundering the Dutch East-India ship, lately lost in Bigbury Bay, were brought to the county gaol under a strong guard of soldiers'. The *Daily Gazetteer* reported in August that

> John Vivian, tried last assize for plundering of a wreck in Bigbury Bay, and the verdict being special, the same has been argued, and the prisoner acquitted of the robbery, but found guilty this assize of two bills preferred against him for a riot, is to remain in gaol for three years, and find sureties for his good behaviour for two years.[71]

No further evidence can be found of this matter.

[71] *London Evening Post*, 22–4 February 1739; *Daily Gazetteer*, 30 August 1739.

The *Boscawen*, Cornwall 1745

Captain George Walker of the thirty-gun privateer *Boscawan* related his dealings with the people of north Cornwall after his ship broke apart on rocks near St Ives late in 1745. The homeward voyage from Madeira had been especially hazardous, with the ship 'almost a wreck upon the sea, every moment expecting to sink forever', before they neared land. Four sailors drowned as the ship foundered, but the rest came safely ashore with the aid of local boatmen. Walker could not say enough to thank his helpers, and to burnish their reputation.

> The people of the sea coast of Cornwall have for some years undergone the censure of being savage devourers of all wrecks that strike against their coasts. How weak a creature is general belief, the dupe of idle fame! Humanity never exercised its virtues more conspicuously than in this instance, in the inhabitants and people of St Ives. They flocked down in numbers to our assistance, and, at the risk of many of their lives, saved ours. Mr Walker... was himself, at last, lifted out by two of the townsmen, strangers to him, who went upon the wreck to bring him off... When they came into the town, everybody's house was open to them in all the offices of assistance.

Walker particularly commended the hospitality of his Cornish hosts, whose 'activity, liberality, and prudence' extended 'down to the lowest man'. The mayor, magistrates, and other gentlemen of St Ives displayed exemplary civility, but Walker and his officers nonetheless thought it necessary the first night to 'sleep under their arms, to be in readiness, in case of any attack against the wreck'. Sure enough, 'in the night the miners came down, and were setting about sharing the wreck amongst them', but the mayor and other officers successfully dispersed the crowd, and took two of the tinners prisoner. Walker allowed that such people were barely human, though he did not call them barbarous. 'These are a people the civil power are scarcely answerable for, at least for their good manners, as they live almost out of the districts of human society, and may be said to be no visible inhabitants of the earth, though they act in the world.' Reputable salvers were distinguishable from disreputable wreckers in this remarkably generous testimonial.[72]

The *Nympha*, Sussex 1747

In March 1747 a British privateering squadron under now-Commodore George Walker captured the Spanish merchantman *Nympha* off Cadiz. (Hostilities with

[72] George Walker, *The Voyages and Cruises of Commodore Walker, during the Late Spanish and French Wars*, 2 vols (1760), i. 222, 228–36; Pearce, *Cornish Wrecking*, 84–5.

Spain were long lasting, with the War of Jenkins's Ear merging into the War of the Austrian Succession.) Bound for Veracruz, Mexico, the *Nympha* was a grand prize, an 800-ton galleon with 36 guns and 260 men, valued above £160,000. Its cargo included 115 tons of quicksilver (mercury, used in the extraction of gold from ore) 'at the common market price worth upwards of £60,000'. After delays and complications at Lisbon, Walker's men brought the ship safely to Portsmouth, where some of its treasure was unloaded, before continuing their voyage to London. Late at night on 29 November 1747 the *Nympha* became separated from its convoy, and came to grief on the coast of Sussex, under the cliffs of Beachy Head.[73] Broken in pieces, the *Nympha* proved a spectacular wreck, commanding administrative, journalistic, and artistic attention for several months. Drawings and paintings as well as newspapers memorialized the scene (see Figure 10).

The account in the *London Evening Post* ignores the mishap that brought the vessel ashore, to focus on the spectacle of scavengers on the beach. The wreck, according to an eyewitness,

Figure 10. 'The Wreck of the Nympha Americana, a Spanish Corsair, near Beachy Head'. © Royal Museums Greenwich Images, PAF7693.

[73] Walker, *Voyages and Cruises*, ii. 100, 105, 294–6; *The British Magazine: Or, The London and Edinburgh Intelligencer* (Edinburgh, 1748), 406, makes it a 700-ton ship with 350 men, valued at £180,000.

> drew some thousands of people to the place for the sake of plundering her. The weather being excessive cold and wet, numbers of them perished on the shore, and on their way homeward, I believe not less than fifty, and a great many more were taken up as dead, but being put into warm beds, have recovered. Among the dead are several women, one in particular having two small children, and as her neighbours were all gone to the wreck, could not leave them, so carried them with her, but soon perished in the cold, and was found dead with the two children crying by her, almost perished with hunger and cold; and indeed, there's hardly a village for several miles round the place, but what have had one or two died, or broke their limbs at the wreck. I must not omit one circumstance because it was a little diverting. A woman at Seaford, whose husband being dead at the wreck, hired a cart and horses to fetch him, in order to bury him, but the carter not knowing him, brought her another man instead of her husband, upon which the woman refused to pay the carter, and he left her the man.

Several papers reprinted this account, to edify and to entertain their readers. One editorialized that 'a story big with the utmost iniquity, as well as misery of human nature, is a very proper subject of diversion'.[74]

Another report a few days later attributes the deaths around Seaford not to cold weather but to alcohol and violence and associates the wreckers with smugglers. Upon hearing of the wreck of the *Nympha*, Mr William Belchier, the member of parliament who had sponsored Walker's privateers,

> went down upon the coast with a warrant from the Secretary of War, requiring all soldiers on that coast to aid and assist him to guard the wreck; and upon coming to the coast, he . . . and a party of soldiers, met about a dozen smugglers loaded from the wreck, which they abandoned upon sight of the soldiers. The next day a great number of the smugglers returned, in order to retake the aforesaid goods; upon which Mr Belchier ordered the soldiers to fire; which they did, and killed two of them, and the rest ran away. It is also said that near thirty of them and the country people were found dead, which is supposed to be owing to their drinking by mistake some liquor out of the said wreck.[75]

One of Belchier's officers told the press that 'we have got above a hundred soldiers, and shall keep the smugglers in awe, who have been very busy about the wreck, and carried off some goods; but by means of a search warrant we have recovered a good deal'.[76]

[74] *London Evening Post*, 5–8 December 1747; *Jacobite's Journal*, 12 December 1747.
[75] *Penny London Post, or Morning Advertiser*, 11–14 December 1747.
[76] *Westminster Journal, or New Weekly Miscellany*, 12 December 1747.

Eight wagonloads of silver had already been unloaded at Portsmouth, but opportunities remained for scavengers and wreckers. Two hundred and fifty chests of quicksilver (mercury) from the *Nympha* were sold in London in February 1748, followed by the offering in June of 3,000 gallons of brandy and 6,000 pounds of cinnamon from the wreck, 'duty free, to pay the salvage'.[77]

Local sources add instructive details. One soldier apparently tried to hide some coins from the wreck by hiding them in his boots. He was caught when the weight of the doubloons prevented him from mounting his horse. Another opportunistic salvor found some mysterious blocks of metal, which he sold to the watchmaker Thomas Harben. These blocks turned out to be virgin gold ingots, which allegedly funded Harben's reinvention as a gentleman. Research in local parish registers finds not a single burial that can be associated with the wrecking of 1747, yet the episode was more than mythic.[78] The engraving *A View of the Wreck of the Nympha, a Spanish Prize*, published in 1748, observes that 'great quantities of her cargo were carried off by people from different parts, sixty of whom perished on the beach, downs, and other places'. Illustrations show the shattered stern of the ship on the beach with wreckage scattered nearby, hundreds of people probing, gathering, and carrying off the merchandize, and one at least falling from the cliffs.[79]

The insurance business by this time had grown in wealth and sophistication, becoming a major participant in the recovery of material from wrecks. Commercial agents from London added their weight to the pull of interest, claims, and adjustments. Disputes involving insurance generated yet another stream of documentation that was not available for earlier periods. Commodore Walker, in his memoir, recalled that his prize the *Nympha*

> was insured for upwards of £103,000; and about £35,000 of her effects and cargo were saved to the underwriters, by the fidelity and activity of one of the managers, who immediately went down to the wreck. But it was said, that there was a deficiency or loss of a large sum in the payment of the money insured, by the failure of some of the underwriters.

Also at stake was the seamen's prize money, said to amount to £50,000.[80] The Spanish side of the story remains untold.

[77] *General Advertiser*, 13 February, 7 and 17 June 1748.

[78] Kevin Gordon, 'Quirky Sussex History', https://sussexhistor.nest/2020/11/29/quicksilver-and-lemons (accessed April 2021).

[79] *A View of the Wreck of the Nympha, a Spanish Prize*, 'published according to Act of Parliament, June the 28, 1748'. See also the painting of the *Nympha* wreck at Marlipins Museum, Shoreham, West Sussex, and the engraving by J. H. Hurdis, *The Wreck of the Nympha Americana, a Spanish Corsair, near Beachy Head* (Newick, Sussex, 1840).

[80] Walker, *Voyages and Cruises*, ii. 295–6; Nicolas Magens, *An Essay on Insurances*, 2 vols (1755), i. 220–44, 'how the loss of a Spanish prize called the *Nympha*, was adjusted with the insurers in London'.

Adjusters were pleased to record that they reached settlement, 'without engaging in any suit at law, very greatly redounding to the honour of the insurers in England'. Their detailed account of receipts and expenditures valued the *Nympha* at £150,000, notes goods saved and recovered worth £39,526, reckons the cost of salvage at £6,608, and registers 'the whole loss is £117,082'.[81] No estimate is possible of the amount retrieved by wreckers, but accounts survive of payments made to the people of Seaford during the months of organized recovery. Local hostelries and provisioners did especially well, as did those with horses, wagons, and boats for hire. Forty men of Seaford received £25 between them on 20 December, with a further £36 distributed a month later. Ann Douglas received £1 11*s.* 6*d.* for her labour. Another woman who recovered a piece of linen was paid 21*s*. Boatmen received rewards for finding the ship's broken bottom, and for recovering cases of quicksilver. Celebrations in January included 'brandy for the boats' and bills run up at the *Star*, the *Tree*, and the *Bear*. The local carpenter earned £25 'for cutting up the decks to get the bales out, and building the house on the battery' for officers and guards. More than £250 was shared between twenty-one named 'farmers at Seaford', presumably for the labour of their employees and tenants. The collector, surveyor, and riding officers of Customs assisted, and received payment for their services, but the agents of the insurers and investors took charge. William Belchier billed the adjusters for 150 days of attendance with soldiers, 'making the proper dispositions' for his commission on the sale of the quicksilver. A Captain Stamper received £42 for 'attending on the wreck, and recovering goods from the country'.[82] The shoremen of Seaford, Sussex, along with assorted dealers and opportunists, benefited from this bounty, as many of their forefathers had done a century and more before.

The *Hope*, Dorset 1749

Bound from Curacao to Amsterdam, 'laden with money and goods', and with seventy-four souls on board, the Dutch merchantman *Hope* was cast away on Chesil Beach, Dorset, on the tempestuous night of 18 January 1749, in the same location as the *Golden Grape* a century earlier. The ship carried more than £50,000 in coin, 'besides a considerable quantity of gold-dust, staple-silver, with other valuable commodities'. Providentially, as the *Hope* shattered in pieces, the main mast fell to the shingle bank, and allowed the mariners to escape; but they were soon overwhelmed and 'plundered by a vast concourse of people', whose 'barbarous behaviour prevented their saving any considerable part of their cargo'. Augustine Elliot, a labourer or quarryman of Portland, allegedly 'a principal in this affair', was

[81] Magens, *Essay on Insurances*, i. 235.

[82] Magens, *Essay on Insurances*, i. 235, 224–35.

indicted at that summer's Dorchester assizes 'for feloniously carrying away part of her cargo', and a detailed but partisan account of the trial soon appeared in print.[83]

Witnesses described the shoremen of Portland, Wyke Regis, and Weymouth coming down to the wreck with crooked knives and hooks tied on sticks, while prosecutors represented them as armed more ominously with cutlasses and clubs. Some spoke of 'three hundred or more', others put their numbers in the thousands. Each community of wreckers had its area of beach, but 'joined together to prevent other companies from taking what they had dug up'. The goods from the ship were scattered, and churned up by the waves, so that 'several bags were found six feet deep under the pebbles'. For ten days the shore was covered with 'these tumultuous plunderers'. The beneficiaries included 'one lord of a manor . . . concerned either in the carrying away part of the property of this ship . . . or in purchasing the same of them that did so'.

Officers and sailors of the *Hope* claimed that their coming ashore alive meant that their ship was 'no wreck'. They attempted to secure their property, to which they still claimed title, but had only one musket and no dry powder between them. They quickly retreated to the village of Fleet, and then to the seaport of Weymouth, seeking help from reputable authorities. Three days passed before Customs officers arrived on the scene, backed by thirty men, 'to take care of the king's interest'. Captain Lisle read a proclamation, fired a pistol, and then retreated, as the wreckers essentially ignored him. Government forces 130-strong eventually imposed order, turning an impromptu mêlée into a programme of recovery. Three justices of the peace belatedly joined them, and with the help of well-armed officers 'traced out the possessors of the spoils of inquity', recovering close to £25,000 for the lawful owners. Most of the Dutch crew travelled home within weeks, but the captain, first mate, and carpenter stayed on to give evidence with the help of interpreters.

Prosecuting Augustine Elliot at the assizes, the counsel for the crown spoke vehemently about his 'heinous . . . horrid, and barbarous' crime. The 'plundering mob', he declaimed, came as 'beasts of prey' for pillage and booty. Instead of succouring strangers in distress, they added 'barbarity to iniquity . . . committing an act exceeding sinful in the sight both of God and man'. Elliot, he thundered, was 'the muster-master, the treasurer, the divider of the prey amongst that his plundering regiment'. Whether this was persuasive to a Dorset jury remained to be seen. An anonymous letter, found near Dorchester's south gate, threatened to murder the clerk of the peace, and to fire the houses of the three justices, if they carried on their prosecution.[84]

[83] *An Authentick Account of the Hope, a Very Rich Dutch Merchant-Ship Laden with Money and Goods, that was Cast-away on Portland-Beach in the County of Dorset* (1749), 4, attributed to 'A Gentleman in the Neighbourhood'.

[84] *London Gazette*, 28 March-1 April 1749.

The case against Elliot began to fall apart when the officer in charge of Portland quarries described him as 'an honest man'. Far from supervising the distribution of loot, 'Elliot was for keeping it together till the owners might call for it'. His intention, said his counsel, was 'to save and not destroy; to preserve for the owners, and not to steal and keep from them'. His was a voice of moderation, not extremity. Far from committing a felony, Elliot had acted 'according to the advertisement in the Sherborne newspapers, brought in the money which fell to his part, and received part of the salvage'. There was no barbarity, no criminality, and after six hours the jury brought in their verdict of 'not guilty'. The judge, Heneage Legge, a son of the Earl of Dartmouth, reflected on 'the injustice and complicated guilt of insulting distressed sailors, and depriving them of their property', but appeared satisfied with the verdict. Not so content was the author of this account, for whom 'the toleration of such proceedings in any nation must soon overturn all the foundations of order, and introduce confusion and every evil work'.[85] Recriminations continued as the Dorset shoremen went about their normal business, many of them enriched by their season's work. Augustine Elliot, his reputation unstained, was able to lease land at Portland in the 1750s, perhaps on the proceeds of wrecking.[86] This case, and others like it, may have quickened demand for a stricter law, enacted four years later.

Conclusion

Shipwrecks were unfortunate concomitants of seaborne traffic, but brought bounty to coastal inhabitants. Merchants had to count them in the cost of doing business. So long as wooden vessels relied on ropes and canvas, and the abilities of the men on board, there would be mishaps. Wind, waves, and rocks could be unforgiving. Mistakes and mishandling added to the toll. An ailing barque in a high wind on a lee shore was bound for trouble. Leakage, foundering, and bilging were all too common. Even modern freighters with advanced equipment are subject to loss, sometimes spilling their loads on shore. The wrecking of RMS *Mülheim* near Land's End in 2003, and the beaching of MSC *Napoli* in Devon in 2007, contributed to a long tradition of informal salvage and plunder.[87]

Emergencies at sea became crises on land when materials and lading reached the tideline. Coastal communities became accustomed to dealing with distressed mariners and broken ships and did not always acquit themselves with honour. Competing claimants tested the bonds of law and order, as shippers, officials,

[85] *Authentick Account of the Hope*, 4–16.

[86] Dorset History Centre, Bettey Collection, D-1801/1/1.

[87] The *Mülheim* was mostly laden with scrap plastic. 'Godsends' from the highly publicized *Napoli* included consumer goods, wines, and BMW motorbikes. *The Times* (London), 4 April 2003, 22 and 23 January 2007.

landowners, and salvors vied for advantage. Opportunities abounded for greed, intimidation, and deceit, as well as negotiation. A wide range of behaviour became manifest, from rowdiness and obstreperousness to diligence and cooperation, as stakeholders of every level engaged with *wreccum maris*.

Many of the reports of shipwrecks depict English coastal commoners at their worst, bent only on plunder, but, I have argued, such accounts are often exaggerated. Far from being 'barbarian savages', the wreckers and shoremen generally maintained cordial relations with lords of manors, droit holders, and most government officials; they knew when to tug their forelocks and when to bend to power. Displays of deference may have been calculated and conditional, but they eased the machinery of community. Shoreline interactions appear to have become more strained in the eighteenth century, as social divisions hardened and the state became more demanding, but not to the point of fracture. Shipwrecks may have tested the social order, but its ligaments held firm. Interest in these events led to the cultural consumption of shipwrecks as art, literature, narratives, and news, items that were 'in turn expurgated, anthologized, sensationalized, [or] turned into secular or ecclesiastical didactic tracts . . . texts drifting from them like flotsam'.[88] As records of the High Court of Admiralty made manifest, shipwrecks produced an abundance of claims, complaints, and stories.

Between the sixteenth century and the eighteenth, England grew from a rising contender at the edge of European commerce to become a major global maritime power. Pivotally placed in the circulation of commodities—as producer, consumer, and entrepot—the English garnered wealth from their expanding trade and empire. Legitimate and conventional traffic flowed through orthodox mercantile channels, but a varying percentage was lost to smuggling, pilferage, and wrecks. The goods that came ashore on English beaches, or that were retrieved from cliffs and sandbanks, were gains for some and casualties for others, and could be considered backwash of the new material world.[89] Global and local cultures intersected as items of exotic provenance became godsends, droits, and loot. This appropriation can be construed in terms of a moral economy, but one that embraced the entire coastal community, not just the rough, the disreputable, and the poor. Shoreline societies everywhere exploited the offerings of the sea that resulted from its perils. Wrecking was part of the ecology of the ocean edge and did not necessarily have pejorative connotations.

[88] Michael Titlestad, 'The Muddy Middle-Ground: Representing the Wreck of the *Wager*', *Journal for Maritime Research*, 15 (2013), 116.

[89] Beverly Lemire, *Global Trade and the Transformation of Consumer Cultures: The Material World Remade, c.1500–1820* (Cambridge, 2018).

APPENDIX

Two Centuries of Shipwrecks

Named ships wrecked on the coasts of England and Wales.
Sources include:

L	Richard Larn and Bridget Larn, *Shipwreck Index of the British Isles*, 7 vols (1995–2005)
HCA	High Court of Admiralty
P	printed pamphlets or newspapers
R	record offices or local archives
SP	State Papers

1559	*Bonaventure* of Dieppe, Northumberland	R, SP
1561	*Pelican* of Hamburg, 400 tons, Kent	R
1563	*Greyhound*, Sussex	L
	Hulke, Sussex	R
1564	*Nicholas* of Danzig, Essex	R
1565	*George* of Flushing, Northumberland	R, SP
1567	*Santa Lucia*, Isle of Wight	L
1569	*Seaven Bargayne* alias *Seven Hylls* of Friesland, Cornwall	R
1572	*Clement* of Southwold	R
1573	*John*, Devon	L
1576	*John Evangelist*, Essex	R
1577	*White Lyon*, Thames	R
1578	*Eagle* of Bremen, Devon	SP
1579	*Symond* of Pomerland, Norfolk	SP
	Angel Gabriel of Antwerp, Cornwall	SP
1580	*George* of Colchester, Essex	HCA
	Mewe of Wismere, Suffolk	HCA
	Sea Brake, S. Wales	L
1581	*Michael* of Hull, Norfolk	HCA
1583	*Anne Frauncis*, S. Wales	R
1584	*Jacques* of Cherbourg, Isle of Wight	SP
1585	*Dolphin* of Flushing, 150 tons, Kent	SP, L
1587	*La Stella Evidale*, Isle of Wight	SP
1588	*Mynyon* of Fowey, Kent	SP
	San Pedro Mayor, 580 tons, Devon	SP, L
1591	*Black Jolly*, Devon	HCA
1592	*Golden Lyon* of Middleburg, Kent	SP, HCA, L, R
	Red Lyon of London, Kent	SP, L, R
	St Peter of Amsterdam, Kent	L, R
1595	*St Crucifix*, S. Wales	L

1596	*Morian* of Nilonse, 160 tons, Kent	HCA
1597	*Sea Cock* of Flushing, 380 tons, S. Wales	HCA, L
	Phoenix of Amsterdam, Devon	HCA
1598	*Pegasus*, Kent	L
1600	*Pelican*, Kent	R
1601	*Black Raven* of London, Yorkshire	HCA
1603	*Wagon* of Emden, Devon	HCA
1604	*Cherubim* of London, Kent	HCA, R
	Nightingall of London, Essex	HCA
1608	*Diamond* of Weymouth, Kent	HCA
	Isaack, Thames	HCA
	Red Hart of Newcastle, Essex	HCA
1609	*Elizabeth*, Essex	HCA
	Sante of Flushing	HCA
	Seahorse, Thames	
1610	*Costlette*, Sussex	HCA
1613	*Hermit* of London, 140 tons, Essex	P
1614	*Carnation* of Ipswich, Yorkshire	HCA
	Elizabeth of Newcastle	HCA
1616	*Abraham* of Hoorn, Kent	L, SP
	Johanne of Bordeaux, Kent	SP
	Jonas of Amsterdam, Kent	L, SP
	Peter of Amsterdam, Kent	SP
	Phenix of Dover, Kent	SP, L
1617	*John* of Southampton, Kent	L, SP
	Supply of London, Scilly	L
	St Cleere of Holland, 160 tons, Kent	SP
1618	*Blind Fortune* of Middleborough, Kent	SP, L
	Sampson, Kent	L
1619	*Golden Wagon* of Emden, Kent	L, SP
1620	*George*	HCA
	Margaret of Scotland, 60 tons, Kent	SP
	Warwick of London	HCA
1621	*Ark Noah* of Hamburg, 200 tons, Kent	L, SP
	Charles	HCA
	Paragon of Leith	HCA
1622	*Angel Ratchell* of Hamburg, 160 tons, Sussex	SP
	Margaret	HCA
	Samaritan, S. Wales	L
1623	*Ann Lyon* of London, Kent	L
	Boon Sperans of Flanders, Kent	SP
	Contente	HCA
	Parrett of Amsterdam	HCA
	St Anthony	HCA
1624	*Alexander* of Leith	HCA
	Bridgitt of London	HCA
	Dolphin of London, Kent	SP, L
	Elizabeth	HCA
	Meremayd, Dorset	SP
	White Swan of Hamburg, 220 tons, Sussex	L, SP
1625	*Golden Rose* of Hamburg, Kent	L
	Little Ann of London	HCA
	Moon of London, 800 tons, Kent	SP, L

1626	*Posthorse* of Copenhagen	HCA
1627	*Anne*, Kent	L
	Bonaventure, Devon	L
	Campen of Amsterdam, Isle of Wight	L, R
	Drake (*Vliegende Draak*) Isle of Wight	L, R
	Green Dragon of Erkhuizen, Isle of Wight	L
	St Mary, S. Wales	L
	St Paule	HCA
1628	*Batchellore*, 150 tons	HCA
	Globe	HCA
	Marigold of London	HCA
	Mary of London	HCA
	Old Flushing of Flushing, S. Wales	HCA, SP
	St Peter of Hoorn, Sussex	SP
1629	*Ann* of Plymouth	HCA
	Mary and Elsabeth of London	HCA
	Phenix of London	HCA
	Santa Maria	HCA
1630	*Hope* of Bristol, Scilly	HCA
	La Janette	HCA
	Mary Constance of London, 350 tons	HCA
	Revenge, Kent	L
	St Peter, Suffolk	L
	Stella of Venice, Kent	SP
	Susann of London, Devon	HCA
	William of London, Cornwall	HCA
1631	*Diligence*, Hampshire	L
	Discovery of London	HCA
	Fame, Dorset	
	Jane of Dartmouth, 40 tons	HCA
	Sea Nimph	HCA
1632	*Angel Gabriel* of Lubeck	HCA
	Anne Catherine of London, Essex	R
	Butterfly of London	HCA
	Catherine of Aldborough, 250 tons	HCA
	Fortune of Dunkirk, Yorkshire	HCA
	Frances of Harwich	HCA
	Playne John of London, Sussex	HCA
	Return, Devon	SP
	Robert of London, Cornwall	HCA
	Salmon of Amsterdam, Dorset	SP
1633	*Besse* of Rainham, Essex	HCA
	Faulcon of Bristol	HCA
	St Andrew of Rotterdam, 120 tons, Sussex	HCA, SP
	William and Rachel of London	HCA
	Unity of London	HCA
1634	*Gift of God* of Liverpool, Lancashire	HCA
	Hopewell of London, Essex	HCA, SP
	Mayflower of Hull	HCA
	Morning Star, Suffolk	
	Rose of Amsterdam, 500 tons, Sussex	HCA, SP
	Samuel of Yarmouth, Suffolk	HCA
	Suzan of London, Kent	HCA
	William and Anne of London, 350 tons, Cornwall	HCA

1635	*Angell* of London	HCA
	Bride Phoenix, Isle of Wight	HCA, L, R
	Expedition of Ipswich, Thames	HCA
	Fortune of Dover, Sussex	HCA
	Griffin of London	HCA
	Henry and John of Weymouth	SP
	Katherine, Suffolk	HCA
	Paragon of London, 180 tons	HCA
	St Luke of Hamburg, Sussex	HCA
	Speedwell of London, Yorkshire	HCA
	Unicorne of Desert, 90 tons, Norfolk	
1636	*Anne Royal*, Thames	SP, L
	Black Eagle, Essex	R
	Bonaventure, Hampshire	L
	Carling, Sussex	HCA
	Fortune of Dartmouth, Sussex	HCA
	Dispatch of London	HCA
	Gift of God of Kirkaldy, Scilly	HCA, L, SP
	Guifte of God of Hull, Sussex	HCA
	Joane of Chichester, Essex	HCA
	Mary Rose of Culross, Sussex	HCA
	Rainbow, Hampshire	L
	Society of London, Kent	HCA
	Star of London, Thames	HCA
	Tamerica of Amsterdam, 60 tons	HCA
	Waterhound, S. Wales	
1637	*Anne*, Yorkshire	HCA
	Caulkman, Thames	HCA
	Expedition of London, Thames	HCA
	Fortune of Dover, Sussex	HCA
	Henry and John of Weymouth, Essex	HCA
	Paulsgrove of London, Devon	L
	Rose of Amsterdam, Sussex	SP
1638	*Elizabeth* of Topsham,	HCA
	Starr of Huizen, Thames	HCA
1639	*Beare* of Londonderry, Kent	HCA
	John and Dorothy of London	HCA
	Le Chauntry	HCA
	Unitie	HCA
1640	*Alice* of Ispwich, Suffolk	HCA
	Charity, 160 tons	HCA
	Falcon	HCA
	Grace of God, Cornwall	R
	Henry and John of Dartmouth	SP
	Joye of Woodbridge	HCA
	Nathaniel of Guernsey, Sussex	HCA, SP
	Plyades, Thames	HCA
	St James of Bordeaux	HCA
	St Peter of London	HCA
	William and Anne	HCA
	William and Thomas, Devon	HCA
1641	*Charles* of London, 300 tons	HCA
	Golden Grape, Dorset	HCA, L, R

	Jane and Judith, 200 tons, Wales	HCA
	Martha of London	HCA
	Merchant Royal of Antwerp, off Cornwall	P, SP
	Phenix of Topsham	HCA
	Whale	HCA
1642	*Charles* of Dartmouth	HCA
	Endeavor, Essex	HCA
	Golden Lyon of London	HCA
	Henry and James, 250 tons	HCA
	Hope of London, 70 tons, Kent	HCA
	Margaret of Cheshire, Wales	
	Margaret Constance	HCA
	Mary of London	HCA
	New Years Gift of London, Wales	HCA
	Peter and Mary, Thames	HCA
	Pleiades	HCA
	Providence, Kent	L
	Seaflower of London, 35 tons	HCA
	Success of Topsham	HCA
	Unity, Devon	HCA
	Vrinessen, S. Wales	L
	William of London	HCA
	William and Sarah of London	HCA
1643	*Henry and James*	HCA
	Jewell, Yorkshire	HCA
	Seaventure of Newcastle	HCA
	St John of Le Havre	HCA
1644	*James* of Berwick	HCA
	Swann, 65 tons	HCA
1645	*Blackhorse* of Amsterdam, Suffolk	HCA
	Fame of London	HCA
	Grace	HCA
	Hope of Hamburg	HCA
	Hopewell of London	HCA
	Isabella and Ellyne of London, 350 tons	HCA
	John, 500 tons, Scilly	L
	Noah's Arke of Amsterdam, Sussex	HCA
	Thomas	HCA
1646	*Gabriel* of Hull	HCA
	Honour, 300 tons	HCA
	Increase of London, 300 tons	HCA
	Zelandia of Magdeburg	HCA
1647	*Frances*, S. Wales	HCA
	Princes of Amsterdam, S. Wales	HCA, L
	St Peter of Amsterdam, Cornwall	HCA
1648	*Constance* of London	HCA
	Peace of Hoorn, Cornwall	HCA
	St Jacob of Danzig, Essex	HCA
	St Peter, Sussex	L
	Willing Minde	HCA
	Ellenor of Newport, Cornwall	
1649	*Charles* of Cork	HCA
	Desire of London	HCA

	Elizabeth of London	HCA
	Garland, Cornwall	L
	Gilliflower	HCA
	John and Elizabeth, S. Wales	SP
	Prosperous Susan	HCA
	Swallowe	HCA
	William and Sarah	HCA
1650	*Ann* of Yarmouth, Cornwall	SP
	Blessing, Essex	HCA
	Increase, S. Wales	L
	Liberty, Essex	SP, L
	Ulysses, Isle of Wight	HCA, L
1651	*Elizabeth*, S. Wales	HCA
1652	*Charity*, Devon	L
	Greene Dragon alias *Greene Whale*, Sussex	HCA
	Lily, 110 tons, Dorset	L, P
1653	*Fortune*, Cornwall	L, HCA
	Hare, Thames	SP, L
	John and Ambrose, Essex	HCA
	Richard of Ipswich, Essex	HCA
1654	*Anne* of Dartmouth, 60 tons, Sussex	SP, L
	Exchange, 240 tons, Essex	HCA
	Imployment, Thames	HCA
	Report, Kent	HCA
	St Jacob of Amsterdam, Sussex	HCA, SP
	Sarah	L
1655	*Hare*, Essex	HCA
	Hope of Queenborough, Essex	HCA
	Stork, Sussex	SP
	Thomas of London, Isle of Wight	HCA
	William of London, Isle of Wight	
1656	*Blackboy*, Isle of Wight	HCA
	James, Kent	L
	Pelican, Hampshire	SP
	Primrose, 287 tons, Scilly	SP
	Reserve, Kent	L
1657	*Endeavour* of Arundel, Essex	HCA
	Half Moon, Kent	L
	Laurel, Norfolk	SP, L
	Peter of Huizen, Norfolk	HCA
	Rochester, Kent	L
1658	*Aleppo Merchant* of London, 350 tons, Cornwall	SP, L
	Isaac, Devon	HCA
	Princess Maria, Kent	SP, L
	Swallow, Cornwall	
	William and Anne, Devon	HCA
1659	*Mayflower*, Kent	L
1660	*Blackamore*, Amsterdam, Norfolk	L
	Catherine of Middleborough, Sussex	
	Green King David of Amsterdam, Sussex	
	King David, of Middleborough, Sussex	
1662	*Constance*, S. Wales	HCA
	Laurel, Norfolk S	

1663	*Hester*, Yorkshire	HCA
1665	*Daniel* of Dover	SP
	Fortune of Bordeaux, Sussex	HCA
	London, Thames	SP, L
	Nathaniel, Norfolk P	
	Providence	
1666	*George* of Bristol, Cornwall	SP, L
	Hope, Cornwall	L
	John, Cornwall	L
	Old James, Essex	L, P, R
	Resolution, Kent	L
	Richard Jerron, Yorkshire	L
	Royal Oak, Scilly	L, P, SP
	St Andrew, Sussex	L, P
	St Nichols, Cornwall	L
	Victory, Dorset	L, SP
	White Rose, Essex, R	
1667	*Anne* of Flushing, Yorkshire	L
	Blessing of Swansea	SP
	Elizabeth of Whitby, Isle of Wight	SP
	Helverston, Kent	L
	John and Elizabeth, Cornwall	
	Mary of Minehead	SP
	Pembroke, 269 tons, Dorset	L
	Peregrine of Hull, 130 tons	SP
	Santo Cristo de Castello of Amsterdam, 800 tons, Cornwall	L, SP
	Sorlings, Kent	L
	Teneriffe Merchant of London, Isle of Wight	L
1668	*Amity* of Southampton, S. Wales	L, R
	Angel of Spain, S. Wales	SP
	Emperor Maximilian of Middleburg, 400 tons, Cornwall	SP
	Hind, Scilly	
	Jeoffords of Hull, Norfolk	L
1669	*Cherubim*, S. Wales	P
	Constant Joanna of Youghall, Somerset	P, SP
	Dragon of London, Yorkshire	SP, L
	Edward, Kent	HCA
	John, Dorset	L
	John, Kent	L
	Little Duck, Durham	L
	Mary of London, Essex	R
	Mousehunter of London, 50 tons, Dorset	SP
	Nicholas, S. Wales	SP
	Phenix, Thames	
	Prosperous of Bristol, Cornwall	P
	Providence of Fowey, S. Wales	SP
	San Salvador, Cornwall	SP
	Thomas, Somerset	SP
1670	*Bear* of Danzig, Cornwall	L
	Diligence, Kent L	
	Dolphin of Topsham, Cornwall S	
	Garden, Cornwall	L
	Happy Entrance, S. Wales	L

	Hope, Cornwall	L
	Lyon of Flushing, Kent	P
	Neptune of Amsterdam, Cornwall	L, SP
	St Salvador of Holland, 500 tons, Cornwall	L, R, SP
	Wapen of Vlissingen, Kent	R
1671	*Francis* of Buness, Cornwall	SP
	Kent, Norfolk	L, SP
	Prosperous, Cornwall	L, R
	Prosperous Adventure of Scarborough, Lincolnshire	R
	Speedwell of London, Cornwall	SP
1672	*Ann* of Cork, Cornwall	L
1673	*Algiers*, Thames	L, R
	Ann, Kent	L
	Fairfax, Kent	L
	Golden Calf, Dorset	R
	Hestor, Kent	L
	Moon, Cornwall	R
	Orange Tree, Sussex	L
	Wapen of Hoorn, Dorset	R
1674	*Delight* of Liverpool, Lancashire	SP
	Dove, Northumberland	L
	Nightingale, Kent	L
	Revenge of London, Scilly	
1675	*Ann* of Bristol, 350 tons, Devon	L, SP
	Anne of London, Cornwall	L
	Charles of London, Cornwall	L
	Florentine of Plymouth, 130 tons, Kent	L, P
	Johanna and Sarah of Boston, 120 tons, Cornwall	SP
	Mary, N. Wales	L
	Port Morant Merchant, Somerset	L, SP
	Rose of Helford, S. Wales	SP
	St Toby, Kent	L
1676	*Castle* of Helford, Cornwall	SP
	Philip and Jacob of Yarmouth, Cornwall	SP
	Rose, S. Wales	P
	Success of London, Cornwall	SP
1677	*Dispatch* of London, 70 tons, Kent	L
	James, Sussex	
	John and Hannah of Deptford, 20 tons, Kent	L, SP
	Morning Star, Kent	L, SP
	Providence of London, 100 tons, Kent	L, SP
	Speedwell of Falmouth, 100 tons, Cornwall	SP
	Submission of London, 150 tons, Kent	L, SP
	Unity of London, 200 tons, Kent.	L, SP
1678	*John* of London, Sussex	
	Judith and Anne, Suffolk	
	Margaret, Kent	L
	Merchants Adventure, Dorset	
	Pearl of Lyme	SP
	Providence of Padstow, Cornwall	
1679	*Fraternity*, Kent	
	Santa Cruz, Wales	L
	St Andrew of Bremen, Sussex	
	Thomas and Sarah of Dover, Kent	R

1680	*Golden Lyon*, Scilly	R
	Phoenix, 450 tons, Scilly	L, R
1681	*Angel Guardian*, Dorset	L
	Anne and Mary of Holland	SP
	Mill, Kent	SP, L
	Success, Dorset	L, SP
	Unity of Bergen, Kent	L, SP
	Worlson, Hampshire	P
1682	*Biscay Merchant* of London, Kent	L
	Catherine, Kent	L
	Gloucester, Norfolk	SP, L, P
	Orange Tree, Kent	L
	Syria Merchant	P
1683	*Hope* of Sweden, Isle of Wight	SP, L
1684	*Burse* of Rotterdam, Hampshire	R
	President, 500 tons, Cornwall	L, P
	Schiedam, Cornwall	L
1685	*Peter*, Dorset	L
1686	*Prinses Maria* of Zeeland, 1140 tons, Scilly	L, R
1687	*Constance*, Dorset	L
	Orange Tree of Holstein, Yorkshire	SP
1689	*Alexander*, Hampshire	L
	Centurion, 530 tons, Devon	L, R
	Charles and Henry, 120 tons, Devon	L, R
	Charles II, Cornwall	L
	Edinburgh, 227 tons, Isle of Wight	L, R
	Harwich, 993 tons, Devon	L
	Henrietta, 763 tons, Devon	L, R
	Pendennis, 1000 tons, Thames	L, R
	Sedgemoor, 660 tons, Kent	L, R
	St Davids, 638 tons, Devon	L, R
	St Francis, Cornwall	L
	St Philip of Holland, Wales	SP
	Unity, 172 tons, Devon	L
1690	*Anne*, Sussex	L
	Coronation, 1400 tons, Cornwall	L, R
	Dragon, 50 tons, Kent	L, R
	Dreadnought, 735 tons, Kent	L, R
	Hopewell, Kent	L
	Resolution, Wales	L
	St David, Hampshire	L
	Supply, Cheshire	L
1691	*Blade of Wheat*, 150 tons, Devon	L, R
	Harwich, Cornwall	L, R
	St Anthony of Padua of Genoa, Isle of Wight	L, SP
	Wolf of Copenhagen, Devon	SP
1692	*America*, Cornwall	R
	Crown, 223 tons, Devon	L
	El Dorado, S. Wales	L
	Southsea Castle, Cheshire	L, R
1693	*Mermaid*, 174 tons, Devon	L
	Peace of Plymouth, Cornwall	L
	Windsor Castle, Kent	L

1694	*Anne* of Southampton, Cornwall	R
	Elizabeth of Lymington, Cornwall	R
	James, Thames	L
	Pembroke, Cornwall	L
1695	*Goodwin*, Kent	L
	Friends Adventure, Kent	L
	Shark, Isle of Wight	L
1696	*Aldborough*, Sussex	L
	Carlisle, Essex	L
1697	*Dove*, Dorset	L
	Hope, Kent	L
	Madre Dios, Kent	L
	Paradise, Kent	
	St Christo of Netherlands, Sussex	SP
1698	*Agreement*, Dorset	L
	Ann and Mary, Devon	L, P
	Palm Tree of Stockholm, 350 tons, Cornwall	P
1699	*Duke of Gloster*, Isle of Wight	P
	Golden Lamb of Arundel, Suffolk	
	Griffin, Cornwall	L
	Nicholas, Cornwall	L
1700	*Carlisle*, Kent	L
	Cornelius of Rotterdam, Devon	L
	Thornton, 500 tons, Cornwall	L, R
1701	*Adventure*, Cornwall	R
	Katherine of Brest, Dorset	L
	Notre Dame de Montaigne, Dorset	L
	Robert and John, Kent	L, P
	Sceptre, 375 tons, S. Wales	R
1702	*Employment*, Lancashire	L
	John and Sarah, S. Wales	P
	Joshuah of Prussia, Devon	SP
1703	*Benbow*, Cornwall	L
	Bonadventure of London, Norfolk	P
	Canterbury, Somerset	L, P
	Concord, Cornwall	L
	Eagle, Sussex	L, P
	George and Grace, Somerset	P
	Hopeful, Devon	P
	Litchfield, Sussex	P
	Mansbridge, Cornwall	P
	Mary, Kent	L, P
	Newcastle, Hampshire	L
	Northumberland, Kent	L, P
	Portsmouth, Thames	L, P
	Reserve, Norfolk	L, P
	Resolution, Sussex	L
	Restoration, Kent	L, P
	Reward, Cornwall	L
	Richard and John, Somerset	P
	Stirling Castle, Kent	L, P
	Vanguard, Kent	P
	Walker Galley of London, Devon	P
	Winchelsea of London, Devon	P
	York, Suffolk	L

1704	*Ann* of Portsmouth, Isle of Wight	HCA
	Colchester, Cornwall	L, P
	John and Anne, Wales	
	Rebecca, Isle of Wight	HCA
1705	*Looe*, Isle of Wight	L
1706	*Golden Fleece* of London, Dorset	L
	Grand Matre de Dios, Cornwall	L
	Hazardous, Sussex	L
	Major, Wales	L
	Nassau, Isle of Wight	
1707	*Association*, 1459 tons, Scilly	L, P
	Devonshire, Cornwall	L
	Dunkerque, Kent	
	Eagle, 1065 tons, Scilly	L
	Enterprise, Lancashire	L
	Firebrand, 268 tons, Scilly	L
	Hastings, Norfolk	L
	La Baleine of Dunkirk, Kent	L
	Romney, 683 tons, Scilly	L
1708	*Albemarle*, 330 tons, Cornwall	L, R
	Samuel, Wales	
1709	*Hind*, Hampshire	L
	Sole Bay, 256 tons, Lincolnshire	L
1710	*Gardner* of Bristol, Cornwall	P
1711	*Greyhound*, Durham	L
	Sea Horse, 161 tons, Devon	L
1716	*Amity*, Kent	P
	Jesus Maria Joseph, Dorset	R
1720	*Betty*, Cornwall	L
	Mary, Scilly	L
	Monck, Suffolk	L, SP
1721	*Aaglekerke*, of Amsterdam, Devon	R
	Hester, Scilly	L
	Josiah and Betty, 1000 tons, Cornwall	L
	Royal Anne, 511 tons, Cornwall	L, P
	St Peter of Amsterdam, 170 tons, Cornwall	L, SP
1723	*Mary*, Kent	P
1724	*Anne*, Kent	P
	Mary, Cornwall	P
1725	*Astrea* of Amsterdam, 800 tons, Devon	L, P
	Hope, Kent	P
	Samuel and James, Kent	P
1726	*Fox*, N. Wales	L
	William and Mary, Scilly	P
1728	*Diligent* of France, Sussex	SP
	Endeavour, Devon	L, P
	Harrison, Cornwall	P
	Peter, Devon	L, P
1729	*Coach*, Hampshire	L, P
	Elizabeth, Kent	P
	John of Waterford, S. Wales	P
	John and Mary, Isle of Wight	P
	Speedwell, Wales	P

1730	*Hedges*, Essex	P
	John and Anne, Lincolnshire	P
	Mary of Dublin, Wales	P
1731	*Globe*, Wales	P
1732	*Exchange*, Norfolk	P
	Molly, Somerset	P
	Postillion, Devon	L
1733	*Charles and Mary*, Suffolk	P
1734	*Dove*, Wales	P
	Emmanuel, Cornwall	R
	Harschundal, Kent	L
	Prowse, Cornwall	P
1735	*Dolphin*, Kent	P
	Friends Adventure, Hampshire	L, P
	Johanna and Mary, Devon	L
	Neptune, Kent	P
	Prince of Orange, Kent	P
	St Dennis of Honfleur, Devon	L, P
	Susannah and Martha, Kent	P
	William of Hamburg, Suffolk	P
	William and Jane of Sunderland, Norfolk	P
1736	*Artillery*, Wales	P
	Bideford, Yorkshire	L
	Clement, Norfolk	P
	Constant, Wales	P
	Flying Fish, Scilly	L
	Loosdrecht of Amsterdam, Kent	R
	St Peter of Amsterdam, Sussex	P
	Triumph, Scilly	P
1737	*Betsy*, Scilly	L
	Endeavour, Scilly	L
	Priscilla, S. Wales	
	Pye, Wales	
1738	*Anna and Helena*, of Amsterdam, Devon	R, L, SP
	Boot of Amsterdam, 650 tons, Devon	L
	Diana, Scilly	P
	Elizabeth and Martha, Isle of Wight	P
	Lintor Ken, Devon	L
	New Intent, Norfolk	P
	Vigilantia of Hamburg, Cornwall	L
	Whale, Northumberland	P
1739	*Adventure*, Kent	L
	Apollo, Sussex	L
	Fenwick, Norfolk	P
	Griffin, Scilly	L
	Johannes Specht of Rotterdam, Kent	L
	Lady Lucy, Cornwall	L
	Mary of Dublin, Cornwall	P
	Mermaid of Plymouth, Scilly	L, P
	Naboth's Vineyard, Cornwall	L
	Phenix of Shields, Suffolk	p
	St Joseph, Scilly	L, P
	William and Elizabeth, Scilly	L

1740	*Diligence*, Scilly	L
	Esther, Suffolk	L
	Friendship, Norfolk	L
	Hannah of London, Scilly	L
	Jane, Scilly	L, P
	Mary and Betty, Lancashire	L
	North Cape of Bristol, Scilly	P
	Pearl, Durham	L
	Prince of Orange, Kent	P
	Rooswijk of Amsterdam, Kent	L, R
	Russell, Northumberland	P
	Speedwell, Cornwall	L
	Townsend, Somerset	R
	Two Brothers, Cornwall	L
	William, N. Wales	L
1741	*Adventure* of Scarborough, Northumberland	L, P
	Anna Maria Margaretta, Kent	L
	Betty, 300 tons, Cornwall	L
	Charming Molly, Wales	L
	Dorothy and Betty, Norfolk	L
	Genge, Kent	L
	Greenwich, Sussex	L
	Hamburg Merchant, Lincolnshire	L
	Hopewell, Durham	L
	Isabella, Cornwall	L
	Joseph and Elizabeth, Cornwall	L
	La Thereisvicaute, Isle of Wight	L
	Liverpool Merchant, Lancashire	L
	Marigold, Scilly	L
	Michael, Norfolk	L
	Prosperous, Norfolk	L
	Reliance, Norfolk	L
	Revolution, Durham	L
	Squirrel, Yorkshire	L
	Susanna, Scilly	L
	Warwick, Norfolk	L
1742	*Charming Widow* of Dublin, Lancashire	P
	John and Mary, Lancashire	P
	Margaret and Sarah, Scilly	L
	Nancy, Scilly	L, P
	Otter, Suffolk	L
1743	*Carolina*, Kent	L
	Catherine, Scilly	L
	Charlot, Kent	L
	Charming Nancy, Cornwall	L
	Diamond, Cornwall	L
	Dolphin, Kent	L
	Draper, Scilly	L
	Elizabeth, Suffolk	L
	Friday, Cornwall	L
	Genoa, Kent	L
	Globe, Kent	L
	Happy Return, Devon	L

	Hollandia of Amsterdam, Scilly	R, P
	Hope, Essex	L
	Industry, Kent	L
	Jennet, Kent	L
	John and Hannah, Yorkshire	L
	Maria, Isle of Wight	L
	Martha, Devon	L
	Mary, Kent	L
	Nottingham, Kent	L
	Oxford, Kent	L
	Providence, N. Wales	L
	Recovery, Kent	L
	St Antonio de Padua, Kent	L
	St Dominic, Isle of Wight	L
	Success, Kent	L
	William and Anne, Cornwall	L
	William and Sarah, Kent	L
1744	*Amoretta* of Bristol, Devon	L, P
	Anne and Betty, Wales	P
	Anne and Elizabeth of Leith, Lincolnshire	P
	Barbadoes Packet, N. Wales	L
	Benjamin, Yorkshire	L
	Chatham, Sussex	L
	Colchester, Thames	L, P
	Colinie van Surinam, Kent	L
	Curten, Isle of Wight	L
	Duke, Kent	L
	Elizabeth, Kent	L
	Endeavour, Norfolk	L
	Fortune, Sussex	L
	Grantham, 480 tons, Kent	L
	Industry, Sussex	L
	Kingston, Northumberland	L
	Maryland Merchant, Devon	L, P
	Neptune, Sussex	L
	Polly, Kent	L
	Prosperous, Dorset	L
	Providence, Kent	L
	Ranger of Poole, Dorset	L
	Robert and John, Lancashire	L
	Rye, Norfolk	L
	Success, Isle of Wight	
	Success, Thames	L
	Terror Bomb, Sussex	P
	Trial of Newcastle, Northumberland	P
	Wackender Boeye, Kent	L
1745	*Boscawen*, Cornwall	L, P
	Cape Coast, Devon	L
	Charming Sally of Boston, Cornwall	P
	Expeditious, Devon	L
	Sarah of Padstow, Dorset	L
	Tiger, Dorset	L

1746	*Content*, 90 tons, Sussex	P
	Fame, Cornwall	
	Friends Goodwill, Cornwall	L
	Griffin, N. Wales	L
	Jane, Cornwall	L
	Little Benjamin, Kent	L
	Loyal Macs, Isle of Wight	L
	Marseilles of Dartmouth, Devon	L
	Panther, Sussex	L
	Providence, Norfolk	L
	Reginald and Jacob, Kent	L
	Robert and Ruth, Durham	L
	Saltash, Sussex	L
	Sophia Louisa, Cumberland	
	Thelma, Scilly	L
	Two Batchelors of Dartmouth, Sussex	P
	Tyger, Isle of Wight	L
	Wager, Devon	L
1747	*Betty*, Kent	L
	Blanchard's Adventure, Kent	L
	Britannia, Wales	L
	Buck, Norfolk	L
	Concord, Yorkshire	L
	De Leifde, Kent	L, P
	Elizabeth, Norfolk	L
	Expedition, Norfolk	L
	Fredericksburg, Cornwall	L
	Friendship, Sussex	L
	Hammond, Yorkshire	L
	Hannah, Suffolk	L
	Invincible, Hampshire	L
	La Nympha Americana, Sussex	L, P, R
	Love Galley, Isle of Wight	L
	Marshall, Sussex	L
	Mayflower, Norfolk	L
	Phenix, Scilly	P
	Portsmouth, Kent	L
	Sheerwater, Cheshire	L
	St Esprit, Kent	L
	Susannah, Norfolk	L
	Three Sisters, Sussex	P
	Virginia Packet, Kent	L
	Willis, Northumberland	L
1748	*Arent and Elizabeth*, Sussex	L
	Basnet, Kent	L
	Elizabeth, Kent	L
	Halsy and Suttle, Lancashire	L
	Happy, Lancashire	L
	Industry, Kent	L
	John and James, Kent	L
	Jonge Alcida, Cornwall	L
	Jonge Princess Carolina, Kent	L
	La Vantese, Kent	L

	Lady Luvibund, Kent	L
	Lagnitus, Dorset	L
	Laura, Kent	L
	Lizard, Scilly	L
	Mary, Dorset	L
	Mary, Lincolnshire	L
	Mayflower, Lancashire	L
	Nancy, Kent	L
	Neptune, Cheshire	L
	Prophet Jonah, Kent	L
	Providence, Sussex	L
	Providence, Kent	L
	Savage, Cornwall	L
	Sea Flower, Scilly	L
	Serpent's Prize, Yorkshire	L
	Squirrel, Dorset	L
	St Domingo of Bilbao, Devon	L
	St George, Kent	L
	Stobbs, Kent	L
	Usro Rebeccah, Kent	L
	Thetis, Cornwall	L
	Young Elizabeth of Bergen, Dorset	L, P
1749	*Alexander*, Thames	R, L
	Amsterdam of Amsterdam, Sussex	L, P, R
	Charming Molly, Dorset	
	Charming Peggy, Cornwall	L
	Content, Norfolk	L
	Expedition, Sussex	L, P
	Hope of Amsterdam, Dorset	L, P, R
	Lisbon Packet, Sussex	L
	Loyal Comfort, Devon	L
	Mary, Dorset	
	Mayflower, Cornwall	L
	Pretty Patsy of London, Isle of Wight	L
	Providence, N. Wales	L
	Rose in June of Barnstable, Cornwall	L
	Salisbury, Devon	L
	Squirrel of Great Yarmouth, Cornwall	
	St George, Lancashire	L, P
	Success, Norfolk	L
	Swallow, Norfolk	L
	Swift, Cornwall	L
	Terra Nova of Amsterdam, Cornwall	L
	Two Friends, 120 tons, Cornwall	L
	Warren, Devon	L
	Wilhelmina, Kent	L
	William and Jane, Devon	L
1750	*Ann*, Essex	L
	Dragon, Yorkshire	L
	Duke, Yorkshire	L
	Endeavour, Cornwall	L
	Fleece, Cornwall	L
	Friends Goodwill, Sussex	L

Holland, 300 tons, Cornwall	L, P
Hope, Lincolnshire	L
Industry, Kent	L
Jonge Hans and Gerten of Friesland, Isle of Wight	L
Lekat, Kent	L
Lorraine, Cornwall	L
Neptune, Lancashire	L
Norwich Merchant, Sussex	L
Oxford, N. Wales	L
Penguin, Devon	L
Reine, Dorset	L
Revenge, Devon	L
Speedwell of Scarborough, Isle of Wight	L
St Johnnes of Gothenburg, Isle of Wight	L
St Kitts Merchant, Cornwall	L
St Laurence of Scarborough, Isle of Wight	
Ulysses, Cornwall	L
Warren of London, Isle of Wight	L
Young Brewer, Norfolk	L

Bibliography

Manuscript Sources

Bodleian Library, Oxford

Jones 27*
Rawlinson A 195

British Library, London

Additional 22,184; 46,501
Egerton 923, 2533
Harley 6990
Harper Collection of Private Bills, 1695–1814
India Office Records
Lansdowne 132, 133, 142, 145, 504/7
Sloane 207

Cornwall Archives and Cornish Studies Service, Redruth

AR15/1–1108 (Arundell Papers)

Devon Archives and Local Studies Service, Exeter

L 1508 M (Courtney Papers)
QS/4/1738/Easter/NO/1–5 (Quarter Sessions)
QS/4/1738/Easter/EX/1–5 (Quarter Sessions)

Dorset History Centre, Dorchester

Bettey Collection, D-1801/1/1

East Sussex Record Office, Falmer

AMS 4606/1 (Birling manorial records)
BH/P/ES/ET/87–91 (Cheynell Papers)
PBT/1/1/60/202 (Probate)
RYE/46, 58 (Cinque Port Papers)
SAS/A593–757 (Pelham Papers)
SAS/G5/49 (Gage Papers)

Essex Record Office, Chelmsford

D/Deb/95 (Bramston Papers)
D/DU/514 (Foulness manorial records)
Q/SR 526/7–8 (Quarter Sessions)

Hatfield House, Hertfordshire

Cecil Papers

Huntington Library, San Marino, California

Ellesmere 9093
Huntington JR 37

Isle of Wight Record Office, Newport

OG/BB/224–334 (Oglander Papers)

Kent History and Library Centre, Maidstone

NR/LB8/1 (Wye manorial records)
QM/SIq/1 (Quarter Sessions)
U442/L1 (Dengemarsh records)

Lambeth Palace Library, London

Carew MS 618
MS 3475 (Sir Mathew Hale's notes, *c.*1652)

The National Archives, Kew

ADM 1, 106 (Navy Board)
C2 (Chancery)
CUST 59, 64, 68, 97 (Customs)
DL 4 (Duchy of Lancaster)
HCA 3, 13, 23, 32, 49 (High Court of Admiralty)
PC 1, 2 (Privy Council)
REQ 2 (Requests)
SP 11, 12, 13, 14, 15, 16, 17, 18, 25, 29, 35, 36, 44, 46, 52, 59, 63, 84 (State Papers)
STAC 2, 4, 5, 8 (Star Chamber)
WO 7, 47 (War Office)

National Library of Wales, Aberystwyth

Penrice and Margam MS 5278

National Maritime Museum, Greenwich

ADL/A/18 (Bishop of Durham claims)
ADM/A/ (Navy Board Orders and Correspondence)
MS JOD/39 (Relation of Moses Bathurst)

Norfolk Record Office, Norwich

BL/Y2/42–4 (Yarmouth letters)
GTN 2/40/35 (Gunton manorial papers)
LEST/Q 37 (Lestrange Estate Rolls)
NAS 1/1/12/Palling/10 (Manorial records)
NAS S2/16/20 (Bacon Papers)

Somerset Heritage Centre, Taunton

DD WO 57/4/8/1 (Trevelyan Papers)
Q/ST/17/2–4 (Quarter Sessions)

West Sussex Record Office, Chichester

Ep/1/55/134 (Chichester Vice-Admiralty records)

Wiltshire and Swindon History Centre, Chippenham
865/404 (Vice-Admiralty of Dorset)

Newspapers

Applebee's Original Weekly Journal, 1721.
Basildon Canvey Southend Echo, 2017.
County Journal, or The Craftsman, 1731.
Daily Courant, 1720, 1721.
Daily Gazetteer, 1738, 1739, 1740.
Daily Journal, 1721, 1736.
The Daily Post, 1736, 1738.
Domestick Intelligence, or News Both from the City and Country, 1679.
Evening Post, 1710, 1721.
Flying Post, 1695, 1698.
Flying Post, or the Post-Master, 1721, 1732.
General Advertiser, 1748, 1749.
Jacobite's Journal, 1747.
London Evening Post, 1738, 1739, 1746, 1747.
London Gazette, 1672, 1678, 1692, 1721, 1749.
London Post, with Intelligence Foreign and Domestick, 1699, 1703.
London Tatler, 1736.
Old England, 1749, 1750.
Penny London Post, or Morning Advertiser, 1747.
Post Boy, 1698, 1721, 1722.
Flying Post, or the Post-Master, 1721.
Remembrancer, 1749.
St James Evening Post, 1735.
Stamford Mercury, 1716, 1722, 1737.
The Times, 2003, 2007.
Universal Journal, 1724.
Weekly Journal or British Gazetteer, 1721.
Weekly Journal, or Saturday's Post, 1724.
Weekly Miscellany, 1735, 1736.
Weekly Packet, 1720.
Westminster Journal, or New Weekly Miscellany, 1747.
Whitehall Evening Post, 1721, 1735.
Whitehall Journal, 1723.

Printed Primary Sources

An Abstract of all such Acts of Parliament, Now in Force, as Relate to the Admiralty, and Navy of England (1715).
The Accomplish'd Sea-Mans Delight (1686).
An Act for the Better Preserving Ships Stranded or Forced on Shore, and the Furniture and Cargoes thereof (1736; British Library, Harper Collection of Private Bills, 1695–1814, no. 32).

Actes des Etats de L'Ile de Guernsey 1605 à 1651 (St Peter Port, 1851).
The Acts of the Parliaments of Scotland, vii. *AD. MDCLXI-MDCLXIX* (Edinburgh, 1820).
Acts of the Privy Council of England, 1542–1631, ed. J. R. Dasent et al., 45 vols (1890–1964).
Anderson, Anthony, 'A Form of Prayer for Sea Men and Passengers', appended to Anderson, *A Godlie Sermon, Preached on Newe Yeers Day Last* (1576).
The Answer of the Masters of the Trinitie-House, to the Special Obiections of the Patentee, for the Keeping of Winterton Lights (1621).
The Answers to the Severall Objections, Made against the Lights for the Goodwin Sands (1641).
Articles Concerning the Admiralty of England, and the Iurisdiction Thereof. 21. Julii. Anno Domini. 1591 (1591).
Articles of Enquirie to be Ministered Concerning the Admiraltie in the County of Sussex (1638).
An Authentick Account of the Hope, a Very Rich Dutch Merchant-Ship Laden with Money and Goods, that was Cast-away on Portland-Beach in the County of Dorset (1749).
B., W., *Seven Dialogues both Pithie and Profitable* (1606).
Bacon, Francis, *Novum Organum* (1620).
Bacon. *The Official Papers of Sir Nathaniel Bacon of Stiffkey, Norfolk as Justice of the Peace 1580–1620*, ed. H. W. Saunders, Camden Society, 3rd ser. 26 (1915).
Bacon. *The Papers of Nathaniel Bacon of Stiffkey*, ed. A. Hassell Smith and Gillian M. Baker, 3 vols (Norwich, 1979–90).
Baldwin, Samuel, *A Survey of the British Customs: Containing the Rates of Merchandize* (1770).
Balfour, Andrew, *Letters to a Friend* (Edinburgh, 1700).
Barlow. *Barlow's Journal of his Life at Sea in King's Ships, East & West Indiamen & Other Merchantmen from 1659 to 1703*, ed. Basil Lubbock, 2 vols (1934).
Beaumont, Francis, and John Fletcher, *Fifty Comedies and Tragedies* (1679).
A Bill for Enforcing the Laws against Persons, who shall Steal or Detain Shipwrecked Goods; and for the Relief of Persons suffering Losses thereby (1753).
Blackstone, William, *Commentaries on the Laws of England*, 11th edn, 4 vols (1791).
Blakhal, Gilbert, *A Brieffe Narration of the Services Done to Three Noble Ladies* (Spalding Club, Aberdeen, 1844).
Blundell. *The Great Diurnal of Nicholas Blundell of Little Crosby, Lancashire. Volume One 1702–1711*, ed. Frank Tyrer and J. J. Bagley, Record Society of Lancashire and Cheshire, vol. 110 (1968).
Booth, A., *Examen Legum Angliae, or, The Laws of England Examined, by Scripture, Antiquity and Reason* (1656).
Boroughs, John, *The Soveraignty of the British Seas* (1651).
Boteler, Nathaniel, *Six Dialogues about Seas-Services* (1685).
Bourne, William, *A Booke Called the Treasure for Traveilers* (1578).
Bourne, William, *Inventions or Devises: Very Necessary for all Generalles and Captains* (1578).
Boys, William, *Collections for the History of Sandwich in Kent* (1792).
Bracton. *Henrici de Bracton de Legibus et Consuetudinibus Regni Angliae* (1569).
Bracton, Henry de, *De Legibus et Consuetudinibus Regni Angliae*, ed. G. E. Woodbine, 4 vols, Selden Society (1968–77).
Bray. *An Account of the Wrecks 1759–1830 on the North Coast of Cornwall. By John Bray*, ed. A. K. Hamilton Jenkin (Truro, 1975).
Brekell, John, *Euroclydon: Or the Dangers of the Sea* (1744).
The British Magazine: Or, The London and Edinburgh Intelligencer (Edinburgh, 1748).

Brome, James, *A Sermon Preached in St Maries Church in Dover* (1694).
Bureau d'addresse et de rencontre, *A General Collection of Discourse of the Virtuosi of France* (1664).
Burroughs, Jeremiah, *A Sea-Mans Direction in Time of Storme* (1640).
Burton, Henry, *Conformitie's Deformity: In a Dialogue between Conformity and Conscience* (1646).
C., J., *The Compleat Collier* (1708).
Calendar of State Papers, Domestic, ed. Mary Anne Everett Green et al., 84 vols (1856–2006).
Calendar of State Papers Foreign Series, of the Reign of Elizabeth, ed. Joseph Stevenson et al., 23 vols (1863–1950).
Calendar of State Papers Relating to Ireland... 1603–1625, ed. Charles William Russell et al., 5 vols (1872–1888).
Calendar of State Papers... Venice, ed. Rawdon Brown et al., 38 vols (1864–1947).
A Calendar of Material Relating to Ireland from the High Court of Admiralty 1641–1660, ed. Elaine Murphy (Dublin, 2011).
Calendar of Treasury Books, 1660–1667, ed. William A. Shaw (1904).
Calendar of Treasury Books 1676–1679, ed. William A. Shaw (1911).
Calendar of Treasury Books, 1679–1680, ed. William A. Shaw (1913).
Calendar of Treasury Books, 1681–1685, ed. William A. Shaw (1916).
Calendar of Treasury Books 1685–1689, ed. William A. Shaw (1923).
Calendar of Treasury Books 1689–1692, ed. William A. Shaw (1931).
Calendar of Treasury Books, 1693–1696, ed. William A. Shaw (1935).
Calendar of Treasury Books 1697–1698, ed. William A. Shaw (1933).
Calendar of Treasury Papers 1556/7–1696, ed. Joseph Redington (1868).
A Calendar of the White and Black Books of the Cinque Ports 1432–1955, ed. Felix Hull (1966).
Calle, Caleb, *On His Royal Highness's Miraculous Delivery, and Happy Return* (1682).
Capt. Inglefield's Narrative, Concerning the Loss of His Majesty's Ship the Centaur (1783).
Cardiff Records, ed. John Hobson Mathews, 6 vols (Cardiff, 1898–1911).
Carew. *The Survey of Cornwall by Richard Carew*, ed. John Chynoueth, Nicholas Orme, and Alexandra Walsham, *Devon and Cornwall Record Society*, NS (2004).
Cawdrey, Daniel, *A Late Great Shipwrack of Faith* (1655).
Charles by the Grace of God... for the Maintenance of Light-Houses at the North and South Forelands (1637).
A Circumstantial Narrative of the Loss of the Halsewell (East-Indiaman) (1786).
Clarke, Samuel, *A Generall Martyrologie Containing a Collection of all the Greatest Persecutions which have Befallen the Church of Christ* (1660).
Clerke, Francis, *Praxis Curiae Admiralitatis Angliae* (1667).
Clerke, Francis, *The Practice of the Court of Admiralty of England* (1722).
Codrington, Robert, *His Majesties Propriety, and Dominion on the British Seas* (1665).
Coke, Sir Edward, *The Fourth Part of the Institutes of the Laws of England: Concerning the Jurisdiction of Courts* (1644).
A Collection of All Such Statutes and Parts of Statutes, as in any Way Relate to the Admiralty (1742).
Collins, Greenvile, *Great Britain's Coasting Pilot: The First Part. Being a New and Exact Survey of the Sea-Coast of England* (1693).
Columne, Jacob, *The Fierie Sea-Columne, wherein are Shewed the Seas, and Sea-Coasts of the Northern, Eastern, and Western Navigation* (Amsterdam, 1640).

Cooper. 'The Journal of Dawtrey Cooper', in *Three Sea Journals of Stuart Times*, ed. Bruce Ingram (1936).

Cosmo. 'The Travels of Cosmo III, Grand Duke of Tuscany, through England', in Alan Gibson and R. Pearse Chope (eds), *Early Tours in Devon and Cornwall* (Newton Abbot, 1967), 92–110.

Cowell, John, and Thomas Manley, *The Interpreter of Words and Terms, Used either in the Common Statute Laws of this Realm* (1701).

Coxere. *Adventures by Sea of Edward Coxere*, ed. E. H. W. Meyerstein (Oxford and New York, 1946).

Dalrymple, Sir John, *Memoirs of Britain and Ireland*, 2 vols (1773).

Dalton, Michael, *The Countrey Iustice, Conteyning the Practise of the Iustices of the Peace* (1618).

Dalton, Michael, *The Country Justice* (1697).

Dame Elizabeth Shovell, Widow and Executrix of Sir John Narborough... The Appellants Case (1718).

De Dominis, Marco Antonio, *The Rockes of Christian Shipwracke, Discovered by the Holy Church of Christ* (1618).

Deane, John, *A Narrative of the Shipwreck of the Nottingham Galley... etc. First Publish'd in 1711*, 4th edn (1738).

A Declaration of His Highness, by the Advice of the Council Setting Forth, on the Behalf of this Commonwealth, the Justice of their Cause Against Spain (1655).

Defoe, Daniel, *The Storm: Or, A Collection of the Most Remarkable Casualties and Disasters which Happen'd in the Late Dreadful Tempest, both by Sea and Land* (1704).

Defoe, Daniel, *The Life and Strange Surprizing Adventures of Robinson Crusoe* (1719).

Defoe, Daniel, *A Tour thro' the Whole Island of Great Britain*, 2 vols (1724–6).

Defoe, Daniel, *An Historical Narrative of the Great and Tremendous Storm which Happened on Nov. 26th, 1703* (1769).

Defoe, Daniel, *A Tour through the Whole Island of Great Britain*, ed. Pat Rogers (1971).

Denton, Thomas, *A Perambulation of Cumberland 1687–1688*, Surtees Society, vol. 207 (2003).

Dickenson, Jonathan, *God's Protecting Providence, Man's Surest Help and Defence* (1700).

Donne. *The Poems of John Donne*, ed. Herbert Grierson (1957).

Dorset Protestation Returns Preserved in the House of Lords, ed. Edward A. Fry and George S. Fry (1912).

The Duties at this Present Time on all Merchandize (1714).

Eden, Robert, *An Address to Depredators & Wreckers on the Sea Coast* (1840).

Elizabethan Court Rolls of Stokenham Manor 1560–1602, ed. W. A. Roberts (Kingsbridge, 1984).

The English Reports Volume XCVIII. King's Bench Division XXVII (1909).

The English reports Volume CLXVI: Ecclesiastical, Admiralty, and Probate and Divorce VI (1924).

Erasmus. *Twenty Select Colloquies, out of Erasmus Roterodamus*, ed. Roger l'Estrange (1680).

Erasmus. *Collected Works of Erasmus: Colloquies*, ed. Craig R. Thompson (Toronto, 1997).

Evelyn, John, *Navigation and Commerce, the Original and Progress* (1674).

An Exact and Perfect Relation of the Arrival of the Ship the James and Mary Captain Phipps Commander (1687).

Exton, John, *The Maritime Dicaeologie, or Sea-Jurisdiction of England* (1656).

Falck, N. D., *A Philosophical Dissertation on the Diving Vessel* (1775).

Falconer, William, *The Shipwreck. A Poem. In Three Cantos. By A Sailor* (1762).
Flavell, John, *A New Compass for Seamen* (1664).
Flavell, John, *The Sea-Mans Companion* (1676).
Flavell, John, *Navigation Spiritualized: Or, A New Compass for Sea-Men* (1682).
Fortrey, Samuel, *Englands Interest and Improvement. Consisting in the Increase of the Store, and Trade of this Kingdom* (Cambridge, 1663).
The Fourth of September: Newes from Sundry Places, both Forraine and Domestique (1622).
Francklyn, Thomas, *Serious Advice and Fair Warning To all the live upon the Sea-Coast of England and Wales* (1756).
A Full and True Account of a Most Dreadful and Terrible Accident (1706).
Fuller, Thomas, *The Historie of the Holy Warre* (Cambridge, 1639).
Gibbon, John, *Prince-Protecting Providences* (1682).
God's Wonders in the Great Deep, or, The Seaman's Danger and Deliverance Exemplified (1710).
Godolphin, John, *Synēgoros Thalassio: A View of the Admiral Jurisdiction* (1661).
Gorges, Sir Ferdinando, *America Painted to the Life: A True History of the Originall Undertakings of the Advancement of Plantations into those Parts* (1658).
Graunt, John, *The Shipwrack of all False Churches* (1652).
The Great and Ancient Charter of the Cinque-Ports of Our Lord the King, and the Members of the same (1682).
Hale, Matthew, *A Treatise Relative to the Maritime Law of England* (1787).
Hale, Sir Matthew, 'Concerning the Prerogative and Franchise of Wreck', in Stuart A. Moore, *A History of the Foreshore and the Law Relating Thereto*, 3rd edn (1888), 406–9.
Halley, Edmund, *An Advertisement Necessary to be Observed in the Navigation up and down the Channel of England* (1701).
Halley, Edmund, 'The Art of Living under Water', *Philosophical Transactions*, 29 (1717), 492–9.
Hayward, Edward, *A Full and Perfect Account of the Size and Lengths of Riggins for all His Majesties Ships and Frigats* (1666).
Heath, Robert, *A Natural and Historical Account of the Islands of Scilly* (1750).
Heather, William, *The Chart of the Entrances to the River Thames* (1801).
Hedges, Charles, *Reasons for Settling Admiralty-Jurisdiction; and Giving Encouragement to Merchants, Owners, Commanders, Masters of Ships, Material-Men and Mariners* (1690),
Heywood, Thomas, *Pleasant Dialogues and Dramas* (1637).
Hickes, Gaspar, *The Advantage of Affliction* (1646).
Historical Manuscripts Commission, *Fourth Report* (1874).
Historical Manuscripts Commission, *Calendar of the Manuscripts of... the Marquis of Salisbury*, 24 vols (1883–1976).
Historical Manuscripts Commission, *Report on the Manuscripts of the Earl of Egmont*, 2 vols (1905).
Hollar, Wenceslaus, *Navium Variae Figurae* Containing the Particular Business of Quarter Sessions *et Formae* (1647).
The Holy Bible: Psalms, Jonah, Acts, 2 Corinthians,
Homer's Odysses, trans. George Chapman (1615).
Houghton, John, *England's Great Happiness, or, A Dialogue between Content and Complaint* (1677).
Hughes, William, *An Exact Abridgement in English of the Cases Reported by Sr Francis More* (1665).

Hutchins, John, *The History and Antiquities of the County of Dorset*, 2 vols (1774).

Hyde. *The Correspondence of Henry Hyde, Earl of Clarendon and of his Brother Lawrence Hyde, Earl of Rochester*, ed. Samuel Weller Singer, 2 vols (1828).

Hyland, William, *The Ship-Wreck: A Dramatick Piece* (1746).

Jacob, Giles, *An Appendix to the Modern Justice: Containing the Particular Business of the Quarter Sessions* (1718).

Jacob, Giles, *Lex Mercatoria: Or the Merchant's Companion* (1729).

Janeway, James, *Mr James Janeway's Legacy to his Friends: Containing Twenty-Seven Famous Instances of God's Providence in and about Sea-Dangers and Deliverances* (1675).

Janeway, James, *A Token for Mainers* (1708).

Jeake, Samuel, *Charters of the Cinque Ports, Two Ancient Towns, and their Members* (1728).

Jeffreys. *The Business and Household Accounts of Joyce Jeffreys, Spinster of Hereford, 1638–1648*, ed. Judith M. Spicksley (Oxford, 2012).

Johnson, John, *Iohnsons Arithmatick* (1623).

Johnson, William, *Deus Nobiscum: Or, A Sermon Preached upon a Great Deliverance at Sea* (1659).

Journal of the House of Commons, 10 vols (1802).

Journals and Narratives of the Third Dutch War, ed. R.C. Anderson (Navy Records Society, vol. 86, 1946).

Justa Edovardo King Naufrago (Cambridge, 1638).

Justice, Alexander, *A General Treatise of the Dominion and Laws of the Sea* (1705).

Justice, Alexander, *A General Treatise of the Dominion of the Sea: And a Compleat Body of the Sea-Laws*, 3rd edn. (1724).

Kessler, Franz, *Unterschiedliche bishero mehrentheils Secreta oder verborgene geheime Künste* (Oppenheim, 1617).

King, John, *Lectures upon Jonas* (Oxford, 1599).

Kitchin, John, *Jurisdictions: Or, The Lawful Authority of Courts Leet* (1651).

Knolles, Richard, *The Generall Historie of the Turkes* (1603).

Lambarde, William, *A Perambulation of Kent* (1576).

Lamentable Newes, Shewing the Wonderfull Deliverance of Maister Edmond Pet Sayler (1613).

Lamentable News from Sea; Being a True Relation how a Ship call'd the Cherry, was Lately Cast Away (1677).

'The Lanisley Letters: to Lt. General Onslow from George Borlase, his Agent at Penzance, 1750–53', ed. Thomas Cornish, *Journal of the Royal Institution of Cornwall*, 6 (1880), 374–9.

The Last Terrible Tempestious Windes and Weather: Truly Relating Many Lamentable Ship-Wracks (1613).

A Late and True Relation from Ireland (1641).

Lauder, George, *Tears on the Death of Evander… Cast away by Storme on the Coast of England upon Goodwin Sands* (The Hague, 1630).

The Laws, Ordinances, and Institutions of the Admiralty of Great Britain, 2 vols (1746).

The Lisle Letters, ed. Muriel St Claire Byrne, 6 vols (London and Chicago, 1981).

List of Witnesses in the High Court of Admiralty, 1619–49, ed. G. G. Harris, List and Index Society (2010).

Liverpool Town Books, i. *1550–1571*, ed. J. A. Twemlow (Liverpool, 1918).

Liverpool Town Books, ii. *1571–1603*, ed. J. A. Twemlow (Liverpool, 1935).

Madox, Richard, *A Learned and Godly Sermon… Especially for all Marryners, Captaynes and Passengers, which Travel the Seas* (1581).

Madox, Thomas, *The History and Antiquities of the Exchequer of the Kings of England* (1711).
Madron. *The First Book of the Parish Registers of Madron, in the County of Cornwall*, ed. George Bown Millett (Penzance, 1877).
Magens, Nicolas, *An Essay on Insurances*, 2 vols (1755).
Mainwaring, Henry, *The Sea-Mans Dictionary: Or, An Exposition and Demonstration of all the Parts and Things Belonging to a Shippe* (1644).
Mainwaring. *The Life and Works of Sir Henry Mainwaring*, ed. G. E. Mainwaring and W. G. Perrin, 2 vols (1920–2).
Markham, Gervase, *A Second Part to the Mothers Blessing: Or a Cure against Misfortunes* (1622).
Mather, Cotton, *The Sailours Companion and Counsellour* (Boston, 1709).
Meriton, Henry, and John Rogers, *A Circumstantial Narrative of the Loss of the Halsewell (East-Indiaman)* (1786).
Miege, Guy, *The Ancient Sea-Laws of Oleron, Wisby, and the Hanse-Towns, Still in Force* (1686).
Milton, John, *Of Reformation* (1641).
Molloy, Charles, *De Jure Maritimo et Navali, or, A Treatise of Affairs Maritime, and of Commerce* (1676).
Moore. *The Journal of Giles Moore 1656–1679*, ed. Ruth Bird, Sussex Record Society, vol. 68 (1971).
Mun, Thomas *A Discourse of Trade, from England unto the East-Indies* (1621).
Mun, Thomas, *England's Treasure by Forraign Trade* (1664).
Nelson, William, *Lex Maneriorum: Or the Law and Customs of England, Relating to Manors and Lords of Manors* (1736).
Neville, Henry, *The Isle of Pines, or, A Late Discovery of a Fourth Island in Terra Australis, Incognita* (1668).
Newes Published for Satisfaction and Information of the People, 17 August 1665.
Nichols, Charles, *The Seamans Summons* (1655).
Ordonnance de la Marine du Mois d'Aoust 1681 (Paris, 1714).
Page, Samuel, *Divine Sea-Service: Containing Sundry Necessary and Uselfull Formes of Prayer and Thanks-giving for the Helpe of Such as Travaile by Sea* (1616).
Parker, Martin, *Neptunes Raging Fury, or, The Gallant Sea-Mens Sufferings* (*c.*1655).
Parker, Thomas, *The Laws of Shipping and Insurance* (1775).
The Parliamentary Survey of the Duchy of Cornwall, part II, ed. Norman J. G. Pounds, Devon and Cornwall Record Society, NS 27 (1984).
Pell, Daniel, *Pelagos. Nec inter Vivos, Nec inter Mortuos: Neither amongst the Living, nor amongst the Dead. Or, An Improvement of the Sea* (1659).
Pepys. *Memoirs of Samuel Pepys... and a Selection from his Private Correspondence*, ed. Richard Lord Braybrooke, 5 vols (1828).
Pepys. *Samuel Pepys's Naval Minutes*, ed. J. R. Tanner, Navy Records Society, vol. 60 (1926).
Pepys. *The Diary of Samuel Pepys*, ed. Robert Latham and William Matthews, 11 vols (Berkeley and Los Angeles, 1970–83).
Pepys. *Samuel Pepys and the Second Dutch War. Pepys's Navy White Book and Brooke House Papers*, Navy Records Society (1995).
Perkins, William, *The Combat between Christ and the Divell Displayed* (1606),
Pett. *The Autobiography of Phineas Pett*, ed. W. G. Perrin, Navy Records Society (1918).
Petty, William, *Political Arithmetick* (1690).
Petyt, William, *Britannia Languens: or, A Discourse of Trade* (1680).

A Poeticall Sea-Piece:. Containing in a Spacious Table the Lively Description of a Tempest at Sea, and Shipwrecks (1633).
Proceedings in the Parliaments of Elizabeth I, ed. T. E. Hartley, 2 vols (Leicester, 1981).
Pulton, Ferdinando, and Sir Anthony Fitzherbert, *De Pace Regis et Regni viz. A Treatise Declaring which be the Great and General Offences of the Realme* (1609).
Purchas, Samuel, *Purchas His Pilgrimes . . . the First Part* (1625).
Rabelais. *Pantagruel's Voyage to the Oracle of the Bottle: Being the Fourth and Fifth Books of the Works of Francis Rabelais* (1694).
Rabelais. *The Complete Works of François Rabelais*, ed. Donald M. Frame and Raymond C. La Charité (Berkeley and Los Angeles, 1991).
Rastell, John, *The Exposicions of the Termes of the Lawes of England* (1563).
Reports of Cases in the Court of Exchequer in the Time of King Charles II, ed. W. H. Bryson (Tempe, AZ, 2017).
Reports of Certain Cases Arising in the Severall Courts of Record (1652).
Risdon, Tristram, *The Chorographical Description or Survey of the County of Devon* (1818).
Roberts. *Accounts of the Roberts Family of Boarzell, Sussex c.1568–1582*, ed. Robert Tittler, Sussex Record Society, 71 (1979).
Robinson, Christopher, *Reports of Cases Argued and Determined in the High Court of Admiralty* (1799).
Roch. 'The Journals of Jeremy Roch', in *Three Sea Journals of Stuart Times*, ed. Bruce Ingram (1936).
Rogers. 'The Journal of Francis Rogers' in *Three Sea Journals of Stuart Times*, ed. Bruce S. Ingram (1936).
Ryther, John, *Sea-Dangers and Deliverances Improved* (1674).
S., T., *A Tragicall Historie of the Troubles and Civile Warres of the Lowe Countries* (1583).
S., W., *An Exact Collection of Choice Declarations* (1653).
A Sad and Deplorable but True Account of the Dreadful Hardships, and Sufferings of Capt. John Dean, and his Company, on Board the Nottingham Galley (1711).
Sad News from the Seas: Being a True Relation of the Losse of that Good Ship Called the Merchant Royall (1641).
Saxby, Mary, *Memoirs of a Female Vagrant* (1806).
Selden, John, *Of the Dominion, or Ownership of the Sea*, trans. Marchamont Nedham (1632).
Select Pleas in the Court of Admiralty, ed. Reginald G. Marsden, 2 vols, Selden Society (vol. 6, 1892; vol. 11, 1897).
Seller, John, *A Description of the Sands, Shoals, Buoyes, Beacons, Roads, Channels and Sea Marks on the Coast of England* (1671).
Shakespeare, William, *Comedy of Errors*; *The Merchant of Venice*; *Pericles*; *Richard III*; *Tempest*; *Twelfth Night*; *Winter's Tale*.
The Ship-Master's Assistant and Owner's Manual (1788).
Sidney, Sir Philip, *The Countesse of Pembrokes Arcadia* (1593).
Skinner, John, *A True Relation of the Uniust, Cruell, and Barbarous Proceedings against the English at Amboyna* (1624).
Smith, G. C., *The Wreckers: Or, A Tour of Benevolence* (1818).
Smith, Henry, *Gods Arrow against Atheists* (1593).
Smith, William, *A Full Account of the Late Ship-Wreck of the Ship called The President* (1684).
Spelman. *John Spelman's Reading on Quo Warranto Delivered in Gray's Inn (Lent 1519)*, ed. J. H. Baker, Selden Society, vol. 113 (1997).

Spenser, Edmund, *The Faerie Queene* (1596).

The Statutes at Large, 3 vols (1706).

Statutes of the Realm, ed. T. E. Tomlins et al., 11 vols (1810–28).

Strachey, William , 'A True Reportory of the Wrack and Redemption of Sir Thomas Gates', in Samuel Purchas, *Purchas His Pilgrimes... the First Part* (1625), 1734–52.

Strange and Terrible News from the Sea. Or: A True Relation of a Most Wonderful Violent Tempest (1678).

Stubs, Philip, *The Religious Seaman, Fitted with Proper Devotions on all Occasions* (1696).

Sturch, John, *A View of the Isle of Wight* (1791).

Sutherland, William, *The Ship-Builders Assistant: Or, Some Essays towards Compleating the Art of Marine Architecture* (1711).

Teonge. *The Diary of Henry Teonge. Chaplain on Board H.M.S.* Assistance, Bristol *and* Royal Oak *1675–1676*, ed. G. E. Manwaring (2005).

Tillinghast, John, *Saint Paul's Ship-Wrack in his Voyage to Rome* (1637).

To the Right Honourable the Lords, Assembled in the Higher House of Parliament, The Humble Petition of John Bulmer Sea-Captaine (1641).

Troutbeck, John, *A Survey of the Ancient and Present State of the Scilly Islands* (1794).

A True Account of the Voyage of the Nottingham Galley (1711).

Turner, John, *Two Sermons, the First Preached upon January the 29, 1687* (1688).

A View of the Wreck of the Nympha, a Spanish Prize (1748).

Viner, Charles, *A General Abridgement of Law and Equity* (1794).

Virgil. *The XII Aeneids of Virgil*, trans. John Vicars (1632).

Virgil. *The Works of Publius Virgilius Maro*, trans. John Ogilby (1675).

Walker, George, *The Voyages and Cruises of Commodore Walker, during the Late Spanish and French Wars*, 2 vols (1760).

Waterhouse, Edward, *A Declaration of the State of the Colony and Affaires in Virginia* (1622).

Webb, William, *An Authentic Narrative of the Loss of the Doddington Indiaman* (1756).

Welwood, William, *The Sea-Law of Scotland* (Edinburgh, 1590).

Welwood, William, *An Abridgement of all Sea-Lawes* (1613).

Westcote, Thomas, *A View of Devonshire in MDCXXX*, ed. George Oliver and Pitman Jones (Exeter, 1845).

Whitelocke, Bulstrode, *Memorials of the English Affairs, or, An Historical Account of what Passed from the Beginning of the Reign of King Charles the First, to King Charles the Second his Happy Restoration* (1682).

Wilkins, John, *Mathematical Magick* (1648).

Wilkinson, John, *The Seaman's Preservation: Or, Safety in Shipwreck* (1759).

Wilkinson, John, *Tutamen Nauticum: Or the Seaman's Preservation from Shipwreck, Diseases, and Other Calamities*, 2 vols (1763).

Wilkinson, Robert, *The Merchant Royall: A Sermon Preached at White-Hall before the Kings Maiestie* (1607).

William Willymat, *The Anchor of Faith upon which, a Christian Man may Repose in all Manner... of Temptations* (1628).

Winthrop. *The Journal of John Winthrop 1630–1649*, ed. Richard S. Dunn, James Savage, and Laetitia Yeandle (Cambridge, MA, 1996).

Wither, George, *Britain's Remembrancer* (1628).

The Wonderful Deliverance at Sea (1675).

A Wonderful History of All the Storms, Hurricanes, Earthquakes, etc. that have Happen'd in England for above 500 Years past (1704).

The Wonderful Preservation of Gregory Crow Being Shipwrackt upon the Coast of Kent (1679).
Wood, Anthony, *Modius Salium* (Oxford, 1751).
The Wreck (c. 1796).
Wright, Edward, *Certain Errors in Navigation. Detected and Corrected* (1657).
Wynne, William, *The Life of Sir Leoline Jenkins, Judge of the High-Court of Admiralty*, 2 vols (1724).
Zouch Richard, *The Jurisdiction of the Admiralty of England Asserted* (1663).

Modern Sources

Anderson, Robert Charles, *The Great Migration Begins: Immigrants to New England 1620–1633*, i. *A-F* (Boston, MA, 1995).
Andrews, Kenneth R., *Ships, Money and Politics: Seafaring and Naval Enterprise in the Reign of Charles I* (Cambridge, 1991).
Anheier, Helmut K., Jürgen Gerhards, and Frank R. Romo, 'Forms of Capital and Social Structure in Cultural Fields: Examining Bourdieu's Social Topography', *American Journal of Sociology*, 100 (1995), 859–903.
Appleby, John C., 'Wars of Plunder and Wars of Profit: English Privateering during the Late Sixteenth and Early Seventeenth Centuries', in David J. Starkey and Morten Hahn-Pedersen (eds), *Bridging Troubled Waters: Conflict and Co-operation in the North Sea Region since 1550* (Esbjerg, 2005), 59–79.
Arel, Maria Salomon, *English Trade and Adventure to Russia in the Early Modern Era: The Muscovy Company, 1603–1649* (Lanham, MD, 2019).
Ashworth, William J., *Customs and Excise: Trade, Production, and Consumption in England, 1640–1845* (Oxford, 2003).
Austin, J. L., *How to Do Things with Words* (Cambridge, MA, 1962).
Bailey, Joanne, 'Voices in Court: Lawyers' or Litigants'?', *Historical Research*, 74 (2001), 392–408.
Banks, Charles Edward, *The Planters of the Commonwealth* (Boston, 1930).
Barbour, Violet, 'Marine Risks and Insurance in the Seventeenth Century', *Journal of Economic and Business History*, 1 (1929), 561–96.
Barbour, Violet, 'Dutch and English Merchant Shipping in the Seventeenth Century', *Economic History Review*, 2 (1930), 261–90.
Bathurst, Bella, *The Wreckers: A Story of Killing Seas, False Lights, and Plundered Ships* (2005).
Bathurst, Bella, *The Wreckers: A Story of Killing Seas and Plundered Shipwrecks: From the 18th Century to the Present Day* (New York, 2005).
Benton, Lauren, *A Search for Sovereignty: Law and Geography in European Empires, 1400–1900* (Cambridge, 2010).
Benton, Lauren, and Nathan Perl-Rosenthal (eds), *A World at Sea: Maritime Practices and Global History* (Philadelphia, 2020).
Benton, Lauren, and Richard J. Ross (eds), *Legal Pluralism and Empires, 1500–1850* (New York, 2013).
Berti, Marcello, 'I rischi nella circolazione marittima tra Europa nordica ed Europa mediterranea nel primo trentennio del seicento e il caso della seconda guerra anglo-olandese (1665–67)', in Simonetta Cavaciocchi (ed.), *Ricchezza del Mare. Ricchezza dal Mare: Secc. XIII–XVIII* (Florence, 2006), 809–39.

Bettey, J. H., 'Manorial Stewards and the Conduct of Manorial Affairs', *Proceedings of the Dorset Natural History and Archeological Society*, 115 (1993), 15–19.

Blackmore, Josiah, *Manifest Perdition: Shipwreck Narrative and the Disruption of Empire* (Minneapolis, 2002).

Blakemore, Richard J., 'The Legal World of English Sailors, *c.*1575–1729', in Maria Fusaro, Bernard Allaire, Richard Blakemore, and Tijl Vannestre (eds), *Law, Labour, and Empire: Comparative Perspectives on Seafarers, c.1500–1800* (Basingstoke, 2015), 100–20.

Blakemore, Richard J., 'Orality and Mutiny: Authority and Speech among Seafarers in Early Modern London', in Thomas V. Cohen and Lesley K. Twomey (eds), *Spoken Word and Social Practice: Orality in Europe (1400–1700)* (Leiden and Boston, 2015), 253–79.

Blakemore, Richard J., 'Pieces of Eight, Pieces of Eight: Seamen's Earnings and the Venture Economy of Early Modern Seafaring', *Economic History Review*, 70 (2017), 1153–84.

Blakemore, Richard J., and James Davey (eds), *The Maritime World of Early Modern Britain* (Amsterdam, 2020).

Blockmans, Wim, Mikhail Krom and Justyna Wubs-Mrozewicz (eds), *The Routledge Handbook of Maritime Trade around Europe 1300–1699: Commercial Networks and Urban Autonomy* (2017).

Blumenberg, Hans, *Shipwreck with Spectator: Paradigm of a Metaphor for Existence* (Cambridge, MA, 1997).

Bohstedt, John, 'The Moral Economy and the Discipline of Historical Context', *Journal of Social History*, 26 (1992), 265–84.

Bowen, H. V., 'The Shipping Losses of the British East India Company, 1755–1813', *International Journal of Maritime History*, 32 (2020), 323–36.

Boxer, C. R. (ed.), *The Tragic History of the Sea 1589–1622: Narratives of the Shipwrecks of the Portuguese East Indiamen* (Cambridge, 1959).

Bracker, Karsten, 'The Lost Ships of the Dutch East India Company—A Cartographic Analysis', https://www.academia.edu/29228296/The_lost_ships_of_the_Dutch_East_India_Company_a_cartographic_analysis (accessed January 2021); www.treasurenet.com.forums/shipwrecks/17237-list-all-653-dutch-voc-shipwrecks-1595-1800-a.html (accessed January 2021); www.vocshipwrecks.nl (accessed January 2021).

Braddick, Michael J., 'Afterword', in Thomas V. Cohen and Lesley K. Twomey (eds), *Spoken Word and Social Practice: Orality in Europe (1400–1700)* (Leiden and Boston, 2015), 446–62.

Brammall, Sheldon, *The English Aeneid: Translations of Virgil 1555–1646* (Edinburgh, 2015).

Brewer, John, *The Sinews of Power: War, Money and the English State*, 1688–1783 (New York, 1989).

Brown, Ruth Rhynas, 'The Thundering Cannon: Guns for the English Navy in the 17th Century', in Gert Groenendijk et al. (eds), *A Farewell to Arms: Studies on the History of Arms and Armour* (Delft, 2004), 123–33.

Burningham, Helene, and Jon French, 'Seabed Dynamics in a Large Coastal Embayment: 180 Years of Morphological Change in the Outer Thames Estuary', *Hydrobiologia*, 627 (2011), 105–19.

Cabantous, Alain, *Les Côtes barbares: Pilleurs d'épaves et sociétés littorales en France (1680–1830)* (Paris, 1993).

Carson, Edward, *The Ancient and Rightful Customs: A History of the English Customs Service* (1972).

Cawley, Robert Ralston, *Unpathed Waters: Studies in the Influence of the Voyagers on Elizabethan Literature* (New York, 1967).

Chandaman, C. D., *The English Public Revenue 1660–1688* (Oxford, 1975).
Clark, Peter, *The English Alehouse: A Social History, 1200–1830* (1983).
Clarke, James Stanier, *Naufragia or Historical Memoirs of Shipwrecks and of the Providential Deliverance of Vessels*, 2 vols (1805–6).
Clay, C. G. A., *Economic Expansion and Social Change: England 1500–1700*, 2 vols (Cambridge, 1984).
Cohen, Thomas V., and Lesley K. Twomey (eds), *Spoken Word and Social Practice: Orality in Europe (1400–1700)* (Leiden and Boston, 2015).
Coindet, Sylvain, 'Les Naufrages sur l'île de Sein au XVIIIe siècle: Une lente évolution vers le sauvetage', *Annales de Bretagne et Pays de l'Ouest*, 113 (2006), 87–109.
Coindet, Sylvain, 'Le Temps du naufrage: Une triple vision de l'événement dans l'amirauté de Cornouaille (1720–1790)', *Annales de Bretagne et Pays de l'Ouest*, 117 (2010), 73–94.
Cook, Ian, and Divya P. Tolia-Kelly, 'Material Geographies', in Dan Hicks and Mary C. Beaudry (eds), *The Oxford Handbook of Material Culture Studies* (Oxford, 2010), 99–122.
Cooke, James Herbert, *The Shipwreck of Sir Cloudesley Shovell, on the Scilly Island in 1707* (Society of Antiquaries, 1883).
Cordes, Albrecht, 'Lex Maritima? Local, Regional and Universal Maritime Law in the Middle Ages', in Wim Blockmans, Mikhail Krom, and Justyna Wubs-Mrozewicz (eds), *The Routledge Handbook of Maritime Trade around Europe 1300–1600: Commercial Networks and Urban Autonomy* (2017), 69–85.
Cormack, Bradin, *A Power to do Justice: Jurisdiction, English Literature, and the Rise of the Common Law, 1509–1625* (Chicago, 2007).
Cousins, Tom, *Erme Estuary Site Conservation Statement & Management Plan* (Bournemouth, 2018).
Cowan, Zélide, 'John Lethbridge, Diver', *History Today*, 28 (December 1978), 825–9.
Cressy, David, *Literacy and the Social Order: Reading and Writing in Tudor and Stuart England* (Cambridge, 1980).
Cressy, David, *Coming Over: Migration and Communication between England and New England in the Seventeenth Century* (Cambridge, 1987).
Cressy, David, *Birth, Marriage and Death: Ritual, Religion and the Life Cycle in Tudor and Stuart England* (Oxford, 1997).
Cressy, David, *England on Edge: Crisis and Revolution 1640–1642* (Oxford, 2006).
Cressy, David, *Charles I and the People of England* (Oxford, 2015).
Cromwell, Jesse, *The Smugglers' World: Illicit Trade and Atlantic Communities in Eighteenth-Century Venezuela* (Chapel Hill, 2018).
Dalyell, John Graham, *Shipwrecks and Disasters at Sea: Or, Historical Narratives of the Most Noted Calamities and Providential Deliverances which have Resulted from Maritime Enterprise*, 3 vols (Edinburgh, 1812).
Davies, Glanville J., 'Wreck and Plunder in 18th Century Portland', *Dorset Natural History and Archaeological Society Proceedings*, 103 (1981), 1–4.
Davis, Ralph, 'English Foreign Trade, 1660–1700', *Economic History Review*, 7 (1954), 150–66.
Davis, Ralph, 'English Foreign Trade, 1700–1774', *Economic History Review*, NS 15 (1962), 285–303.
Davis, Ralph, *The Rise of the English Shipping Industry in the Seventeenth and Eighteenth Centuries* (1962).
Davison, Caroline, and Ronnie Pestell, *Wild Waxham* (Norwich, 2004).

Derriman, James, 'The Wreck of the *Albemarle*', *Journal of the Royal Institution of Cornwall*, NS 1 (1992), 128–48.

Dolan, Frances E., *True Relations: Reading, Literature and Evidence in Seventeenth-Century England* (Philadelphia, 2013).

Dorey, Graham, 'Rights to Wreck in Norman Customary Law', *Guernsey Law Journal*, 15 (1993), 63–6.

Du Boulay, Juliet, 'Wrecks in the Isles of Scilly', *Mariner's Mirror*, 46 (1960), 88–112.

Duffy, James, *Shipwreck and Empire: Being an Account of Portuguese Maritime Disasters in a Century of Decline* (Cambridge, MA, 1955).

Duncan, Archibald, *The Mariner's Chronicle: Being a Collection of the Most Interesting Narratives of Shipwrecks, Fires, Famines, and other Calamities Incident to a Life of Marine Enterprise*, 6 vols (1804–8).

Duncan, Brad, and Martin Gibbs, *Please God Send Me a Wreck: Responses to Shipwreck in a 19th Century Australian Community* (New York, 2015).

Durston, Gregory, *The Admiralty Sessions, 1536–1834: Maritime Crime and the Silver Oar* (Newcastle, 2017).

Earle, Peter, *The Wreck of the Almiranta: Sir William Phips and the Hispaniola Treasure* (1979).

Earle, Peter, *The Treasure of the Concepción: The Wreck of the Almiranta* (New York, 1980).

Earle, Peter, 'English Sailors, 1570–1775', in Paul van Royen, Jaap Bruijn, and Jan Lucassen (eds), *'Those Emblems of Hell'? European Sailors and the Maritime Labour Market, 1570–1870* (St John's, Newfoundland, 1997), 73–82.

Eliav, Joseph, 'Guglielmo's Secret: The Enigma of the First Diving Bell used in Underwater Archaeology', *International Journal for the History of Engineering and Technology*, 85 (2015), 60–9.

Falvey, Heather, 'Relating Early Modern Depositions', in Carl J. Griffin and B. McDonagh (eds), *Remembering Protest in Britain since 1500* (2018), 81–106.

Farrington, Anthony, *Catalogue of East India Company Ships' Journals and Logs 1600–1834* (1999).

Fassin, Didier, 'Les Économies morales revisitées', *Annales HSS*, 6 (Novembre-Décembre 2009), 1237–66.

Fox, Frank L., 'The *London* of 1656: Her History and Armament', *Journal of the Ordnance Society*, 23 (2011), 15–44.

Fox, Frank L., 'The Quex Park 12-Pounder', *Journal of the Ordnance Society*, 25 (2018), 67–81.

Francis, A. D., *The Wine Trade* (1972).

Franson, J. Karl, 'The Fatal Voyage of Edward King, Milton's Lycidas', *Milton Studies*, 25 (1989), 43–67.

Fury, Cheryl A., *Tides in the Affairs of Men: The Social History of Elizabethan Seamen, 1580–1603* (Westport, CT and London, 2002).

Fury, Cheryl A. (ed.), *The Social History of English Seamen, 1485–1649* (Woodbridge, 2012).

Fury, Cheryl A., 'The Work of G. V. Scammell', in Cheryl A. Fury (ed.), *The Social History of English Seamen, 1485–1649* (Woodbridge, 2012), 27–45.

Gewirtz, Paul, 'Narrative and Rhetoric in the Law', in Peter Brooks and Paul Gewirtz (eds), *Law's Stories: Narrative and Rhetoric in Law* (New Haven, 1996), 2–13.

Glete, Jan, *Navies and Nations: Warships, Navies and Nations in Europe and America, 1500–1860*, 2 vols (Stockholm, 1993).

Gordon, Kevin, 'Quirky Sussex History', https://sussexhistor.nest/2020/11/29/quicksilver-and-lemons (accessed April 2021).

Gould, Richard A., *Shipwreck Anthropology* (Albuquerque, 1983).

Green, Adrian, 'Consumption and Material Culture', in Keith Wrightson (ed.), *A Social History of England, 1500–1750* (Cambridge, 2017), 242–66.

Greenstreet, Colin, 'What was a C17th Commercial Ship Worth per Ton of Cargo Burden?', https://marinelives.academia.edu/ColinGreenstreet (accessed October 2019).

Gunn, Simon, 'Translating Bourdieu: Cultural Capital and the English Middle Class in Historical Perspective', *British Journal of Sociology*, 56 (2005), 49–64.

Hailwood, Mark, *Alehouses and Good Fellowship in Early Modern England* (Woodbridge, 2014).

Hamil, Frederick C., 'Wreck of the Sea in Medieval England', in A. E. R. Boak (ed.), *University of Michigan Historical Essays* (Ann Arbor, 1937), 1–24.

Hanna, Mark, *Pirate Nests and the Rise of the British Empire, 1570–1740* (Chapel Hill, 2015).

Hanna, Mark G., 'Well-Behaved Pirates Seldom Make History: A Reevaluation of the Golden Age of English Piracy', in Peter C. Mancall and Carole Shammas (eds), *Governing the Sea in the Early Modern Era: Essays in Honor of Robert C. Ritchie* (San Marino, CA, 2015), 129–68.

Harris, G. G., *The Trinity House of Deptford 1514–1660* (1969).

Harris, Simon, *Sir Cloudesley Shovell: Stuart Admiral* (Staplehurst, 2001).

Harrison, Christopher, 'Manor Courts and the Governance of Tudor England', in Christopher Brooks and Michael Lobban (eds), *Communities and Courts in Britain 1150–1900* (London and Rio Grande, 1997), 43–59.

Hartnett, Alexandra, and Shannon Lee Dawdy, 'The Archaeology of Illegal and Illicit Economies', *Annual Review of Anthropology*, 42 (2013), 37–51.

Healey, Jonathan, 'The Political Culture of the English Commons, c.1550–1650', *Journal of Agricultural History*, 60 (2012), 266–87.

Healey, Jonathan, 'The Northern Manor and the Politics of Neighbourhood: Dilston, Northumberland, 1558–1640', *Northern History*, 51 (2014), 221–41.

Hebb, David D., 'Profiting from Misfortune: Corruption and the Admiralty under the Early Stuarts', in Thomas Cogswell, Richard Cust, and Peter Lake (eds), *Politics, Religion and Popularity in Early Stuart Britain. Essays in Honour of Conrad Russell* (Cambridge, 2002), 103–23.

Helmholz, R. H., *Natural Law in Court: A History of Legal Theory in Practice* (Cambridge, MA, 2015).

Henningsen, Henning, 'Legends about "Wreckers"', *Mariner's Mirror*, 71 (1985), 215–18.

Hershenzon, Daniel, *The Captive Sea: Slavery, Communication, and Commerce in Early Modern Spain and the Mediterranean* (Philadelphia, 2018).

Hindle, Steve, 'Persuasion and Protest in the Caddington Common Enclosure Dispute 1635–1639', *Past & Present*, 158 (1998), 37–78.

Hindle, Steve, 'A Sense of Place? Becoming and Belonging in the Rural Parish, 1550–1650', in Alexandra Shepard and Phil Withington (eds), *Communities in Early Modern England: Networks, Place, Rhetoric* (Manchester, 2000), 96–114.

Hindle, Steve, *The State and Social Change in Early Modern England, 1550–1640* (Basingstoke and New York, 2002).

Hoare, Christobel M., (ed.), *Records of a Norfolk Village, Being Notes on the History of the Parish of Sidestrand* (Bedford, 1914).

Hoare, Christobel M., *The History of an East Anglian Soke: Studies in Original Documents* (Bedford, 1918).

Holdsworth, William, *A History of English Law*, 17 vols (1903–72).
Hori, Motoko, 'The Price and Quality of Wine and Conspicuous Consumption in England 1646–1759', *English Historical Review*, 123 (2008), 1457–69.
Horsfield, Thomas W., *The History, Antiquities, and Topography of the County of Sussex*, 2 vols (Lewes, 1835).
Hubbard, Eleanor, 'Sailors and the Early Modern British Empire: Labor, Nation, and Identity at Sea', *History Compass*, 14 (2016), 348–58.
Hubbard, Eleanor, *Englishmen at Sea: Labor and the Nation at the Dawn of Empire 1570–1630* (New Haven and London, 2021).
Hurdis, J. H., *The Wreck of the Nympha Americana, a Spanish Corsair, near Beachy Head* (Newick, Sussex, 1840).
Huxley, H. H., 'Storm and Shipwreck in Roman Literature', *Greece and Rome*, 21 (1952), 117–24.
Ireland, J. de Courcey, 'Wreckers', *Mariner's Mirror*, 70 (1984), 44.
James. *Stuart Royal Proclamations Volume I: Royal Proclamations of King James I 1603–1625*, ed. Paul L. Hughes, and James F. Larkin (Oxford, 1973).
Johnson, Tom, 'Medieval Law and Materiality: Shipwrecks, Finders, and Property on the Suffolk Coast, ca. 1380–1410', *American Historical Review*, 120 (2015), 407–32.
Johnson, Tom, 'The Economics of Shipwreck in Late Medieval Suffolk', in James P. Bowen and A. T. Brown (eds), *Custom and Commercialization in English Rural Society: Revisiting Tawney and Postan* (Hatfield, 2016), 121–38.
Johnson, Tom, *Law in Common: Legal Cultures in Late-Medieval England* (Oxford, 2020).
Jones, W. J., *The Elizabethan Court of Chancery* (Oxford, 1967).
Jowitt, Claire, Craig Lambert, and Steve Mentz (eds), *The Routledge Companion to Marine and Maritime Worlds, 1400–1800* (Abingdon and New York, 2020).
Karraker, Cyrus H., 'Spanish Treasure, Casual Revenue of the Crown', *Journal of Modern History*, 5 (1933), 301–18.
Karraker, Cyrus H., *The Hispaniola Treasure* (Philadelphia, 1934).
Kaukiainen, Yrjö, 'Wreck-Plundering by East Finnish Coastal People—Criminal Tradition or Popular Culture?', in Lars U. Scholl and Merja-Liisa Hinkkanen (eds), *Sail and Steam: Selected Maritime Writings of Yrjö Kaukiainen* (Liverpool, 2004), 151–62.
Kelleher, John, 'The Mysterious Case of the Ship Abandoned off Sark in 1608: The Customary Law Relating to *choses gaives*', in Gordon Dawes (ed.), *Commise 1204: Studies in the History and Law of Continental and Insular Normandy* (St Peter Port, 2005), 171–90.
Kennedy, D. E., 'The Establishment and Settlement of Parliament's Admiralty, 1642–1648', *Mariner's Mirror*, 48 (1962), 276–91.
Kepler, J. S., 'The Value of Ships Gained and Lost by the English Shipping Industry during the Wars with Spain and France, 1624-1630', *Mariner's Mirror*, 59 (1973), 218–19.
Kepler, J. S., 'The Operating Potential of London Marine Insurance in the 1570s', *Business History*, 17 (1975), 44–55.
Kirby, Thomas Frederick, *Annals of Winchester College: From its Foundation* (1892).
Lamb, Hubert, *Historic Storms of the North Sea, British Isles and Northwest Europe* (Cambridge, 1991).
Lambert, Craig L., and Gary P. Baker, 'An Investigation of the Size and Geographical Distribution of the English, Welsh, and Channel Islands Merchant Fleet: A Case Study of 1571–72', in Richard J. Blakemore and James Davey (eds), *The Maritime World of Early Modern Britain* (Amsterdam, 2020), 81–103.
Land, Isaac, 'Tidal Waves: The New Coastal History', *Journal of Social History*, 40 (2007), 731–43.

Land, Isaac, 'The Urban Amphibious', in David Worthington (ed.), *The New Coastal History: Cultural and Environmental Perspectives from Scotland and Beyond* (Cham, Switzerland, 2017), 31–48.

Lane, Frederic C., 'Tonnages, Medieval and Modern', *Economic History Review*, 2nd ser., 17 (1964), 213–29.

Langford, Paul, *A Polite and Commercial People: England 1727–1783* (Oxford, 1992).

Larn, Richard (ed.), *'Poor England has lost so many men': The Loss of Queen Anne's Man o' War Association* (St Mary's, Isles of Scilly, 2006).

Larn, Richard, and Bridget Larn, *Shipwreck Index of the British Isles*, 7 vols (1995–2005).

Larn, Richard, et al., *Cornish Shipwrecks*, 3 vols (New York, 1969–71).

Le Bouedec, Gérard, 'La Pluriactivité dans les sociétés littorales XVIIe–XIXe siècle', *Annales de Bretagne et des Pays de l'Ouest*, 109 (2002), 61–90.

Le Juez, Brigitte, and Olga Springer (eds), *Shipwrecks and Island Motifs in Literature and the Arts* (Leiden, 2015).

Lein, Clayton D., 'Donne's "The Storme": The Poem and the Tradition', *English Literary Renaissance*, 4 (1974), 137–63.

Lemire, Beverly, 'The Theft of Clothes and Popular Consumerism in Early Modern England', *Journal of Social History*, 24 (1990), 255–76.

Lemire, Beverly, '"Men of the World": British Mariners, Consumer Practice, and Material Culture in an Era of Global Trade, c. 1660–1800', *Journal of British Studies*, 54 (2015), 288–319.

Lemire, Beverly, *Global Trade and the Transformation of Consumer Cultures: The Material Word Remade, c.1500–1820* (Cambridge, 2018).

Levack, Brian P., *The Civil Lawyers in England 1603–1641: A Political Study* (Oxford, 1973).

Lincoln, Margarette, 'Shipwreck Narratives of the Eighteenth and Early Nineteenth Century: Indicators of Culture and Identity', *British Journal for Eighteenth-Century Studies*, 20 (1997), 155–72.

Lobban, Michael, Joanne Begiato, and Adrian Green (eds), *Law, Lawyers and Litigants in Early Modern England* (Cambridge, 2019).

Lower, Mark Antony, and William Durrant Cooper, 'Further Memorials of Seaford', *Sussex Archaeological Collections*, 17 (1865), 141–63.

Lust, Kersti, 'Wrecking Peasants and Salvaging Landlords—Or Vice Versa? Wrecking in the Russian Baltic Provinces of Estland and Livland, 1780–1870', *International Review of Social History*, 62 (2017), 67–93.

McBride, P., R. Larn, and R. Davis, 'A Mid-17th Century Merchant Ship Found near Mullion Cove: 3rd Interim Report on the *Santo Christo de Castello*, 1667', *International Journal of Nautical Archaeology*, 4 (1975), 237–52.

McCarthy, William J., 'Gambling on Empire: The Economic Role of Shipwreck in the Age of Discovery', *International Journal of Maritime History*, 23 (2011), 69–84.

McGrath, Patrick, 'Merchant Shipping in the Seventeenth Century: The Evidence of the Bristol Deposition Books', *Mariner's Mirror*, 41 (1955), 23–37.

Mack, John, *The Sea: A Cultural History* (2011).

MacMillan, Ken, *Sovereignty and Possession in the English New World, 1576–1640* (Cambridge, 2006).

Marsden, R. G., 'Admiralty Droits and Salvage—Gas Float Whitton, No. II', *Law Quarterly Review*, 15 (1899), 353–66.

Marsden, R. G., 'The Vice-Admirals of the Coast', *English Historical Review*, 23 (1908), 736–57.

Martin, Colin, and Geoffrey Parker, *The Spanish Armada* (1988).

Marx, Robert F., *History of Underwater Exploration* (New York, 1990).

Mathiasen, Joanne, 'Some Problems of Admiralty Jurisdiction in the 17th Century', *American Journal of Legal History*, 2 (1958), 215–36.

Matthews, G. Forrester, *The Isles of Scilly: A Constitutional, Economic and Social Survey* (1960).

Melikan, Rose, 'Shippers, Salvors, and Sovereigns: Competing Interests in the Medieval Law of Shipwreck', *Journal of Legal History*, 11 (1990), 163–82.

Mentz, S. R., 'Reason, Faith, and Shipwreck in Sidney's *New Arcadia*', *Studies in English Literature, 1500–1900*, 44 (2004), 1–18.

Mentz, Steve, *At the Bottom of Shakespeare's Ocean* (2009).

Mentz, Steve, 'God's Storms: Shipwreck and the Meanings of Ocean in Early Modern England and America', in Carl Thompson (ed.), *Shipwreck in Art and Literature* (New York, 2014), 77–91.

Mentz, Steve, *Shipwreck Modernity: Ecologies of Globalization, 1550–1719* (Minneapolis, 2015).

Mentz, Steve, '"We Split!": Shipwreck in Early Modern European History and Culture', in Claire Jowitt, Craig Lambert, and Steve Mentz (eds), *The Routledge Companion to Marine and Maritime Worlds, 1400–1800* (Abingdon and New York, 2020), 580–97.

Millard, A. M., 'London's Imports 1587–1640', *Blackmansbury*, 4 (1967), 14–22.

Mitchell-Cook, Amy, *A Sea of Misadventures: Shipwreck and Survival in Early America* (Columbia, SC, 2013).

Moore, Stuart A., *A History of the Foreshore and the Law Relating Thereto*, 3rd edn (1888).

Morrill, J. S., and J. D. Walter, 'Order and Disorder in the English Revolution', in Anthony Fletcher and John Stevenson (eds), *Order and Disorder in Early Modern England* (Cambridge, 1985), 137–66.

Morrison, James V., *Shipwrecked: Disaster and Transformation in Homer, Shakespeare, Defoe, and the Modern World* (Ann Arbor, 2014).

Muldrew, Craig, *Food, Energy and the Creation of Industriousness: Work and Material Culture in Agrarian England, 1550–1780* (Cambridge, 2011).

Muldrew, Craig, and Stephen King, 'Cash Wages and the Economy of Makeshifts in England, 1650–1800', in Peter Scholliers and Leonard Schwartz (eds), *Experiencing Wages: Social and Cultural Aspects of Wage Forms in Europe since 1500* (New York, 2003), 155–80.

Murray, K. M. E., *The Constitutional History of the Cinque Ports* (Manchester, 1935).

Musa, Shavana, 'Victims of Maritime Conflict, Compensation Claims and the Role of the Admiralty Court in the Early Modern Period', *Comparative Legal History*, 5 (2017), 125–41.

O'Hara, Glen, '"The Sea is Swinging into View": Modern British Maritime History in a Globalised World', *English Historical* Review, 124 (2009), 1109–34.

Oliver, Jennifer H., *Shipwreck in French Renaissance Writing: The Direful Spectacle* (Oxford, 2019).

Oppenheim, M., 'Maritime History', in *The Victoria History of the County of Dorset*, ii, ed. William Page (1908), 193–223.

Pagratis, Gerassimos D., '"Le fortune di mare": Incidenti della navigazione mercantile nei mari Ionio e Adriatico (1611–1765)', in Simonetta Cavaciocchi (ed), *Ricchezza del Mare. Ricchezza dal Mare: Secc. XIII–XVIII* (Prato, 2006), 841–61.

Parker, Geoffrey, *Global Crisis: War, Climate Change and Catastrophe in the Seventeenth Century* (London and New Haven, 2013).

Pascoe, Daniel, 'Forensic Archaeology, Gun Carriages and Bronze Guns from the Wreck of the *London* (1665)', *Journal of the Ordnance Society*, 24 (2017), 43–61.

Pattison, S. R., 'Sir Cloudesly Shovel', *Journal of the Royal Institution of Cornwall*, 1 (1864–5), 61–4.

Pearce, Cathryn J., review of Bella Bathurst, *The Wreckers: A Story of Killing Seas, False Lights, and Plundered Ships* (2005), in *International Journal of Maritime History*, 17 (2005), 411–12.

Pearce, Cathryn, 'Neglectful or Worse: A Lurid Tale of a Lighthouse Keeper and Wrecking in the Isles of Scilly', *Troze: The Online Journal of the National Maritime Museum of Cornwall*, 1 (2008), 3–15.

Pearce, Cathryn, *Cornish Wrecking 1700–1860: Reality and Popular Myth* (Woodbridge, 2010).

Pearce, Cathryn, 'The Cornish Arundells and the Right of Wreck: A Case Study of Landlord–Tenant Relations in the Long Eighteenth Century', in Philip Payton, Alston Kennerley, and Helen Doe (eds), *The Maritime History of Cornwall* (Exeter, 2014), 209–17.

Pearson, Michael N., 'Littoral Society: The Concept and the Problems', *Journal of World History*, 17 (2006), 353–73.

Perkins, Dave, 'Stirling Castle: Goodwin Sands', *Archaeologia Cantiana*, 119 (1999), 410–12.

Pickwell, J. G., 'Improbable Legends Surrounding the Shipwreck of Sir Clowdisley Shovell', *Mariner's Mirror*, 59 (1973), 221–3.

Place, Geoffrey W., 'Wreckers: The Fate of the *Charming Jenny*', *Mariner's Mirror*, 76 (1990), 167–8.

Pool, P. A. S., 'The Penheleg Manuscript', *Journal of the Royal Institution of Cornwall*, NS 3 (1959), 163–228.

Poulson, George, *The History and Antiquities of the Seignory of Holderness*, 2 vols (Hull, 1840).

Press, Jonathon, *The Merchant Seamen of Bristol, 1747–1789* (Bristol, 1976).

Price, Richard, *British Society 1680–1880* (Cambridge, 1999).

Raich, Susan, 'Wreck of the Sea in Law and Practice in Eleventh- and Twelfth-Century England', in Elizabeth van Houts (ed.), *Anglo-Norman Studies XXXVIII: Proceedings of the Battle Conference 2015* (2016), 141–54.

Randall, Adrian, and Andrew Charlesworth (eds), *Moral Economy and Popular Protest: Crowds, Conflict and Authority* (Basingstoke, 2000).

Reid, Phillip F., 'Something Ventured: Dangers and Risk Mitigation for the Ordinary British Atlantic Merchant Ship, 1600–1800', *Journal of Transport History*, 38 (2017), 196–212.

Roberts, Luke S., 'Shipwrecks and Flotsam: The Foreign World in Edo-Period Topesa', *Monumenta nipponica*, 70 (2015), 83–122.

Roddie, Alan, 'Jacob, the Diver', *Mariner's Mirror*, 62 (1976), 253–69.

Roding, Juliette, and Lex Herman van Voss (eds), *The North Sea and Culture (1550–1800)* (Hilversum, 1996).

Rodger, N. A. M., *The Command of the Ocean: A Naval History of Britain, 1649–1815* (2004).

Rosier, Barrington, 'The Construction Costs of Eighteenth-Century Warships', *Mariner's Mirror*, 96 (2010), 161–72.

Rossi, Anthony, 'A Tale of Two Barns: Paston and Waxham', *Transactions of the Ancient Monuments Society*, 56 (2012), 33–54.

Rule, John G., 'Wrecking and Coastal Plunder', in Douglas Hay, Peter Linebaugh, John G. Rule, et al. (eds), *Albion's Fatal Tree: Crime and Society in Eighteenth-Century England* (1975), 167–88.

Rule, J. G., 'Social Crime in the Rural South in the Eighteenth and Early Nineteenth Centuries', *Southern History*, 1 (1979), 135–53.

Rule, John, 'Smuggling and Wrecking', in Philip Payton, Aston Kennerly, and Helen Doe (eds), *The Maritime History of Cornwall* (Exeter, 2014), 195–208.

Rushton, Peter, 'Local Laws, Local Principles: The Paradoxes of Local Legal Process in Early Modern England', in Michael Lobban, Joanne Begiato, and Adrian Green (eds), *Law, Lawyers and Litigants in Early Modern England* (Cambridge, 2019), 185–206.

Scammell, G. V., 'Shipowning in the Economy and Politics of Early Modern England', *Historical Journal*, 15 (1972), 385–407.

Schivelbusch, Wolfgang, *Tastes of Paradise: A Social History of Spices, Stimulants, and Intoxicants* (New York, 1992).

Scott, James C., *Weapons of the Weak: Everyday Forms of Peasant Resistance* (New Haven, 1985).

Senior, William, 'The Judges in the High Court of Admiralty', *Mariner's Mirror*, 13 (1927), 333–47.

Shammas, Carole, *The Pre-Industrial Consumer in England and America* (Oxford, 1990).

Sharpe, Kevin, *The Personal Rule of Charles I* (New Haven and London, 1992).

Shepard, Alexandra, 'Honesty, Worth and Gender in Early Modern England, 1560–1640,' in Henry French and Jonathan Barry (eds), *Identity and Agency in England, 1500–1800* (Basingstoke and New York, 2004), 87–105.

Shepard, Alexandra, and Judith Spicksley, 'Worth, Age, and Social Status in Early Modern England', *Economic History Review*, 64 (2011), 493–530.

Smith, David Chen, 'Fair Trade and the Political Economy of Brandy Smuggling in Early Eighteenth-Century Britain', *Past & Present*, 251 (May 2021), 75–111.

Spooner, Frank C., *Risks at Sea: Amsterdam Insurance and Maritime Europe, 1766–1780* (Cambridge, 1983).

Spufford, Margaret, *The Great Reclothing of Rural England: Petty Chapmen and their Ware in the Seventeenth Century* (1984).

Steckley, George F., 'Merchants and the Admiralty Court during the English Revolution', *American Journal of Legal History*, 22 (1978), 137–75.

Steckley, George F., 'Instance Cases at Admiralty in 1657: A Court "Packed up with Sutors"', *Journal of Legal History*, 7 (1986), 68–83.

Steckley, George F., 'Collisions, Prohibitions, and the Admiralty Court in Seventeenth-Century London', *Law and History Review*, 21 (2003), 41–67.

Steckley, George F., 'Freight Law in the Seventeenth-Century Admiralty Court', *Journal of Legal History*, 27 (2006), 175–97.

Steckley, George F., 'The Seventeenth-Century Origins of Modern Salvage Law', *Journal of Legal History*, 35 (2014), 209–30.

Stephens, W. B., 'English Wine Imports *c*.1603-40, with Special Reference to the Devon Ports', in Todd Gray and Margery M. Rowe (eds), *Tudor and Stuart Devon: The Common Estate and Government* (1992), 141–72.

Stevenson, David, 'The English and the Public Records of Scotland, 1650–1660', in David Stevenson, *Union, Revolution and Religion in 17th-Century Scotland* (Aldershot and Brookfield, VT, 1997), 156–68.

Stobart, Jon, 'Making the Global Local? Overseas Goods in English Rural Shops, *c*.1600–1760', *Business History*, 59 (2017), 1136–53.

Styles, John, '"Our traitorous money makers": The Yorkshire Coiners and the Law, 1760–83', in John Brewer and John Styles (eds), *An Ungovernable People: The English and their Law in the Seventeenth and Eighteenth Centuries* (New Brunswick, 1980), 209–10.

Sutherland, Lucy S., *A London Merchant 1695–1774* (Oxford, 1933).

Tanner, J. R. (ed.), *A Descriptive Catalogue of the Naval Manuscripts in the Pepysian Library at Magdalene College, Cambridge* (1903).

Tellis, Gerard. J., and Stav Rosenzweig, *How Transformative Innovations Shaped the Rise of Nations* (Cambridge, 2018).

Thompson, Carl (ed.), *Shipwreck in Art and Literature* (New York, 2014).

Thompson, E. P., 'The Moral Economy of the English Crowd in the Eighteenth Century', *Past & Present*, 50 (1971), 76–136.

Thomson, David Whittet, 'Two Thousand Years under Sea: The Story of the Diving Bell', *American Neptune*, 7 (1947), 261–80.

Titlestad, Michael, 'The Muddy Middle-Ground: Representing the Wreck of the *Wager*', *Journal for Maritime Research*, 15 (2013), 115–28.

Tomlinson, H. C., *Guns and Government: The Ordnance Office under the Later Stuarts* (1979).

Tomlinson, William Weaver, *Life in Northumberland during the Sixteenth Century* (1897).

Traugott, Mark (ed.), *Repertoires and Cycles of Collective Action* (Durham, NC, 1995).

Trentmann, Frank, 'Materiality in the Future of History: Things, Practices, and Policies', *Journal of British Studies*, 48 (2009), 283–307.

Trentmann, Frank, *Empire of Things* (New York, 2016).

Trivellato, Francesca, '"Amphibious Power": The Law of Wreck, Maritime Customs, and Sovereignty in Richelieu's France', *Law and History Review*, 33 (2015), 915–44.

Unger, Richard W., 'The Tonnage of Europe's Merchant Fleets, 1300–1800', in Richard W. Unger (ed.), *Ships and Shipping in the North Sea and Atlantic, 1400–1800* (Aldershot and Brookfield, VT, 1997), 253–61.

Unger, Richard W. (ed.), *Shipping and Economic Growth 1350–1850* (Leiden, 2011).

Unger, Richard W., 'Ships and Sailing Routes in Maritime Trade around Europe 1300–1600', in Wim Blockmans, Mikhail Krom, and Justyna Wubs-Mrozewicz (eds), *The Routledge Handbook of Maritime Trade around Europe 1300–1699: Commercial Networks and Urban Autonomy* (2017), 17–35.

Usher, Abbot Payson, 'The Growth of English Shipping 1572–1922', *Quarterly Journal of Economics*, 42 (1928), 465–78.

Van Zanden, Jan Luiten, 'Early Modern Economic Growth: A Survey of the European Economy, 1500–1800', in Maarten Prak (ed.), *Early Modern Capitalism: Economic and Social Change in Europe, 1400–1800* (2001), 69–87.

Vazquez, Juan José Ponce, *Islanders and Empire: Smuggling and Political Defiance in Hispaniola, 1580–1690* (Cambridge, 2020).

'VOC Shipwreck Archaeology: VOC Shipwrecks and Archives', https://www.maarer.com/voc-shipwrecks.html (accessed January 2021).

Waddell, Brodie, 'Governing England through the Manor Courts, 1550–1850', *Historical Journal*, 55 (2012), 279–315.

Waddell, Brodie, *God, Duty and Community in English Economic Life, 1660–1720* (Woodbridge, 2012).

Walter, John, 'Public Transcripts, Popular Agency and the Politics of Subsistence in Early Modern England', in Michael J. Braddick and John Walter (eds), *Negotiating Power in Early Modern Society: Order, Hierarchy and Subordination in Britain and Ireland* (Cambridge, 2001), 123–48.

Walter, John, '"Law-Mindedness" Crowds, Courts and Popular Knowledge of the Law in Early Modern England', in Michael Lobban, Joanne Begiato, and Adrian Green (eds), *Law, Lawyers and Litigants in Early Modern England* (Cambridge, 2019), 164–84.

Wells, Elizabeth M. P., 'Civil Litigation in the High Court of Admiralty, 1585–1595', in Christopher Brooks and Michael Lobban (eds), *Communities and Courts in Britain 1150–1900* (London and Rio Grande, 1997), 83–97.

Willan, T. S., *The English Coasting Trade, 1600–1750* (Manchester, 1938).

Williams, Glanmor, 'The Affray at Oxwich Castle, 1557', *Gower. Journal of the Gower Society*, 2 (1949), 6–9.

Williams, N. J., 'Francis Shaxton and the Elizabethan Port Books', *English Historical Review*, 66 (1951), 387–95.

Williams, N. J., *The Maritime Trade of the East Anglian Ports 1550–1590* (Oxford, 1988).

Williams, Selwyn, *Treasure of the Golden Grape. 11th December 1641. A Chesil Beach Wreck* (Dorchester, 2012).

Wood, Andy, *Faith, Hope and Charity: English Neighbourhoods, 1500–1640* (Cambridge, 2020).

Woodcroft, Bennet (ed.), *Subject-Matter Index... of Patents of Invention*, 2 vols (1854).

Worthington, David (ed.), *The New Coastal History: Cultural and Environmental Perspectives from Scotland and Beyond* (Cham, Switzerland, 2017).

Wreck Chart of the British Isles for 1859: Compiled from the Board of Trade Register (1860).

'Wreck Chart of the British Isles for the Year 1873–4', *Lifeboat*, 9/98 (November 1875).

Wrightson, Keith, 'Two Concepts of Order: Justices, Constables and Jurymen in Seventeenth-Century England', in John Brewer and John A. Styles (eds), *An Ungovernable People: The English and their Law in the Seventeenth and Eighteenth Centuries* (1980), 21–46.

Wrightson, Keith, 'The Politics of the Parish in Early Modern England', in Paul Griffiths, Adam Fox, and Steve Hindle (eds), *The Experience of Authority in Early Modern England* (1996), 10–46.

Wrightson, Keith, 'Mutualities and Obligations: Changing Relationships in Early Modern England', *Proceedings of the British Academy*, 139 (2006), 157–94.

Wrightson, Keith, and David Levine, *Poverty and Piety in an English Village: Terling 1525–1700* (New York, 1979).

Index

For the benefit of digital users, indexed terms that span two pages (e.g., 52–53) may, on occasion, appear on only one of those pages.